"As long as there are borders and money to be made off the backs of migrants seeking freedom via the state, we must continue to expose the profit-makers and share our stories of resistance. *Asylum for Sale* does exactly this. It reminds us that our people will never be truly free under capitalism—and that we must not only challenge the capitalist state but destroy it and open borders for all. It is an urgent, inspiring, and necessary volume."
—Jamila Hammami, founder of the Queer Detainee Empowerment Project

"A very important book. With a potent mix of theoretical rigor, empirical detail and vivid human witness, it helps to move the debate about asylum seekers beyond suffering and compassion to rights and resistance. In the process, it exposes the nature of the industry growing around asylum application systems: an industry of those demanding extortionate payments to overcome border fences, those erecting the fences, those detaining asylum seekers while they wait, the lawyers, the NGOs—all with a self-interest in treating asylum seekers as voiceless victims without agency or capacity, pitted against citizens. This book conveys the possibilities of global citizenship, involving active solidarity with those who are crossing borders, whether by choice or as a refusal of oppression. It is a vital resource for the struggle for global human rights—a struggle often led by those who are denied them."
—Hilary Wainwright, author of *A New Politics from the Left* (Polity, 2018)

"As the frontiers of disaster capitalism expand, the same systems that drive migration are finding ever more harrowing ways to criminalize and exploit the displaced. This book is part of how we fight back: connecting the extraordinary stories and insights of people studying, personally navigating, and creatively resisting the global asylum industry. An unparalleled resource."
—Naomi Klein, author of *On Fire: The Burning Case for the Green New Deal* (Simon & Schuster, 2019)

D1377867

Asylum for Sale

KAIROS

In ancient Greek philosophy, *kairos* signifies the right time or the "moment of transition." We believe that we live in such a transitional period. The most important task of social science in time of transformation is to transform itself into a force of liberation. Kairos, an editorial imprint of the Anthropology and Social Change department housed in the California Institute of Integral Studies, publishes groundbreaking works in critical social sciences, including anthropology, sociology, geography, theory of education, political ecology, political theory, and history.

Series editor: Andrej Grubačić

Recent and featured Kairos books:

Building Free Life: Dialogues with Öcalan edited by International Initiative

The Sociology of Freedom: Manifesto of the Democratic Civilization, Volume III by Abdullah Öcalan

In, Against, and Beyond Capitalism: The San Francisco Lectures by John Holloway

Anthropocene or Capitalocene? Nature, History, and the Crisis of Capitalism edited by Jason W. Moore

We Are the Crisis of Capital: A John Holloway Reader by John Holloway

Re-enchanting the World: Feminism and the Politics of the Commons by Silvia Federici

Autonomy Is in Our Hearts: Zapatista Autonomous Government through the Lens of the Tsotsil Language by Dylan Eldredge Fitzwater

The Battle for the Mountain of the Kurds: Self-Determination and Ethnic Cleansing in the Afrin Region of Rojava by Thomas Schmidinger

Beyond the Periphery of the Skin: Rethinking, Remaking, and Reclaiming the Body in Contemporary Capitalism by Silvia Federici

Facebooking the Anthropocene in Raja Ampat by Robert Ostertag

For more information visit www.pmpress.org/blog/kairos/

Asylum for Sale

Profit and Protest in the Migration Industry

Edited by
Siobhán McGuirk and Adrienne Pine

ISBN: 978-1-62963-782-2 (print)
ISBN: 978-1-62963-818-8 (ebook)
Library of Congress Control Number: 2019946107

Cover by John Yates / www.stealworks.com
Interior design by briandesign

10 9 8 7 6 5 4 3 2 1

PM Press
PO Box 23912
Oakland, CA 94623
www.pmpress.org

Printed in the USA.

Contents

FOREWORD   xi
Seth M. Holmes

ACKNOWLEDGMENTS   xvii

Introduction   1
Siobhán McGuirk and Adrienne Pine

I   CROSSINGS

On Seeking Refuge from an Undeclared War   21
José López

The Business of Selling Life: Reflections from a Rescue Ship in the
Mediterranean Sea   29
Alva, Uyi, and Madi

Trump and the USMCA: From Free Trade to Gassing Migrants   41
Garry Leech

Outsourcing, Responsibility, and Refugee Claim-Making in
Australia's Offshore Detention Regime   47
Sara Dehm

Kidneys without Borders—Asylum without Kidneys   67
Nancy Scheper-Hughes

II WAITING GAMES

From Paris to Lampedusa: The New Business of Migrant Detention
in Europe 79
Louise Tassin

Detained Voices on Labor 95
Detained Voices

The Poetics of Prison Protest 101
Behrouz Boochani and Omid Tofighian

Displacement, Commodification, and Profitmaking in Nigeria 113
Sidonia Lucia Kula and Oreva Olakpe

A Guard's Story 127
Sam Wallman, Nick Olle, Pat Grant, Pat Armstrong, and Sam Bungey

III COMPLEX INDUSTRIES/ INDUSTRIAL COMPLEXES

The Military and Security Industry: Promoting Europe's Refugee
Regime 149
Mark Akkerman

Making a Refugee Market in the Republic of Nauru 165
Julia Morris

The Cost of Freedom 181
Marzena Zukowska

Making Profits in Hostile Environments: Asylum Accommodation
Markets in the UK and Ireland 193
John Grayson

An "Expert" View of the Asylum Industry 203
Adrienne Pine

IV "NONPROFIT"/"NONGOVERNMENTAL"

In the Best Interest of Whom? Professional Humanitarians and
Selfie Samaritans in the Danish Asylum Industry 219
Annika Lindberg

The Marketization of Asylum Justice in the UK   231
Jo Wilding

Free Wireless Network Activism and the Industrial Media
Infrastructures of Forced Migration   241
Tim Schütz and Monic Meisel

Surmounting the Hostile Environment: Reflections on Social Work
Activism without Borders   253
Lynn King, Bridget Ng'andu, and Lauren Wroe

Neoliberalism and LGBT Asylum: A Play in Five Acts   267
Siobhán McGuirk

V AFTERMATHS?

Border Militarization in a Warming World: Climate Adaptation for
the Rich and Powerful   281
Todd Miller

Beds, Masks, and Prayers: Mexican Migrants, the Immigration
Regime, and Investments in Social Exclusion in Canada   287
Paloma E. Villegas

Contesting Profit Structures: Rejected Asylum Seekers between
Modern Slavery and Autonomy   297
Jorinde Bijl and Sarah Nimführ

Grounded: Power, Profit, and the Deportation Industrial Complex 309
Ruth Potts and Jo Ram

Kuja Meri?   319
Joël van Houdt

INDEX   335

Foreword

Seth M. Holmes

> A commodity appears at first sight an extremely obvious, trivial thing. But its analysis brings out that it is a very strange thing, abounding in metaphysical subtleties.
> —Karl Marx[1]

What does it mean for a person to be seen as a commodity? For a whole category of people to be treated as objects for profit? How is this (strange, metaphysical) transformation experienced, navigated, and resisted? Who profits from such transmogrification,[2] and who facilitates or allows it? At what cost does such grotesque and bizarre commodification of people occur? To whom? And what alternate futures may be possible?

This book analyzes the commodification of the growing number of displaced people in many parts of the world who are seeking refuge from violence and harm. The broader context for the book is the intensifying conjuncture of neoliberal capitalism, structural racism, nationalism, and colonialism, all "with increasingly fascist hues."[3] Neoliberal capitalism is here defined both as the political economic system of privatization of public goods and the symbolic system of the privatization of risk and responsibility.[4] Policy bolsters markets above people, and discourse bolsters the individual above the collective.[5] In these political, economic, and social contexts, profits flow in steep, uneven patterns at unbelievable rates and magnitudes. While, in many ways, it is true that "human suffering is irrelevant when commerce is at stake,"[6] it is also true that the intense suffering of some is making immense profit for others.

The authors of the volume are an inspiring collection of scholars, advocates, activists, artists, and asylum seekers—some of whom have been deported, some of whom have been legitimized as refugees, and some of whom remain incarcerated at the time of this writing. In different settings from Papua New Guinea to Turkey, Australia to the United States, Italy to Narau, Libya to Greece, and far beyond, the authors trace the production of violence and displacement, the treatment of persons seeking asylum as (dangerous) objects from which to make profit, the diffusion of responsibility for blatant human rights abuses, the grave human cost of these realities, and the multiple—sometimes contradictory—means by which such processes are lived and resisted. Their writing, painting, photographing, interviewing, and organizing invite the reader into conversation and praxis. Thank you to Siobhán McGuirk, Adrienne Pine, and all the contributors for this powerful invitation into reflection and action.

Poignantly, the authors reflect on their own complicated positions vis-à-vis the multiple forms of profit extracted at great cost from asylum seekers. Through their own reflexivity,[7] they remind us that we all exist in some relation to the *asylum industry*. We must consider our complicity and the ways in which we can join in solidarity with people seeking refuge and others who are actively imagining and working toward different social, political, human, and environmental realities.

> A commodity has a value because it is a crystallization of social labor. The greatness of its value ... depends upon the greater or less amount of that social substance contained in it; that is to say, on the relative mass of labor necessary for its production.
> —Karl Marx[8]

As made clear in this volume, there are multiple levels on which people are rendered and treated as commodities in the asylum process. First, racial capitalism seeks continual growth through "predatory accumulation" of land and resource grabs through violence and war,[9] directly displacing large populations. Racial capitalism's hunger for growth, including through fossil fuels, also generates environmental destruction with escalating (un)natural disasters and expanding zones of uninhabitability. These environmental causes of displacement are increasing in frequency and scale,[10] without being taken into account in most asylum policies and conventions worldwide.

Second, displaced people must pay smugglers, traffickers, guides, drivers, ship captains, kidnappers, lawyers, doctors, and nonprofiteers along their journey in search of refuge.[11] Analyzing the extractive processes along the dangerous—sometimes fatal—route, one asylum seeker explains in this volume, "You pay to die."[12] In violent and gendered ways, asylum seekers are forced to pay for fleeting safety or survival with money or even their bodies.[13] As analyzed in detail in several chapters in this book, many of the lawyers and nonprofiteers providing services to asylum seekers work for or are connected to corporations that contribute to the violence of displacement in the first place.

Third, governments increasingly outsource and externalize adjudication, detention, and deportation through contracts with private firms—which often subcontract to other private firms. This multilayered (sub) contracting allows a bad faith diffusion of responsibility,[14] avoidance of monitoring, functional impunity, and—through it all—profit for some at the cost of violence against others.

Fourth and finally, some of the same firms (as well as some of the same nonprofit service organizations) involved in these processes then rely on the low-paid, flexible labor of racialized, minoritized refugees and deportees. In the words of José López, vividly describing his own journey seeking asylum, "It's a vicious cycle with profit at every stage, from detention and deportation to relying on immigrants to accept poorly paid jobs that make bosses rich."[15]

The *social labor* (playing off Marx) that produces and treats people as commodities is inherent to each of these levels—violent displacement, costly services on the road toward asylum, processing, certification, incarceration, or deportation, and then precarious employment. On another level, this social labor involves the narratives that justify displacement, exploitation, detention, and deportation. These narratives represent specific categories of people as "preemptive suspects" or as expendable, portray their cases for asylum as "bogus,"[16] and legitimize the exploitation of their flexible labor.

How can we work against these violent processes of profit-making for many at the social, bodily, psychic, and material expense of even more "others"? Following Bourdieu's explication that social structures and symbolic structures can either reproduce or transform one another,[17] it is critical to work on both levels. In solidarity with and following the leadership of asylum seekers and others already organizing, we must work against the structural—including nationalist and racist—violence that leads to displacement and environmental degradation and, for many, to incarceration, deportation, and exploitation.[18] This means disinvestment from "security firms,"[19] organizing for change in asylum policy and practice, pushing against neoliberal transnational agreements, forming mutual aid networks, and more. At the same time, it is imperative that we challenge representations of asylum seekers as undeserving, as well as narratives that justify inclusion of some at the expense of the violent and sometimes fatal exclusion of others. Following the insights of asylum seekers themselves, we must utilize alternative images, "in opposition to the image created by the system."[20]

The diverse voices included in this volume push us to acknowledge our own relationships to the commodification of people seeking refuge. Within the structures of racial capitalism, even our attempts to do good are often complicit and contradictory. Knowing full well the interrelationship between all of us writing about, reading about, profiting from, and experiencing displacement and exploitation, the only viable option is solidarity across difference to imagine and organize for alternative futures. If solidarity is both a feeling and practice of interdependence among people that is capable of changing both the way society is structured[21] and each of the people involved,[22] we must engage with the reflexivity demonstrated by the authors in this volume. Learning from the Combahee River Collective, Keeanga-Yamahtta Taylor,[23] and others, we must develop solidarity as coalition building that recognizes connections between different forms of inequity and exploitation and highlights the need to stand together for the good of all. And we must respond to Frantz Fanon's demand that "solidarity must be a solidarity of fact, a solidarity of action, a solidarity concrete in [people], in equipment, in money."[24]

Seth M. Holmes is a cultural and medical anthropologist and physician at the University of California Berkeley and San Francisco, author of *Fresh Fruit, Broken Bodies: Migrant Farmworkers in the United States* (University of California Press 2013), and a Margaret Mead Award recipient. He works collaboratively with scholars, practitioners, migrants, and refugees on displacement, social and health inequities, and the ways each is justified and resisted.

Notes

1   Karl Marx, *Capital: A Critique of Political Economy*, vol. One, Ben Fowlkes trans. (London: Penguin Books, 1990[1867]), 163.

2   "To change or transform into a different shape, esp. a grotesque or bizarre one." *Collins Dictionary*, accessed March 29, 2020, https://www.collinsdictionary. com/dictionary/english/transmogrify.

3   Siobhán McGuirk and Adrienne Pine, "Introduction," this volume, 1–18.

4   Craig Calhoun, "The Privatization of Risk," *Public Culture* 18, no. 2 (Spring 2006): 257–63, accessed March 29, 2020, https://eportfolios.macaulay.cuny. edu/alterman2014/files/2014/02/The-Privatization-of-Risk-Craig-Calhoun. pdf; Seth M. Holmes and Heide Castañeda, "Representing the 'European Refugee Crisis' in Germany and Beyond: Deservingness and Difference, Life and Death," *American Ethnologist* 43, no. 1 (February 2016): 1–13, accessed March 29, 2020, https://escholarship.org/uc/item/0xr0m9rr.

5   Wendy Brown, "American Nightmare: Neoliberalism, Neoconservatism, and De-Democratization," *Political Theory* 34, no. 6 (December 2006): 690–714.

6   Nancy Scheper-Hughes, "Kidneys without Borders—Asylum without Kidneys," this volume, 67–76.

7   Adrienne Pine, "An 'Expert' View of the Asylum Industry," this volume, 203–15; Siobhán McGuirk, "Neoliberalism and LGBT Asylum: A Play in Five Acts," this volume, 267–77.

8   Karl Marx, *Value, Price and Profit* (New York: International Co., Inc., 1969 [1865]), accessed March 20, 2020, https://www.marxists.org/archive/marx/ works/1865/value-price-profit.

9   Philippe Bourgois, "Decolonising Drug Studies in an Era of Predatory Accumulation," *Third World Quarterly* 39, no. 2 (February 2018): 385–98, accessed March 20, 2020, https://www.ncbi.nlm.nih.gov/pmc/articles/ PMC5976441.

10 Todd Miller, "Border Militarization in a Warming World: Climate Adaptation for the Rich and Powerful," this volume, 281–86.

11 Also see Wendy Vogt, "Crossing Mexico: Structural Violence and the Commodification of Central American Migrants," *American Ethnologist* 40, no. 4 (November 2013): 764–80.

12 Alva, Uyi, and Madi, "The Business of Selling Life: Reflections from a Rescue Ship in the Mediterranean Sea," this volume, 29–39.

13 Sidonia Lucia Kula and Oreva Olakpe, "Displacement, Commodification, and Profitmaking in Nigeria," this volume, 113–25.

14 Jean-Paul Sartre, *Being and Nothingness* (London: Methuen & Co., 1956); Nancy Scheper-Hughes, *Death without Weeping* (Berkeley: University of California Press, 1992).

15 José López, "On Seeking Refuge from an Undeclared War," this volume, 21–28.

16 Lynn Stephen, "Creating Preemptive Suspects: National Security, Border Defense, and Immigration Policy, 1980–Present," *Latin American Perspectives* 45, no. 6 (November 2018): 7–25; Seth M. Holmes, "Marking Preemptive Suspects: Migration, Bodies, Exclusion," *Latin American Perspectives* 45, no. 6 (November 2018): 30–36; also see Siobhán McGuirk and Adrienne Pine, "Introduction," this volume, 1–18.

17 Pierre Bourdieu and Loic J.D. Wacquant, *An Invitation to Reflexive Sociology* (Chicago: University of Chicago Press, 1992).

18 María L. Cruz-Torres, "The US-Mexican Border, Immigration, and Resistance," *Latin American Perspectives* 45, no. 6 (November 2018): 26–29.

19 Marzena Zukowska, "The Cost of Freedom," this volume, 181–91.

20 Behrouz Boochani and Omid Tofighian, "The Poetics of Prison Protest," this volume.

21 Emile Durkheim, *The Division of Labour in* Society, W.D. Halls trans. (New York: Free Press, 1997).

22 Paulo Freire, *Pedagogy of the Oppressed*, Myra Bergman Ramos trans. (New York: Continuum, 2006).

23 Keeanga-Yamahtta Taylor, ed., *How We Get Free: Black Feminism and the Combahee River Collective* (Chicago: Haymarket Books, 2017).

24 Franz Fanon, "Unity and Effective Solidarity Are the Conditions for African Liberation," *Toward the African Revolution: Political Essays*, Haakon Chevalier trans. (New York: Grove Books, 1988[1960]), 173.

Acknowledgments

We extend immense gratitude to all of the contributors featured for their patience and dedication to this project. We also thank Sarah Leister, Pablo Melchor, and the team at PM Press for their support.

This volume exists only because hundreds of people chose to share aspects of their lives, opinions, and experiences with us, often at great risk. The book is dedicated to them and to all who continue to resist the pernicious expansion of capitalism into every facet of our lives in the pursuit of justice for all.

Humanity is not for sale, and no one is illegal.

March 2020
Siobhán McGuirk and Adrienne Pine

Introduction

Siobhán McGuirk and Adrienne Pine

Throughout the so-called Mediterranean refugee crisis of 2015–2016, public sympathy, government policy, and media coverage swirled around an apparent debate: Were the people arriving to European borders "refugees" or "economic migrants"? The same question arose with reference to the US-Mexico border, as caravans of asylum seekers arrived from Central America in 2018–2019. It has been a recurrent refrain in Australian parliamentary discussions regarding offshore immigrant detention and globally in migration debates for decades.[1] The more the dichotomy is evoked, the more successfully the economic realities of asylum are obscured. Yet, under the neoliberal capitalist status quo that defines the current era, the ability to seek asylum can no longer be considered a universal human right. It is a product up for sale. And, in true capitalist form, an entire industry has developed around it.

Today's drivers of global capitalism are also among the most potent "push factors"—to borrow from demographers' lexicon—compelling people to migrate: wars for geopolitical and economic influence; catastrophic climate change caused by the fossil fuel industry; financial collapse provoked by "free trade" deals and global recession; social stratification and identity-based persecution that erode the potential for class solidarity. The resultant forced migration takes place in a context of "disaster capitalism," with human-made crises and catastrophes used to justify the adoption—or imposition—of neoliberal economic policies that further consolidate wealth and power in elite hands, leading to yet more suffering.[2] It is a profitable cycle.

Expansion is necessary to the survival of capitalism—new markets, new opportunities. Ongoing and discrete instances of violence create space for "growth." The consistent flow of migration that such violence produces does not constitute a spectacular event, however, despite dominant narratives suggesting otherwise. Neither are the pathways taken only linear, recent, or pointed northward. Many people caught in the gaze of the latest migrant "crisis" have been displaced and moving—some constantly, some intermittently—for years, even decades or generations. As they are held at borders or in encampments, news cameras, spotlights, and NGO-branded relief teams shift from one global frontier zone to the next, leaving behind the growing tendrils of a complex and diversifying asylum industry that is produced and sustained by the everyday realities of global capitalism. And as border crossings and petitions for protection become ever more costly for the people who make them, they are ever more lucrative for those seeking to profit from the massive human displacement that characterizes the world today.[3]

When unlivable conditions force people to flee their homes, only those with substantial resources can obtain the passports, visas, and plane tickets needed to avoid long and often perilous journeys over land and over sea. Financial and social capital can secure attentive lawyers, social supports, and endorsements in destination countries. The superrich need not worry about asylum at all: investor visas are far easier to obtain, at least for millionaires facing exile. For the rest, brokers, forgers, coyotes, traffickers, and smugglers demand extortionate payments to facilitate escapes. Contractors and "security" firms receive billion-dollar contracts to stop them in their tracks—erecting walls, fences, and watchtowers or running patrol boats and coast guards to bar potential asylum seekers from entering territories and making claims.

Those who make it across the border are frequently placed into detention centers, jails, encampments, or crumbling housing complexes, all run by multinational corporations, with investment from the biggest global banks. Agencies compete for government contracts to provide stipulated services to asylum seekers and refugees,[4] often while placing them into new regimes of monitored vulnerability. Private doctors produce medical and psychoanalytical examination certificates to bolster claims with bodily "proof" of persecution.[5] Expert witnesses and think tank staff create testimonies and reports that further shape case outcomes—and establish archetypes of "genuine" claimants. Specialized NGOs similarly

2

mobilize million-dollar revenues and professionalized workforces (overwhelmingly middle-class and/or citizens of the Global North) to advocate for select categories of "deserving" persecuted people. Their constructions win asylum for some, while excluding others unable to fit imaginaries of ideal victimhood that are shaped by class, gender, racial, religious, and other prejudices. Private immigration lawyers charge exorbitant fees, while powerful law firms use pro bono asylum work to sanitize reputations tarnished by their day-to-day work reinforcing disaster capitalism. Businesses profiting from immigrant detention likewise make large, tax-deductible donations to asylum charities, adding humanitarian sheen to their philanthropic portfolios.[6] The same corporations building the warplanes that cause human displacement profit from the deportation of "failed" asylum claimants.[7]

Meanwhile, governments cite "austerity measures" in their efforts to defund or privatize legal and social aid—measures framed in the language of "efficiency" and "cost saving" for the taxpayer. While such rhetoric further pits citizens against migrants—particularly useful in the aftermath of a global recession triggered by elite greed—creeping xenophobia paradoxically justifies huge spending on border enforcement and the expansion of immigrant detention estates. In the Global South, transnational private actors work with state governments to buoy the UNHCR's expansive bureaucratic "refugee protection regime," which functions in part to keep the most impoverished asylum seekers encamped far from northern borders.[8]

The expansion of neoliberal capitalism not only causes forced migration, it requires the vulnerable itinerant workforce such migration creates. The production of exploitable, generally racialized "others" is the bedrock of our current economic system—the figure of the "illegal" immigrant laborer is just one recent incarnation of this long-standing historical process.[9] Forced migration is frequently intertwined with forced labor, leading to the creation of new, "hyperprecarious" categories of migrant. The "rejected asylum seeker," for example, is linguistically and symbolically constructed to be hyperexploitable in ways that build upon extant racisms.[10] As Nicholas De Genova argues, the production of migrant "illegality"—including through imaginaries of "bogus" and "failed" asylum seekers—is "crucial for the creation and maintenance of a . . . reliable, eminently mobile, flexible, and ultimately disposable source of labor power."[11]

3

The aim of this volume is to expose and examine profit-making as a significant force driving contemporary asylum regimes. This perspective is a product not only of contributors' work as researchers, academics, and journalists but also their experiences as people directly engaged with the industry: as activists, advocates, "experts," organizers, and people who have themselves sought asylum. Moving beyond the questions of moral, ethical, and legal obligation that have come to dominate scholarship and activism concerning asylum seekers, we approach the actors and institutions forming around asylum adjudication systems and individuals seeking asylum globally as an industry—one that is thriving at grave human cost, and one that must be opposed.

Shifting Asylum Norms

To understand how neoliberal capitalism has come to define asylum as a concept and as a bureaucratic process, we must first review how the meaning and contours of asylum have evolved over time. Asylum existed as a historical norm for millennia before its codification in modern international legal conventions,[12] culminating in the United Nations 1951 Convention Relating to the Status of Refugees and its 1967 Protocol Relating to the Status of Refugees,[13] and has always posed a challenge to nation-state sovereignty by asserting a position of concern for the "other/outsider." The interpretation and implementation of legal conventions are subject to political, cultural, and material realities, however, and the praxis of asylum has changed radically in the nearly seventy years since the signing of the 1951 convention. These shifts have, in turn, exposed the inherent tensions, contradictions, and limitations of asylum in different ways.

The context of the 1951 convention is, of course, the end of World War II and the start of the Cold War. A series of international treaties preceded and framed it, including the 1948 Universal Declaration of Human Rights and the Geneva Conventions and North Atlantic Treaty of 1949[14]—all part and parcel of the postwar project that was shaping and justifying a new kind of US-led empire. Through Hannah Arendt and other influential thinkers of the day (many of them, like her, European refugees), the modern origins of asylum came to be widely understood as a response to the Holocaust. In practice, however, the more potent underlying logic (and implementation) of the convention had much to do with institutionalizing the Cold War ideological framework that positioned capitalism as the savior for political refugees seeking an escape from communism. Charles B. Keely argues that two distinct refugee regimes subsequently developed, one for the industrialized capitalist North and another for the rest of the world:

> The Northern regime was designed for political purposes of the Cold War . . . an instrument to embarrass communist states. . . . At a minimum, the program could be used to demonstrate the bankruptcy of a system from which people had to escape, often at great peril. In Europe, the asylum systems put into place basically assumed that applicants would be from the East. Fairly generous assistance, commensurate with the welfare state policy generally pursued . . . and an adjudication system that provided the benefit of the doubt to the applicant prevailed. In this scheme, the UNHCR had virtually no role. . . . It quickly became an agency operating in the third world.[15]

The two regimes had paradoxical objectives: while the UNHCR sought to defuse "explosive situations" so that locally displaced citizens might return safely home, the northern regime intended explicitly to destabilize states by permanently resettling an intentionally small number of political refugees.[16] Thus, as the institutional project as a whole was being reinforced, in the Global North, its imagined ideal subject transformed from an agentive (white) European exile from fascism to a freedom-seeking (white) victim of human rights–abusing Soviet or Soviet-allied communist governments.

This shift was further complicated by racist and colonialist logics, with greater agency imputed to individuals from the Soviet bloc compared to people fleeing Soviet-allied countries in the Global South—Nicaragua, Cuba, Vietnam and Cambodia, and Angola, for example—who were readily associated with stereotypes of weakness and passivity or threatening otherness.[17] In keeping with this context, actual levels of state-sponsored violence have historically had very little to do with the likelihood of targeted individuals being granted asylum by nation-state-based adjudicators: individuals interpreted as victims of "enemy" states have been—and continue to be—far more likely to receive asylum than those suffering persecution at the hands of allied governments.[18]

It is important to note that it required subsequent protocols, declarations, and agreements to expand the internationally legally enshrined concept of refugees beyond post–World War II imaginaries. It was not until the 1967 protocol that the UN removed the temporal and geographic restrictions of its 1951 convention, which defined refugees as people impacted by "events occurring in Europe" prior to that year. That is to say, the forcible displacement of over ten million people due to the partition of India in 1947 and the exodus of nearly one million people from Palestine in 1948—among countless examples of violent colonial upheaval—were intentionally omitted from the original definition.[19] The United States went further, explicitly defining "refugee" in relation to communist countries in its Refugee Relief Act of 1953[20]—language that remained in place until 1980. Over the same period, it repeatedly targeted non-white immigrants for deportation through explicitly racist policy initiatives, building the foundations for careful legal and linguistic differentiations of immigrant categories that remain potent today in the granting—and, more often, denial—of asylum.[21]

Leading up to and following the fall of the USSR, the ideal subject of asylum shifted again to become the apparently docile target of humanitarian intervention—a figure imagined as being and belonging far from European borders. By the 1990s, large population displacements associated with civil wars and famines across the African continent dominated popular imaginaries of refugees. Not incidentally, the contexts of such displacement included the fallout from anticolonial liberation struggles, Cold War–era proxy wars between East and West, and the disastrous consequences of neoliberalizing conditions attached to World Bank and International Monetary Fund loans. These political realities were obscured, however, by dominant narratives of "ethnic conflicts" and "natural disasters."[22] As a result, terminology that previously indexed exiles from "specific political, historical, cultural contexts" became depoliticized and conventionalized through bureaucratic humanitarian practices such that refugees "stop[ped] being specific persons and bec[a]me pure victims in general."[23] Meanwhile, in the Global North, governments "changed the rules of the game in reaction to changes in geopolitical structure,"[24] creating "fortress Europe" and erecting ever-bigger walls while demonizing the asylum seekers who reached their territories as "bogus," "illegal," or "criminal."[25]

Liisa Malkki (as others since) has focused on the ways in which these dynamics silence refugees,[26] stripping them of the authority to speak credibly about their own experiences and instead bestowing that authority on the professional staff of humanitarian agencies and adjacent NGOs.[27] These external creators of "expert knowledge" not only come to dictate policy decisions and influence individual case adjudications regarding asylum seekers and refugees, they are also rewarded for their actions in salaries, status, and social capital—rewards of the professionalization that has accompanied asylum industry growth.

Concurrent with the longer-term shift in the imagined archetypal asylum seeker from Arendt's white European intellectual to the silenced brown or black victim Malkki describes, agency has transferred from people seeking asylum to their "saviors"—asylum technicians, humanitarians, academics, and other "experts." These latter categories form a global elite of "knowledge creators" about asylum seekers—knowledge that can be sold at a high price to other actors within (and beyond) migration industries. As the stock of these predominantly white, Western, and highly educated professionals who "do good" has risen, the conception that people seeking refuge are informed, political subjects has been steadily eroded—along with their ability to command financially rewarding work, status, and social capital. Even as understandings and practices of asylum have evolved, they have thus consistently served to reinforce white supremacy.

The accepted grounds for claiming asylum continue to shift beyond the late-twentieth-century emphasis on suffering and compassion and away from an erstwhile focus on rights and entitlements under the law.[28] Leading up to and following 9/11, and especially post-ISIS, the framing of the ideal asylum-seeking subject transformed again in conjunction with political and discursive moves toward securitization and militarization—predicated on new nationalist campaigns—and the technologized scrutiny of masses of potential terrorists.[29] However, in the current neoliberal moment—in which a smaller, more consolidated global oligarchy exerts far greater control over the technologies and processes of displacement from and incorporation into nation-states—asylum has become more readily obtainable through the performance of identity-based persecution.

In their attempts to support people seeking asylum, NGOs and legal advocates have worked especially hard to promote a new model of deserving asylum seekers as "innocent," passive individuals fleeing persecution on the basis of illness, gender, or sexuality, for example, rather than agentive members of a collective engaged in political struggle.[30] Particularly in such cases, the individual claimant is expected to present harrowing evidence of personalized suffering and violence—via photographs, video footage, and/or testimonies—to elicit compassion and subsequent positive action (be it case decisions, donations, or public sympathy). In this framework—thoroughly neoliberal in its elevation of "exceptional" cases—the asylum industry renders dispensable would-be applicants who do not conform to the expectations of normative identity categories prescribed by cultural and financial capital.[31]

But suffering narratives do not guarantee asylum—not even for compliant defectors from "enemy" states or those who are suitably grateful and able to assimilate.[32] The racialized, classed specters of the terrorist threat, the "bogus" claimant, the criminal element, the potential welfare "scrounger," and the "public charge" loom too large.[33] Adjudicators and publics are responding to asylum seekers' testimonies with increasing suspicion.[34] Rather than their own testimonies, products and technologies outside the applicant's control—medical evaluations, psychoanalytical documentation, police records, news reports, and "expert" witnesses—are now heavily weighted forms of "truth" that asylum seekers must provide to state authorities. Each of these "truths" is a commodity forged and sold within the asylum industry, created and collated by actors engaged in the coproduction of new asylum norms.

Ultimately, under neoliberal capitalism, shifting attitudes toward asylum are always tied to ideological and practical commitments—to cutting welfare spending, privatizing state services, facilitating "frictionless" movement, and valorizing the individual over society, such that the notion of "deservingness" is tied to entrepreneurialism. Neoliberal faith in self-sufficiency and individual responsibility, not to mention "free movement," renders the very concept of asylum illogical. Unless, of course, it is for sale.

Profit *and* Protest

The first purpose of this volume is to identify and explain how current practices of asylum align with the neoliberal moment more broadly. The second is to examine how radical-minded, predominantly grassroots activists worldwide are fighting for reform and attempting to fill gaps in service provision, even under such constraints. In bringing together international scholars, journalists, artists, activists, and people directly impacted by the asylum industry, we aim to inform strategy debates and identify pathways to transnational collaborations that recognize how forced transnational migration operates in the context of neoliberal capitalism with increasingly fascist hues.[35]

This is not a theoretical discussion. Although our analyses are rooted in and build upon existing scholarship, we are equally focused on presenting and debating visions for radically alternative systems and processes—and committed to reflecting on the real work already underway to create them. In highlighting protest as well as profit, we strike a balance of critical analyses and proposed solutions for resisting and reshaping current and emerging immigration norms.

It has been a long road to completing this volume. When we first began work on it, Barack Obama sat in the White House, overseeing an immigration policy that earned him the nickname "Deporter in Chief." The Mediterranean "refugee crisis" was dominating headlines and providing distressing visual resources for countless NGO fundraising campaigns. Austerity Britain was a member of a seemingly robust European Union, working multilaterally to fortify borders and "manage" asylum claimants. Protests in or responding to Australia's offshore detention camps were ubiquitous, catalyzing national debates and political fractures within as well as between parties.[36] Back then, in 2015, neoliberal mindsets and market-driven restructuring were already shaping experiences of seeking asylum. By 2020, they have come to define them.

In the intervening years, an increasing number of right-wing authoritarian leaders—Trump, Bolsonaro, Modi, Netanyahu, Duterte, Orbán, Erdoğan—have risen to or consolidated power on the basis of ethnonationalist, anti-immigrant agendas. These ideological positions have dovetailed neatly with a shared opposition to human rights and corresponding efforts to diminish the power and status of the United Nations, eroding further the already unstable international norm of asylum. Despite posturing as "anti-establishment" and espousing "citizens first" and "anti-globalist" rhetoric, international right-wing forces remain resolutely neoliberal at heart. New trade deals, new wars, new allies and alignments, new extremes of climate catastrophe—these, too, are transforming access to, and even the concept of, asylum. They will continue to do so in ways we cannot fully anticipate.

As activists engaged with the defense of immigrants' rights, including in many cases their own, the past few years have proven challenging for many of our contributors. We have been working in the midst of the expanding and evolving asylum industry, not simply viewing it from the outside. Authors have themselves been forced to move to different countries, have taken on casework for increasing numbers of asylum seekers, have been compelled to action—in some cases risking arrest and long-term imprisonment—in response to urgent needs and sudden shifts in immigration law and policy. Those who work within the industry, even as they are critical of it, have faced funding cuts and job losses. As profit margins have grown, so has the need for protest. We are not disheartened, though there remain many battles to be fought and won. We hope that this volume provides both inspiration and insight toward that end.

Why Asylum?

We recognize and situate this volume within a growing body of literature on migration industries,[37] just as we recognize how profit-making around asylum seekers connects to broader contexts of neoliberal industrialization and commodification. Contributors to this volume emphasize those links, which include but are not limited to: criminal (in)justice systems and the prison industrial complex;[38] nonprofit organizations and the maintenance of imperialist capitalist structures;[39] paradoxes of elite mobility, citizenship, and investment; new bureaucratic forms in, and the governmentality of, neoliberal states.[40] We have chosen to focus on asylum, however, because it is a category so often held apart from other areas of migration, which are more readily associated with economics. Nowhere is this clearer than with the dichotomous metric of "asylum seeker *or* economic migrant." The discursive insistence that the two categories are not intertwined supports the comforting fiction that asylum is a question of moral and legal obligations alone.[41] The related assertive distinction between "genuine" (granted) and "bogus" (denied) asylum claimants similarly reinforces the reassuring notion that there exists the possibility of objective and infallible determinations of who "deserves" refuge; that asylum adjudication is an arbiter of "truth." Protesters and scholars alike have worked to dispel that fantasy.[42] We focus on asylum to similarly push conversations and readers beyond those comfort zones, and because we reject the categorical imperative—dictated from above and always subject to change in accordance with elite interests—upon which asylum adjudications are based.

We further recognize that dominant narratives and taxonomies not only pit citizens against migrants, they also pit categories of migrants against each other in competition for resources that are only apparently limited. In their respective chapters, the contributors to this volume use a variety of terms and categories and provide justifications and definitions for their choices. The resultant diversity of terminology and approaches to categorizing people who migrate highlights the slipperiness of labels. Taken together, the following chapters thus reveal the expansiveness of the category "asylum seekers" rather than pointing to its ostensible limits. As editors, we share this perspective and regard this book as concerning all people who seek refuge from harm, regardless of the legal, social, political, or other ways in which they may have been categorized.

This volume focuses on the Global North—home to the global asylum industry's most lucrative sites and where the overwhelming majority of asylum claims are made.[43] We have chosen to concentrate on nation-states that maintain their own adjudication systems and devise their own asylum policies. That is to say, with the exception of one chapter, this volume does not concern the UNHCR, a singular institutional body that oversees or supports refugee status determination processes in approximately seventy nation-states, the majority of which are "non-industrialized" countries located in the Global South.[44] In choosing this geographical focus, we do not wish to imply that profit-making around people seeking asylum does not occur everywhere or that significant and varied resistance to unjust asylum practices is not taking place in the Global South. Neither do we want to add credence to popular imaginaries of migration in general as flowing predominantly South to North, East to West. This impression is patently false: world migration patterns are complex, fluctuating, and nonlinear, and nearly four out of five of the world's displaced people live in countries neighboring their countries of origin.[45] A great deal stands to be written about the economics of the UNHCR. Profiteering from Palestinian refugees could likewise constitute a volume on its own, as could the dynamics of asylum capitalism between, for example, North Korea and South Korea or Venezuela and Colombia. China has no refugee resettlement policy or national legislation on asylum, yet a de facto industry has been forming in that absence.[46] In fact, this volume's limited focus cries out for further works exploring the ways in which the asylum industry functions in different locations. We encourage others to push the insights and analyses shared here further still.

Chapter Overview

We have organized this book into five sections, each addressing different points and practices encountered on attempted pathways toward asylum.

Together, the chapters provide an in-depth exploration of complex international networks, policies, and norms that impact and implicate people around the world. Reflective of the overlapping interests and crisscrossing trajectories found and experienced within the asylum industry, many chapters could also find a fitting home in another section. Readers are encouraged to move between them as they choose, following cross-references or pursuing their own lines of interest.

In "Crossings," contributors focus on the costs and experiences of traveling across borders—and of being "intercepted" on the way to intended destinations. The section addresses journeys across three routes that have been at the fore of Western political and public consciousness in recent years—through Central America toward the United States (López, Leech), across the Mediterranean Sea toward mainland Europe (Alva, Uyi, and Madi), and between islands and atolls toward Australia (Dehm). The final chapter in the section highlights a less commonly discussed journey, through private hospital operating theaters (Scheper-Hughes). In each case, the profit-making and exploitative practices of traffickers, smugglers, and illicit "security services" in transit countries are immediately clear—with state investments in privatization, outsourcing, and "cost-cutting" an ever-present backdrop.

Privately run detention, perhaps the most readily and widely understood source of profit within the migration industry, is the focus of "Waiting Games." Moving beyond the well-established fact of for-profit companies in receipt of lucrative government contracts, contributors examine the finer details of the profit extraction that takes place within these prison and camp walls. These include the labor abuses of both asylum seekers (Detained Voices) and staff (Tassin, Wallman et al.), compounded by the threat of bodily commodification (Kula and Olakpe). Resistance runs through these scenes, however, from subtle obstructions to explicit and creative disavowals (Boochani and Tofighian) of systems that are embedded in colonialism and capitalism alike.

The third section, "Complex Industries/Industrial Complexes," looks beyond detention to examine the corporations, small businesses, and states profiting from—and investing heavily in—efforts to prevent people from accessing asylum in Europe (Akkerman) and Australia (Morris), extracting money from asylum claimants via offers of "freedom" (Zukowska) and "expertise" (Pine), or by engaging in a race to the bottom in substandard "service" provision (Grayson).

We turn attention more fully to NGO actors in "'Nonprofit'/ 'Nongovernmental.'" Here, contributors examine which forms of political activism are accorded legitimacy over others within the asylum industry, assessing NGO engagements with state apparatuses through a critically reflective lens (Wilding) and detailing the paradoxes and challenges of working adjacent to governmental (King, Ng'andu and Wroe), corporate (Schütz and Meisel), and NGO (Lindberg, McGuirk) goals.

The final section, "Aftermaths?" addresses the experiences of (un)settled, rejected, and returned asylum seekers who continue to experience uncertainty (Villegas) and exploitation (Bijl and Nimführ) at the edges of the asylum industry—as well as those profiting from and battling against deportation regimes (Potts and Ram). The closing chapters look ahead to likely future entrants to the asylum industry, prompted by climate change (Miller) and postwar instability (van Houdt), while echoing themes that have preceded them and emphasizing the circularity of experience within an ever-expanding industrial frontier.

Notes

1   See, e.g., William Deane Stanley, "Economic Migrants or Refugees from Violence? A Time-Series Analysis of Salvadoran Migration to the United States," *Latin American Research Review* 22, no. 1 (1987): 132–54; Monica den Boer, "Moving between Bogus and Bona Fide: The Policing of Inclusion and Exclusion in Europe," in Robert Miles and Dietrich Thränhardt, eds., *Migration and European Integration: The Dynamics of Inclusion and Exclusion* (Vancouver, BC: Fairleigh Dickinson University Press, 1995); Danielle Every and Martha Augoustinos, "'Taking Advantage' or Fleeing Persecution? Opposing Accounts of Asylum Seeking," *Journal of Sociolinguistics* 12, no. 5 (October 2008): 648–67; Susan E. Zimmermann, "Reconsidering the Problem of 'Bogus' Refugees with 'Socio-economic Motivations' for Seeking Asylum," *Mobilities* 6, no. 3 (September 2011): 335–52; Raia Apostolova, "Of Refugees and Migrants: Stigma, Politics, and Boundary Work at the Borders of Europe," *American Sociological Association Newsletter*, September 14, 2015, accessed March 21, 2020, https://asaculturesection.org/2015/09/14/of-refugees-and-migrants-stigma-politics-and-boundary-work-at-the-borders-of-europe.

2   Naomi Klein, *The Shock Doctrine: The Rise of Disaster Capitalism* (New York: Metropolitan Books, 2007).

3   According to UNHCR estimates, as of 2018, there were seventy-one million forcibly displaced people worldwide—an estimate that we take as conservative, given the strict definitions that body employs. For up-to-date statistics, see "Figures at a Glance," UNHCR, accessed March 21, 2020, https://www.unhcr.org/uk/figures-at-a-glance.html.

4   Following the Migration Policy Institute definition, "Refugees and asylees are individuals who are unable or unwilling to return to their country of origin or nationality because of persecution or a well-founded fear of persecution." The differences between each category—in terms of admission processes, rights, and status—varies from country to country, but often concerns "the location of the person at the time of application. Refugees are usually outside of [a country] when they are screened for resettlement, whereas asylum seekers submit their applications while they are physically present in [the country] or at a port of entry. See "Refugees and Asylees in the United States," MPI, June 13, 2019, accessed May 28, 2020, "https://www.migrationpolicy.org/article/refugees-and-asylees-united-states

5   Didier Fassin and Estelle D'Halluin, "The Truth from the Body: Medical Certificates as Ultimate Evidence for Asylum Seekers," *American Anthropologist* 107, no. 4 (December 2005): 597–608.

6   Barclays Bank, for example, has sponsored the asylum-focused NGO Immigration Equality as part of its philanthropic portfolio, while investing in military aircraft production and profiting from corporations that run private immigration detention facilities; see "Our Financials," Immigration Equality, accessed March 21, 2020, https://www.immigrationequality.org/about-us/our-financials/#.Xme9bi1ocWp; Marina Gerner, "Barclays' Impact Fund: Should It Be Investing in Military Aircraft?" Money Observer, December 11, 2017, accessed March 21, 2020, https://www.moneyobserver.com/our-analysis/barclays-impact-fund-should-it-be-investing-military-aircraft; Elizabeth Rembert, "Barclays Is Latest to Cut Finance Ties with Private Prisons," Bloomberg, July 31, 2019, accessed March 21, 2020, https://www.bloomberg.com/news/articles/2019-07-31/barclays-is-latest-to-cut-finance-ties-with-private-prison-firms.

7   See "Raytheon Wins DHS ICE Investigative Case Management Modernization Contract" (press release), Raytheon Company, November 14, 2011, accessed March 21, 2020, http://investor.raytheon.com/phoenix.zhtml?c=84193&p=irol-newsArticle&ID=1629873; Jefferson Morley, "Raytheon's Profits Boom Alongside Civilian Deaths in Yemen," Salon, June 27, 2018, accessed March 21, 2020, https://www.salon.com/2018/06/27/raytheons-profits-boom-alongside-civilian-deaths-in-yemen_partner.

8   Charles B. Keely, "The International Refugee Regime(s): The End of the Cold War Matters," *International Migration Review* 35, no. 1, Special Issue: UNHCR at 50: Past, Present and Future of Refugee Assistance (Spring 2001).

9   Nicholas De Genova, "Migration and the Mobility of Labor," in Matt Vidal, Tony Smith, Tomás Rotta, and Paul Prew, eds., *The Oxford Handbook of Karl Marx*, (Oxford: Oxford University Press, 2018).

10 See Jorinde Bijl and Sarah Nimführ, "Contesting Profit Structures: Rejected Asylum Seekers between Modern Slavery and Autonomy," this volume, 297–308.

11 De Genova, "Migration and the Mobility of Labor."

12 The concept of providing sanctuary from persecution, particularly but not only on religious grounds, existed in numerous ancient and medieval

civilizations and religious traditions worldwide. The modern concept of territorial asylum has been discussed and enshrined in documents, including the French Constitution of 1793, the Convention on the International Penal Law adopted in 1889 by the First South American Congress on Private International Law in Montevideo, the Convention on Political Asylum signed by the International Conference of American States in Havana in 1928, and the Universal Declaration of Human Rights, proclaimed by the UN General Assembly in Paris in 1948. For a detailed history of asylum, see S. Prakash Sinha, "History of Asylum," in *Asylum and International Law* (Dordrecht, NL: Springer, 1971), 5–49.

13   For both the Convention and the Protocol, see Convention and Protocol Relating to the Status of Refugees, UNHCR, accessed March 29, 2020, https://www.unhcr.org/protection/basic/3b66c2aa10/convention-protocol-relating-status-refugees.html.

14   Universal Declaration of Human Rights (1948), United Nations, accessed March 29, 2020, https://www.ohchr.org/EN/UDHR/Documents/UDHR_Translations/eng.pdf; Geneva Conventions of 1949 and Additional Protocols and Their Commentaries, International Committee of the Red Cross, accessed March 29, 2020, https://ihl-databases.icrc.org/applic/ihl/ihl.nsf/vwTreaties1949.xsp; North Atlantic Treaty (1949), North Atlantic Treaty Organization, accessed March 29, 2020, https://www.nato.int/cps/en/natolive/official_texts_17120.htm.

15   Keely, "The International Refugee Regime(s)," 307.

16   Ibid.

17   Aihwa Ong, *Buddha Is Hiding:* (Berkeley: University of California Press, 2003), 81–90; Yêên Lêê Espiritu, "Toward a Critical Refugee Study: The Vietnamese Refugee Subject in US Scholarship," *Journal of Vietnamese Studies* 1, no. 1–2 (February–August 2006): 410–33, accessed March 21, 2020, https://vs.ucpress.edu/content/1/1-2/41.full.pdf+html; Susan Bibler Coutin, "Falling Outside: Excavating the History of Central American Asylum Seekers," *Law & Social Inquiry* 36, no. 3 (Summer 2011): 569–96. For an example of popular Western media representation of Angolan refugees, see James Brooke, "Angolans Flee Both Sides in Civil War" *New York Times*, February 10, 1987, accessed March 21, 2020, https://www.nytimes.com/1987/02/10/world/angolans-flee-both-sides-in-civil-war.html.

18   Susan Gzesh, "Central Americans and Asylum Policy in the Reagan Era," Migration Policy Institute, April 1, 2006, accessed March 21, 2020, https://www.migrationpolicy.org/article/central-americans-and-asylum-policy-reagan-era; Melly Cooper, "Afghanistan as a 'Safe Country': The Fallacy Behind Deportations," Choose Love, Help Refugees, February 1, 2018, accessed March 21, 2020, https://helprefugees.org/news/afghanistan-unlawful-deportations.

19   In 1949, the United Nations created its Relief and Works Agency for Palestine Refugees in the Near East (UNRWA), which has historically used its own definition of "refugee." The UN continues to count Palestinian refugees separately from other refugee populations in its statistical reports. See, e.g., "Figures at a Glance," UNHCR.

20 Refugee Relief Act of 1953, Documents of American History 2, M2010, accessed April 21, 2020, http://tucnak.fsv.cuni.cz/~calda/Documents/1950s/Refugee_53. html.

21 Sarah Lazar, "How the Red Scare Shaped the Artificial Distinction Between Migrants and Refugees," *In These Times*, February 5, 2018, accessed March 21, 2020, http://inthesetimes.com/article/20888/cold-war-anti-communism-political-refugee-economic-migrant-war-poverty.

22 James C. McKinley Jr., "Rwanda's Paralyzing Wound: Hutu-Tutsi Killings," *New York Times*, December 22, 1997, accessed April 7, 2020, https://www.nytimes.com/1997/12/22/world/rwanda-s-paralyzing-wound-hutu-tutsi-killings.html; David Rieff, "Dangerous Pity," *Prospect Magazine*, July 23, 2005, access April 7, 2020, https://www.prospectmagazine.co.uk/magazine/dangerouspity.

23 Liisa H. Malkki, "Speechless Emissaries: Refugees, Humanitarianism, and Dehistoricization," *Cultural Anthropology* 11, no. 3 (August 1996): 377–78.

24 Keely, "The International Refugee Regime(s)," 306.

25 Monish Bhatia, "Researching 'Bogus' Asylum Seekers, 'Illegal' Migrants and 'Crimmigrants,'" in Karen Lumsden and Aaron Winter, eds., *Reflexivity in Criminological Research* (London: Palgrave Macmillan, 2014), 162–77.

26 See, e.g., Miriam Ticktin, *Casualties of Care: Immigration and the Politics of Humanitarianism in France* (Berkeley: University of California Press, 2011); Erica Bornstein and Peter Redfield, eds., *Forces of Compassion: Humanitarianism between Ethics and Politics* (Santa Fe, NM: School for Advanced Research Press, 2011).

27 Malkki, "Speechless Emissaries," 378.

28 Didier Fassin, "The Precarious Truth of Asylum," *Public Culture* 25, no. 1 (Winter 2013): 39–63, accessed March 21, 2020, https://static.ias.edu/morals. ias.edu/files/Truth-PC-VO.pdf.

29 Natascha Klocker and Kevin M. Dunn, "Who's Driving the Asylum Debate? Newspaper and Government Representations of Asylum Seekers," *Media International Australia Incorporating Culture and Policy* 109, no. 1 (January 2003): 71–92, accessed March 21, 2020, https://pdfs.semanticscholar.org/9479/f1f5d4 fbdde3b33ac57373896cefd0c84c9f.pdf; Michael Welch, "Quiet Constructions in the War on Terror: Subjecting Asylum Seekers to Unnecessary Detention," *Social Justice* 31, no. 1–2 (2004): 113–29; Ambalavaner Sivanandan, "Race, Terror and Civil Society," *Race & Class* 47, no. 3 (Spring–Summer 2006): 1–8, accessed March 21, 2020, http://ieas.unideb.hu/admin/file_9717.pdf.

30 This has occurred notably with regard to illness, (Fassin, "The Precarious Truth of Asylum"), sexuality (Siobhán McGuirk, "(In)credible Subjects: NGOs, Attorneys, and Permissible 'LGBT Asylum Seeker' Identities," *PoLAR: Political and Legal Anthropology Review* 41[S1] [September 2018]: 4–15), and gender-based violence (Ticktin, *Casualties of Care*).

31 McGuirk, "(In)credible Subjects."

32 On narratives of "suitable" multiculturalism in relation to migration, see Sara Ahmed, "Multiculturalism and the Promise of Happiness," *New Formations* 63 (Winter 2007–2008): 121–37, accessed March 21, 2020, https://webadmin.mcgill. ca/igsf/files/igsf/Ahmed1_multiculturalism.pdf.

33 Kerry Moore, "'Asylum Shopping' in the Neoliberal Social Imaginary," *Media, Culture & Society* 35, no. 3 (April 2013): 348–65. "Fact Sheet: President Donald J. Trump Is Ensuring Non-Citizens Do Not Abuse Our Nation's Public Benefit," White House, August 12, 2019, accessed March 21, 2020, https://www.whitehouse.gov/briefings-statements/president-donald-j-trump-ensuring-non-citizens-not-abuse-nations-public-benefit.

34 Bhatia, "Researching 'Bogus' Asylum Seekers"; Andrew Markus and Dharmalingam Arunachalam, "Australian Public Opinion on Asylum," *Migration and Development* 7, no. 3 (May 2018): 435–47; Shenilla Mohamed l, "South Africa: Failing Asylum System Is Exacerbating Xenophobia," Amnesty International, October 29, 2019, accessed March 21, 2020, https://www.amnesty.org/en/latest/news/2019/10/south-africa-failing-asylum-system-is-exacerbating-xenophobia.

35 Adrienne Pine, "Forging an Anthropology of Neoliberal Fascism," *Public Anthropologist* 1, no. 1 (January 2019): 20–40.

36 Helen Davison, "Asylum Seeker Rallies across Australia Draw Thousands in Support of Refugees," *Guardian*, October 11, 2015, accessed March 29, 2020, https://www.theguardian.com/world/2015/oct/11/asylum-seeker-rallies-across-australia-draw-thousands-in-support-of-refugees; Jessica Longbottom, "Hundreds Protest in Melbourne against Offshore Detention of Asylum Seekers," ABC News, April 30, 2016, accessed March 29, 2020, https://www.abc.net.au/news/2016-04-30/hundreds-protest-in-melbourne-against-offshore-detention/7373094; Katharine Murphy, "Labor's Left Wing Growing Uneasy about Nauru Children and Pacific Trade Deal," *Guardian*, October 6, 2018, accessed March 29, 2020, https://www.theguardian.com/australia-news/2018/oct/07/labors-left-wing-growing-uneasy-about-nauru-children-and-pacific-trade-deal; "Australia Government Loses Bill Blocking Sick Asylum Seekers," BBC News, February 12, 2019, accessed March 29, 2020, https://www.bbc.co.uk/news/world-australia-47193899.

37 See, e.g., Thomas Gammeltoft-Hansen and Ninna Nyberg Sørensen, eds., *The Migration Industry and the Commercialization of International Migration* (London: Routledge, 2013); Sophie Cranston, Joris Schapendonk, and Ernst Spaan, eds., "New Directions in Exploring the Migration Industries: Introduction to Special Issue," *Journal of Ethnic and Migration Studies* 44, no. 4 (March 2018): 543–57, accessed March 26, 2020, https://www.tandfonline.com/doi/full/10.1080/1369183X.2017.1315504.

38 Angela Y. Davis, "The Prison Industrial Complex" (speech), Colorado College, Colorado, May 5, 1997; Julia Chinyere Oparah, *Global Lockdown: Race, Gender, and the Prison-Industrial Complex* (New York: Routledge, 2005); Patrisia Macías-Rojas, *From Deportation to Prison: The Politics of Immigration Enforcement in Post-Civil Rights America* (New York: New York University Press, 2016).

39 Laura María Agustín, *Sex at the Margins: Migration, Labour Markets and the Rescue Industry* (London: Zed Books, 2007); INCITE! Women of Color against Violence, eds., *The Revolution Will Not Be Funded: Beyond the Nonprofit Industrial Complex* (Cambridge, MA: South End Press, 2007).

40 James Ferguson and Akhil Gupta, "Spatializing States: Toward an Ethnography of Neoliberal Governmentality," *American Ethnologist* 29, no. 4 (November 2002): 981–1002; Jon Stratton, "Uncertain Lives: Migration, the Border and Neoliberalism in Australia," *Social Identities* 15, no. 5 (September 2009): 677–92.

41 Apostolova, "Of Refugees and Migrants"; Zimmermann, "Reconsidering the Problem of 'Bogus' Refugees with 'Socio-economic Motivations' for Seeking Asylum."

42 Susan Bibler Coutin, "Smugglers or Samaritans in Tucson, Arizona: Producing and Contesting Legal Truth," *American Ethnologist* 22, no. 3 (August 1995): 549–71; Fassin, "The Precarious Truth of Asylum."

43 This is in part due to the difference between a nation-state's adjudicating asylum claims directly and consequently offering (or refusing) refuge within its own territory, and the UNHCR-supported "refugee status determination" (RSD) process, which generally leads to refuge and resettlement in a third country, if the application is successful; see "Figures at a Glance," UNHCR.

44 The distinction between "industrialized" and "non-industrialized" is used by the UNHCR in its asylum reporting, which specifies: "The 44 industrialized countries are: the 28 member states of the European Union, Albania, Bosnia and Herzegovina, Iceland, Liechtenstein, Montenegro, Norway, Serbia and Kosovo, Switzerland, the former Yugoslav Republic of Macedonia, and Turkey, as well as Australia, Canada, Japan, New Zealand, the Republic of Korea, and the United States of America."; *UNHCR: Asylum Trends 2014: Levels and Trends in Industrialized Countries,* (Geneva: UNHCR, 2015), 4, accessed March 21, 2020, https://www.unhcr.org/uk/statistics/unhcrstats/551128679/asylum-levels-trends-industrialized-countries-2014.html. We do not regard this distinction uncritically and use it here to demonstrate the UNHCR's own definitional categories. Which and how many countries the UNHCR supports in RSD processes fluctuates year by year; see, e.g., *UNHCR Statistical Yearbook 2014,* (Geneva: UNHCR, 2015), accessed March 21, 2020, https://www.unhcr.org/56655f4cb.html.

45 See, e.g., "World Migration Report 2020," IOM UN Migration, accessed March 21, 2020, https://www.iom.int/wmr/2020#block-views-block-world-migration-report-2020-infosheet-block-1; "Global Trends," UNHCR, accessed March 21, 2020, https://www.unhcr.org/globaltrends2018.

46 Jessica Meyers, "China Once Welcomed Refugees, but Its Policies Now Make Trump Look Lenient," *LA Times*, October 18, 2017, accessed March 21, 2020, https://www.latimes.com/world/asia/la-fg-china-forgotten-refugees-2017108-story.html.

I
Crossings

On Seeking Refuge from an Undeclared War

José López

My journey toward becoming an asylum seeker began with a series of violent assaults in my hometown of Tegucigalpa, Honduras, where I was a small business owner.[1] One day in 2015, I noticed I was being followed by a group of men on my way to and from work. This continued for a while, until they attacked me twice in one week. Even as part of the anti-government resistance movement and a gay man, nothing like that had ever happened to me before. I was afraid, so I moved to a new apartment. The same men found me soon after and attacked me for a third time.

Eventually, the violence subsided. Then, the following summer, I was carjacked. My boyfriend and I immediately reported it to the police, but carjackings are extremely common in Honduras. Insurance companies find reasons not to pay out on the claims, as they did with me once my car was found, abandoned and wrecked. Then, two weeks later, my boyfriend received a Facebook threat from a fake profile saying that they were going to kill both of us. The message said, "You're dating José. Get ready, because we're going to kill you both."

This type of violence has always been well-organized in Honduras, but it's such a small country, and we don't want to be *perceived* as violent. Most of the violence comes from the state and national security structures. They decide who the victim is, who the perpetrator is, and where (and where not) to sow fear. Honduras is, effectively, in a state of undeclared and unrecognized civil war.

After the carjacking and the Facebook threat, I was *really* afraid and thought about leaving Honduras for the first time. I had suffered five violent incidents in one year. The sixth one came soon after, at the hands of Frank, a big guy in the neighborhood.

When I first opened my store, Frank showed up every day asking for work. I had my reservations: he was a hard worker, but he was openly homophobic, very right-wing, and explicitly anti-communist. Eventually, I agreed to hire him. While we never spoke about politics, he knew my family was with the resistance movement. Over time, Frank became hostile. He dropped hints about working as a hit man and being involved with an organized crime mafia in Tegucigalpa. His Facebook profile showed pictures of him holding weapons, and I suspected he engaged in extortion. He would sneer publicly at my politics, and my brother later told me that he'd made comments about my store behind my back, like "this place is full of faggots."

Once again, I started to worry about my safety. I fired Frank, explaining that there wasn't enough money to pay him. That was a mistake. A few days later, he came back and said, "You fired me so you could buy a car." That was a threat. It became clear to me that Frank was a walking war tax; we hadn't employed him to protect us from outside dangers but to keep us safe *from him*.

I knew then that my life was in danger. I had to leave Honduras.

The Consequences of Fear

I knew nothing about asylum when I was in Tegucigalpa. It's not something people talk about. It's not something anyone wants to do—unless they have to. I chose to go to the United States, because it's close to Honduras, jobs are available, LGBT people have more rights there, and I had friends I could stay with for a while. But I didn't *want* to go there. In the United States, there is so much stigmatization of immigrants and people from Latin America. But it was my best option.

I left Honduras in 2016 in a state of fear and shock. I had no time to plan. When a situation is this fucked and you're in the middle of it, you can't prepare as you do when calmly applying for a visa. For two months after I arrived in New York, I was mentally blocked. It was only when I started calling human rights organizations that I learned about the asylum process. I was told that New York was a good city to be in when seeking asylum, but I had a hard time getting help. I went to LGBT rights organizations, spoke with attorneys who do pro bono work, visited state offices, even the Department of Homeland Security (DHS). No one would help me. A woman working at DHS told me: "Asylum is for Russians and Chinese people, not for Hondurans."

The most useful information I found was online. I printed the application form and my I-94 Arrival/Departure Record, filled everything out, and stuck it in the mail. Then I traveled back to Honduras to clear out my apartment, take care of my work (and my ten employees), and pick up my personal documents. I had no idea I wasn't allowed to go back to my home country after submitting the asylum application.

I went back because I had left behind a mess that was affecting my family. Between the muggings, the carjacking, moving frequently to new apartments to evade being found by my attackers, and fleeing to the United States, I had racked up a debt of over $12,000. I was afraid to go home but believed I could avoid danger if I stayed just a few days.

Less than a week later, I headed back to the United States. When I arrived at Atlanta airport for my flight connection to New York, airport security took me aside and began to look through my luggage. They interrogated me and searched my phone to see "if I had been looking for work." As soon as I said I was seeking asylum, their demeanor changed. I was already in their system. At first, I thought that was a good thing.

I was held for twelve hours and was made to do a mini credible fear interview on the spot,[2] where an immigration officer wrote down every aspect of my story. Afterward, I was given a choice: voluntary deportation back to Honduras or speak with a judge in a couple of weeks. I chose the latter. They took my suitcase and put me on a bus. I had no idea I was being transferred to one of the worst immigration prisons in the country.

Detention

On September 9, 2016, I arrived at Atlanta City Detention Center. It was awful. A lot of people got sick there. People were dying. One man went to the emergency room, and we never heard from him again. His parents in Guatemala didn't hear from him either. I later found out that the city of Atlanta was paid $78 a day by the US federal government for each ICE (Immigration and Customs Enforcement) detainee held in the jail. That means Atlanta made $7,020 off my suffering. In total, the city's profits from the jail added up to millions of dollars per year.[3] I am glad that Mayor Keisha Lance Bottoms decided to shut the jail down in 2019.

When I arrived, I was put in a "pod"—a cell with two small bunk beds and a tiny window. It was awful. The entire prison area was about two

The view from my cell window

thousand square meters (approximately 6,500 square feet). There was no outdoor recreational area. Apart from eating in the common space, most of the time we were locked in our cells. The food was terrible, and it was never enough.

At the airport they said I'd speak to an immigration judge within weeks. I was detained for months before I got the chance. Daily life was rough. As soon as I arrived, a gay Venezuelan man told me, "It's not going to work out for you. Give up your right to see a judge and go back to Honduras." I saw people placed in solitary confinement for up to twelve days. The United Nations says that fifteen days or more solitary is "torture."

In immigration prison, everything costs money. From attorneys to phone calls to extra food, everything is expensive. I spent over $500 in three months there—money I borrowed from from a friend of my brother. It's an entire economic system. Nearly all immigration prisons are run by the private sector. There is massive money in asylum. The state pays corporations to provide food and services according to how many prisoners are there. I found out that the US government *requires* that over thirty thousand people be held in detention facilities every day.[4] That money goes straight to prison companies and investors. Central Americans and Mexicans make up the majority of people they put in detention. Some people ended up in prison because of minor traffic infractions, like driving without a driver's license. In Georgia, if you don't have the right immigration papers, things like that can put you in prison for years.

In detention, violence was an everyday reality. The place was overcrowded. People were transported there from across the entire South and even places like Calexico, California. You felt the hatred in how the guards looked at you. Georgia has a history of anti-immigrant and anti-Black laws, and there are even white supremacists within the court system. You can tell. Some prisoners were allowed to bring in razor blades and knives. Along with the guards, they conspired against other prisoners they didn't like to send them to solitary confinement.

We had very limited access to pro bono lawyers. I made attempts to find one and so did my family, but we had no luck. Being proficient in English, I decided to prepare my case myself. I spent a lot of time in front of the jail computer, doing research and writing down relevant information about immigration law. I helped other prisoners write letters in Spanish and English, and I explained aspects of their cases to them. It became my currency, my capital. One guy who had bullied me stopped when he saw that I could help him.

I also read books and wrote about my experiences, some of which was published in a popular alternative media website in Honduras. That was the only way to pass the time. Otherwise, I would have died of depression. It was forty-five days before I finally saw an immigration judge.

Courting Deportation

On November 6, 2016, I arrived in an immigration court that was just fifteen minutes away from my prison. I knew my case would be complicated to explain—a mix of political oppression, extortion, and homophobia. Plus, I was representing myself pro se—without a lawyer.

Everyone was surprised that I had come to court alone and even more surprised that I spoke English well. The court usually has three main players: the DHS lawyer making the case to deport you, the judge as the arbiter hearing both sides, and your lawyer—or in my case, me.

I stood in front of the judge in handcuffs. Always handcuffs. He began to review my application. He was visibly impressed. Based on my research, I should have gotten an asylum hearing date for the beginning of December, four weeks later. Instead, he said, "Very good, your papers are in perfect order. I'm putting your next hearing date for January 25." An additional two months in jail, with everything in "perfect order." I could not believe it.

Shocked and upset, I said to the judge: "No. I cannot wait any longer." I told him that I was withdrawing my application. He tried to calm me down. He said it was the best pro se application he had seen in his seventeen years working on immigration cases. It felt like the judge was trying to say I had a good shot at getting asylum. But who was he to guarantee that? Just 2 percent of applicants in Atlanta are granted asylum.[5]

Another reason I withdrew my application was for my own security. My pod, unlike the other pods in the prison, had a mix of asylum seekers coming from abroad and outbound deportees detained on criminal charges, some of whom were dangerous criminals. One of these, a man who clearly had privileges granted by staff, had secured the expulsion of a Black man he did not like from the pod. Shortly afterward, as I was lining up for my dinner, he loudly said to me: "Let's see who's next." He had been caught before, during one of the midnight internal prison police raids, with a knife made from razor blades.

Knowing that the odds were stacked against me and feeling that my life was at risk, I made my decision. I sat in the back of the courtroom in handcuffs crying, as I waited for the guard to take me and the other detainees back to detention.

Over the next few days, I was just freaking out. I didn't want to go back to Honduras. Even though I had just requested a voluntary deportation, it did not feel voluntary. It took me another couple of weeks before I finally submitted the paperwork. Then another month in detention before I was deported. You never know when you are actually going to leave. You find out on the morning of the flight, at 5:00 a.m., when the guards make the announcement.

The morning my name was called, I rode in the back of a car to the airport, along with another Honduran, a Colombian, and a Guatemalan. I boarded my aircraft from the runway, ascending the stairs to where passengers were heading onto commercial flights. It was a humiliating, awful experience. From the airplane gates, everyone saw me, in handcuffs, getting onto the plane. Two ICE officers stood by the gate door until the plane started to move.

I was deported on December 7, the day before my birthday.

The Mark of Asylum

As soon as I was back in Honduras, Frank showed up. I was staying in my mother's home and only left the house to go to work. I only went to my store once or twice, but he was always there, in the parking lot with a friend of his. They always knew where I was. I knew I had to leave again for my safety.

Today, I live in Barcelona, Spain. After waiting two and a half years for a decision on the claim I filed here, I was finally granted asylum in

December 2019. The process was slow, and life continues to be hard. I have been depressed. The economic conditions in Spain are horrible, and the general quality of life is poor. There is pervasive discrimination against Latin Americans. I work at a call center and half of my earnings go toward rent.

Every day, I carry the mark of asylum, an emotional and financial burden. Back home, my business is a disaster, on the brink of collapse. I still owe 600,000 Honduran lempiras (approximately US$24,000) for my past debts, which I need to pay back within six years. My family is suffering the consequences. My boyfriend lives the United States, and we want to get married, but getting a fiancé (K-1) visa is complicated, especially after my deportation. It's in the works, but our lawyers in San Francisco keep asking for more money without producing anything new.

Meanwhile, the immigration profit-making machine keeps turning. As the US government funds military interventions in Honduras, my people continue to be extorted and harassed by their own government and forced to flee their homes. The same violence that forces people in one country to seek asylum enables another country to fill its detention cells and fill prison contractors' pockets. It's a vicious cycle with profit at every stage, from detention and deportation to relying on immigrants to accept poorly paid jobs that make bosses rich. And even Donald Trump knows that.

José López (pseudonym) is an agronomist, small business owner, and member of the Honduran resistance movement. He was granted asylum in Spain, where he now lives.

Notes

1   "José López" is a pseudonym.
2   Editors' note: a credible fear interview is an interview of the asylum applicant following initial contact with US Customs and Border Protection, conducted by an asylum officer from the United States Citizenship and Immigration Services (USCIS) Asylum Division to determine whether the applicant has a prima facie case that makes it plausible that they could be granted asylum.
3   Editors' note: see Jeremy Redmon, "Atlanta Mayor Under Fire Amid Debate Over Illegal Immigration," *Atlanta Journal-Constitution*, November 17, 2017, accessed March 29, 2020, https://www.ajc.com/news/state--regional-govt--politics/atlanta-mayor-under-fire-amid-debate-over-illegal-immigration.
4   Editors' note: The infamous "bed quota" was eventually removed in mid-2017. However, under the Trump administration, the number of people held per

night in immigration detention has continuously risen above the original quota of thirty-four thousand.

5   Editors' note: Planning, Analysis, and Statistics Division, *Statistics Yearbook Fiscal Year 2018* (Washington, DC: US Department of Justice, 2018), 28, accessed March 29, 2020, https://www.justice.gov/eoir/file/1198896/download; For more on the Atlanta asylum statistics, see Jeremy Redmon, "Georgia's Immigration Court Judges among Toughest in Nation for Asylum," *Atlanta Journal-Constitution*, July 25, 2019, accessed March 21, 2020, https://www.ajc.com/news/breaking-news/georgia-immigration-court-judges-among-toughest-nation-for-asylum/svQ2CmRGXS5Hgi2utVTmrO.

The Business of Selling Life: Reflections from a Rescue Ship in the Mediterranean Sea

Alva, Uyi, and Madi

The *Aquarius*

The *Aquarius* was a search and rescue ship that patrolled the Mediterranean Sea from February 2016 to October 2018.[1] It was funded by donations, operated by Médecins Sans Frontières (MSF), and run by volunteers. It takes ships like the *Aquarius* three days to cover the three-hundred-mile stretch of water that separates Libya and Italy. In Libya, smugglers tell people waiting to cross that the journey takes three hours.

A rubber vessel carrying approximately one hundred people, seen from the *Aquarius*. Often, only men are visible at first. Women and children on board usually sit in the middle of the boat, where they are at risk of suffocation if the floor cracks. Corrosive puddles of fuel and salt pool on the floor and burn people's skin.

Most of the vessels intercepted by rescue ships in the Mediterranean are flimsy rubber boats designed for forty people and loaded with over a hundred. They are not intended to withstand the journey to Europe, carrying just enough fuel to sail a few miles from the coastline. They are either intercepted by Libyan authorities and returned to Libya, rescued by a nongovernmental organization (NGO) ship, or they sink.

NGO ships play an important role in the Mediterranean, one that was previously filled by European states. In 2014, the European Union pressured the Italian government to end its Mare Nostrum (Our Sea) program, which had previously provided rescue boats, food, and medical and legal services to migrants rescued at sea. Frontex, the EU's border security agency, replaced Mare Nostrum with Operation Triton and a new mandate: "search and rescue" became "border control." Triton patrols the Italian coast—too far from Libya to reach vessels in distress before they and their passengers sink.

In 2017, the Italian government introduced a code of conduct for NGO-sponsored boats, in an attempt to ban the transfer of refugees to larger rescue ships and to force NGO crews to allow police officers on board.[2]

Such policies have been met with dismay by human rights advocates. The German charity Sea-Watch accused the EU of "willfully letting refugees drown," while Amnesty International characterized the code as a "concerted smear campaign" against NGO rescue operations.[3]

Governmental decisions to defund rescue operations and to "cooperate" with Libyan authorities—all under the rubric of "border control"—have had deadly consequences. In 2016, an estimated five thousand people died attempting to cross the Mediterranean to Europe.[4] Thousands more drowned in boats that sank unseen. People intercepted by the Libyan authorities or deemed by Frontex adjudicators to be "irregular migrants"—the vast majority of those who survive the journey and make it to Italy—are "sent back" to state-run detention centers in Libya,[5] where they face enslavement, captivity, and violent exploitation.[6]

Critics argue that rescue boats incentivize crossings. State governments and EU bodies promote this view, critiquing and intervening in independent search and rescue operations. People making the crossings tell a very different story.

"You Pay to Die"

On June 29, 2016, the *Aquarius* intercepted a vessel in distress carrying 111 passengers. Uyi,[7] an artist from Nigeria, was on board. A few hours after the rescue, he drew these images and asked us to photograph them, "so people can see how hard it was making this journey and how we were maltreated."

Uyi: This picture shows the start of the journey crossing the border between Nigeria and Niger by motorbike. It was not an easy decision to leave Nigeria, and getting money to embark on the journey was not easy. It took a lot of time and determination. I spent two months on the road from Nigeria to Libya, and it was terrible, horrible. You pay for every step you take. You have to pay. If you don't pay, you cannot go to the next place. You see people dying on the road. I never knew it would be so dangerous to leave Nigeria.

Uyi: We reached Agadez in Niger. That's where you meet the people who will take you on to the next stage, the smugglers who will take you to Libya. From Agadez, we took a vehicle to Libya. It took us through the Sahara Desert to Qatrun. There were twenty-five people in the vehicle. Women and children too. You can see how we were sitting. Each of us was sitting holding these wooden sticks. If someone falls off, they keep driving. I was in that car for over five days. No water for days while you are in the desert. I felt so bad and so weak. When I got down [from the vehicle], I couldn't even stand. My legs were shaking. It was a bad experience.

Uyi: I was in Libya for close to four months. I was in Sabha, and then in Tripoli, where I did some small jobs. To raise money there was not easy. Then I fell into the hands of other men. They maltreated us. We stayed in a house that was like a prison, where you could not go out; you could not take a shower. I ended up in this house after I met some African guys in Libya. I wanted to make this journey to Europe, and I asked them where they were going. They were also heading this direction, so I thought I would give them the money, and they would bring us here. I didn't know that after giving them the money they would take us to this prison and keep us there for months. They treated us like prisoners and slaves. They were not humans who kept us. They gave us a handful of pasta and saltwater from the sea to drink. They beat people so much. So much. Why? They beat us for talking. They beat you for money. They don't have a reason to beat you. They beat you for no just cause. Because they don't hear you speak English, they beat you. When they wanted us to work, they put us in a van and took us to work somewhere. There were over six hundred people in that place, all different nationalities. Some of those rescued here today [by the *Aquarius*] were in that prison too. From there, they took us to the beach at night and put us in a *lampedusa* [a rubber dinghy, named after the Italian island where many boats land]. You couldn't raise your head to look. If you did, they beat you.

Uyi: A lot of thoughts were going through my mind on this boat, like: "If this thing explodes now, I will die. The water will not help me. Oh, God, please send a rescue. Come save me. Oh, why did I put myself in this mess? No land to put my leg on." Look this way, that way—all sea. A lot of thoughts on my mind that day. It was not easy being on that boat. We stayed on that boat for what felt like days. It was so horrible. You pay to die. That is how it is: you pay to die. We prayed for rescue.

Engendered Dangers

A common misconception is that most people attempting the crossing are adult men. The UNHCR estimates that nearly half are women or children.[8] Smugglers advise people to say that they are over twenty, because adults are taken to less secure processing centers in Italy—from which it is easier to "disappear." Fifteen-year-old Madi travelled alone from Mali.

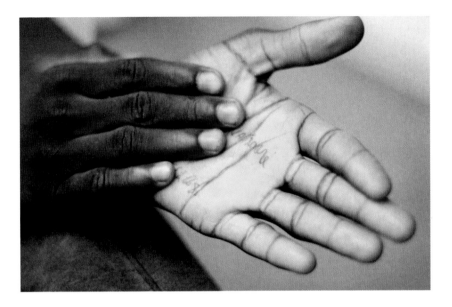

Madi: I went to primary school and I worked on a farm. I travelled in a big truck from Mali to Libya, with sixty-one others. First, I went from Mali to Algeria, and then to Libya. I paid money to get to Libya. On the first day of Ramadan, they put me in prison. They beat me a lot. Under my feet and on my body. No good food and very bad treatment. It was like a very large prison with a metal roof over the top and no windows. Just one door and a little bit of light from where the sun could get in on the sides of the roof. Bandits ran the prison, carrying small pistols and big long guns. I saw dead bodies in that prison. They died of starvation or illnesses. [The guards] held me at gunpoint in the prison to give them money. I paid them so that I could escape. My father is in France. He has been there for eight years. I have his phone number written on my hand. I spoke to him when I was in Mali, and he told me not to make this journey. I said I want to come. My father said that it is too dangerous. But I chose to come. He does not know that I made the journey over the sea. How else could I come?

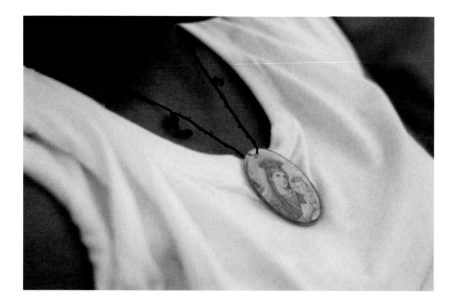

During their journeys, women are exposed to high levels of sexual violence at the hands of smugglers, private individuals, armed groups, militias, criminals, and traffickers. Young Eritrean women told medics on the *Aquarius* that they had been advised to use injectable contraception before starting the journey, as the risk of rape was so high—particularly in the desert and in Libya. Other women did not receive such advice. While on board, they were offered pregnancy tests. Some found out they were pregnant as a result of the rape they had endured reaching Europe. One woman on the ship wanted to take her own life after finding out that she was pregnant.

Fortress Europe
After intercepting a boat in distress, the *Aquarius* travelled back to Europe. When the ship pulled close to port, all on board fell quiet. The mood sank from elation at surviving the crossing to uneasy anticipation. A wealth of hopes, dreams, skills, resilience, and youthful vision arrived in the port—met by administration tents and officials ready to "vet" their owners.

In December 2018, MSF and its partner SOS Méditerranée were forced to terminate operation of the *Aquarius*. MSF announced that the decision "was the result of a sustained campaign, spearheaded by the Italian government and backed by other European states, to delegitimize, slander and obstruct aid organizations providing assistance to vulnerable people."[9]

Eritrean women arriving at the port of Catania, Sicily, on August 23, 2016. The *Aquarius* had taken them aboard, along with over four hundred other people who had been crammed into an unseaworthy old wooden fishing boat. This was their first sight of Europe.

As of January 2019, no dedicated rescue boats were operating in the Central Mediterranean. The UNHCR has warned that while the overall number of people attempting the journey was decreasing, the rate of those dying at sea was rising. In 2018, six people a day died trying to cross the Mediterranean.[10] The UNHCR concludes that cuts in rescue operations by European countries and restrictions on humanitarian boats are pushing up the death toll. By reducing documentation and publicity of vessels in distress, as well as rescue operations themselves, Europe can claim "successes on migration," while thousands continue to drown in its waters.[11]

Alva White works as a BBC journalist when she is not on assignment as a field communications manager for Médecins Sans Frontières.
Uyi is an artist from Nigeria.
Madi is a student from Mali.

Notes
1   All photos by Alva White.
2   Lizzie Dearden, "EU Accused of 'Willfully Letting Refugees Drown' as NGOs Face Having Rescues Suspended in the Mediterranean," *Independent*, July 29, 2017, accessed March 21, 2020, http://www.independent.co.uk/news/world/

europe/refugee-crisis-ngo-rescue-ships-mediterranean-sea-italy-libya-eu-code-of-conduct-deaths-2300-latest-a7866226.html.

3   Dearden, "EU Accused of 'Willfully Letting Refugees Drown' as NGOs Face Having Rescues Suspended in the Mediterranean."

4   "Desperate Journeys: Refugees and Migrants Entering and Crossing Europe via the Mediterranean and Western Balkans Routes," UNHCR Bureau for Europe, February 2017, accessed March 21, 2020, https://www.unhcr.org/news/updates/2017/2/58b449f54/desperate-journeys-refugees-migrants-entering-crossing-europe-via-mediterranean.html.

5   Alan Travis, "EU Summit to Offer Resettlement to Only 5,000 Refugees," *Guardian*, April 23, 2015, accessed March 21, 2020, https://www.theguardian.com/world/2015/apr/22/most-migrants-crossing-mediterranean-will-be-sent-back-eu-leaders-to-agree.

6   *A Perfect Storm: The Failure of European Policies in the Central Mediterranean*, (London: Amnesty International, 2017), accessed March 21, 2020, https://www.refworld.org/pdfid/597f0fed4.pdf.

7   Both Uyi and Madi requested to use their first names only.

8   "Desperate Journeys."

9   "Aquarius Forced to End Operations as Europe Condemns People to Drown," Médecins Sans Frontières, December 6, 2018, accessed March 21, 2020, https://www.msf.org/aquarius-forced-end-operations-europe-condemns-people-drown.

10 "Desperate Journeys."

11 "Aquarius Forced to End Operations as Europe Condemns People to Drown."

Trump and the USMCA: From Free Trade to Gassing Migrants

Garry Leech

On November 25, 2018, US Border Patrol agents fired tear gas at hundreds of migrants protesting on the Mexican side of the border.[1] The men, women, and children targeted were among six thousand asylum seekers who had fled violence and poverty in Central America by forming a caravan, which had recently reached the Mexico-US border. Five days later, the leaders of the United States, Mexico, and Canada signed the United States-Mexico-Canada Agreement (USMCA) at the G20 summit in Argentina. The two events were related: many of the migrants gassed at the border were economic refugees who made evident a major contradiction in this and all supposed "free trade" agreements. To facilitate free trade in capital and products these agreements violate one of the basic tenets of the free market: the free movement of *all* commodities—including labor. In addition to signing the USMCA, President Trump also sought to restrict the mobility of workers by building a border wall, deploying troops to the border, and using military force against migrant job seekers. Given this reality, the USMCA could be more accurately called the United States Migrant Control Agreement.

Neoliberal free trade agreements are not about creating free markets so much as they are designed to establish favorable conditions for multinational corporations to maximize profits through access to low-wage labor. By not allowing the free movement of workers across borders, the USMCA, like its predecessor the North American Free Trade Agreement (NAFTA), ensures that corporations can exploit workers in the Global South. Under both the USMCA and NAFTA, for example, an automobile manufacturer can close down an assembly plant in Detroit and lay off thousands of $30-per-hour workers and open up a factory in Mexico, where wages are $2 per hour.[2]

The Trump administration's token protectionist policies, including aspects of the USMCA, claim to address this issue but fail to do so. If the USMCA were to actually create a free market, then workers would be able to move freely across borders. Such a scenario would lower wages in the United States and Canada but raise them in Mexico, because the movement of workers to regions where wages are higher would theoretically eventually equalize wage levels between the three countries. Instead of auto workers earning $30 an hour in the United States and Canada, and $2 an hour in Mexico, they might earn $15 an hour in all three countries. This would serve corporate interests in lowering wages in the United States and Canada, but would still not be as profitable as the current arrangement of keeping a surplus of impoverished workers trapped in places where wages are staggeringly low.

An inevitable consequence of the neoliberal free trade model in Latin America and throughout most of the Global South is the immiseration of millions of people, many of whom cannot find jobs, while most of those who do earn poverty-level wages. Not surprisingly, many people choose to flee the structural and political violence that has been imposed on them by undertaking the arduous and dangerous journey to a country where they might be able to earn a living wage and have a better chance at physical survival: the United States. The thousands of refugees in caravans that arrived at the US border in late 2018 were just the latest of many waves of migrants that have fled the violence of neoliberal free trade agreements. We need only look at the history of NAFTA to see how this has played out over the past twenty-five years.

NAFTA dramatically reduced the tariffs and quotas that a country could impose on imports from a NAFTA partner. The agreement still permitted agricultural subsidies, however—largely at the insistence of the US government—in theory allowing the three governments to support their agricultural producers.[3] In actuality, the United States and Canada could provide subsidies, but Mexico could not, a discrepancy caused by the broader neoliberal framework of global capitalism: conditions placed on loans provided to Mexico by both the International Monetary Fund (IMF) and the United States during the 1980s and early 1990s stipulated that the Mexican government reduce its subsidies to the agricultural sector.[4] As such, neoliberal austerity measures imposed on the country actually ensured that Mexico could not exercise the same NAFTA "allowances" as its partners.

The biased structure favored US and Canadian agribusinesses, constituting further structural violence that shattered the lives of millions of Mexican small farmers through NAFTA-sanctioned dumping of heavily subsidized US food products onto the Mexican market. Between 1997 and 2005, for example, US agricultural subsidies to domestic corn producers averaged $4.5 billion a year.[5] This corn was then sold in Mexico at far below cost; unsubsidized Mexican farmers could not compete. Imports from the United States quickly came to dominate the Mexican market, devastating local producers of Mexico's principal food staple.[6]

For supporters of NAFTA, this outcome was unproblematic. In their imagined scenario, Mexican farmers who could no longer compete would, in theory, abandon agriculture to become wage laborers in Mexico's manufacturing sector—at which point they would begin purchasing imported food. The prediction was only partly right: Mexican farmers did abandon their lands, in startling numbers. By 2006, an estimated two million Mexican farmers had quit farming.[7] Many of those displaced farmers joined the exodus of other poor people from rural areas across the country to cities in northern Mexico, which experienced a manufacturing boom in the early years of the trade agreement. By 2000, NAFTA had created seven hundred thousand manufacturing jobs in maquiladoras, or assembly plants. The massive displacement of peasants from the countryside to the cities ensured sufficient surplus labor to keep wages low—an average of $1.74 per hour.[8] By 2003, however, more than three hundred thousand of those jobs had moved overseas, primarily to China, where the interests of multinational corporations were better served by even lower labor costs.[9] Even at its height, NAFTA failed to create enough manufacturing jobs to accommodate—never mind fairly pay—the farmworker population it had displaced. The devastating economic impacts of NAFTA forced millions of Mexicans to seek survival elsewhere, with the United States the most logical destination for many.

Creating Refugees, from NAFTA to CAFTA

For most of the twentieth century, Mexican migration to the United States constituted little more than a trickle. In 1994, the year that NAFTA went into effect, there were only 4.8 million Mexican-born residents living in the United States. By 2000, that number had almost doubled, to 9 million. It continued to grow after that.[10] The economic refugees who cross the increasingly militarized Mexico-US border are criminalized and targeted for violence by the US government, but these factors have not deterred many impoverished Mexicans when weighed against the dire circumstances they face at home. According to the US government's own statistics, more than two thousand migrants died trying to cross the border during the first decade of NAFTA.[11]

In 2006, the Central American Free Trade Agreement (CAFTA-DR) extended the agricultural provisions in NAFTA to Guatemala, Honduras, El Salvador, Nicaragua, Costa Rica, and the Dominican Republic. CAFTA has devastated farmers in Honduras, Guatemala, and El Salvador in the same manner that NAFTA destroyed the livelihood of farmers in Mexico. The massive displacement of rural farmworkers in these Central American countries ensured a surplus labor force that kept wages low in garment sweatshops that produce clothing for US-based brand name designers.[12]

By 2017, however, clothing exports from Honduras—the largest Central American exporter of clothing—to the United States had fallen by 24 percent, while Guatemala saw its apparel exports plummet by 40 percent.[13] As had happened with Mexico's maquiladoras, corporations using garment sweatshop labor in Honduras and Guatemala simply moved operations further overseas to even more profitable locations. So after destroying the livelihoods of Central American farmers, CAFTA also led to thousands of Honduran and Guatemalan garment workers losing their jobs. The worsening economic reality has been compounded by the extreme levels of violence that have plagued Honduras since the US-supported military coup in 2009. As a result, millions of Hondurans have had little choice but to flee the country's rampant corruption, state-sanctioned violence, unemployment, and poverty.[14]

The thousands of asylum seekers who travelled toward the United States in migrant caravans in 2018 were not "hardened criminals," as President Trump declared.[15] Nearly half were women and children, refugees of neoliberal free trade agreements. It is worth noting that while the mainstream US media openly blamed Venezuela's socialist policies for people leaving that South American country, they very rarely pointed out that "hordes" of refugees arriving from Honduras and other Central American nations are fleeing the failures of capitalism in those places. This discrepancy was echoed by politicians; as Mexican and Central American asylum seekers faced repression at the southern border, Republican senators were calling for special immigration protections for Venezuelans in the United States.[16]

When President Trump met with the leaders of Mexico and Canada to smile for the cameras, shake hands, and sign the USMCA, thousands of refugees were desperately waiting at the US border, hoping and praying that the richest and most powerful country in the world would open its doors to them. It is a potent irony that they sought asylum in the very country responsible for their dire predicament. Yet they were not allowed to enter the United States. Despite being workers in the "free market," these migrants did not have the same right as capital or the commodities produced by labor to move freely across borders. A majority of those at the border were further denied their legal right to apply for asylum.

The migrants in that caravan and thousands of others since have found themselves trapped on the Mexican side of a heavily guarded frontier, from where they can watch thousands of trucks full of new cars, televisions, computers, clothing, and other commodities cross freely into the United States. The USMCA has not changed this reality; it has not eliminated the trade barrier that restricts the free movement of workers. After all, giving labor the same right to free movement as other commodities fetishized under capitalism would infringe on the "right" of multinational corporations to exploit workers to maximize profits. And what if gassing men, women, and children is necessary to safeguard those profits? Under the Trump administration's United States Migrant Control Agreement, so be it.

Garry Leech is an independent journalist and the author of numerous books about human rights and economic globalization. He also teaches international politics at Cape Breton University in Canada.

Notes

1   Daniel González and Rafael Carranza, "US Border Agents Fire Tear Gas as Some Migrants Protesting Slow Asylum Process Try to Breach Fence," *USA Today*, November 25, 2018, accessed March 21, 2020, https://www.usatoday.com/story/news/2018/11/25/immigrant-caravan-us-agents-fire-tear-gas-slow-migrants/2110267002.
2   Michael Wayland, "UAW-FCA Deal Sets $29 Top Wage for Entry-Level Workers," *Detroit News*, October 8, 2015, accessed March 21, 2020, https://detroitnews.com/story/business/autos/chrysler/2015/10/08/new-uaw-fca-contract-includes-cap-entry-level-workers/73593558; Mark Stevenson, "In

Mexico, $2 Per Hour Workers Make $40,000 SUVs," Associated Press News, September 25, 2017, accessed March 1, 2020, https://www.apnews.com/a9866 4091478482e90b739766a1c5857.

3   Timothy A. Wise, "The Impacts of U.S. Agricultural Policies on Mexican Producers," in Jonathan Fox and Libby Haight, eds., *Subsidizing Inequality: Mexican Corn Policy Since NAFTA* (Washington, DC: Woodrow Wilson International Center for Scholars, 2010), 165.

4   Steve Suppan, "Mexican Corn, NAFTA and Hunger, May 1996, Fact Sheet 3," Institute for Agriculture and Trade Policy, May 15, 1996, accessed March 21, 2020, https://www.iatp.org/documents/mexican-corn-nafta-and-hunger-may-1996-fact-sheet-3.

5   Wise, "The Impacts of U.S. Agricultural Policies on Mexican Producers," 165.

6   Ibid., 166.

7   Roger Bybee and Carolyn Winter, "Immigration Flood Unleashed by NAFTA's Disastrous Impact on Mexican Economy," Common Dreams, April 25, 2006, accessed March 21, 2020, https://www.commondreams.org/views06/0425-30.htm.

8   Collin Harris, "NAFTA and the Political Economy of Mexican Migration," ZNet, June 7, 2010, accessed March 21, 2020, https://zcomm.org/znetarticle/nafta-and-the-political-economy-of-mexican-immigration-by-collin-harris.

9   Ibid.

10 Ibid.

11 *Report to the Honorable Bill Frist, Majority Leader, U.S. Senate: Illegal Immigration: Border-Crossing Deaths Have Doubled Since 1995; Border Patrol's Efforts to Prevent Deaths Have Not Been Fully Evaluated*, (Washington, DC: United States Government Accountability Office, 2006), 16.

12 Héctor Perla Jr., "The Impact of CAFTA: Drugs, Gangs, and Immigration," telesurtv.net, March 1, 2016, accessed March 29, 2020, https://www.telesurenglish.net/opinion/The-Impact-of-CAFTA-Drugs-Gangs-and-Immigration-20160301-0008.html.

13 Public Citizen's Global Trade Watch, "CAFTA's Tragic Legacy in Central America: Failed Trade Policy That Drove Millions from Their Homes," Public Citizen, August 22, 2018, accessed March 29, 2020, https://www.citizen.org/article/caftas-tragic-legacy-in-central-america-failed-trade-policy-that-drove-millions-from-their-homes.

14 See José López, "On Seeking Refuge from an Undeclared War," this volume, 21–28.

15 "Trump: Migrants Headed to US Hardened Criminals," *US News & World Report*, October 19, 2018, accessed March 21, 2020, https://www.usnews.com/news/best-states/arizona/articles/2018-10-19/the-latest-trump-calls-senate-hopeful-mcsally-brilliant.

16 Franco Ordoñez, "Amid Border Crackdown, White House May Shield Venezuelans from Deportation," NPR, August 2, 2019, accessed March 21, 2020, https://www.npr.org/2019/08/02/747734905/amid-border-crackdown-white-house-may-shield-venezuelans-from-deportation.

Outsourcing, Responsibility, and Refugee Claim-Making in Australia's Offshore Detention Regime

Sara Dehm

On October 31, 2017, the Australian-run Manus Island Regional Processing Centre (RPC) located at the Lombrum Naval Base in Papua New Guinea (PNG) officially ceased operations. At the time, 606 men still lived there. All had been forcibly transferred from Australia to PNG by Australian authorities and detained at the center at some point during the preceding four years. Most had subsequently been found to be refugees by PNG immigration authorities. As part of the center's closure, PNG and Australian authorities insisted that the men either return to their state of origin (an unviable option for people recognized as having a well-founded fear of persecution in their home state) or relocate to a new temporary accommodation facility—the then-unfinished East Lorengau Refugee Transit Centre (RTC)—in the hope of being resettled in a third country. The fallacy of this "choice" was exacerbated by a lack of available third-country resettlement options: either await the slim possibility of formal resettlement under a fledging (and much-criticized) arrangement with the United States or accept integration into the local PNG community, which offered few prospects of employment or long-term livelihood. Instead, most men opted to remain inside the RPC after its closure and continue protesting their prolonged state of legal limbo and political abandonment.

Organizing collectively around the center's closure, the group publicly demanded that the Australian government recognize its political, legal, and moral responsibility toward them. Materially, the center's closure meant that the provision of essentials like food, water, and medical supplies to the men, who refused to leave the center's grounds, effectively ceased. The decision to remain in the center thus instigated three weeks of intense resistance within the RPC, characterized by state-orchestrated starvation, creative self-reliance, organized protest, and imminent terror. The prominent award-winning Kurdish journalist and filmmaker Behrouz Boochani, detained as a refugee on Manus Island from July 2013 until November 2019, vividly chronicled the center's closing in his "Diary of a Disaster," published in the *Guardian*.[1] In it, Boochani outlined the mantra that united the men during this time: "We will never retreat and leave this prison of hell. We will never move to another prison. We will never settle for anything less than freedom. Only freedom."[2]

In this chapter, I locate struggles around the closure of the Manus Island RPC in the context of broader legal, political, and economic contestations surrounding Australia's punitive offshore refugee detention regime in PNG. I argue that Australia's draconian offshore processing policies have increasingly sought to place the economics of immigration detention outside of the realm of domestic political debate and to obfuscate the Australian state's obligations under international refugee law. This has occurred through the two key strategies of outsourcing and offshoring, which have both, in different ways, devolved legal and practical responsibility for the management and processing of asylum seekers to private corporations and external state authorities.

In the most recent iteration of Australia's offshore detention regime, this mix of external public and private actors, has included two neighboring island states (PNG and Nauru), transnational private companies (Group 4 Securicor [G4S], International Health and Medical Services, Transfield, and Wilson Security), and nongovernmental organizations (Salvation Army and Save the Children). However, as the events of October 2017 demonstrate, the Australian government's practices of exclusion and expulsion have been met with mass refugee protests and claim-making practices from the men held within the Manus Island RPC, who asserted the political, legal, and moral responsibility of the authorities that exercise control over their lives and futures.

One site of these forms of refugee claim-making has been court litigation, both in Australia and PNG. I examine two recent legal challenges initiated by and on behalf of the affected refugees that have shaped the political struggle around the legality and legitimacy of Australia's regional offshore detention regime. At the time of writing, this combined litigation has not (yet) been successful in bringing an end to Australia's offshore processing regime, and the plights and protests of the asylum seekers and refugees who are subjected to this violent and harmful regime continue.

Australia's Deterrence Paradigm: The Structural Violence of Outsourcing, the Diffusion of Responsibility

Australia has maintained a policy of mandatorily detaining asylum seekers who arrive in its territory by boat without a valid visa ("unauthorized") since 1992. Initially adopted in response to rising unauthorized boat arrivals of Indochinese asylum seekers from the late 1980s onward, this mandatory detention policy has become a central pillar of Australia's increasingly draconian approach to asylum seekers. At the time of its introduction, the policy was justified as a temporary practice necessary to maintain the "integrity" of Australia's migration program, modeled on state practices of asylum seeker deterrence elsewhere.[3] Successive Australian governments have maintained this policy in the face of sustained domestic and international criticism. The UN Human Rights Committee, for example, has repeatedly stated that mandatory indefinite detention of certain asylum seekers and refugees amounts to systematic human rights breaches and has "cumulatively inflict[ed] serious, irreversible psychological harm."[4] Domestic political opposition to these centers has been expressed through, for instance, widespread detainee protests, including hunger strikes and riots within detention facilities, and accompanying mass civil society mobilizations in the early 2000s.[5]

The introduction of mandatory detention quickly gave rise to a complex institutional infrastructure of immigration detention centers, including in notoriously remote locations like the Woomera Immigration Reception and Processing Centre (1999–2003) in the Australian central desert. Initially, these immigration detention centers were run by an agency within the Australian Department of Immigration and Multicultural and Indigenous Affairs (DIMIA). A significant shift occurred in 1996, when the conservative government under Prime Minister John Howard announced its intention to engage private companies to manage the network of centers with the stated aim of "deliver[ing] quality detention services with ongoing cost reduction."[6] In February 1998, the first contract for running Australia's then network of seven immigration detention centers was awarded to Australasian Correctional Services (ACS), an Australia-based company that would eventually become a subsidiary of the multinational G4S.[7] ACS ran the so-called Detention Services Contract for six years, at a cost of over half a billion Australian dollars (approximately US$307 million).[8] Despite this huge expenditure, the number of people traveling to Australia unauthorized by boat during the first decade of mandatory detention remained relatively low compared to global asylum trends.[9]

Australia was among the first states to fully privatize the running of immigration detention centers, following earlier moves to outsource some immigration detention functions in the UK and the US.[10] Like elsewhere, the privatization of Australia's immigration detention network has had two key effects: first, the use of public funds to generate increasing profits for private companies, and, second, the formal devolution and diffusion from the state to the private contractor of practical and legal responsibility for "delivering" certain "services" to asylum seekers.[11] However, the use of private companies to run immigration detention centers has not resulted in reduced government bureaucracy, the provision of quality care to asylum seekers, or the evasion of legal liability on the part of the government. For example, a 2004 government review of the ACS contract found that it failed to define the nature, quality, and level of services required of ACS and lacked sufficient mechanisms to allow DIMIA to monitor ACS conduct.[12] Similarly, despite the privatization of services, Australian courts have held that the Australian government still retains a legal duty of care to reasonably ensure the safety of asylum seekers in detention, a duty that cannot be contracted to external providers.[13] Consequently, the Australian government paid out over AU$5 million (approximately US$3.5 million) between 1999 and 2012 in compensation to former detainees who suffered physical or psychological harm while in detention.[14]

More recently, successive Australian governments have further sought to externalize their responsibility toward asylum seekers and refugees through the implementation of a policy of "offshore processing." This policy has had two distinct phases: the Pacific Solution Mark I (2001–2008, implemented under the coalition government led by Prime Minister Howard) and the Pacific Solution Mark II (2012–present, first implemented under the Gillard Labor government and maintained under the subsequent governments).[15] When the newly elected Rudd Labor government announced the end of the first Pacific Solution in 2007, the immigration minister denounced the policy of offshore processing as a "cynical, costly and ultimately unsuccessful exercise."[16] Over the previous seven years, the Australian government had contracted the International

Organization for Migration to administer the detention facilities on Manus Island and Nauru—at an estimated cost of AU$289 million (approximately US$220 million)—while the Australian immigration authorities conducted refugee status determinations.

The reintroduction of Australia's offshore detention regime in August 2012 signaled a new phase in Australia's approach to asylum seeker deterrence, instrumentalizing humanitarian concerns about migrant deaths to further border securitization. Justified under the rhetoric of "saving lives at sea," following an increase in migrant drownings alongside a rise in unauthorized arrivals,[17] the reestablishment of offshore processing was soon accompanied by a military-led campaign to turn back asylum seeker boats at sea and a political pledge to never allow asylum seekers arriving unauthorized by boat to settle in or even visit Australia.[18] As Michael Grewcock argues, central to Australia's draconian deterrence model is a "conceptual approach to refugees that deprives them of agency and vests legitimacy only in those willing to comply with border controls."[19]

The revamped offshore detention regime was implemented through a series of agreements with two small Pacific Island neighboring states to Australia's north and private contractors willing to provide a range of services, including those classified as "garrison," welfare, and health in the newly reestablished RPCs. In mid-2012, the Australian government concluded two Memorandums of Understanding, one with PNG and the other with Nauru,[20] for the transfer and detention of asylum seekers from Australia.[21] Under both memoranda, the Australian government bears all costs incurred for implementing regional detention and processing (including construction and operations), while the PNG and Nauruan governments are responsible for instituting the refugee status determination process in accordance with their respective domestic laws. Australian officials often criticize this jurisdictional arrangement as deflecting legal responsibility for the predicament of the people subject to offshore detention.[22] In exchange, Australia significantly increased its aid to both states, including funding major infrastructure projects.

While the RPCs are officially "operated" by the PNG and Nauruan governments, the Australian government has practical authority over their running and management via contracts with private companies and NGOs. Initially, the Australian government contracted G4S to manage the Manus Island RPC, with welfare services provided by the Salvation Army and Save the Children Australia. From mid-2014 to October 2017, a lucrative contract for combined services was awarded to the Australian-listed company Transfield (known as Broadspectrum from November 2015), worth over AU\$3 billion (approximately US\$2.3 billion).[23] Under the terms of this contract, Transfield became responsible for the day-to-day operations of the RPCs, including security, cleaning, catering, and individual welfare and health services. As a result, the company exercised practical and quasi-sovereign authority over the lives of the people living in RPCs, making "decisions about detainee welfare, placement, movement, communication, accommodation, food, clothing, water, security and environment on a daily basis."[24] A 2015 report authored by a group of Australian lawyers, researchers, and human rights activists under the No Business in Abuse initiative held that, while the Australian authorities appeared to "have ultimate authority for some decisions under the terms of the contracts, there can be no doubt that without Transfield and its subcontractors the operation of the ODCs [Offshore Detention Centers] would be impossible."[25] At the peak of the transfers, in November 2013, the number of men detained in the Manus Island RPC reached 1,339. The following year, an Australian Senate report noted that conditions at the RPC were "harsh, inadequate and inhumane," including "cramped and over-heated sleeping quarters, exposure to the weather, poor sanitation and sewage blockages, unhygienic meals, and poorly managed service of meals."[26]

In recent years, the logic of border security has coexisted ambivalently alongside global discourses of austerity and fiscal responsibility. The findings of the National Commission of Audit, established by the Australian Treasurer in 2013, with the purpose of examining the "scope and efficiency" of government finances, present an example. While asserting that the government faced a "substantial budgetary challenge" and required a reduction in state spending, the commission failed to question the legitimacy or underlying basis of expenditure on immigration detention per se. Although it recognized that Australia's immigration detention regime was the "fastest growing" government program in recent years, the commission merely recommended the renegotiation of contracts and "better targeting of services" to reduce the cost of detaining people within both onshore and offshore facilities rather than a more radical overhaul of the contractual relationships or the costly policy of mandatory immigration detention and offshore processing.[27] Border security is thus presented as an economic and technocratic necessity that must be accepted and managed rather than eliminated, even by proponents of austerity.

In contrast, refugee sector advocates have sought to delegitimize Australia's punitive offshore detention policies, using an economic cost-benefit framework. Since 2012, the cost of Australia's offshore detention regime has been a routine target of civil society and media critique. For example, in September 2016, Save the Children and UNICEF Australia released a joint report, *At What Cost?* that documents the human, economic, and strategic costs of Australia's offshore processing regime. The report authors estimated that Australia spent at least AU$9.6 billion (approximately US$7.3 billion) between 2013 and 2016 funding "deterrence" policies, including boat turnbacks, offshore processing, and mandatory immigration detention.[28] Paradoxically, this criticism was articulated by one of the very NGOs previously contracted by the Australian government to provide "welfare services" to asylum seekers on Nauru between 2013 and 2015.[29]

In making the case for a less punitive policy approach, civil society efforts have also drawn attention to the economic and other contributions that refugee communities do and could further make, if Australia abandoned mandatory offshore processing and allowed asylum seekers and refugees greater labor market participation and community integration. One risk with this campaign strategy is that hospitality becomes connected to economic motivations and the validity of a person's presence in a host country linked to their economic productivity—thus imposing additional expectations on asylum seekers and refugees. This shift in public debate from legal to economic arguments has also been exploited by successive Australian governments to delegitimize the claims of refugees and to justify the exclusionary approach toward asylum seekers. For example, successive Australian governments have depicted asylum seekers traveling to Australia unauthorized by boat as profit-seeking actors rather than rights-claiming individuals.[30] In this model, asylum seekers become trapped in a binary framework as either deserving individuals who generate profit for and benefit the Australian state or undeserving individuals who seek to exploit it.

#SOSManus: Refugee Protests, Court Litigation, and Articulating Relations of Responsibility

The global proliferation of neoliberal policies from the 1990s onward has not led to a reduction in punitive or disciplinary state functions.[31] While neoliberalism purports to create a liberalized economy and self-regulating market, it in fact rests upon practices of criminalization, confinement, and risk-dissemination. Such strategies also animate Australia's offshore processing regime, wherein the government seeks to export risks and escape responsibility for processing asylum claims and protecting refugees. While this "ambiguous architecture of risk" has made it increasingly difficult for affected asylum seekers to challenge Australia's practices of refugee deterrence and border control,[32] its offshore detention regime has been contested through civil and constitutional litigation in Australian and PNG courts. Two court cases in particular—initiated by or on behalf of asylum seekers and refugees at the Manus Island RPC and brought against state authorities and the corporations running the offshore detention camps—have transformed the broader political terrain.

The first case, initiated in December 2014, was a class action for negligence instigated in the Victorian Supreme Court by Iranian asylum seeker Majid Kamasaee on behalf of all people who had been detained at the Manus Island RPC over the previous two years.[33] The torts claim was brought against the Australian government and the two private contractors (Transfield/Broadspectrum and G4S) that had been responsible for the management of the Manus RPC over the claim period.[34] Mr. Kamasaee had himself been forcibly transferred to PNG around August 2013 but had been returned to Australia in July 2014 for medical treatment. A key argument was that the responsible parties had failed to provide people detained at the RPC with a reasonable standard of services—measured in relation to Australian community expectations—or a reasonable level of protection from "physical violence or intimidation, discrimination, ostracisms, bullying or other anti-social behavior" from other detainees or third parties.[35] This failure, the claim alleged, was particularly harmful given the shared characteristics of the individuals detained, namely people with "complex" asylum claims who had or were likely to have fled violence and travelled to Australia under dangerous circumstances.[36]

In July 2017, just one day before the case was due to be heard (and livestreamed) in the Victorian Supreme Court, it was announced that an out-of-court settlement had been reached, with the Australian government agreeing to pay a reported AU$70 million (approximately US$53.2 million) in compensation and damages to the affected class of asylum seekers.[37] Said to be the largest human rights class action settled by the Australian government to date, 1,905 people detained on Manus Island between 2012 and 2016 were eligible for financial compensation.

Speaking to the Australian media at the time, Mr. Kamasaee said, "Our voices have never been listened to, but today we are finally being heard and I hope everyone's suffering can be over as quickly as possible."[38] Other affected asylum seekers and refugees stressed the symbolic importance of the action as a powerful public acknowledgment that the conditions in Australia's offshore detention regime are abusive, harmful, and ultimately unlawful.[39]

As the case was resolved through an out-of-court settlement, however, volumes of evidence documenting the conditions and experiences of the asylum seekers and refugees on Manus Island went unheard in open court, allowing the Australian government to maintain the fallacy that the settlement is not an admission of legal liability nor wrongdoing but rather a "prudent" use of taxpayer dollars to avoid a lengthy trial.[40] Most importantly, the out-of-court settlement did nothing to commit the Australian government to redressing ongoing harm inflicted upon those who remained in the RPC, specifically the political uncertainty about their legal status or their futures. As Pakistani refugee Naeem stated, expressing his disappointment in the settlement, "Money cannot [give me] back the four years of my life that I have lost without committing any crime."[41] While the case was brought against the government and private contractors alike, it is unclear whether the settlement committed Transfield/Broadspectrum or G4S to pay any compensation—demonstrating yet again how the legal architecture of outsourcing allows for public funds to generate private profit, while legal liability for compensation rests with public authorities and comes at public expense.

A second case concerning the legality of the Manus Island RPC was brought before the PNG courts in 2015 by Belden Namah, the then PNG opposition leader. In April 2016, the PNG Supreme Court declared the Manus Island RPC to be unconstitutional, in part because it limited the right to freedom of movement enshrined in the PNG constitution.[42] At that point, the RPC was a "closed" center with secure fencing that resembled a prison and detained men on an indefinite basis with only a few limited so-called "excursions" allowed. A day after the court ruling, PNG prime minister Peter O'Neill announced the impending closure of the Manus Island RPC and urged Australia to "immediately" make alternative arrangements for the affected men.[43] As an interim measure, the RPC was transformed into an "open" center, allowing those living there to leave the compound during the day.[44] While some transport was provided for the men to access the nearby Lorengau township, ongoing tensions in the local community over the politics and socioeconomic impact of the Manus Island RPC meant that the men's movement was constrained by security concerns. Given this change in the center's operation, in March 2017, the PNG Supreme Court Chief Justice declared that the Manus Island RPC had as a matter of law been closed, and that the "transferees" were, in fact, being accommodated at the Lombrum Navy base by the PNG government, with the assistance of the Australian government.[45] His declaration effectively removed any legal obligation to relocate the refugees to a different facility in PNG. Nonetheless, in April 2017, the PNG and Australian prime ministers jointly announced that the Manus Island RPC would cease its operations on October 31 that year, a move partly seen as a way of accelerating the integration of refugees into the PNG community.[46] The closure date coincided, not coincidentally, with the end of Broadspectrum's contract with the Australian government.

The physical closure of the RPC was protracted and brutal. Australian government-contracted service providers, at the behest of the state, attempted to force the asylum seekers and refugees to "voluntarily" relocate to the new facilities by dismantling sections of the RPC and denying services. By May 2017, five months ahead of the official closure, facilities, including the telephone room, had been removed, and the provision of power, water, cleaning services, and food had been reduced across the RPC.[47] Small "luxuries," such as cigarettes, tea, sugar, coffee, fruit, English language classes, internet and gym access, also ceased. This deliberate withdrawal of essential services authorized by both Australian and PNG authorities and the companies contracted to run the RPC manifested a form of "slow violence" that deprived the affected asylum seekers and refugees of the necessary conditions for life over a protracted period.[48]

In response, at the start of August 2017, the men living in the Manus Island RPC began a daily protest that called upon the Australian government to acknowledge its responsibility for their basic rights, conditions of detention, and future resettlement. Each day, the men uploaded photos and at times videos of their collective protests on social media, using handwritten signs in English highlighting the brutality and hypocrisy of the Australian government's purported humanitarianism. The messages included: "Australia, why are you killing us?" "The Government of Australia evades its responsibility toward us," and "The Government of Australia claims humanity, but where its humanity?"

In anticipation of the Manus Island RPC closure, the Australian government contracted multinational global logistics company Toll Group to expand an existing facility—the East Lorengau RTC—and build two additional centers, in order to transfer men from the Manus Island RPC. The contract was valued at AU$30 million (approximately US$23 million).[49] Yet, by the Australian government's own admission, the new accommodation remained unfinished just days prior to the RPC's closure, prompting the UNHCR to condemn the relocation policy, stating as late as November that the new facilities were still "incomplete, sub-standard . . . and unsanitary."[50] As an inducement to move, the refugees were told that those who relocated to the East Lorengau RTC would be given a weekly allowance. Yet many of the refugees expressed concerns that the new temporary accommodation was not a viable or safe alternative, citing fears about their personal safety, given the local lack of prospects for future livelihoods, as well as escalating tensions between Manus locals and refugees.[51] One violent incident in February 2014 had resulted in the murder of Kurdish asylum seeker Reza Barati, who was beaten to death by local G4S employees while inside the Manus Island RPC.

By the time Broadspectrum and Wilson Security staff left on the official October 31 closure date, the protests were in their ninety-first consecutive day. The men had developed a sustained campaign of collective resistance from within the Manus Island RPC that was connected with refugee advocates and supporters in PNG, Australia, and elsewhere. In the days that followed, the men occupied the decommissioned RPC, enduring starvation, infections, threats, and incursions from the PNG military into the center to sabotage already limited water and food supplies. Nonetheless, through their embodied protest the men asserted a form of autonomy against the authorities who had controlled their lives in the RPC, refusing to be yet again relocated against their will. As one Sudanese refugee and human rights advocate, Abdul Aziz Muhamat, shared via a collaborative podcast he made with Australian journalist Michael Green, the occupation of the RPC provided an opportunity for people to become "united" through their endurance of hardship and acts of defiance and self-determination:

> We are looking after each other more than even before. It's been like more than four and a half years we never had any opportunity to do so. . . . Every single man in detention now is contributing [for

example, by building wells or doing security].... We are using that kind of resistance and the resilience that we have.... We are paying the price of our freedom.[52]

On November 7, 2017, a week after the official closure of the Manus Island RPC, the PNG Supreme Court rejected a last-ditch legal application lodged on behalf of Behrouz Boochani to force PNG to restore essential services to the center, including power, water, food, sanitation, and medical services.[53] Responding to the decision, Boochani wrote on social media: "We the refugees in Manus are outside of law and justice. There is no justice for the refugees and we are used to the court decisions going against us."[54]

The defiant standoff lasted three weeks, until the PNG used the military to violently evict the men, forcing them to relocate to the new facilities. Amnesty International termed the standoff a "humanitarian crisis of the Australian and PNG governments' own making," noting that the forced relocation of the men

> was carried out in a demeaning and deeply humiliating manner— with refugees forced to relocate to newer, but still temporary, sites that were also poorly equipped, overcrowded, unsafe and lacking in basic services such as water and power. In effect, the refugees and asylum seekers have been shuttled from one prison-like centre to several others, with no improvement to their situation.[55]

Ultimately, the forced relocations merely replaced one visible crisis with another, characterized by the underlying structural violence and ongoing legal uncertainty and political abandonment surrounding the future of the asylum seekers and refugees on Manus Island. As Iranian refugee Mehdi Maleknia reportedly said in the wake of the forced relocation, "Yes, it's a nicer prison. But what we want is not a nice place, we want our freedom."[56]

Conclusion

The forced closure of the Manus Island RPC in October 2017 made visible the physical brutality and suffering that animates Australia's paradigm of asylum seeker deterrence. Less visible was the enduring structural violence that informed how the Australian state, through the dual strategies of contracting private for-profit service providers and enrolling neighboring states into its offshore detention regime, had created a situation of calculated legal limbo and prolonged abandonment for the refugees on Manus Island and Nauru. In this chapter, I have traced the evolution of Australia's offshore processing regime in relation to broader trends concerning the privatization of Australian immigration detention centers since the 1990s and the contested economics of asylum in Australia today. Boochani, for example, refused to pathologize his emotional experience of Australia's offshore detention regime and instead located his pain and that of his fellow refugees within Australia's neocolonial relations with PNG authorities and people, including the logics of imperial profit-seeking and extraction:

> Only a meta-historical and transhistorical approach can unpack the peculiarities associated with the issue of Manus and Nauru. Only a rigorous analysis of a colonial presence in Australia and its tactics in the region can disclose the reality of violence in these island prisons. . . . This form of affliction, inflicted on people in similarly vulnerable situations, has always existed in the history of modern Australia. Pain and suffering systematically inflicted on defenseless and vulnerable bodies.[57]

As Maurice Stierl has argued, holding on to the ambiguities of migrant struggles allows for an understanding of migrant protagonists as "complex subjects . . . able to be traumatized and resistant, scared and hopeful, captured and recalcitrant."[58] Similarly, as I suggest in this chapter, refugee claim-making in legal settings constitutes a form of political action that feeds into broader struggles to articulate the political, moral, and legal responsibilities of state authorities and the private corporations they contract, in an attempt to outsource liability toward asylum seekers and refugees. While legal actions of negligence or false imprisonment rest upon a claim of injury, the men detained at Manus Island RPC strategically mobilized their claims to reshape the broader political contestations around the Australia's detention regime's legality and legitimacy. Using a range of tactics to amplify their struggles and demands, the men subject to Australia's carceral violence challenged the state of legal limbo and political abandonment to which they had long been subjected.

Sara Dehm is a lecturer at the Faculty of Law, University of Technology Sydney. She researches and writes about forms of violence authorized through international migration and refugee law.

Notes

1   See Behrouz Boochani and Omid Tofighian, "The Poetics of Prison Protest," this volume, 101–11.

2   Behrouz Boochani, "Manus Is a Landscape of Surreal Horror," *Guardian*, November 2, 2017, accessed March 21, 2020, https://www.theguardian.com/commentisfree/2017/nov/02/manus-is-a-landscape-of-surreal-horror.

3   Daniel Ghezelbash, *Refuge Lost: Asylum Law in an Interdependent World* (Cambridge: Cambridge University Press, 2018).

4   *FKAG v Australia*, UN Doc CCPR/C/108/D/2094/2011 and *MMM v Australia*, UN Doc CCPR/C/108/D/2136/2012, August 20, 2013, accessed April 22, 2020, https://www.humanrights.gov.au/our-work/asylum-seekers-and-refugees/publications/casenote-fkag-v-australia-and-mmm-v-australia.

5   See Lucy Fiske, *Human Rights, Refugee Protest and Immigration Detention* (London: Palgrave, 2016).

6   Australian National Audit Office, *Management of the Detention Centres Contracts—Part A* (Canberra: Department of Immigration Multicultural and Indigenous Affairs, 2004), 13, accessed March 21, 20202, https://www.anao.gov.au/sites/default/files/ANAO_Report_2003-2004_54.pdf.

7   While the Australian government contract was with ACS, the detention centers were run through its operational subsidiary Australasian Correctional Management (ACM). At the time, ACS was a subsidiary of the American-based company Wackenhut Corrections Services (WCC). The initial contract was for three years, with a possibility of extension.

8   Australian National Audit Office, *Management of the Detention Centres Contracts—Part B*, 2005 (Canberra: Department of Immigration Multicultural and Indigenous Affairs, 2005), 12, accessed March 21, 2020, https://www.anao.gov.au/sites/default/files/ANAO_Report_2005-2006_01.pdf. In 2003, DIMIA entered into a three-year detention services contract with a new provider, GSL, valued at AU$100 million per year (approximately US$65 million); Australian National Audit Office, *Management of the Detention Centres Contracts—Part B*, 18.

9   Government statistics indicate that in 1995–1996 there were only 693 people in immigration detention, although this number would rise significantly to peak at 9,321 people (including 1,224 children) in 2001–2002; Janet Phillips and Harriet Spinks, "Immigration Detention in Australia," Parliament of Australia, March 20, 2013, accessed March 22, 2020, https://www.aph.gov.au/About_Parliament/Parliamentary_Departments/Parliamentary_Library/pubs/BN/2012-2013/Detention.

10 Michael Flynn and Cecilia Cannon, "The Privatization of Immigration Detention: Toward a Global View," Global Detention Project, September 2009, accessed March 22, 2020, https://papers.ssrn.com/sol3/papers.cfm?abstract_id=2344196.

11 Michael Welch, "Economic Man and Diffused Sovereignty: A Critique of Australia's Asylum Regime," *Crime, Law and Social Change* 61, no. 1 (February 2014): 81, 88.

12 Australian National Audit Office, *Management of the Detention Centres Contracts—Part B.*

13 See, e.g., *Behrooz v Secretary, Department of Immigration and Multicultural and Indigenous Affairs* [2004] HCA 36, accessed March 30, 2020, http://eresources. hcourt.gov.au/downloadPdf/2004/HCA/36; *AS v Minister for Immigration and Border Protection* [2014] VSC 593, accessed March 30, 2020, https://jade.io/ article/352579.

14 This number is much higher for compensation claims concerning unlawful detention, amounting to over $18 million for the same period; see Department of Finance and Deregulation, Australian Government, "Compensation Claims Made by Immigration Detainees between 1999 and 2011" (FOI Request, 2012). It is difficult to ascertain the precise details of these cases, as most successful compensation cases have been settled out of court.

15 For an overview of these two distinct phases, see Anthea Vogl, "Sovereign Relations: Australia's 'Off-shoring' of Asylum Seekers on Nauru in Historical Perspective," in Charlotte Epstein, ed., *Norming the World: Postcolonial Perspectives on the Use of Norms in International Relations* (London: Routledge, 2017), 158.

16 Paul Maley, "Pacific Solution Sinks Quietly," *Australian*, February 9, 2008, accessed March 22, 2020, http://www.theaustralian.com.au/archive/news/ pacific-solution-sinks-quietly/news-story/507ebc9ecc06316fe3eb131a9333583a

17 Australian Human Rights Commission, "Expert Panel on Asylum Seekers," July 2012, 9, accessed March 22, 2020, https://www.humanrights.gov.au/sites/ default/files/content/legal/submissions/2012/20120720_asylum_seekers.pdf.

18 In July 2013, the Australian government under new prime minister Kevin Rudd announced that no asylum seeker or refugee subject to offshore processing would be resettled in Australia. In addition, since the election of the coalition government in November 2013, Australia has adopted a policy of turning back asylum seeker boats at sea. While in clear breach of the fundamental international norm of non-refoulement, this practice has drastically reduced the number of people able to travel to the Australian mainland by boat to seek asylum. As a result, Australia has not transferred new arrivals to PNG or Manus Island since 2014. See Sara Dehm and Max Walden, "Refugee Policy: A Cruel Bipartisanship," in Anika Gauja, Peter Chen, Jennifer Curtin, and Juliet Pietsch eds., *Double Disillusion: The 2016 Australian Federal Election*, (Canberra: ANU Press, 2018).

19 Michael Grewcock, "'Our Lives Is in Danger:' Manus Island and the End of Asylum," *Race & Class* 59, no. 2 (July 2017): 70, 75.

20 Boochani and Tofighian, "The Poetics of Prison Protest."

21 "Memorandum of Understanding between the Government of the Independent State of Papua New Guinea and the Government of Australia, relating to the Transfer to and Assessment of Persons in Papua New Guinea, and Related Issues," September 2012, accessed March 22, 2020, https://parlinfo.aph.gov.au/ parlInfo/search/display/display.w3p;query=Id%3A%22media%2Fpressrel%2F1 906352%22;src1=sm1, was superseded by the Memorandum of Understanding between the Government of the Independent State of Papua New Guinea and

the Government of Australia, relating to the Transfer to, and Assessment and Resettlement in, Papua New Guinea of Certain Persons, and Related Issues, July 19, 2013, accessed March 22, 2020, https://www.kaldorcentre.unsw.edu.au/sites/default/files/australia-png-mou-2013.pdf.

22 Nonetheless, under these arrangements, refugees and asylum seekers on Manus Island and Nauru may be temporarily brought back to Australia in certain circumstances, such as to give birth or receive specialized medical treatment.

23 "Offshore Processing Centres in Nauru and Papua New Guinea: Procurement of Garrison Support and Welfare Services," Australian National Audit Office, September 13, 2016, accessed March 22, 2020, https://www.anao.gov.au/work/performance-audit/offshore-processing-centres-nauru-and-papua-new-guinea-procurement. This figure is until March 2016. In reality, the contract between the Australian government and Transfield was a series of contracts, starting in 2012, for the running of the Nauru RPC, before signing another single contract to become the sole provider of garrison support and welfare services for both RPCs in October 2015. This contract was extended on two occasions, February 2016 and August 2016.

24 Shen Narayanasamy, Rachel Ball, Dr. Katie Hepworth, Brynn O'Brien, and Claire Parfitt, *Business in Abuse: Transfield's Complicity in Gross Human Rights Abuses within Australia's Offshore Detention Regime* (Sydney: No Business in Abuse, 2015), 22.

25 Ibid.; also see Brynn O'Brien, "Extraterritorial Detention Contracting in Australia and the UN Guiding Principles on Business and Human Rights," *Business and Human Rights Journal* 1, no. 2, (July 2016): 333, accessed March 22, 2020, https://bit.ly/2wZdh6u.

26 "Incident at the Manus Island Detention Centre from 16 February to 18 February 2014," Parliament of Australia, chapter 3, accessed March 22, 2020, https://www.aph.gov.au/parliamentary_business/committees/senate/legal_and_constitutional_affairs/manus_island/Report/c03.

27 "Toward Responsible Government: The Report of the National Commission of Audit," Australian Government National Commission of Audit, lviii, accessed March 22, 2020, https://www.ncoa.gov.au.

28 Lisa Button and Shane Evans, *At What Cost? The Human, Economic and Strategic Cost of Australia's Asylum Seeker Policies and the Alternatives* (East Melbourne/Sydney: Save the Children Australia/UNICEF Australia, 2016), accessed March 22, 2020, http://www.unicef.org.au/Upload/UNICEF/Media/Documents/At-What-Cost-Report.pdf; also see *Islands of Despair: Australia's "Processing" of Refugees on Nauru* (London: Amnesty International, 2016), accessed March 22, 2020, https://www.amnesty.org.au/wp-content/uploads/2016/10/ISLAND-OF-DESPAIR-FINAL.pdf.

29 Save the Children's initial one-year contract, awarded in 2013, was valued at approximately AU$30 million (approximately US$19 million) and was not renewed when it expired on October 31, 2015. Transfield (now Broadspectrum) took over the contractual responsibility for providing "welfare services" to refugees and asylum seekers on Nauru.

30 See, e.g., ministerial comments about Sri Lankan asylum seekers as "economic migrants"; Lenore Taylor, "Bob Carr's Comments Foreshadow Labor Asylum Seeker Clampdown," *Guardian*, June 28, 2013, accessed March 22, 2020, https://www.theguardian.com/world/2013/jun/28/rudd-government-asylum-seeker-policy. Also see "wealthy" Iranian "economic refugees"; Ben Doherty "Peter Dutton Launches Extraordinary Attack on 'Economic Refugees' Sent to US," *Guardian*, September 28, 2017, accessed March 22, 2020, https://www.theguardian.com/australia-news/2017/sep/28/peter-dutton-lets-fly-at-armani-clad-economic-refugees-sent-to-us.

31 Georg Menz, "Neo-Liberalism, Privatization and the Outsourcing of Migration Management: A Five-Country Comparison," *Competition & Change* 15, no. 2 (July 2011): 116, 117, accessed March 22, 2020, http://citeseerx.ist.psu.edu/viewdoc/download?doi=10.1.1.854.7498&rep=rep1&type=pdf.

32 Leanne Weber and Sharon Pickering, *Globalization and Borders: Death at the Global Frontier* (London: Palgrave Macmillan, 2011), 163; also see Sharon Pickering and Leanne Weber, "Hardening the Rule of Law and Asylum Seekers: Exporting Risk and the Juridical Censure of State Illegality," in Elizabeth Stanley and Jude McCulloch, eds., *State Crime and Resistance* (London: Routledge, 2013), 183.

33 The claim initially concerned personal injury but was later expanded to cover the additional count of false imprisonment; see: Gabrielle Holly, "Transnational Tort and Access to Remedy under the UN Guiding Principles on Business and Human Rights: Kamasaee v Commonwealth," *Melbourne Journal of International Law* 19, no. 1 (2018), accessed March 22, 2020, http://classic.austlii.edu.au/au/journals/MelbJIL/2018/3.html.

34 Wilson Security was also joined at a later stage as a third party to the litigation.

35 Statement of Claim, *Kamasaee v Commonwealth*, Victorian Supreme Court, No 06770, 2014, accessed March 30, 2020, https://www.supremecourt.vic.gov.au/news/kamasaee-v-commonwealth-of-australia-and-ors.

36 Ibid.

37 Ben Doherty and Calla Wahlquist, "Government to Pay $70m Damages to 1,905 Manus Detainees in Class Action," *Guardian*, June 14, 2017, accessed March 30, 2020, https://www.theguardian.com/australia-news/2017/jun/14/government-to-pay-damages-to-manus-island-detainees-in-class-action.

38 Ibid.

39 See interview with Behrouz Boochani, in Martin McKenzie-Murray, "The Wrong Kind of Settlement," *The Saturday Paper*, June 17, 2017, accessed March 22, 2020, https://www.thesaturdaypaper.com.au/news/politics/2017/06/17/the-wrong-kind-settlement/14976216004800.

40 See Immigration Minister Peter Dutton's remarks that "an anticipated six-month legal battle for this case would have cost tens of millions of dollars in legal fees alone, with an unknown outcome," in Michael Koziol, "Court Approves $70 Million Compensation Payout to Manus Island Detainee," *Sydney Morning Herald*, September 6, 2017, accessed March 30, 2020, https://www.smh.com.au/politics/federal/court-approves-70-million-compensation-payout-to-manus-island-detainees-20170906-gybpjy.html.

41   Stefan Armbruster, "Refugees Afraid, Confused as Manus Detention Centre Shutdown Begins," *ABC News,* July 9, 2017, accessed March 22, 2020, https://www.sbs.com.au/news/refugees-afraid-confused-as-manus-detention-centre-shutdown-begins.

42   *Namah v Pato* [2016] PGSC 13; SC1497 (26 April 2016). For a detailed earlier analysis of the case, see Azadeh Dastyari and Maria O-Sullivan, "Not for Export: The Failure of Australia's Extraterritorial Processing Regime in Papua New Guinea and the Decision of the PNG Supreme Court in Namah (2016)," *Monash University Law Review* 42, no. 2 (2016): 308, accessed March 22, 2020, https://bit.ly/2WvRFsS.

43   Stephanie Anderson, "Manus Island Detention Centre to Be Shut, Papua New Guinea Prime Minister Peter O'Neill Says," *ABC News,* April 28, 2016, accessed March 22, 2020, http://www.abc.net.au/news/2016-04-27/png-pm-oneill-to-shut-manus-island-detention-centre/7364414.

44   Their movement was limited to the Manus Province area, and the men still required permission to travel to, say, Port Moresby at the time of going to press.

45   *Boochani v Independent State of Papua New Guinea* [2017] PGSC 4 (March 13, 2017).

46   "Manus Island Immigration Detention Centre to Close by Year's End," SBS News, April 10, 2017, accessed March 22, 2020, https://www.sbs.com.au/news/manus-island-immigration-detention-centre-to-close-by-year-s-end.

47   The first part of the RPC to close was N Block in the Foxtrot compound on May 28, 2017; "Power, Water Cut to Manus Island Detention Centre," Radio New Zealand, August 1, 2017, accessed March 22, 2020, http://www.radionz.co.nz/international/pacific-news/336227/power-water-cut-to-manus-island-detention-centre; Behrouz Boochani, "Days Before the Forced Closure of Manus, We Have No Safe Place to Go," *Guardian,* October 27, 2017, accessed March 22, 2020, https://www.theguardian.com/australia-news/2017/may/15/manus-island-detention-centre-to-close-by-30-june-detainees-told.

48   Rob Nixon, *Slow Violence and the Environmentalism of the Poor* (Cambridge, MA: Harvard University Press, 2013); Thom Davies, Arshad Isakjee, and Surindar Dhesi, "Violent Inaction: The Necropolitical Experience of Refugees in Europe," *Antipode* 49, no. 5 (November 2017), accessed March 22, 2020, https://onlinelibrary.wiley.com/doi/10.1111/anti.12325.

49   According to government statistics, the East Lorengau RTC and West Lorengau Haus could accommodate around four hundred and three hundred refugees respectively, while Hillside House was designed to accommodate under two hundred people who had not been recognized as refugees.

50   United Nations High Commissioner for Refugees Regional Representation in Canberra, "Medical Expert Mission Papua New Guinea 10 to 16 November 2017," UNHCR, accessed March 22, 2020, http://www.unhcr.org/5a3b0f317.pdf.

51   Boochani, "Days Before the Forced Closure of Manus."

52   Abdul Aziz Muhamat and Michael Green, "We Are Looking After Each Other " (podcast), Wheeler Centre, November 21, 2017, accessed March 22, 2020, https://www.wheelercentre.com/broadcasts/podcasts/the-messenger/we-are-looking-after-each-other.

53 Fergus Hunter, "PNG Court Quashes Detainees' Last-Ditch Bid to Keep Manus Centre Open," *Age*, November 7, 2017, accessed March 22, 2020, http://www.theage.com.au/federal-politics/political-news/png-court-quashes-detainees-lastditch-bid-to-keep-manus-centre-open-20171107-gzgbe3.html.

54 Behrouz Boochani, Facebook post, November 7, 2017 (on file with author).

55 *Punishment Not Protection: Australia's Treatment of Refugees and Asylum Seekers in Papua New Guinea* (London: Amnesty International, 2018).

56 "All Manus Island Refugees Evicted from Detention Centre," RNZ, November 24, 2017, accessed March 22, 2020, https://www.radionz.co.nz/international/pacific-news/344619/all-manus-island-refugees-evicted-from-detention-centre.

57 Behrouz Boochani, "I Write from Manus Island as a Duty to History," *Guardian*, December 6, 2017, accessed March 22, 2020, https://www.theguardian.com/commentisfree/2017/dec/06/i-write-from-manus-island-as-a-duty-to-history.

58 Maurice Stierl, "Excessive Migration, Excessive Governance: Migrant Entanglements in Greek EU-rope," in Nicholas De Genova, ed., *The Borders of "Europe": Autonomy of Migration, Tactics of Bordering* (Durham, NC: Duke University Press, 2017), 210, 231.

Kidneys without Borders— Asylum without Kidneys

Nancy Scheper-Hughes

The Interzone

Pirates, smugglers, traffickers, refugees, migrants, babies torn away from mothers or washed up on the shore, sea disasters, detention centers, prisons, borders, deaths in the desert, dehydration, snakes, immigration officers—all exist in the real and imaginary line between the dead and the living, as indistinguishable as the line between dream and waking, auto-biography and fiction, past and present. Kafka on the one hand, Trump on the other. The stateless versus the global citizen, who amasses passports as a symbol of geographical and social mobility and strides across borders unfettered in pursuit of prosperity—or, perhaps, like the stateless, just longs for a better life.[1]

Kidneys without Borders

Moshe Tati was among the first of several hundred Israelis who would eventually sign up for a kidney "transplant tour" package organized by a syndicate of local and international transplant brokers and their surgeons between 1999 and 2010.[2] The $120,000 package included: travel to an undisclosed exotic foreign location; five-star hotel accommodation; surgery in a private hospital unit; a kidney supplied by a paid, anonymous, living donor brought in from a third country.

The plan behind the package was simple: the patient would come from one country, the kidney provider from another, and the transplant surgery would take place in a third country, overseen by local surgeons. It was always a quick and dirty operation safeguarded by bribes and police protection. Patients flew on charter planes without being told where they would land and were sent home as soon as possible post-surgery with almost no aftercare. As "stateless" crimes, the clandestine operations were almost impossible to prosecute.

In 2001, Tati and his wife, accompanied by their broker, visited Dr. Zaki Shapira at Shapira's clinic in Tel Aviv. The surgeon reassured Tati that he was healthy enough for a transplant, then sent him to a lab at a local hospital where his blood was drawn for crossmatching with potential donors. The broker did not share any details of the transplant tour with Tati, not even the destination, explaining, "What we are doing, it's not legal, it's not illegal. We have to be quiet." Tati agreed to the conditions. Pulling together $58,000 from his insurance program, donations from his co-workers at the Sanitation Department, and a $33,000 bank loan, cosigned by sponsors, Tati paid for the trip. His wife was ecstatic. They were hardworking people who knew only the tensions of daily life in Jerusalem, relieved by the occasional weekend trip to the beach in Tel Aviv. This adventure, as she saw it, would be her first "tourist" experience. She bought a cheap set of matching suitcases, beach towels, brightly colored shirts, and Bermuda shorts. Tati's brother-in-law borrowed a video camera to document the holiday.

Tati showed me video from the trip on his small screen TV during his long recuperation, providing a running commentary. The small charter plane flight from the Tel Aviv airport was short—time just for a quick meal and round of drinks. In the footage, Tati is smiling but subdued, waving weakly to the camera. Four other transplant patients, each accompanied by a family member, were also on board the plane. Only after they had landed at a small airport and been hustled into waiting vans did they discover they were in Turkey, en route to the port city of Adana, where they would stay at the Hilton. That night, Tati and the group partied in their rooms. The video shows them bouncing on soft hotel beds, running in and out of the shower in their hotel bathrobes, fiddling with the radios and the color TV set, and belly dancing to "exotic" Turkish music playing on local stations. Having the time of their lives.

Tati talked me through the rest of the trip. Each night, two patients were selected for surgery. Tati's surgery took place on day two. He told me later that he'd had some qualms. The surgeries were done after midnight with patients smuggled into the hospital through a dark basement entrance, which made Tati feel like a thief in the night. In the corridor, he was briefly introduced to his seller, an Iraqi soldier, AWOL from Saddam's army, who had slipped across the border into Turkey without papers. Tati had some doubts about his "kidney man," but Dr. Shapira was reassuring. They had found a seller who was a perfect match, "like a brother." But the surgery didn't go well. Tati had a heart attack during the operation. When he emerged from the anesthesia the next day, he was hit by a wall of pain that caused him to lose consciousness again. The first crisis was followed by kidney rejection. He had a fever and a likely infection. "It was a poison kidney, and it almost killed me," Tati told me.

The holiday was over. Tati's wife continued to roll the film, capturing their frantic leave-taking at the Turkish airport, Tati's body on a stretcher, his face covered by an oxygen mask. On arrival in Tel Aviv, an anxious broker raises his hands to shield his face from the camera as he directs Tati's stretcher into a waiting ambulance. On arrival at Hadassah Hospital, Tati's regular doctor, Dr. F., is waiting, furious. He exclaims, "So my patient, against my orders, goes abroad to get a 'botched' transplant and now he is back here as an expensive basket case. He arrived from the Turkish hospital with a blank sheet of paper, no address, no letterhead, stating the obvious: 'failed Kidney transplant; myocardial infarction.'"

Tati spent six months in hospital before being released home to recover. By the time we talked, he was mortally ill, back on dialysis and living with his now estranged wife, their adult daughter, and her family in a cramped apartment in a public housing project in Jerusalem. Tati had a lot of complaints to air about his careless Turkish and Israeli surgeons—"one who took out, and one who put in"—and his deadly kidney exchange with a runaway Iraqi soldier. He died three years after his transplant holiday. As his story was told in the newspapers, the idea of transplants abroad spread, and Tati became a poster boy for transplant tourism. More brokers entered the game, competing viciously with each other. A public survey recorded that during the early years of organ trafficking, 70 percent of Israelis who had kidney transplants had acquired their kidney overseas.[3]

Transplant tourism, despite a spate of deaths, scandals, and medical infighting, soon became the new norm. With increasing demand, new destinations emerged, including China, the Philippines, Korea, South Africa, Kosovo, Azerbaijan, Argentina, Costa Rica, and the United States— where Levy Izhak Rosenbaum (aka Isaac Rosenbaum) ran a syndicate that managed to infiltrate reputable US hospitals and transplant units in New York, Philadelphia, and Baltimore, and later in Minnesota and Los Angeles.[4]

From 2001 to 2004, the trans-Atlantic "Brazil-South Africa-Israel" tri-angle was by far the most dramatic of the transplant schemes. It was also the first to be prosecuted, starting in Brazil, where eleven people were arrested and convicted of trafficking poor Afro-Brazilians from Recife to Durban, South Africa, where they were kept in a safe house awaiting the call to forfeit a kidney for as little as $6,000. The transplant tourists, primarily from Israel but also from Europe and the United States, were in contrast housed at the Holiday Inn by the Durban waterfront. A private hospital, Saint Augustine, owned by the Netcare Corporation, rented surgical rooms to the syndicate. In 2010, Netcare—South Africa's largest private hospital group—pleaded guilty to facilitating "an illegal organ trafficking syndicate in a scam that included the removal of kidneys from [among others] five children."[5]

One hundred and nine illicit transplants were performed at Saint Augustine, including five in which the "donors" were minors. A police sting resulted in several plea bargains being granted to various brokers and their accomplices. Netcare pleaded guilty to facilitating transplants,[6] causing their stocks to immediately—but only temporarily—plummet. The four surgeons and two transplant coordinators who were indicted held fast to their not guilty pleas, claiming that they had been deceived by the company and its lawyers who had stated these international surgeries were legal. In December 2012, the six defendants were given a permanent stay of prosecution, and the state was ordered to pay their legal costs.

Borders without Kidneys (and a Wolf among the Sheep)

Homo homini lupus est.
Man is a wolf to man.
—Latin proverb

In December 2015, a Ukrainian-Israeli man named Boris Wolfman (or Volfman) was arrested in Istanbul, where he had been recruiting Syrian refugees to sell their organs to foreign medical tourists willing to pay over $100,000 for a transplant.[7] The operations took place in private trans-plant units in Turkish hospitals. Wolfman was wanted in Israel, where he had been indicted for setting up illegal transplant operations in shadowy clinics in Kosovo, Azerbaijan, and Sri Lanka.[8]

Known among kidney sellers and transplant tourists alike to be totally ruthless, Wolfman collaborated with nefarious organized crime networks, with the help of Dr. Shapira in Israel. Wolfman began his career recruiting "spare kidney" immigrants, including refugees to Israel from economically devastated countries in Eastern Europe (mostly former Soviet states). He offered a small payment along with a deceitful promise to help them settle permanently in Israel. In the "great migration" of political refugees from Syria, Wolfman saw another business opportunity. An easy touch, dazed and disoriented, the Syrians seemed to be willing to do anything to get themselves and their children to safe ground. Parting with a kidney would be the least of what they had to suffer getting to "the West"—or at least as far as Turkey. Syrians, like countless others, have long been exposed to kidney trafficking inside and outside of their home country—selling organs an ugly last resort when facing extreme poverty.

In 2010, a Druze Syrian refugee to California contacted me in my role as director of Organs Watch to assist his petition for political asylum following what he described as a coerced nephrectomy (kidney removal) at the world-famous Cleveland Clinic Transplant Unit. The man, Mr. Salah G., had submitted to a San Franciscan lawyer a large file including medical evidence of his coerced trafficking to the United States from Qatar to serve, unbeknown to himself, as a living kidney donor to a relative of his employer. I agreed to investigate the case, after which I agreed to serve as a pro bono witness.

Mr. G. was never really a free man. As a child of thirteen he was apprenticed to an uncle in Lebanon. From there, his family more or less sold him as a bonded servant to a royal family in Qatar. As his period of bondage was coming to an end, his employers asked him to assist the family on a visit to the United States, after which, they promised, he would be returned to Syria. Salah did not know that his service to the family would include the donation of one of his kidneys to a young princess related to Salah's employer.

Cleveland Clinic staff paid scant attention to Salah's panic, and the kidney removal proceeded without his consent. He later managed, through a lawyer, to obtain his medical records. These supported his case for asylum, but the surgeons involved had both left the hospital and were working elsewhere by the time I interviewed them. One had been a surgical resident at the time. He confirmed to me that Salah had protested the nephrectomy as he was being intubated, but the senior surgeon had dismissed his distress as a minor panic attack. The current transplant chief of staff at Cleveland Clinic refused to hear the complaint of a person who was, after all, an undocumented person. He noted that Salah's signature was on the consent form. Salah did not speak English, however, and was assisted by an interpreter in each of our meetings. In the end, his case was dismissed, and Salah was denied asylum. He has since dropped out of sight.

Since the beginning of the war in Syria in 2011, huge numbers of religious and cultural minorities in ISIS-controlled areas have made the trek known as the "great migration" across the borders of Syria to Turkey, to Lebanon, to Italy, to Scandinavia, by foot, bicycle, taxi, and most notoriously by dinghy or raft—vessels I call "boats of wrath." Vulnerable and stateless people are unwanted even in nations recently thought of as democratic, secular, and humanist, like Hungary, Italy, Germany, and Denmark. While such European Union member states pour money into funding new border fences and guards,[9] impoverished asylum seekers are selling their organs to survive.

In 2015, Raïd, a nineteen-year-old Syrian who fled Aleppo to Lebanon with his family of six siblings, was picked up in Beirut by a kidney hunter known as "Abu Hussain." The broker had sent kidney runners to locate newly arrived refugees and offer them several thousand dollars for their organ—"expenses" deducted for the broker's help with the immigration authorities. A kidney for a visa, what could be better?

Lebanon has been a facilitating site for illegal transplants for many years, serving thousands of Arab transplant tourists, mostly from the Persian Gulf. Once it was Palestinian refugees in Lebanon who provided the kidneys, but Syrian war refugees soon became the new catch—cheaper and more desperate. Raïd told his story to *Der Speigel*.[10] He said he was happy to help his parents purchase the basics they needed to survive for a few months. Raïd was deposited on a curb after his surgery, without pain medication or antibiotics. "I don't care if you die," his broker told him. A sale is a sale, and Raïd went into it with his eyes shut.

Prosecutions and Protected Crime

Following decades of denial, human trafficking for the removal of kidneys from living "suppliers" to meet the needs and demands of transplant patients is now recognized as a real, resilient, flexible, mobile, and disturbing intrusion of criminal networks and syndicates into the field of global medical transplant programs and practices. "Transplant trafficking" best defines what is being sold to consumers: an illicit transplant in which the organ—a kidney or a half liver—and the person supplying the biological material are part of the package. While new laws have been put in place in Europe to combat human trafficking for the purpose of organ retrieval, illegal surgeries still comprise at least 20 percent of all global transplant operations.[11]

The new generation of organs traffickers is also more ruthless. Under the gaze of international media attention during the Beijing Olympics, brokers had their supply cut off after the Chinese government shut down foreign access to organs harvested from executed prisoners. Undeterred, brokers began to pursue transplants from living donors, some of them trafficked Vietnamese people, others naive villagers from parts of China where blood-selling programs had groomed people to accept kidney selling as another possibility.[12] The sites of illicit transplants have since expanded within Asia, as well as across the Middle East, Eastern Europe, Latin America, Europe, and the United States. As for the recruitment of kidney sellers, they can be found in almost any nation. One crisis after another has supplied the market with countless political and economic refugees, who fall like ripe, low-hanging fruit into the hands of the human traffickers.

Prosecutions are rare and extremely difficult. In most instances, only a few culprits—usually lower-ranking brokers and kidney sellers—are convicted. Surgeons, without whom no organ-trafficking crimes can be facilitated, and hospital administrators often escape by pleading igno-rance. The Netcare trial in South Africa is a case in point.[13] It is fair to state that rogue transplant surgeons operate with considerable impunity, despite the fact that they are the primary link in the organ-trafficking business.

Because human trafficking for organs is seen to benefit some very sick people at the expense of other, less visible or more dispensable people, prosecutors and judges have treated it as a victimless crime. For example, in 2009, when New Jersey federal agents charged Levy Izhak Rosenbaum—the above-mentioned hyperactive international kidney trafficker who had sold transplant packages for upward of $180,000—the FBI had no idea what a "kidney salesman" was. The prosecutors could not believe that prestig-ious US hospitals and surgeons had been complicit with the scheme, or that the trafficked sellers had been deceived and at times coerced into a serious medical procedure. The federal case ended in 2011 with a plea bargain; Rosenbaum admitted guilt to just three incidents of brokering kidneys for payment—while acknowledging that he had been in the busi-ness for over a decade.

At Rosenbaum's sentencing, however, the judge was impressed by a powerful show of support from his transplant clients, who had arrived to praise the trafficker and appeal for mercy. Only one of Rosenbaum's victims was presented as a witness by the prosecution, subpoenaed at the last minute and a surprise to the defense. Elan Quick, a young black Hebrew Israeli, had been recruited to travel to a hospital in Minnesota to sell his kidney to one Mr. Cohen, a seventy-year-old man from Brooklyn. None of Mr. Cohen's eleven adult children had been disposed to donate a life-saving organ to their father, later claiming that "none of them matched." They were, however, able to pay $20,000 to a stranger.

Quick testified that he agreed to the deal because he was unemployed at the time, alienated from his community, and hopeful that a meritorious act would improve his social standing. On arrival at the transplant unit, however, he had misgivings. Quick told Ito, his "minder" and the Israeli enforcer for the trafficking network, that he had changed his mind and wanted to get out of the deal. Those were the last words he uttered before going under anesthesia. Quick's testimony had no impact whatsoever on the sentencing judge, who stated that she hated to send Rosenbaum to a low security prison in New Jersey for thirty months, because she was convinced that, deep down, he "was a good man." The judge added that Elan Quick had not been defrauded; he was paid what he was promised. "Everyone," she said, "got something out of this deal."

Rosenbaum was treated as a white-collar commercial criminal— rather than a human trafficker—because his case was prosecuted as a felony regulatory violation of a law that prohibits "any person to knowingly acquire, receive, or otherwise transfer any human organ for valuable consideration for use in human transplantation if the transfer affects interstate commerce."[14] Under this law, it is the bartered kidneys at issue, not the trafficking of persons deceived into selling them. Human suffering is irrelevant when commerce is at stake. The kidney has become the blood diamond of our times.

Conclusions

Today, in the US-Mexico borderlands, migrants from Mexico and Central America face geographical and political barriers put into place by the US policy of "prevention through deterrence," which forces "illegals" to cross hostile sections of the Sonoran Desert where the likelihood of death— from heat and dehydration, poisonous snakes and reptiles, or rape and murder—is high. An increase in fatalities is seen as an indicator of policy success. More than 2,600 dead bodies have been recovered in the Arizona desert since 2000. In 2015, while scouring the desert for material objects left behind by migrants crossing into the United States—backpacks, caches of food, messages, maps, and clothing—Jason De León instead found a human arm, stripped of flesh, among the scattered remains of other decaying corpses. In his book, *The Land of Open Graves*, De León made public the official policy of US Border Patrol: to set the stage for undocumented migrants to fall victim to human, animal, and environmental conditions.[15]

The policy is a war on the living and on the dead, necroviolence, as bodies quickly turned into bones and dust cannot be retrieved for burial. It is a US version of the Argentine dirty war, which was backed by the CIA: designed to make unwanted aliens disappear. And while devalued refugees face incredible difficulty finding security or asylum across international borders, their commodified human organs—like any other valuable commercial product—travel freely, following the flows of capital and power, unhindered by their "alien" status.

Nancy Scheper-Hughes is Chancellor's Professor Emerita at the University of California Berkeley. Her lifework concerns the violence of everyday life examined from a radical existentialist and politically engaged perspective.

Notes

1   Aihwa Ong, *Flexible Citizenship: The Cultural Logics of Transnationality* (Durham, NC: Duke University Press, 1999), 123.

2   Before 2000, the problem of trafficking in human organs (mainly kidneys) was primarily limited to the Indian subcontinent and Southeast Asia. Recipients of these organs came mainly from the Gulf states, Japan, and other Asian countries. The EU and the USA issued sporadic reports about patients traveling overseas to obtain kidneys. However, since 2000, trafficking in organs has started to spread globally, to a large extent driven by Israeli doctors and patients who explored opportunities to seek transplants in Eastern Europe, Turkey, Russia, and the Philippines. Following the Istanbul Conference and Declaration in 2008 (see The declaration of Istanbul on Organ Trafficking and Transplant Tourism, *Indian Journal of Nephrology* 18, no. 3 [July 2008]: 135–140, accessed March 30, 2020, https://www.ncbi.nlm.nih.gov/pmc/articles/PMC2813140), Israel began to pay attention to Israeli citizens who traveled abroad for illegal transplants, especially following two prosecutions of Israeli organ trafficking schemes, one in Northeast Brazil in 2008 (see Nancy Scheper-Hughes, "Black Market: Gaddy Tauber, Organs Trafficker, Holocaust Survivor," *Business Today* [Spring 2009]: 62–67) and another simultaneous prosecution

of Israeli transplant tourists to Durban, South Africa, in 2010 (see David Smith, "South African Hospital Firm Admits 'Cash for Kidney' Transplants," *Guardian*, November 10, 2010, accessed March 22, 2020, https://www.theguardian.com/ world/2010/nov/10/south-africa-hospital-organ-trafficking). Both prosecutions included the author, Scheper-Hughes, who gave testimony to the governments. Today the trafficking in organs has shifted to Latin America, North Africa, Cypress, Turkey, and other regions where economic crises alongside social and political instability create opportunities for organ traffickers.

3   Michael Friedlaender, "The Right to Sell or Buy a Kidney: Are We Failing Our Patients?" *Lancet* 359, no. 9310 (April 2002): 971–73, accessed March 22, 2020, https://hods.org/pdf/The%20right%20to%20Sell%20or%20Buy%20a%20Kidney. pdf.

4   Nancy Scheper-Hughes, "The Rosenbaum Kidney Trafficking Gang," *CounterPunch*, November 30, 2011, accessed March 22, 2020, https://www. counterpunch.org/2011/11/30/the-rosenbaum-kidney-trafficking-gang.

5   Smith, "South African Hospital Firm Admits 'Cash for Kidney' Transplants."

6   Ibid.

7   Chase Winter, "Suspected Israeli Organ Trafficker Arrested in Turkey: Reports," Deutsche Welle, May 5, 2015, accessed March 22, 2020, https://www.dw.com/en/ suspected-israeli-organ-trafficker-arrested-in-turkey-reports/a-18896905-0.

8   For coverage of Boris Wolfman/Volfman's criminal activities, see Kevin Sack, "Transplant Brokers in Israel Lure Desperate Kidney Patients to Costa Rica," *New York Times*, August 17, 2014, accessed March 20, 2020, https://www. nytimes.com/2014/08/17/world/middleeast/transplant-brokers-in-israel-lure- desperate-kidney-patients-to-costa-rica.html.

9   Jon Stone, "EU Plans to Triple Spending on Border Control in Response to Refugee Crisis," *Independent*, June 13, 2018, accessed March 22, 2020, https:// www.independent.co.uk/news/world/europe/eu-border-control-spending- refugee-crisis-austria-coast-guard-mediterranean-a8397176.html.

10   Ulrike Putz, "Syrian Refugees Sell Organs to Survive," *Spiegel International*, November 12, 2013, accessed March 22, 2020, https://www.spiegel.de/ international/world/organ-trade-thrives-among-desperate-syrian-refugees- in-lebanon-a-933228.html.

11   Nancy Scheper-Hughes, "Organ Trafficking during Times of War and Political Conflict," *Current Anthropology* 41, no. 2 (April 2000): 191–224, accessed March 22, 2020, http://www.ia-forum.org/Files/HDSQLC.pdf.

12   Nancy Scheper-Hughes, "Perpetual Scars," *New Internationalist* 472 (May 2014), accessed March 22, 2020, https://digital.newint.com.au/issues/88/articles/1890.

13   "South African Hospital Pleads Guilty to Organ Trafficking Case," *Telegraph*, November 10, 2010, accessed March 22, 2020, https://www.telegraph.co.uk/ news/worldnews/africaandindianocean/southafrica/8124710/South-African- hospital-pleads-guilty-to-organ-trafficking-case.html.

14   42 US Code § 274e accessed March 30, 2020, https://www.law.cornell.edu/ uscode/text/42/274e.

15   Jason De León, *The Land of Open Graves: Living and Dying on the Migrant Trail* (Berkeley: University of California Press, 2015).

II
Waiting Games

From Paris to Lampedusa:
The New Business of Migrant Detention in Europe

Louise Tassin

Far from the image of "Sieve Europe" so often mentioned in the media, the European Union (EU) increasingly militarized its external borders in the 2000s, compensating for the creation of the Schengen Area (in which free movement across national borders is permitted).[1] After the Seville Summit of June 2002, the fight against so-called illegal immigration was established as an EU priority.[2] Over the next ten years, a series of legal, material, and human systems aimed at securing the external border spread throughout the continent. These included forcible returns of people intercepted at sea and land crossings, the building of new walls and fences, the establishment of new detention facilities, and increased use of high-end technologies (thermal cameras, heartbeat detectors, etc.) for surveillance and "securitization."[3]

Consequently, a market in migratory control has emerged, responding to the converging interests of European political leaders and leading economic players in defense and security.[4] Privatized to varying degrees in different countries, detention centers—where migrants are held while government administrators assess their immigration status or asylum claims or organize their deportation—constitute a flourishing sector of this new business. As of 2017, there were more than 360 detention facilities in forty-four countries in Europe and at its borders, with a total capacity of forty-seven thousand beds.[5] This development raises financial and, most importantly, humanitarian questions about migrant detention: degrading treatment, violations of human rights, suicide attempts, and revolts are frequently reported.[6] Furthermore, despite the tightening of migration control policies, these facilities are inefficient in achieving their stated goals. In 2014, for example, the European Commission observed that fewer than 40 percent of detained migrants subject to forcible return had been expelled from EU territory.[7] In this context, migrant detention has been interpreted as a symbolic policy: an instrument for EU member states to deter migrants from irregularly crossing its borders and to reassure their political constituencies.[8]

The subcontracting of detention facilities has developed in various forms and to different degrees throughout EU territory. From the construction of facilities to their administration and upkeep, detention involves both businesses and nonprofit organizations. The system is sometimes completely privatized, as in the United Kingdom, where most sites are entirely managed by companies providing surveillance, logistics, and even escort during deportations. But privatization can also be limited, as in France and many other countries where only specific services are delegated to external providers, such as building upkeep, food, and cleaning services, or—as in the center where I conducted my research—the "reception" of detainees. This official term is a euphemism to describe various activities of stewardship and control, as I explain below. Finally, there are more hybridized forms of subcontracting. In Italy, for example, centers have been managed by local nongovernmental organizations (NGOs) and, increasingly, in the 2010s, by private companies. However, police and security forces are still in charge of keeping the detainees under surveillance.

The outsourcing of migrant detention has received increased media coverage in recent years, especially in the United Kingdom, where numerous abuses by guards in private facilities—including sexual assault, beatings, and violence during deportation, which in a few cases have led to deaths—have been exposed.[9] Publications by NGOs and academics alike have shown that privatization leads to degradation in the conditions of detention, the jeopardizing of detainees' rights, and the diluting of responsibility for problems when they arise.[10] However, as empirical studies are difficult to conduct in these areas, the concrete effects of subcontracting practices remain underreported.

In France, other than a few brief newspaper articles on the employment of undocumented workers on a construction site for a detention center in 2008 and some coverage of an employee's strike in 2013, the little information and analysis available are products of activist work,[11] which include notable critical zines that accurately describe the growth of the detention market.[12] In Italy, the 2014 Mafia Capitale scandal generated considerable media attention. It revealed the existence of a vast corruption and embezzlement network involving detention facilities and migrant shelters. In 2017, the two ringleaders of the organization, Massimo Carminati and Salvatore Buzzi, were sentenced to up to twenty years in prison. However, the implications of subcontracting in this context were not publicized or studied much further. Nevertheless, several publications on Italian reception centers for asylum seekers have shown how, in a state of permanent emergency, civil society actors have become extensions of the state security apparatus.[13]

My research aims to fill gaps in this area. The situations in France and Italy are particularly interesting. In France, although private subcontracting is officially limited to logistical management, external providers appear to play a far more central and more ambivalent role than just stewardship. Private employees—the majority of whom are working-class immigrants or descendants of immigrants—sometimes serve as intermediaries between staff and detainees, performing a kind of mediation that is essential to maintaining order within the institution. In Italy, competition for contracts between NGOs, and more recently between private actors, has lowered standards of reception. Far from preventing nepotistic relations, competition seems to have favored opaque practices at the expense of detainees' rights.

In this chapter, drawing from ethnographic studies conducted in Paris and Lampedusa detention centers, I explore the impact of migrant detention outsourcing to non-state actors—private companies and NGOs—with a focus on the practices of those who implement it on a daily basis.[14] Drawing on Virginie Guiraudon,[15] I interrogate the extent to which the subcontracting of tasks that are not key to state sovereignty affect the implementation of detention and deportation policies. This involves understanding how the delegation of these tasks helps to reshape the conditions of care and control of confined foreign nationals, particularly how informal intermediaries contribute to both the pacification of detained people and the symbolic normalization of a very violent environment.

Private-Sector Staff in France: An Immigrant Workforce in a Central Role

The Centre de rétention administrative (Administrative Detention Center) in Vincennes is located in Paris but commonly referred to by the name of the woodland where it stands. It is one of the better known CRAs in France, because it made media headlines in June 2008, when revolts broke out in reaction to the death of a Tunisian detainee, leading to a fire in the buildings. Today, the center imprisons up to 180 people in three buildings of sixty beds each. The site resembles a prison: yards fenced in with ceilings or mounted with barbed wire, sentry walks, security booths, surveillance cameras, alarms, automatic doors, security gates, etc. (see figure 6.1). The detainees are not locked in their cells and can freely access collective spaces, including an exterior courtyard. They, however, cannot leave the securitized area except under the escort of police officers and private staff, and then only to access the center's various services (medical team, legal advisers, administration) or to travel to external locations (trials, consulates, or airports).

In 2015, nearly 3,800 people were detained in Vincennes, for an average stay of fifteen days. Seventy-one percent of them were freed without having their immigration status regularized, and 29 percent were deported— about half of them to countries within EU territory under the Dublin Agreement, which stipulates immigrants may only apply for asylum in the EU country they first entered.[16] The detainees held in Vincennes are of diverse nationalities, including Tunisian, Algerian, Moroccan, Romanian, Indian, Senegalese, Egyptian, Gabonese, Eritrean, and Sudanese. These statistics are representative of the other twenty-three CRAs in the country. In France, CRAs are officially intended to organize deportations of undocumented migrants (persons who entered the territory illegally, whose visas have expired, or who have been denied asylum), but anyone detained may apply for asylum in the center if they have not done so before.

The process for detaining people is as follows: people are stopped during immigration raids (in a neighborhood, home, or workplace) on the order of a prosecutor, or they may be intercepted at the prefecture, in border zones, during "routine" identity checks, or upon arrest.[17] Following an "administrative detention" at the police station of up to sixteen hours, they are transferred to one of twenty-four CRAs. Upon arrival, they are searched and must leave most of their belongings in "storage"—a small room of lockers. Telephones with cameras are not admitted; only some personal possessions and a small amount of money are authorized inside. Once escorted by a police officer into the building, they are brought before a "reception agent." This is an employee of a subcontractor, GEPSA, which specializes in detention facilities management. This employee is responsible for filling out the detained person's "identification card" (photograph, serial number, and name), handing them a hygiene kit, explaining the organization of the center, and placing them in a room. Although tasks delegated to the private sector are officially circumscribed, these staff are the only workers constantly present in the facility and serve as intermediaries between state or NGO employees (police, medical team, and legal advisers) and detainees: the same employee "reception agent" may later serve the detainee in the canteen or laundry and will likely be on hand to answer their requests for information, for access to personal belongings in storage, to see a doctor, or to buy a phone card.

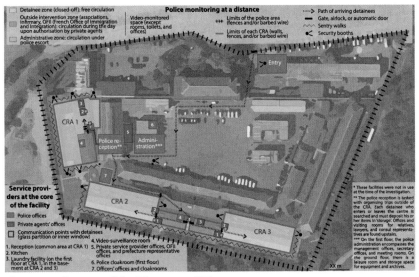

Figure 6.1: Site map of the Vincennes CRA
(Source: field study, autumn 2014. Map background courtesy of GoogleMap. © Louise Tassin, 2016)

Detained migrants can be locked up for up to ninety days at a time. Their deportation is subject to two conditions: identification of their country of origin and the securing of a "laissez-passer" (i.e., an authorization, or pass card) from the authorities of that country. If the detained person has not been deported within ninety days, they are released from detention without regularization of their immigration status and are obliged to leave the country by their own means within seven days. Once this period has expired, they can be arrested and locked up again, often creating a painful cycle of detention and release. One Tunisian man I met in the Vincennes CRA was in the middle of his sixth stay in detention.

While the outsourcing of French CRAs may seem insignificant at first glance, my research in the Vincennes center shows that in a multitiered subcontracting system private companies are embedded at many levels, directly or through their subsidiaries. ENGIE, Air France, Bouygues, VINCI, Compass—multinationals that have amassed their wealth through globalization and the circulation of capital and goods—also now reap financial benefits from the restriction of the movement of human beings. At Vincennes, GEPSA—a subsidiary of ENGIE (formerly GDF-Suez)—has won all the contracts in "multiple services" at the center since the first call for tender in 2007. It has also won contracts to manage several other centers, making it an "industry leader" at the national level. Responsible for providing food, laundry services, cleaning, and detainee reception, the company itself employs a subcontractor, Onet, to clean the premises and to organize weekend activities. Moreover, GEPSA negotiates contracts with other service providers for meals, as well as for laundry services and vending machines, thus increasing the number of companies with a stake in the market.

This pursuit of financial gain at multiple levels raises many questions. First, because of budgetary restrictions, it leads to a degradation of detention conditions. Subcontractors tend to rank priorities according to criteria defined by the prefecture, which are not always favorable to the detainees. Various means of minimizing costs are implemented, be it delaying repairs, refusing to replace damaged games or educational resources, or distributing meals on the day of or the day before their expiration date. During my research, no activities were offered in the center, leaving people bored and frustrated, while the quality and quantity of the meals were often the subject of complaints, and facilities were often defective (broken sinks, leaks in the roof during heavy rain, toilets overflowing near the canteen).

The recourse to subcontractors has also exacerbated the deterioration of working conditions, including low pay, reduced hours, precarious contracts, and increased workloads, particularly for the subcontractors of subcontractors. These changes have altered the profile of the workforce, which had previously been composed of ex-soldiers contracted to the Ministry of Justice. In keeping with the national context of increasing labor segregation, in which immigrants are overrepresented in so-called unskilled jobs, detention center management companies employ a "flexible" workforce primarily made up of descendants of immigrants and foreigners holding a temporary residence permit (usually valid for one year or for ten years). Forced to accept these jobs for lack of better opportunities—the result of discriminatory social structures—these employees hardly flourish in their minimum-wage positions but find some compensation in relative job stability, close-knit teams, and the material benefits of the job.

Given their socioeconomic insecurity, their immigrant background, and their temporary legal status, these employees' lives often reflect those of the detainees. Many have been undocumented themselves or have undocumented relatives. Some employees I spoke to had encountered friends or acquaintances detained in the CRA. In a striking coincidence, one GEPSA employee even learned that two of his uncles had been incarcerated in their youth at the Vincennes Identification Center, which had been used to confine Algerians in the 1960s and was located on a site situated approximately where the Vincennes CRA now stands.[18]

Such examples stress two sociohistorical continuities. The first is as a location where foreign nationals are held, which over decades and under varying conditions have perpetuated a system of confinement and relegation of undesirable populations. The second continuity is the commonality between those confined and those responsible for managing them: to remove unauthorized foreign nationals, the French state has enlisted immigrant workers who often fit the same profiles as those whose expulsion they facilitate. This is a reminder, if one were needed, of the contradictions between policies hostile to immigration and common practices among multinational companies and state institutions, for which undocumented immigrants and foreigners also represent (to various degrees) a highly useful and flexible workforce.

Finally, my research reveals that subcontracting activities are not limited to their official domain of material assistance. Privatization has produced a partial, but nevertheless decisive, transfer of the monitoring of detainees to private-sector staff. At the heart of the CRA, between the closed-off zone and the personnel area, non-state employees have become an essential component of the system. Going far beyond the tasks officially assigned to them, they are key intermediaries between state staff and detainees; I see non-state employees as "small-time performers of police work." Inside their office, which looks out over the closed off zone, they monitor common areas, observe "risky" behavior, and inform administrators of any problems. Moreover, as they are the only employees to interact daily with the detainees, they build personal relationships and play an essential role in maintaining order in the center, defusing many tense situations, even while surveilling those detained.

The gap between assigned and actual responsibilities reveals how private employees supplement and even sometimes replace state actors in carrying out tasks traditionally under the purview of state—but without the training or supervision allotted to official administrators. Not only do certain employees sometimes lack the training or means to carry out their assigned tasks correctly, but their response to their working conditions can also impact detainees. Staff may leave early, fall asleep during morning shifts, or study on the job. Their lack of interest and professionalism may be understood as resistance to poor working conditions. It is also often to the detriment of people in detention.

The Booming Immigrant Confinement Market in Italy: Corruption and Symbolism

The Italian situation reveals other problems that can arise from subcontracting immigration control, in this case to nonprofit actors. In Italy, civil society associations are, in effect, similarly forced to compete for contracts via government calls for tender—a process geared toward securing the lowest-cost services. The sums allocated by provinces for the management of detention centers tend to diminish year after year, since the most economically attractive offers are almost always sought by local governments. GEPSA, which had previously established its name in private prison management, won contracts to manage three detention centers in Italy between 2012 and 2014, offering prices 20 to 30 percent below those proposed by its predecessors. Similarly, the social cooperative LampedusAccoglienza took over provision for first aid and reception centers in Lampedusa in 2006 by proposing a price 40 percent lower than that of the preceding manager, Misericordia. In the whole of Italy during 2014, the cost per day per detainee cited in corporate and nonprofit proposals oscillated between €20 and €40 (approximately US$26 and US$52)—a two-fold difference. The result is a high risk of differentiated treatment according to the location and its management (see figure 6.2).

However, it is difficult to draw conclusions about service quality based on these numbers alone. In a mafia-ridden system wherein several managers have been accused of reaping illegal benefits from their activities, a higher daily expenditure is not a certain sign of quality. "You have

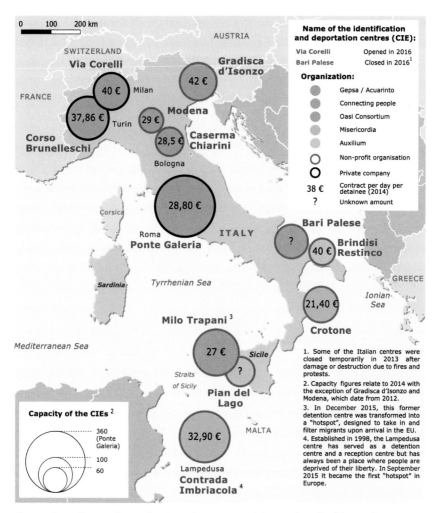

Figure 6.2: Migrant detention in Italy: a competitive and profitable market
(Sources: Campagne LasciateCIEentrare; Close the Camps: www.closethecamps.org;
Macerie: www.autistici.org; MEDU: "The CIE Archipelago: Inquiry into the Italian Centres
for Identification and Expulsion," May 4, 2013; Migreurop; Prefecture of Rome (information
note); Senate Report on Italian CIE's by the special Human Rights Committee, XVII
legislature, 2014. © Louise Tassin, 2016)

no idea how much we've made off of immigrants. Drug-trafficking is less
profitable," affirmed Salvatore Buzzi, a key figure in a national scandal
known as Mafia Capitale, to an accomplice over the telephone in 2014.[19]
In bugged conversations, Buzzi inadvertently revealed the existence of
an enormous Mafia network—led by Massimo Carminati, an extreme
right-winger and former associate of the neofascist terrorist group,

Nuclei Armati Rivoluzionari—that allotted contracts for the management of asylum seeker reception centers to favored companies and inflated population figures to augment profit margins. This scandal revealed that the management of migrants in open or semi-open centers (where people are held during the processing of their asylum applications) and in civil society associations were also prone to corruption. Concerning Lampedusa, a body of evidence indicates that the contract between LampedusAccoglienza and the state was settled before the call for tender was announced, thanks to the organization's political affiliations and nepotistic relationships. The assistant director of LampedusAccoglienza had previously been indicted in 2011 for "aggravated fraud" and "illegal profit." He was also accused of embezzling nearly €500,000 (approximately US$695,000 in 2011 dollars) by "registering" detainees who did not exist or by detaining migrants for longer than required—sometimes up to three hundred days—in one of his reception centers, the CARA in Sant'Angelo di Brolo, near Messina.[20]

Subcontracting, in addition to being an appealing cost-saving measure, also facilitates state disengagement from and dilution of responsibility toward migrants and asylum seekers. Multiple cases of sexual abuse and degrading treatments by private staff have been discovered, mainly in Italy and the United Kingdom.[21] In each case, state authorities have blamed and punished management organizations, companies, and associations for individual failures, never questioning the logic of privatization. In turn, companies have blamed individual staff for abuses. For example, the company G4S—a self-proclaimed "global leader" in security, with operations in 125 countries—was implicated in numerous controversies in England, where some of its guards have been sued for negligence and assault.[22] G4S was also recently criticized in Lesbos, Greece, where it provides security for the Moria migrant camp. The Mytilene association of lawyers accused the company of preventing migrants from accessing the European Asylum Support Office (EASO) to file their requests for asylum.[23] These scandals have had little impact on G4S's ability to win detention center management contracts.

A key issue raised by the subcontracting phenomenon concerns its symbolic aspects. What is the representational effect of resorting to companies specializing in weapons, security, or prison administration to "manage" foreign nationals without proper documentation? Inversely, what happens when humanitarian actors or service providers specializing in social assistance are introduced into mainly coercive institutions? Lampedusa is a case in point.

Boats carrying migrants that are intercepted at sea by the Italian Coast Guard or Guardia di finanza (financial police), sometimes several hundred kilometers from the Italian Coast, have for decades disembarked their passengers on the island of Lampedusa, on a quay closed to the public. After a medical screening, they are transferred by bus to the center, where they are subjected to a brief interview with the police. They are then categorized as asylum seekers, economic migrants, or vulnerable people and, depending on their situation, transferred to another center on the continent, either to assess their claim or to organize their deportation. The maximum length of detention in the Lampedusa center is officially seventy-two hours, but migrants have often been locked up for weeks and even months. The transformation of the center into a "hotspot" in September 2015 did not significantly change the organization of procedures, aside from the looming presence of the European agencies Frontex and EASO.

Abuses in Lampedusa (lack of privacy, hygiene problems, difficulty in accessing medical services, lack of interpreters, and the impossibility of filing appeals, as well as those mentioned above) were repeatedly denounced by nonprofit and parliamentary actors long before the reception crisis of 2015.[24] The center suffered from a negative reputation in the 2000s and became a symbol of migrants' rights violations in 2005, when an undercover journalist revealed the shameful conditions of confinement, then overseen by Misericordia.[25]

To deflect criticism, the government announced changes intended to "humanize" the institution.[26] It assigned the management of the center to the charitable NGO LampedusAccoglienza, limited the length of confinement to a few days, and granted site access to a consortium of international organizations. These changes marked a turning point in the history of the island. By helping to displace and reframe debates about the center, they transformed questions of the legitimacy of detention into less controversial debates over the material conditions of confinement. The repellent image of the center was thus replaced after 2006 by what parliamentarians and journalists called "the Lampedusa model."[27] In short, the subcontracting of the center to an NGO allowed a security apparatus of disputed legitimacy to become publicly acceptable.

However, problems once again arose in early 2009, when the center became overpopulated following the Berlusconi government's decision to stop transfers to the continent, and, in spring 2011, when the assistant director of LampedusAccoglienza was indicted for fraud. Even then, local and national authorities did not cease to promote the "nonprofit" management of the center, to such an extent that official, sanitizing terminology was adopted into popular representations: the detention center became a "reception" center, and its occupants became *ospite*, meaning *guests*. The site, however, continues to be an area of deprivation of freedom without legal monitoring, where degrading treatment is the norm.

In December 2013, a detained migrant succeeded in secretly filming LampedusAccoglienza employees as they forced naked men to wait in single file in an outside courtyard before spraying them with a scabies control substance from a powerful hose. This much publicized event was widely condemned, with one report comparing the site—and its employees—to a Nazi-run camp.[28] The government suspended its contract with LampedusAccoglienza and replaced it with Misericordia—the very same cooperative that had managed the site in the early 2000s, until it was similarly ousted following outcry prompted by an undercover report.[29]

The history of the Lampedusa site is riddled with scandal, and the government has long known of the rights violations occurring there. The only political response has been a cosmetic change imposed by media pressure, illustrating how the practice of subcontracting immigration detention to civil society and private actors allows the state to delegate away responsibility for abuses, while placing itself beyond reproach. The symbolic impact of governmental interventions has only strengthened this position; whereas the establishment of the first Lampedusa center was met with fierce opposition, the maintenance of a space (re)conceived and promoted as an area for assistance, open to national and international nonprofit actors, has been widely received as a satisfactory solution that minimizes migrants' presence, while preserving the island's welcoming image.[30] These developments reveal how state disengagement from migrants' detention centers by subcontracting services is far from a retreat of state power in these areas. On the contrary, it helps to legitimize it.

Louise Tassin is a PhD student at the Migration and Society Research Unit (URMIS), University of Nice Sophia Antipolis and a teaching assistant at the School for Advanced Studies in the Social Sciences in Paris, France. She is a member of the Migreurop network.

Notes

1   Smaïn Laacher, *Ce qu'immigrer veut dire: Idées reçues sur l'immigration* (Paris: Éditions le Cavalier Bleu, 2012).

2   Measures against human trafficking and a common approach to immigration dominated the agenda of this two-day EU summit in June 2002. The fight against illegal immigration was defined as an "absolute priority."

3   See Mark Akkerman, "The Military and Security Industry: Promoting Europe's Refugee Regime," this volume, 149–63.

4   Claire Rodier, *Xénophobie business: À quoi servent les contrôles migratoires?* (Paris: La Découverte, 2012); Thomas Gammeltoft-Hansen and Ninna Nyberg Sørensen, eds., *The Migration Industry and the Commercialization of International Migration* (London: Routledge, 2013); Ruben Andersson, *Illegality, Inc.: Clandestine Migration and the Business of Bordering Europe* (Oakland: University of California Press, 2014).

5   Migreurop, *Atlas des migrants en Europe: Géographie critique des politiques migratoires européennes* (Paris: Armand Colin/Migreurop, 2017).

6   Olivier Clochard, "Révoltes, protestations et 'résistances du quotidien': Des étrangers à l'épreuve de la détention," *Migrations Société* 164, no. 2 (June 2016): 57–72, accessed March 30, 2020, https://www.cairn.info/revue-migrations-societe-2016-2-page-57.htm.

7   European Union: European Commission, "Communication of the Commission to the European Parliament and the Council: EU Action Plan on Return," EUR-Lex, September 9, 2015, accessed March 22, 2020, https://eur-lex.europa.eu/legal-content/EN/TXT/?uri=COM%3A2015%3A453%3AFIN.

8   Rodier, *Xénophobie business*.

9   "G4S: Company Profile 2018," Corporate Watch, June 2018, accessed March 22, 2020, https://corporatewatch.org/g4s-company-profile-2018.

10 Michael Flynn and Cecilia Cannon, "The Privatization of Immigration Detention: Toward a Global View," Global Detention Project, September 2009, accessed March 22, 2020, https://papers.ssrn.com/sol3/papers.cfm?abstract_id=2344196; Michael Flynn, "Kidnapped, Trafficked, Detained? The Implications of Non-State Actor Involvement in Immigration Detention," *Journal on Migration and Human Security* 5, no. 3 (July 2017), accessed March 22, 2020, https://cmsny.org/publications/jmhs-kidnapped-trafficked-detained; Rodier, *Xénophobie business*; Andersson, *Illegality, Inc.*; Lydie Arbogast, "Migrant Detention in the European Union: A Thriving Business" (Brussels: Migeurop, 2016); Georg Menz, "Neo-Liberalism, Privatization and the Outsourcing of Migration Management: A Five-Country Comparison," *Competition & Change* 15, no. 2 (July 2011): 116–35, accessed March 22, 2020, http://citeseerx.ist.psu.edu/viewdoc/download?doi=10.1.1.854.7498&rep=rep1&type=pdf.

11 Arbogast, "Migrant detention in the European Union"; Olivier Clochard and Claire Rodier, "Circulez, c'est privé," *Plein Droit* 101 (January 2014): 26–30, accessed March 22, 2020, https://halshs.archives-ouvertes.fr/halshs-01098086/document.

12 See Non Fides, accessed March 22, 2020, http://non-fides.fr; Infokiosques, https://infokiosques.net.

13 Marie Bassi, "Politiques de contrôle et réalités locales: le cas du centre d'accueil (pour demandeurs d'asile) de Mineo en Sicile," *L'Espace Politique* 25, no. 1 (April 2015), accessed March 22, 2020, https://journals.openedition.org/ espacepolitique/3354.

14 This chapter is drawn from a PhD in sociology on public and private actors in the detention of migrants in the EU, comparing three case studies in Paris (France), Lampedusa (Italy), and Lesbos (Greece). It offers only a brief glimpse into two empirical research projects. The first was a nearly three-month ethnographic field study in the Vincennes center, with daily observations and about one hundred interviews with the detainees and personnel, particularly police officers and private employees. The second, in Lampedusa, was a field study supplemented by analysis of archives in the island's municipal council, intermittent observations in the center, and fifty interviews with center employees and security, political, economic, and activist actors linked to immigration control. This work is complemented by an analysis of press and institutional and civil society associate reports. A first and shorter version of this paper was published in French in Babels auteur collectif (ed.), *De Lesbos à Calais, comment l'Europe fabrique des camps* (Paris: Editions du Passager Clandestin, 2017).

15 Virginie Guiraudon, "Logiques et pratiques de l'Etat délégateur: les compagnies de transport dans le contrôle migratoire à distance," *Cultures et conflits* 45 (Spring 2002), accessed March 22, 2020, part 1, https://journals.openedition. org/conflits/771; part 2, https://journals.openedition.org/conflits/773.

16 During the reception crisis (see n24 below) of 2015–2017, the number of people detained in France and deported within the Dublin Agreement framework multiplied by four, rising from 834 to 3723 detained, and from 405 to 1719 deported; see "Centres et locaux de rétention administrative, 2018 rapport" Paris: Rapport, 2018, La Cimade, June 2019, accessed March 22, 2020, https://www.lacimade. org/publication/rapport-2018-centres-locaux-retention-administrative.

17 Open Society Justice Initiative, "Ethnic Profiling in France: A Well-Documented Practice," Open Society Foundations, May 2011, accessed March 22, 2020, https://www.justiceinitiative.org/uploads/c4cab2a3-1889-4e19-9e5b-23f755686daf/ethnic-profiling-in-france-a-well-documented-practice-english-2011-05-23.pdf.

18 Emmanuel Blanchard, "L'internement avant l'internement Commissariats, centres de triage et autres lieux d'assignation à résidence (il)-légale," *Matériaux pour l'histoire de notre temps* 4, no. 92 (2008): 8–14, accessed March 22, 2020, https://www.cairn.info/revue-materiaux-pour-l-histoire-de-notre-temps-2008-4-page-8.htm.

19 Lucie Geffroy, "Corruption. 'Mafia capitale,' l'énorme scandale qui secoue l'Italie," *Courrier International*, December 10, 2014, accessed March 22, 2020, https://www.courrierinternational.com/revue-de-presse/2014/12/09/ mafia-capitale-l-enorme-scandale-qui-secoue-l-italie.

20 Antonio Mazzeo, "Cono Galipò richiesta di rinvio a giudizio per 'illeciti profitti' sui richiedenti asilo del centro di accoglienza migranti che gestiva. Vergogna tutta italiana," *Annalisa Melandri*, July 25, 2011, accessed March 22, 2020, http://www.annalisamelandri.it/2011/07/cono-galipo-richiesta-di-rinvio-a-

giudizio-per-%E2%80%9Cilleciti-profitti%E2%80%9D-sui-richiedenti-asilo-del-centro-di-accoglienza-migranti-che-gestiva-vergogna-tutta-italiana.

21 Arbogast, "Migrant detention in the European Union."

22 Rhiannon Curry, "Five More Arrested Over G4S Child Detention Centre Scandal," *Telegraph*, June 9, 2016, accessed March 22, 2020, https://www.telegraph.co.uk/business/2016/06/09/five-more-arrested-over-g4s-child-detention-centre-scandal.

23 Apostolis Fotiadis, "New Security on Greek Islands Reduces Access," News Deeply: Refugees Deeply Digital Project, June 15, 2016, accessed March 30, 2020, https://www.newsdeeply.com/refugees/community/2016/06/15/new-security-on-greek-islands-reduces-access.

24 I use "reception crisis" rather than "refugee crisis" to underline the nature of this period; see Annalisa Lendaro, Claire Rodier, and Youri Lou Vertongen, *La crise de l'accueil: Frontières, droits, résistances* (Paris: La Découverte, 2019).

25 Fabrizio Gatti, "Io clandestino a Lampedusa," *L'Espresso*, October 7, 2005, accessed March 22, 2020, https://espresso.repubblica.it/palazzo/2005/10/07/news/io-clandestino-a-lampedusa-1.594.

26 Cono Galipò and Federico Miragliotta, *Rotta 0.05 Modello Lampedusa: Cosa accade nei centri per immigrati?* (Florence: Bonnano Editore, 2010), 14.

27 Conseil de l'Europe, "Les 'boat people' de l'Europe: arrivée par mer de flux migratoires mixtes en Europe du Sud," Assemblée parlementaire, 2008, accessed March 22, 2020, http://assembly.coe.int/nw/xml/XRef/Xref-XML2HTML-FR.asp?fileid=17692&lang=FR.

28 "Cie Lampedusa, il video-shock del Tg2 indigna e scuote le coscienze," *La Repubblica*, December 17, 2013, accessed March 22, 2020, https://www.repubblica.it/solidarieta/immigrazione/2013/12/17/news/cie_lampedusa-73848222.

29 Paolo Cuttitta, *Lo spettacolo del confine: Lampedusa tra produzione e messa in scena della frontiera* (Milan: Mimesis, 2012).

30 Louise Tassin, "Accueillir les indésirables: Les habitants de Lampedusa à l'épreuve de l'enfermement des étrangers," *Genèses* 96, no. 3 (January 2014): 110–131, accessed March 22, 2020, https://www.cairn.info/revue-geneses-2014-3-page-110.htm.

Detained Voices on Labor

Detained Voices

In March 2015, a solidarity protest led by an ad hoc group of unaffiliated activists was held outside Harmondsworth and Colnbrook, two adjacent immigrant detention centers in West London. The protesters made contact with people detained in Harmondsworth, who were demonstrating in response to a recently broadcast Channel 4 television program that had documented racist treatment by guards and inhumane conditions inside the center. While previous protests outside the detention center had often coincided with protests inside, it quickly became clear that on this occasion a larger mass detainee protest was stirring. The phone used by activists outside to speak to those inside was overwhelmed with calls from people wanting to make demands to the Home Office (the government agency in charge of immigration) and to share their stories of mistreatment. The resulting detainee-led protest took the form of yard occupations and hunger strikes. It lasted for two weeks, drawing in people held in other detention centers across the country, in Dover, Dungavel, and Morton Hall.

A number of things were striking to those of us in contact with protesters inside the center. First, they were fully aware of and eager to articulate the exploitative conditions in which they were held, the inherent unfairness of the immigration process, and the intrinsic racism of their treatment as individuals, and of the immigration system as a whole. Second, widespread discontent about the conditions of detention was being successfully harnessed by organizers on the inside—and, therefore, collective grassroots action could generate both a powerful critique of the detention system and effective resistance against the smooth running of the detention estate, including stopping individual deportations. Third, we realized that few people were listening. The government ignored the protests. More worryingly, the mainstream anti-detention movement had not yet learned how to respond in solidarity with protests led by people held in detention. The NGO community was primarily focused on convincing politicians to adopt reforms. Civil disobedience by those inside simply did not fit with their campaign priorities.

These insights prompted us to create Detained Voices, a collective that provides an online platform (www.detainedvoices.com) for people inside to share their experiences, demands, and critiques of detention. The statements are published in their own words, as dictated to a Detained Voices member over the phone or sent to us by fax. Since 2015, we have published over two hundred posts detailing abuse by guards, exploitative labor conditions, inadequate health care, poor food, the frustration of waiting, and the fear of violence during and after deportation. The project thus challenges elements of the anti-detention movement that present people in detention solely as vulnerable and voiceless. The three posts below highlight profit-making—through labor exploitation and bail systems, for example—and protest in the UK asylum industry. Detained Voices continues to work with detainee protesters to amplify their words and actions and to build solidarity and coordination between those fighting to end detention from outside and inside.

—Tom Kemp, Detained Voices, April 10, 2019.

Double Standards in the "Right" to Work

I want to talk about work. I am paid £1 [approximately US$1.30] per hour for any job. I was specifically told that I had no right to work outside of detention. If a company out there employs an "illegal migrant," the company gets prosecuted and fined and the migrant gets arrested and jailed. But G4S, GEO, SERCO, and MITIE all run these detention centers, contracted by the Home Office, and all employ "illegal migrants." They should be prosecuted and fined. They make lots of profit and pay us under minimum wage, while treating us like slaves. I find this very disgusting. Why are we being treated in this inhuman way?

People work as cleaners, in the kitchen, some people who wash pans, some that work in the library as an attendant, clean tables, clean the showers. Every essential part of the center apart from security is all done by detainees who are paid £1 an hour. The health and safety situation is poor as well. . . . In normal circumstances, the first thing that gets done when you're employed is induction. There is no induction for people who start work in detention. There are no induction packs whatsoever. No one knows their right from their left. I'm quite educated, but for most people in here, the system is shambolic.

[Detention] is a place where they cage people just to remove them. Everyone is classified as a "danger to the public," yet they've committed no crime, and they come from a war-torn area. I've seen lots of [people's] papers, and it's like a template, they just classify people. . . . It's not the Britain I used to live in. It's all politically motivated. Nobody is talking about this. We are being used to make profit, as cash cows for the Home Office and for the security companies. G4S: £148 million in 2014 [approximately US$245 million]. Where are they making this profit? They are making it from those in prison, from detainees. If they employed people outside to work here, they would be paid £6–7 an hour. Any other job, [the government] would punish people for paying £1 an hour. I think this is double standards. I'm allowed to work in here. If I get released, I will not be allowed to work.

Why do I say that the Home Office is involved in this? Because before you get a job in a detention center, the Home Office has to clear you. So they know! If they don't clear you, then you don't get a job. They know how much they pay us. They know exactly what is going on. The Home Office, the medical care providers, and the companies are all involved in this. They know about it. Why is it different for us? Why should we be marginalized and almost enslaved?

—Anonymous, Brook House Detention Centre, published March 16, 2015.

Rice, Chips, and Bail

They have kept me in detention for nine months for no reason. I left my country to seek a better life, not to be in here. They feed us chips and rice every day. Every day. We are humans, we need to eat good food. They treat young nationals from other countries like animals. We only want freedom. . . . I want people to know that when some people say they are spending money on refugees, what they really do is buy rice and chips and give it to you in here.

I've seen people in here with mental problems because of what the Home Office does. They think every day that they are going to get released.

I don't want that to happen to me. There are people with no support, and they get released. And some people who have friends and girlfriends outside, they don't get out. They say you have to have friends who are working and earning money to get bail. The Home Office says I have to have friends with a £1,000 [approximately US$1,300] in their bank accounts. I have friends, but they're all in university, and those that are working are not earning that much, so they can't be a surety for me.

I should be out. I should be enjoying myself. I should be doing something with my life. I am wasting my life. I should be out doing something for my life and for my girlfriend. When I was out, I was at college studying information and communications technology and business. In here, they just offer English as a Second Language, but obviously I can already speak English. I want people to know what they're doing to refugees.

—Anonymous, Colnbrook Detention Centre, published November 11, 2015.

The Strikers Demands

In February–March 2018, over 120 women took part in a month-long hunger strike at Yarl's Wood Immigration Removal Centre to protest UK immigration detention practices. At the time of the hunger strike, former immigration minister and Conservative MP Brandon Lewis erroneously claimed that "The people in detention centers are people who are illegally in this country and are there for a period of time until they go back to their own country."[1] In fact, many are asylum seekers detained while awaiting the processing and outcomes of their claims. In 2017, Women for Refugee Women found that 85 percent of women at Yarl's Wood were survivors of sexual or other gender-based violence.[2] The same year, the Inspector of Prisons found that 70 percent of the women detained at Yarl's Wood were later released back into the community, not deported as Lewis claimed, raising concerns about why they had been detained at all.[3] The UK is the only European country that has no time limit on how long a person may be held in immigration detention. These conditions prompted action.

—the editors

After an initial three-day hunger strike, which the Home Office refused to acknowledge, it is clear that they are not listening to us. On Monday February 26, 2018, we will cease to participate in detention. We will not eat, use their facilities, or work for them. The detainees are thus staging an all-out strike to protest the Home Office's continued immoral practices.

Our demands are for a fair system and an end to the "hostile environment" policy toward people with legitimate reasons to remain in the UK.

- We want an end to indefinite detention and a return to the original plan of the 28-day time limit.
- We want the Home Office to respect Article 8 [of the European Convention on Human Rights, which protects a person's right to respect for their private and family life].
- We want the Home Office to respect the European Convention of Human Rights regarding refugees and asylum seekers.
- We want the Home Office to respect due process and stop deporting people before their cases are decided or appeals are heard.
- We want due process before we are imprisoned on immigration matters.
- We want a fair bail process and the Home Office to end the process of selective evidence disclosure to the immigration tribunal courts and instead disclosure of all evidence to ensure a fair judgement is reached.
- We want adequate health care and especially the mental health nurse to stop operating as an extension of the Home Office, asking people such questions as, "did you know you were going to stay in the UK when you entered?"
- We want the Home Office to stop detaining the vulnerable people, that is victims of rape, all forms of torture, trafficking, forced labor, the disabled, the mentally ill and so on.
- We want amnesty for all people who have lived in the UK for more than 10 years and an end to the exiling of those who came as children and are culturally British.
- We want an end to the Home Office's practice of employing detainees to do menial work for £1 per hour. It preys on the vulnerable and forces them to participate in their own detention.
- We want an end to charter flights and the snatching of people from their beds in the night and herding them like animals.

I want to stress that there are as many demands as there are detainees. Everyone in detention is unfairly treated, and all we want is a fair process. This is the only option we are left with to express how we feel. We will not eat till we are free.

—An open letter from the Yarl's Wood Detention Centre Hunger Strikers, published February 25, 2018.

On March 27, 2019, a UK high court judge ruled that £1 per hour wages for people held in immigration detention were "lawful," because "the purpose of the types of jobs being done, such as cleaning, hairdressing and welfare support, was 'to provide meaningful activity and alleviate boredom.'" [4] *The case had been brought by five people previously held in detention, who termed the pay "slave labour wages." One journalist covering the case, Diane Taylor, reported: "In 2016–17, detainees carried out 887,073 hours of work, for which they were paid £887,565."* [5]
—the editors

Detained Voices (www.detainedvoices.com) is a UK-based collective that provides an online platform to people inside to share their experiences, demands, and critiques of detention.

Notes

1   Brandon Lewis, quoted in Ash Sarkar, "By Demeaning Refugees, Tories Have Caused the Yarl's Wood Hunger Strike," *Guardian*, February 28, 2018, accessed April 17, 2020, https://www.theguardian.com/commentisfree/2018/feb/28/refugees-tories-yarls-wood-hunger-strike.

2   Gemma Lousley and Sarah Cope, *We Are Still Here: The Continued Detention of Women Seeking Asylum in Yarl's Wood* (London: Women for Refugee Women, 2017), accessed March 23, 2020, https://www.libertyhumanrights.org.uk/sites/default/files/We-are-still-here-report-WEB.pdf.

3   HM Chief Inspector of Prisons, *Report on an Unannounced Inspection of Yarl's Wood Immigration Removal Centre, 5–7, 12–16 June 2017* (London: Her Majesty's Inspectorate of Prisons, 2017), accessed March 23, 2020, https://www.justiceinspectorates.gov.uk/hmiprisons/wp-content/uploads/sites/4/2017/11/Yarls-Wood-Web-2017.pdf.

4   Diane Taylor, "Judge Rules £1/hr Wages for Immigration Detainees are Lawful," *Guardian*, March 27, 2019, accessed March 23, 2020, https://www.theguardian.com/uk-news/2019/mar/27/judge-rules-1hr-wages-lawful-for-immigration-centre-detainees.

5   Ibid.; approximately US$1,171,585.

The Poetics of Prison Protest

Behrouz Boochani and Omid Tofighian

This chapter highlights the poetics and critical thought of Behrouz Boochani and his collaborator and translator Omid Tofighian. Behrouz was incarcerated in an Australian-run immigration detention center on Manus Island from August 2013 to November 2019. The excerpts that constitute this piece are examples of creative and intellectual protest and of fundamental elements of what we refer to as "Manus Prison theory." The excerpts are necessarily fragmented, reflective of the conditions of Behrouz's imprisonment and resistance. The philosophical thought quoted here was originally published between late November 2018 and May 18, 2019, the day of the Australian federal election.

Omid: Like in most nation-states, Australian border politics are particularly violent. Consecutive leaders and governments have constantly reconfigured the relationship between three fundamental elements of the sociopolitical imagination: "Australian values," "national security," and "national interest." The border is both an ideological and physical location where this reconfiguration is tested. Therefore, as domestic and international political events and discourses change, politicians introduce and enforce new varieties of interconnected techniques for controlling the movement of bodies. The values-security-interest nexus justifies and maintains violent border regimes, while the reality of bordering practices is modified in accordance with it—a sleight of hand that also functions to conceal the violence.

In his November 28, 2018, article for the *Guardian*, Behrouz paid tribute to his late friend and confidant Poruan "Sam" Malai, a Baluan man who lived on Manus Island. Sam featured in the 2017 film *Chauka, Please Tell Us the Time*, which Behrouz codirected with Arash Kamali Sarvestani,[1] as well as making significant contributions to cultural and intellectual dimensions of the movie.

> One day I made plans to see Sam at his place but when I arrived, I only saw his niece who was smoking outside. She said: "Sam had heart pains a few days ago and died." It was one of the most painful moments during my time on Manus Island. This feeling was the same as the pain I felt every time a refugee died on this island of medical neglect. His niece explained: "Sam could have been saved. The GP said that had he encountered this pain anywhere else other than Manus he could have been treated with ease." The problem was that he was extremely poor and it was not easy for him to travel to Port Moresby. Sam's tragic death made me contemplate. I still think of his wonderful laugh and kindness, I think about his life, I think about his untimely death. . . . These things will always remain with me.
>
> Over and over again, incidents such as this one have occurred through the years we have been imprisoned here. The people on Manus have died even though hundreds of millions of dollars have been paid to companies who are assigned to run the prison camp. According to the agreement between PNG and Australia the main road of Manus must be repaired, a police station must be built and the hospital on the island must be adequately equipped. But after years the hospital has fallen into disrepair. A few months ago the roof of the primary school was destroyed by a storm and the school requested assistance from the community. But no one had the capacity to help rebuild the school. For months the children had to attend their lessons within a hazardous zone and under the rain. The condition of the hospital is getting worse by the day.[2]

Tweeting as Protest

Omid: Behrouz used social media throughout his years imprisoned on Manus Island, live reporting events and processes that the Australian government sought to hide from view to tens of thousands international followers.[3]

Behrouz Boochani ✔
@BehrouzBoochani

Yesterday a refugee was beaten up by a guard on Manus. Another performance of the cruelty of this system that strengthens itself through our humiliation. In reality, it's you that you are humiliating and your grand values and morals that you take so much pride in.#Manus #auspol

3:43 AM · Jan 6, 2019 · Twitter for Android

399 Retweets **501** Likes

Behrouz Boochani ✔
@BehrouzBoochani

The guards on Manus and Nauru have been beating up innocent refugees in the past six years, over hundred times maybe. This shows how sadistic this system is. Shame on those who are running and supporting this system.#Manus #auspol

3:46 AM · Jan 6, 2019 · Twitter for Android

95 Retweets **113** Likes

Behrouz Boochani ✔
@BehrouzBoochani

One of the major problems we have on Manus & Nauru is that there's nowhere for us to go to and complain when we are mistreated. The police and juridical system have been at the service of those who exiled and tortured us. We are standing outside the law but still subject to it.

3:50 AM · Jan 6, 2019 · Twitter for Android

125 Retweets **152** Likes

Behrouz Boochani ✔
@BehrouzBoochani

A human may be able to survive physical torture and prison, but he/she can never get over humiliation. When you beat up a refugee, you are not hurting them physically only, you're taking their humanity and identity. Humiliation is the ultimate torture.#auspol #Manus

3:53 AM · Jan 6, 2019 · Twitter for Android

112 Retweets **186** Likes

Behrouz Boochani ✔
@BehrouzBoochani

The guard who beat up a refugee yesterday proved that he's nothing but a coward puppet, a slave of this sadistic system, a bastard, void of human qualities. I'm wondering if those serving this system will ever be punished for their animalistic treatment of the refugees.#Manus

4:01 AM · Jan 6, 2019 · Twitter for Android

119 Retweets   **183** Likes

Behrouz Boochani ✔
@BehrouzBoochani

The Paladin staff are protesting in Manus right now. This company has made $423m while paying local staff only $450 per month.People are very angry at this company and want to be respected. The big companies made the refugees and locals victims while they have made so much money.

11:36 PM · Feb 25, 2019 · Twitter for Android

639 Retweets   **1K** Likes

Behrouz Boochani ✔
@BehrouzBoochani

The only reason people are ill on Manus & Nauru is that they've been kept in an indefinite prison camp,six years so far, and nothing else. Transferring them to Christams island prison camps does't cure them, just worsen it.Stop carrying our broken bodies from one cage to another.

6:45 AM · Feb 20, 2019 · Twitter for Android

1.1K Retweets   **2.2K** Likes

Behrouz Boochani ✔
@BehrouzBoochani

Australian Paladin officer was arrested and jailed in Manus because of allegations of sexual assault. He is a former G4S officer who was sacked in 2014 but remployed and returned to Manus to work for Paladin #Auspol #Manus

9:06 AM · Apr 4, 2019 · Twitter for Android

600 Retweets   **693** Likes

Behrouz Boochani ✓
@BehrouzBoochani

Today a rally is happening across Australia to call out for an end to the barbaric policy of exiling asylum seekers. Please don't be silent in this grand moment. This is not a protest for supporting the refugees only, but for the Aus people too, who are standing against this gov.

2:18 AM · Apr 14, 2019 · Twitter for Android

482 Retweets   **1.3K** Likes

Behrouz: The issue here is that the people working in this system are its instruments, they are also being sacrificed. By defining them in this way as a sacrifice I mean they are victims. It is not just the imprisoned refugees who suffer affliction, the employees of the system have relinquished their human agency. They have no choice but to serve this system in order to take money. They are made to do inhumane things just for money, and these same people return to their homes and families and bring that same violence with them.

A Prize Platform

Omid: On January 31, 2019, Behrouz won both the Victorian Premier's Awards for Literature and for Non-Fiction, for his book *No Friend but the Mountains: Writing from Manus Prison.*[4] The book has been released internationally, translated into numerous languages, and will be made into a film. Behrouz was unable to attend the ceremony in Melbourne, as he could not leave Manus Island. The absurdity and irony of the situation was remarkable: Behrouz "won" an award from the same political system that imprisoned him, including prize money that he could not access due to that imprisonment. I accepted the awards on his behalf. Behrouz engaged with the audience via WhatsApp video call.

I thought the most appropriate way to represent Behrouz was to come on stage while communicating with him via WhatsApp at the same time. This reflects something of the surreal and horrific nature of the entire situation and gives some sense of the translation process. Behrouz and I understand each other particularly well, because we both have complicated histories of displacement, exile, and interlocking forms of marginalization—a reality that has also affected our family networks. But, unlike Behrouz, I have been able to spend most of my life in Australia.

This is in many ways the result of chance—a strong element of luck distinguishes our current situations. While he was writing in prison on a remote island, I was translating and regularly crossing many borders without any trouble. The experience of working with Behrouz has been both beautiful and tragic. The translation process, like the narratives in *No Friend but the Mountains*, are both surreal and horrific. A gross paradox of this modern, globalized world.

Behrouz's acceptance speech:

> When I arrived at Christmas Island six years ago, an immigration official called me into the office and told me that they were going to exile me to Manus Island, a place in the middle of the Pacific Ocean. I told them that I am a writer. That same person just laughed at me, and ordered the guards to exile me to Manus.
>
> I kept this image in my mind for years, even while I was writing my novel—and even right now, as I'm writing this acceptance speech. It was an act of humiliation. When I arrived in Manus, I created another image for myself. I imagined a novelist in a remote prison. Sometimes I would work half naked beside the prison fences and imagine a novelist locked up right there, in that place. This image was awe-inspiring. For years I maintained this image in my mind. Even while I was forced to wait in long queues to get food, or while enduring other humiliating moments. This image always helped me uphold my dignity and keep my identity as a human being. In fact, I created this image in opposition to the image created by the system.
>
> After years of struggling against the system that has completely ignored our individual identities, I am happy that we have arrived at this moment. This proves that words still have the power to challenge inhumane systems and structures. I have always said that I believe in words and literature. I believe that literature has the potential to make change and challenge structures of power. Literature has the power to give us freedom. Yes, it is true.
>
> I have been in a cage for years but throughout this time my mind has always been producing words, and these words have taken me across borders, taken me overseas and to unknown places. I truly believe words are more powerful than the fences of this place, this prison.

This is not just a basic slogan. I am not an idealist. I am not expressing the views of an idealist here. These words are from a person who has been held captive on this island for almost six years. A person who has witnessed an extraordinary tragedy unfold in this place. These words allow me to appear there with you, tonight.

With humility, I would like to say that this award is a victory. It is a victory not only for us, but for literature and art and above all, it is a victory for humanity. A victory for human beings, for human dignity. A victory against a system that has never recognized us as human beings. It is a victory against a system that has reduced us to numbers. This is a beautiful moment. Let us all rejoice tonight in the power of literature.[5]

The Kyriarchal System and Manus Prison Theory

Omid: Behrouz analyzes Manus Prison as an extension of the Australian state. For him, the conditions created, the techniques used, and the history of detaining refugees—especially offshore detention—are linked to Australia's exploitative colonial past and its neocolonial, neoliberal present. Even though Manus Island and Nauru are politically independent, and the detained refugees have been held there to keep them out of Australia, we want to draw attention to the fact that Manus Island and Nauru are integral parts of Australian society and history. This feature of Manus Prison theory is important, because it helps explain the way vulnerable people in Australia are treated by their government, guided by a neoliberal capitalist ideology. The inhumane treatment of people in immigration detention is actually a feature of their own institutions.

Behrouz, writing for the *Guardian*, in February 2019:

Recently, the Paladin controversy has dominated political discussions. The company was contracted to provide security for the refugees detained on Manus Island. The questions at the center of this debate relate to the conditions under which this contract was made and the ways in which the agreed $423m were spent. However, all the focus of the media has been directed only at this one company, simply questioning the figure in the contract. For years I have been scrutinising the security companies and medical service providers on Manus.

...From all the companies working on Manus during these years it is International Health and Medical Services (IHMS) that has the worst record. . . . [It] has been operating on Manus for four-and-a-half years—throughout this time a number of refugees have lost their lives due to medical neglect. . . . [Paladin] took over from IHMS in November 2017. I have already detailed how they play with the health of refugees.[6] They employ the same approach that IHMS had been implementing for years. Their strategy involves nothing more than issuing painkillers and referring refugees mainly to the public hospital in Lorengau—which is just a decrepit building with no real use. . . .

During these years the Australian government has always used propaganda to influence public opinion and prove that they have been providing refugees with welfare and medical services. However, what they portray in the media is in stark contrast with the reality on Manus and Nauru. The most convincing evidence we can use to justify this accusation is the deaths of 12 individuals.[7] The only things these companies have achieved during these years has been to assist immigration [officials] in torturing refugees psychologically and emotionally. They have not only withheld services from refugees but have in fact been a significant element in a system aimed at stripping people of their humanity and afflicting suffering.[8]

Omid: It is extremely difficult to fully comprehend and analyze the significant aspects of the lived experience in immigration detention, the emotional and psychological power dynamics of the system, and the ideological dimensions of the border regime. Many people know that there are detention centers on Manus Island and Nauru, that people are living in difficult conditions. They know about the corruption and mismanagement. But they are unaware of the extent of systemic torture perpetrated there.

Behrouz identifies "off-shore asylum processing" as a kyriarchal system,[9] working to create a prison that orchestrates a system of torture and to distort perceptions of the situation so that it becomes palatable to the public. Politicians and media conglomerates thus saturate popular discourse, while minimizing the extreme levels of harm inflicted on refugees through euphemism. They constantly repeat selective facts and narratives about how detained individuals are provided, for instance, "three meals every day" or offered "facilities for recreation and health." This distorts people's capacity to interpret the kind of violence taking place, which has its own particular prolonged, psychological, emotional, and spiritual dimensions. It was difficult for Behrouz's journalism to communicate this perverse form of torment and violence. Behrouz has been saying for quite some time that his journalism, film, and public speeches have not been successful in convincing people of the extent of persecution refugees are facing. For him, literature has been the only way to explain systematic torture and the kyriarchal system.

Behrouz, writing for the *Saturday Paper*, April 2019:

> After a lot of political tumult the medivac bill was eventually passed on February 12. According to this law, all sick refugees on Manus and Nauru now have the opportunity to be transferred to Australia for medical assistance.... According to the bill, if two doctors confirm that a sick refugee needs to be transferred to Australia then the government must comply with their advice. However, a big problem with this bill is that a clear mechanism has not been designed so that a refugee can access two doctors. In fact, dozens of sick refugees either do not know how or have no way to apply for a transfer....
>
> The thing that has made this process excruciating is that these human rights organisations [Refugee Council of Australia, Asylum Seeker Resource Centre, Amnesty International, National Justice Project, and Human Rights Law Centre] are following the same path the government has been carving out all these years regarding the treatment of sick refugees. This is nothing more than subjecting refugees to a bureaucratic game—a very drawn-out administrative process and complex structure.
>
> At this point in time, a refugee has to sign many forms and send his documents and information to these groups. Then he has to wait for them to act on his behalf. But this is an extremely tortuous process. Many people signed papers months and months ago and are still waiting for attention.
>
> If we were to calculate the length of time necessary for all the sick refugees to leave this island, based on the [current] rate of two people every two-and-a-half months, we can conclude that it would take about 128 years. You are right to laugh. You would be right, also,

to conclude that the government has tried to exploit this bill for its own political purposes.

They reopened the Christmas Island detention center at a massive cost and then closed it again after a short period. Home Affairs Minister Peter Dutton announced that hundreds of refugees would be transferred to Australia and would fill up hospital beds. Of course, that didn't happen. With all the political ruckus and propaganda this bill is a failure. [10]

Omid: On May 18, 2019, the Liberal/National Coalition was reelected at the Australian federal election. The current prime minister is Scott Morrison, who launched Operation Sovereign Borders (OSB) in 2013, as minister for immigration and border protection. OSB made the situation for people seeking asylum in Australia more tortuous and hopeless. In November 2019, after more than six years detained on Manus Island, Behrouz managed to escape to New Zealand. His future, however, remains uncertain.

Behrouz Boochani is adjunct associate professor in social sciences, University of New South Wales, and a visiting professor at Birkbeck, University of London. He is a filmmaker, journalist, and author, including of the book *No Friend but the Mountains: Writing from Manus Prison* (Pan Macmillan-Picador, 2018).
Omid Tofighian is adjunct lecturer in the School of Arts and Media, University of New South Wales, and honorary research associate at the University of Sydney. He is author of *Myth and Philosophy in Platonic Dialogues* (Palgrave Macmillan, 2016) and the translator of *No Friend but the Mountains: Writing from Manus Prison*, by Behhouz Boochani.

Notes

1   Arash Kamali Sarvestani and Behrouz Boochani, *Chauka, Please Tell Us the Time* (Eindhoven, NL: Sarvin Productions, 2017).

2   Behrouz Boochani, "'Sam Could Have Been Saved': Where Does the Money for Healthcare Go on Manus?" trans. Omid Tofighian, *Guardian*, November 28, 2018, accessed March 23, 2020, https://www.theguardian.com/commentisfree/2018/nov/28/sam-could-have-been-saved-where-does-the-money-for-healthcare-go-on-manus.

3   Behrouz Boochani, "Yesterday a refugee was beaten up by a guard on Manus," Twitter, January 6, 2019, accessed March 23, 2020, https://twitter.com/BehrouzBoochani/status/1081758110140645377.

4   Behrouz Boochani, *No Friend but the Mountains: Writing from Manus Prison*, trans. Omid Tofighian (Sydney: Pan Macmillan-Picador, 2018).

5   For full transcript, see Behrouz Boochani, "Behrouz Boochani's Literary Prize Acceptance Speech: Full Transcript," *Guardian*, February 1, 2019, accessed March 23, 2020, https://www.theguardian.com/world/2019/feb/01/behrouz-boochani-on-literary-prize-words-still-have-the-power-to-challenge-inhumane-systems.

6   Helen Davidson, "Self-Harm and Suicide Worsening under Australian Detention Regime, Report Finds," *Guardian*, November 21, 2018, accessed March 23, 2020, https://www.theguardian.com/australia-news/2018/nov/22/self-harm-and-suicide-worsening-under-australian-detention-regime-report-finds.

7   Ben Doherty, Nick Evershed, and Andy Ball, "Deaths in Offshore Detention: The Faces of the People Who Have Died in Australia's Care," *Guardian*, June 17, 2018, accessed March 23, 2020, https://www.theguardian.com/australia-news/ng-interactive/2018/jun/20/deaths-in-offshore-detention-the-faces-of-the-people-who-have-died-in-australias-care.

8   Behrouz Boochani. "The Paladin Scandal Is Only a Drop in the Ocean of Corruption on Manus and Nauru," trans. Omid Tofighian, *Guardian*, February 27, 2019, accessed March 23, 2020, https://www.theguardian.com/commentisfree/2019/feb/27/the-paladin-scandal-is-only-a-drop-in-the-ocean-of-corruption-on-manus-and-nauru.

9   A kyriarchy is a matrix of interlocking social systems that keep oppressions in place, defined by Elisabeth Schüssler Fiorenza as "a complex pyramidal system of intersecting multiplicative social structures of superordination and subordination, of ruling and oppression"; Elisabeth Schüssler Fiorenza, *Wisdom Ways: Introducing Feminist Biblical Interpretation* (New York: Orbis Books, 2001).

10 Behrouz Boochani, "Medivac Missteps Rack Sick Refugees," trans. Omid Tofighian, *Saturday Paper*, April 27, 2019, accessed March 23, 2020, https://www.thesaturdaypaper.com.au/news/politics/2019/04/27/medivac-missteps-rack-sick-refugees/15562872008056.

Displacement, Commodification, and Profitmaking in Nigeria

Sidonia Lucia Kula and Oreva Olakpe

Academic discussions on the commodification of asylum and displacement are often focused on the privatization of migration control in Western countries.[1] These discourses center on how Western countries cut the cost of and responsibility for migration control by outsourcing to private companies, which then profit from immigration systems.[2] In this chapter, we argue that commodification comes in other additional forms and occurs in other spaces around the world. In our analysis of the displacement, security, and asylum industry in Nigeria, we approach displaced people, humanitarian aid, security, and access to support as commodifiable products.

We look at how profit is made within the context of human trafficking, the actors involved, and the beneficiaries of the socioeconomic disparities caused by insecurity and displacement. We then explore the narratives of women and girls who suffer within the system and explain what their experiences signify. Our aim is to analyze the profit-making constructs that feed off displaced persons, refugees, and asylum seekers and to explain their impacts. Though internally displaced persons (IDPs) are usually overlooked in the traditional conception of "refugees," their experiences of exploitation are similar.

Refugee and IDP camps are filled with people marginalized by states and often forgotten in coverage of global "refugee crises." As a result, extreme forms of exploitation and abuse of power persist within camps. With a huge power differential between refugees and camp officials, these abuses manifest in corruption and the commodification of necessities or services, access to which are controlled by authority figures who may use their positions for personal gain or gratification.

In these spaces of displacement, the provision of refuge—whether temporary or permanent—takes the form of a series of transactions in which certain goods or services are exchanged between authority figures and displaced people, often to the detriment and dehumanization of the latter. These transactions may be in cash or in kind, involving sellers, intermediaries, and buyers. A wide range of individuals and institutions benefit from the exploitation of asylum seekers and displaced people, including governments, local communities, camp officials, nongovernmental organizations, and so on. Each group profits from the displaced in different ways. Depending on the context, the contours of exploitation and commodification change. We look to Nigeria as a case study for lessons on the commodification of asylum and its impact on the displaced.

Profiteers
Actions taken by the jihadist militant organization Boko Haram in northeastern Nigeria led to over ten thousand civilian deaths from 2009 to 2014 and the abduction of more than two thousand women and children. They also led to the displacement of an estimated 2.5 million people, many of whom have sought refuge in thirteen IDP camps in Nigeria, as well as in neighboring countries like Cameroon.[3] Ensuing conflicts have further compounded the exploitation of refugees through human trafficking and forced labor.

From its inception in 2009 until 2012, Boko Haram attacked army and police officers, politicians, and those the organization's leaders deemed corrupt.[4] In 2012, however, Boko Haram changed tactics. It began attacking and kidnapping women and children with the aim of discouraging "Western education" and forcing non-Muslims to convert to Islam. These abductions also became profitable for Boko Haram in a number of ways. For example, abducted women and children have been used as bargaining chips in negotiations with the government for the release of captured militants. Boko Haram leaders have also forced abducted girls and women to work in their camps as cooks or maids, to act as recruits for suicide bombings, and to marry new recruits in an effort to incentivize loyalty. Many of the girls and women have been raped by combatants.[5] In some cases, Boko Haram has paid dowries to the families of women and girls it has kidnapped.[6] These payments exacerbate existing power dynamics in the region by silencing family members and the community at large. Dowries are common in Northern Nigeria, where rising bride prices may have indirectly contributed to the rise of Boko Haram; evidence suggests it provides inexpensive weddings as a recruitment strategy.[7]

Products

How do we measure how profit is made within a context of violence, displacement, and trafficking? The process of trafficking is defined by the United Nations as a transaction between the trafficker and a "buyer," involving the use or threat of force, abduction, and abuse of power for forced labor, prostitution, and/or slavery.[8] Wheaton et al. state that "the human trafficking market is a monopolistically competitive industry with many sellers (human traffickers) offering many buyers (employers) differentiated products (vulnerable individuals) based on price and preferences of the individual employers."[9] In this market, Boko Haram is both a trafficker (producer) and a beneficiary (consumer) of different forms of forced labor.

Trafficking has become an especially important means of funding Boko Haram's activity, because it provides the group with nonmonetary benefits, including labor, unlike other revenue streams like money laundering or kidnapping for ransom. The process of building these new financial and labor reserves can also attract new recruits and expand the group's networks. In a local context of endemic impoverishment, violence, and a lack of access to education, the promise of compensation or better opportunities in exchange for participating in the capture and exploitation of others can be enticing. Participation in trafficking and related processes of exploitation—illicit as they may be—can also be understood as a survival strategy.

The complex nature of how different people are victimized and put at the service of Boko Haram makes it difficult for them to escape the group and return to their previous lives. Sexual violence in particular has a deep impact on female escapees, who often face exclusion, stigma, and distrust in their new communities. The Federation of Muslim Women's Associations in Nigeria (FOMWAN) and the Herwa Community Development Initiative are two Nigerian advocacy organizations that, having identified these impacts, are actively seeking to dismantle the stigmatization associated with sexual violence by facilitating dialogues in IDP communities.[10]

Within the Nigerian legal system, responses to trafficking are shaped by cultural norms and attitudes toward survivors based on their socioeconomic status and means and their gender.[11] Nigerian institutional systems, weakened by corruption, often fail survivors of trafficking. In 2016, for example, Orodata researchers uncovered evidence of camp officials and aid workers collaborating in child trafficking in IDP camps and identified a "conspiracy of silence" among government officials regarding the problem.[12] In September 2018, the National Agency for the Prohibition of Trafficking in Persons (NAPTIP) announced the dismissal of six officers for a litany of corruption charges, including bribery, the exchange of services for sex, and "sabotage and gross indiscipline."[13]

As the Boko Haram example demonstrates, trafficking and related complex forms of profit-making operate both within and between areas separated by national borders. Internal displacement, however, continues to be frequently overlooked in discussions of forced and exploitative migrant labor,[14] in part because IDPs are categorically not "asylum seekers" or "refugees" under international law. Beyond Boko Haram, numerous other profit-making structures impact refugee asylum seekers and IDPs alike in Nigeria—and the roots of the dynamic cannot be associated with just one group. Structural violence and the interplay of political economic dynamics in the North East, and in Nigeria as a whole, also shape this reality. Addressing the problem is not just a question of removing Boko Haram. Other actors and dynamics are also implicated.

Markets

People seeking refuge from violence encounter multiple forms of exploitation in camps for the displaced, including forced marriage, rape, and human trafficking.[15] For example:

> In late July 2016, Human Rights Watch documented sexual abuse, including rape and exploitation, of 43 women and girls living in seven internally displaced persons (IDP) camps in Maiduguri, the Borno State capital. Four of the victims told Human Rights Watch that they were drugged and raped, while 37 were coerced into sex through false marriage promises and material and financial assistance. Many of those coerced into sex said they were abandoned if they became pregnant. They and their children have suffered discrimination, abuse, and stigmatization from other camp residents. Eight of the

victims said they were previously abducted by Boko Haram fighters and forced into marriage before they escaped to Maiduguri. A situational assessment of IDPs in the northeast in July 2016 by NOI Polls, a Nigerian research organization, reported that 66 percent of 400 displaced people in Adamawa, Borno, and Yobe states said that camp officials sexually abuse the displaced women and girls.[16]

IDP camps have become spaces for the continued capitalist exploitation of refugees/asylum seekers and IDPs, where they must pay to access material and other forms of assistance. Shortages of supplies like food and medicine, as well as the imposition of restricted movement, have been used by camp officials, security operatives, and local community members to bargain for sex. Camp residents' ability to leave the camps remains particularly restricted by the army due to "security concerns." Ironically, confinement inside the camp can be just as unsafe as venturing outside.[17] This restriction further impacts IDPs ability to access specialized services and means of livelihood in surrounding areas, resulting in their economic marginalization and subsequent vulnerability, which officials and traffickers alike are liable to exploit.

Human trafficking persists in IDP and refugee camps, with reports of trafficking of hundreds of girls for sex and labor.[18] The National Agency for the Prohibition of Trafficking in Persons alleges that camp officials accept payments for smuggling children out of the camps, threatening their parents with expulsion from the camps and out of safe areas if they speak out.[19] This type of exploitation is not limited to the camps in Nigeria. There have also been similar reports about soldiers in a refugee camp in neighboring Cameroon using the threat of deportation and/or of limiting access to necessities to put pressure on Nigerian refugees and asylum seekers for sex.[20] Nigerian government officials have also been caught appropriating funds meant to support refugees,[21] further contributing to the cycle of exploitation that exists within the camps.

Structural violence and complex socioeconomic and governmental dynamics contribute to the creation of groups like Boko Haram, which in turn leads to further violence and exploitation and the displacement of people to camps. In those camps, resources are scarce, in part because of misappropriation of funds and corruption. As a result, camp officials and security operatives make demands on displaced people—citizens and asylum seekers alike—in exchange for resources and services. The costs can include loss of health, well-being, social support, dignity, family, and, in some cases, life.

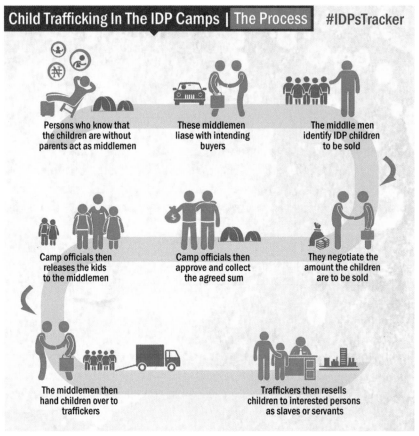

Child Trafficking In The IDP Camps | The Process   #IDPsTracker

Persons who know that the children are without parents act as middlemen

These middlemen liase with intending buyers

The middlle men identify IDP children to be sold

Camp officials then releases the kids to the middlemen

Camp officials then approve and collect the agreed sum

They negotiate the amount the children are to be sold

The middlemen then hand children over to traffickers

Traffickers then resells children to interested persons as slaves or servants

(Source: International Center for Investigative Reporting. Data Visualization created by Orodataviz, reprinted with permission.)

Exploitability

Not only are refuge and asylum commodified, they are also gendered. Sex is one of the gendered commodities that service providers in refugee settlements and camps demand in exchange for providing refugees and asylum seekers with the services they need. This form of coerced transactional sex is facilitated by the fact that majority of the refugee population are women and children, while a majority of the security operatives, camp officials, and other authority figures are men.

The abuse that female IDPs and trafficked women endure is informed by patriarchal colonial and postcolonial structures that have brought turmoil, disorder, and displacement to cultures and communities across the continent. Structured sexual violence cannot be understood in isolation from political violence, which is a frequent occurrence in sub-Saharan Africa, driven in part by the imperialist imposition of divisive, arbitrary boundaries that created nation-states by cutting lines through ethnic, cultural, and religious groups.[22] In such contexts, ideologically motivated groups such as—but not limited to—Boko Haram are able to construct particular people as exploitable based on their gender, ethnicity, religion, or other features of perceived difference.[23] Within the camp, understood as an exceptional space where "everything is possible," displaced people are often understood as being stripped of their rights and status and, therefore, subjectable to exploitation—a perspective born out of Western notions of displacement, borders, and belonging,[24] which seems to apply as much to citizen IDPs as it does to refugees and asylum seekers.

Focusing on the narratives of the women who have felt the exploitative nature of displacement is important, because it centers the discussion on those who are directly affected by the system, illuminating how exploitation impacts their experience of refuge and how women's position can be used as a source of "profit." Regarding forced marriage and rape, Human Rights Watch researchers have uncovered numerous incidents of abuse committed by security operatives, both within the Nigerian military and the Civilian Joint Task Force. The report also uncovered women's perspectives on the commodification of basic necessities. One young female IDP from Damasak, Borno, explained:

> Life is terrible here in this camp. For the past three days we have not eaten because there is no firewood to cook the food. To make it worse, they will not even allow us to go out to fend for ourselves. Most times you have to beg the camp officials to intervene with the guards before they will give you the pass to go out. Why will you refuse if any of those people ask you for marriage? You have to survive.[25]

These words reveal the options that female refugees are often presented with for the sake of food, security, financial independence, and freedom of movement. That is not to say that men or children are not similarly exploited or expected to bargain sex, though this occurs less commonly than it does with women. Without money as an intermediary of exchange within the context of the camp, sex may be exchanged for basic necessities.[26] In theory, refuge and asylum services should center on protecting the rights and dignity of refugees and IDPs, whether or not they have something to offer in exchange. Within the refuge and asylum industry, currency—in the form of money, services, material goods, or other substitutes—dictates protection. These dynamics are not limited to "internal" or "international" displacements. As noted above, across the border in Cameroon, soldiers have demanded money or sex from female refugees in exchange for protection from detention and deportation.[27] IDPs and refugees alike are required to have something to offer to receive protection.

Women also report other abuses of power in refugee camps, where camp managers and other authority figures can determine who has access to basic resources, how much, and how often.[28] There is often little accountability or reliable third-party monitoring of resource distribution in camps. The power to control access to resources creates an environment ripe for multiple, often exploitative, forms of profit-making and the creation of new markets and commodities within the asylum industry. In addition to historical, political, patriarchal, and ideological factors, camp-specific power dynamics inform the emergent patterns of commodification and commodity circulation.

Women's narratives of insecurity also encompass experiences outside camps. IDPs living in a host community in Shokari, for example, have reported being harassed by their hosts, who have sought to trade water and other resources for sex, labor, or material goods.[29] Here, beyond the camp, host communities become another space where power imbalances, scarce resources, and local attitudes toward the displaced all shape the experiences of IDPs and refugees—a space where new markets and spaces of exploitation and bodily commodification emerge.

Conclusion
In Nigeria, the commodification of asylum involves structural violence and complex socioeconomic and governmental dynamics—factors that also contribute to the formation of groups like Boko Haram, which in turn create new forms of violence. From the resultant displacement of people emerge new spaces of exploitation that are structured by and inform the logics of the growing asylum industry, like IDP camps, where resources are scarce and the demand for necessities like food and water is high. Authority figures within camps—whether employed or appointed by the

Nigerian government or military, international relief organizations, or NGOs—perpetuate cycles of profit-making and exploitation by requiring refugees and IDPs alike to pay for access to support and necessities for survival.

Refugees, asylum seekers, and IDPs are severely impacted by the commodification of their bodies, as well as by their lack of access to security, food, water, and freedom of movement. Sex is often the currency that authority figures seek in exchange for these necessities. As a result, women and children—particularly girls—often become targets. This commodification further marginalizes women and children within the camps and in the wider society.

There are countless other narratives of how different groups profit from displacement, particularly that of women and children. Understanding how people experience exploitation in the asylum and refuge industry can point to the best ways of combating parasitic structures. Identifying the specific scenarios in which officials and community members abuse their power can offer policymakers insight about which changes might have the most impact. The foremost way to combat these forms of exploitation is to address root causes of the conflict in the North East, including structural violence leading to widespread poverty, conflict, and displacement. The redistribution of wealth in the region and improved access to education must be core aspects of any solution. Without these interventions, the structurally imposed cycle of violence, displacement, and exploitation will continue.

At the camp level, the first necessary move is to establish more robust systems of accountability and transparency, which are crucial with regards to how necessities and funds are distributed to refugees. As long as local government agencies continue to demonstrate a lack of will to address exploitation, locally led NGOs and women's rights groups, academics, journalists, and international organizations all have roles to play in naming and shaming those groups and officials who are appropriating funds, facilitating trafficking, or otherwise forcing displaced people into exploitative arrangements.

Second, refugees and IDPs must participate meaningfully in the distribution of resources to avoid the diversion of supplies. Direct access to necessities can potentially and usefully destabilize power dynamics that lead to exploitation. Refugee communities have leadership structures and these structures need to be represented in the distribution process, as well as in any decision-making processes that affect them. Most importantly, women refugees need to be meaningfully involved in these processes, not least because female-headed households constitute a large majority of the IDP population.[30] A recent UN-sponsored Global Protection Cluster report supports this view and suggests that to avoid diversions distributions be made household by household in the camps rather than to individuals.[31]

Third, information sharing among refugees/IDPs and human rights/ humanitarian groups must be improved for people to feel comfortable reporting exploitation, and doing so promptly. Open communication and transparency can make it difficult for individuals to exploit others—but organizations must work to demonstrate that they are trustworthy and able to respond effectively before this can occur.

Fourth, academics and other researchers must look deeper into the economics of trafficking and sex within the context of internal displacement in Nigeria, as opposed to focusing solely on religion, politics, or historical conflict as causes of violence. Focusing on the complex, overlapping root causes of exploitation is a step toward understanding and redressing the abuse of people for financial gain, both during and after armed conflicts. Research focused on structural violence and how it leads to exploitation and commodification in the context of displacement in Africa and other non-Western spaces is also much needed.

Fifth, and most important, women's experiences must take center stage in any attempt to address this exploitation. Policymakers must recognize the damage caused in the everyday lives of women and children by the commodification and gendering of displacement and asylum processes. In Nigeria, those who abuse asylum seekers, refugees, and IDPs face few consequences, creating a structure in which survivors are doubly victimized by the denial of justice. The protection of women and girls is crucial to ending exploitation. This can only be achieved if processes of profit-making are taken seriously and exploitation and trafficking are addressed as part of the agenda on displacement and asylum in Nigeria.

Sidonia Lucia Kula is an Angolan-Dutch doctoral researcher and teaching fellow in law at SOAS, University of London. Her research focuses on an interdisciplinary study of international law, forced migration, and gendered violence.
Oreva Olakpe holds a PhD in Law from SOAS, University of London, and focuses on approaches to migrations in the Global South, the law from below, and informal justice mechanisms in migrant communities.

Notes

1 Georg Menz, "The Neoliberalized State and the Growth of the Migration Industry," in Thomas Gammeltoft-Hansen and Ninna Nyberg Sørensen, eds., *The Migration Industry and the Commercialization of International Migration* (London: Routledge, 2013), 108–27.

2 Tendayi Bloom, "The Business of Noncitizenship," *Citizenship Studies* 19, no. 8 (December 2015): 892–906.

3 Mausi Segun and Samer Muscati, "'Those Terrible Weeks in Their Camp': Boko Haram Violence against Women and Girls in Northeast Nigeria," Human Rights Watch, October 27, 2014, accessed March 23, 2020, https://www.hrw.org/report/2014/10/27/those-terrible-weeks-their-camp/boko-haram-violence-against-women-and-girls. Note: We are using Human Rights Watch here as a source of data on the number occurrences of abuse in IDP camps specifically. This is not an endorsement of the organization, its position on Nigeria, or its funders and affiliations.

4 Ibid.

5 Valerie M. Hudson and Hilary Matfess, "In Plain Sight: The Neglected Linkage between Brideprice and Violent Conflict," *International Security* 42, no. 1 (Summer 2017): 7–40, accessed March 23, 2020, https://www.mitpressjournals.org/doi/pdf/10.1162/ISEC_a_00289. In places like Garta, Northeastern Nigeria, families were forced to collect brideprices for their abducted daughters; see "Boko Haram Abducts More Women, Pays N1,500 Dowry," *PM News*, October 23, 2014, accessed March 23, 2020, https://www.pmnewsnigeria.com/2014/10/23/boko-haram-abducts-more-women-pays-n1500-dowry.

6 Hudson and Matfess, "In Plain Sight."

7 Ibid.

8 UN General Assembly, "Protocol to Prevent, Suppress and Punish Trafficking in Persons, Especially Women and Children, Supplementing the United Nations Convention against Transnational Organized Crime," November 15, 2000, article 3, paragraph (a), accessed March 23, 2020, http://www.refworld.org/docid/4720706c0.html.

9 Edward M. Wheaton, Edward J. Schauer, and Thomas V. Galli, "Economics of Human Trafficking," *International Migration* 48, no. 4 (August 2010): 114–41, accessed March 23, 2020, https://www.amherst.edu/media/view/247221/original/Economics+of+Human+Trafficking.pdf.

10 For more information about these groups' work, see their respective websites: Federation of Muslim Women's Associations in Nigeria, accessed March 23, 2020, https://www.international-alert.org/partners/federation-muslim-womens-associations-nigeria-fomwan; Herwa Community Development Initiative, accessed March 23, 2020, https://herwacdi.org.

11 Osita Agbu, "Corruption and Human Trafficking: The Nigerian Case," *West Africa Review* 4, no. 1 (2003), accessed March 23, 2020, https://pdfs.semanticscholar.org/ab84/544291af64bdd21d4d99ea4e68ea4c7f26cd.pdf.

12 Danielle Ogbeche, "IDP Officials Allegedly Sell Children for up to N100,000," *Daily Post*, August 26, 2016, accessed March 23, 2020, https://dailypost.ng/2016/08/26/idp-officials-allegedly-sell-children-n100000.

13   Adekoye Vincent, "Six (6) NAPTIP Officers Sacked for Corruption, Unproffessional [sic] Conducts," Press and Public Relations Unit, *NAPTIP*, September 20, 2018, accessed March 23, 2020, https://www.naptip.gov. ng/?p=1809.

14   Hein de Haas, "International Migration, National Development and the Role of Governments: The Case of Nigeria," in Aderanti Adepoju, Ton van Naerssen, and Annelies Zoomers, eds., *International Migration and National Development in Sub-Saharan Africa: Viewpoints and Policy Initiatives in the Countries of Origin* (Leiden, NL: Brill Publishers, 2007), 161–81.

15   Senator Iroegbu, Omololu Ogunmade, and Ejiofor Alike, "Nigeria: Soldiers Rape Starving Women in IDP Camps, Says Amnesty International," allAfrica, May 24, 2018, accessed March 23, 2020, https://allafrica.com/stories/201805240182.html.

16   Segun and Muscati, "Those Terrible Weeks in Their Camp."

17   "Nigeria: Officials Abusing Displaced Women, Girls: Displaced by Boko Haram and Victims Twice Over" Human Rights Watch, October 31, 2016, accessed March 23, 2020, https://www.hrw.org/news/2016/10/31/nigeria-officials-abusing-displaced-women-girls.

18   "Nigeria to Investigate Alleged Abuses at Refugee Camps," BBC News, February 10, 2015, accessed March 23, 2020, http://www.bbc.com/news/world-africa-31386340.

19   Ogbeche, "IDB Officials Allegedly Sell Children for up to N100,000."

20   "'They Forced Us onto Trucks Like Animals': Cameroon's Mass Forced Return and Abuse of Nigerian Refugees," Human Rights Watch, September 27, 2017, accessed March 23, 2020, https://www.hrw.org/report/2017/09/27/they-forced-us-trucks-animals/cameroons-mass-forced-return-and-abuse-nigerian.

21   Yomi Kazeem, "An $8 Million Refugee Fund Scandal Shows Buhari's Anti-Corruption Drive in Nigeria Is Not Going to Plan," Quartz Africa, December 9, 2016, accessed March 23, 2020, https://qz.com/858019/a-new-8m-scam-of-relief-funds-shows-nigerias-buhari-anti-corruption-drive-is-not-going-to-plan.

22   Rangira Béa Gallimore, "Militarism, Ethnicity, and Sexual Violence in the Rwandan Genocide," *Feminist Africa* 10 (August 2008): 9–29, accessed March 23, 2020, http://www.agi.ac.za/sites/default/files/image_tool/images/429/feminist_africa_journals/archive/10/fa_10_feature_article_1.pdf.

23   Temitope B. Oriola and Olabanji Akinola, "Ideational Dimensions of the Boko Haram Phenomenon," *Studies in Conflict & Terrorism* 41, no. 8 (August 2018): 595–618, accessed March 23, 2020, https://www.ualberta.ca/-/media/A2A64C977126473B9BC2AA4C577FD609.

24   Giorgio Agamben, *Homo Sacer: Sovereign Power and Bare Life*, trans. Daniel Heller-Roazen (Stanford, CA: Stanford University Press, 1998), 170–71.

25   "Nigeria," Human Rights Watch.

26   Elizabeth G. Ferris, "Abuse of Power: Sexual Exploitation of Refugee Women and Girls," *Signs* 32, no. 3 (Spring 2007).

27   Simpson, "They Forced Us."

28 Diane Cole, "Safe from Boko Haram but at Risk of Sexual Abuse," NPR, November 3, 2016, accessed March 23, 2020, http://www.npr.org/sections/goatsands oda/2016/11/03/500221012/safe-from-boko-haram-but-at-risk-of-sexual-abuse.

29 Protection Sector Working Group Nigeria, *Rapid Protection Assessment Report, Borno State, Nigeria*, UNHCR, (Geneva, UHNCR, May 2016), accessed March 23, 2020, https://reliefweb.int/sites/reliefweb.int/files/resources/ rapid_protection_assessment_report_pswg_borno_may_2016.pdf.

30 Ibid.

31 "North East Nigeria Vulnerability Screening Report, Round II," UNHCR, June 2016, accessed March 23 2020, http://www.globalprotectioncluster.org/_assets/ files/vulnerability-screening-report-round-ii-june-2016_en.pdf.

A Guard's Story

Sam Wallman, Nick Olle, Pat Grant, Pat Armstrong, and Sam Bungey

This is a firsthand account of life inside an Australian immigration detention facility, told from the perspective of a former employee of Serco, the ubiquitous multinational service provider that runs the nation's onshore centers. It was produced in early 2014 and originally published in the *Global Mail*. Realized in a comic-book style and drawn from exclusive interviews with and diary entries of the ex-employee, "A Guard's Story" offers rare insight into how Australia's outsourced detention facilities were run at that time.

Like all Serco employees, our informant signed a confidentiality agreement and has taken a significant personal risk by talking to us. Prior to being employed by Serco, our source was sympathetic to the plight of asylum seekers in Australia's detention facilities and took on a job as a "client support worker" to try to help people from inside the system. What follows is our source's experience, illustrated.

Sam Wallman, Nick Olle, Pat Grant, Pat Armstrong, and Sam Bungey produced "A Guard's Story" for the now defunct *Global Mail*. Their collaborative piece was nominated for a Walkley Award and won the 2014 Australian Human Rights Award. They work in journalism, graphic design, production, and illustration and are based in Melbourne, Australia.

at work inside our detention centres
a guard's story

I ALWAYS UNDERSTOOD THAT INDEFINITE DETENTION DID TERRIBLE THINGS TO PEOPLE.

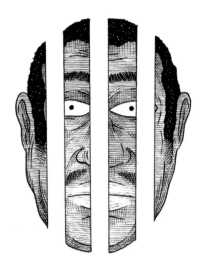

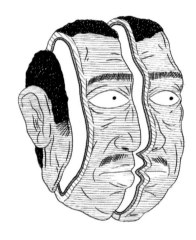

I THOUGHT, WELL, THE SYSTEM EXISTS,

THERE'S NOTHING I CAN DO ABOUT IT

SO MAYBE THE BEST WAY TO SUPPORT PEOPLE WHO ARE IN DETENTION IS TO WORK INSIDE THE SYSTEM

AND THE ONLY WAY YOU CAN WORK IN DETENTION CENTRES IN AUSTRALIA IS TO WORK FOR THIS COMPANY CALLED SERCO.

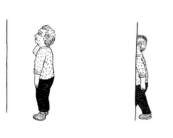

SO THAT'S WHAT I DID.

serco

Bringing service to life

SERCO IS A MULTINATIONAL SERVICES COMPANY THAT DOES EVERYTHING FROM MANAGING THE UK'S ATOMIC WEAPONS ESTABLISHMENT TO INSTALLING SPEED CAMERAS IN BAHRAIN.

AND IT'S RESPONSIBLE FOR RUNNING ALL OF THE IMMIGRATION DETENTION CENTRES ON THE AUSTRALIAN MAINLAND.

I'M HERE TO APPLY FOR —

YOU'RE HIRED

IT'S NOT HARD TO GET A JOB WITH SERCO.

THEY HIRE PEOPLE QUICKLY AND IN BIG GROUPS

YOU DON'T HAVE TO HAVE QUALIFICATIONS OR ANYTHING.

THIS GUY CAME IN AND INTRODUCED HIMSELF AS OUR TRAINER.

HIS LAST JOB WAS IN THE PRISON SYSTEM.

HE TOLD US:

"THE ONLY THING THAT'S DIFFERENT IS THE CLOTHES WE LET THEM WEAR.

THE DEPARTMENT WANTS US TO CALL THEM CLIENTS SO WE CALL THEM CLIENTS.

IF THEY TOLD US TO CALL THEM HAMSTERS WE'D CALL THEM HAMSTERS

BUT WE KNOW THAT THEY'RE DETAINEES."

THE TRAINER TOLD US TO
BE CAREFUL GIVING OUT RAZORS.

IF A DETAINEE
GETS A WEAPON AND
STABS ANOTHER

IT CREATES
A LOT OF WORK FOR
SERCO STAFF.

IT'S HAPPENED
AGAIN

BLOODY HELL

I REMEMBER ONE DAY
THEY WERE TEACHING US HOW
TO PHYSICALLY RESTRAIN PEOPLE.
IT WAS LIKE A ROLE PLAY.
I VOLUNTEERED.

OKAY YOU'RE THE
MISBEHAVING CLIENT,
AND THE REST OF YOU
ARE SERCO OFFICERS —
RESTRAIN HIM.

AS IT WAS HAPPENING
AND THE 'OFFICERS'
WERE RESTRAINING ME

SITTING ON TOP OF ME

AND SQUEEZING MY
PRESSURE POINTS

ALL I COULD THINK
WAS THAT THIS WAS HAPPENING
TO A REFUGEE INSIDE THE CENTRE
OR A TAMIL GUY WHO HAD LIVED
THROUGH A WAR AND WAS
FLEEING TORTURE.

I COULDN'T HANDLE IT

I KEPT
HAVING TO DISAPPEAR
OUT OF THE ROOM.

WHEN TRAINING WAS OVER
THEY SENT US OUT TO WORK
IN DETENTION CENTRES.

MY CO-WORKERS
WERE GOOD PEOPLE

BUT TO BE ABLE
TO SLEEP AT NIGHT

THEY HAD TO
CONVINCE THEMSELVES THAT THE
PEOPLE THEY WERE GUARDING
WERE DANGEROUS

NONE OF THE
SERCO STAFF HAD ANY
UNDERSTANDING OF WHAT THE
PEOPLE HAD BEEN THROUGH
BEFORE THEY ARRIVED
IN AUSTRALIA.

THE DETAINEES
DID CRAZY THINGS TO EXPRES
THEIR FRUSTRATION

I REMEMBER THIS ONE OCCASION WHERE SOME OF THE GUYS DECIDED TO DIG THEMSELVES GRAVES IN ONE OF THE COMMON AREAS.

I THINK IT WAS A VOLLEYBALL COURT OR SOMETHING

YOU HAD TO WALK PAST IT EVERY DAY.

ANOTHER TIME
THERE WERE THESE TWO
ROHINGYAN GUYS ON THE ROOF
I DON'T KNOW HOW LONG
THEY WERE THERE FOR

YOU COULD SEE THEM
SQUATTING UNDER
THE EAVES

WE WERE TOLD
NOT TO LOOK AT THEM
OR SPEAK TO THEM
TO PRETEND THEY
WEREN'T THERE

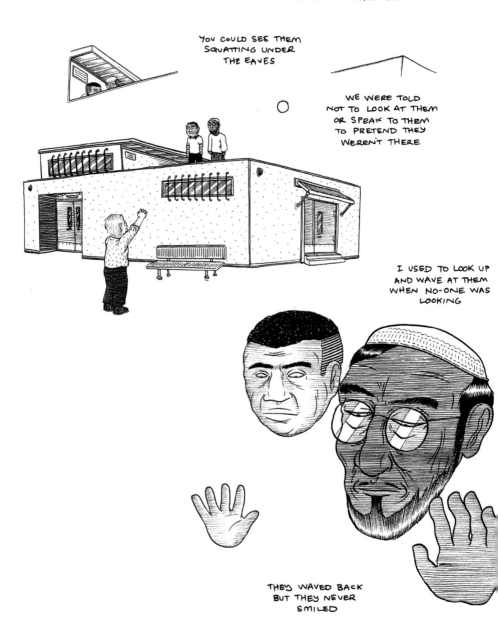

I USED TO LOOK UP
AND WAVE AT THEM
WHEN NO-ONE WAS
LOOKING

THEY WAVED BACK
BUT THEY NEVER
SMILED

ONE DAY, THERE WAS AN EMERGENCY CODE ON THE RADIO

I WALKED AROUND A CORNER

AND THERE WAS A GUY WITH A WHOLE BUNCH OF BROKEN GLASS IN HIS MOUTH

HE SAID HE WOULD SWALLOW IT IF WE DIDN'T MEET HIS DEMANDS.

HIS DEMANDS WEREN'T MUCH

FROM MEMORY, ALL HE WANTED WAS TO SEE HIS CASE MANAGER

THE SERCO OFFICERS TOLD ME TO KEEP WALKING.

THIS KIND OF SELF-HARM WAS REALLY COMMON IN THE DETENTION CENTRES

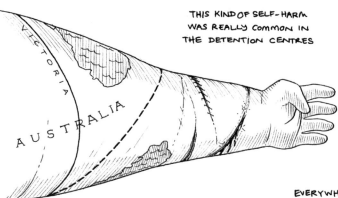

EVERYWHERE YOU LOOKED THERE WERE PEOPLE WITH FRESH CUTS AND SCARS UP THEIR ARMS.

I REMEMBER
HEARING ABOUT ONE KID

HE CUT HIS HEAD OPEN
ON THE WAY HOME
FROM SCHOOL

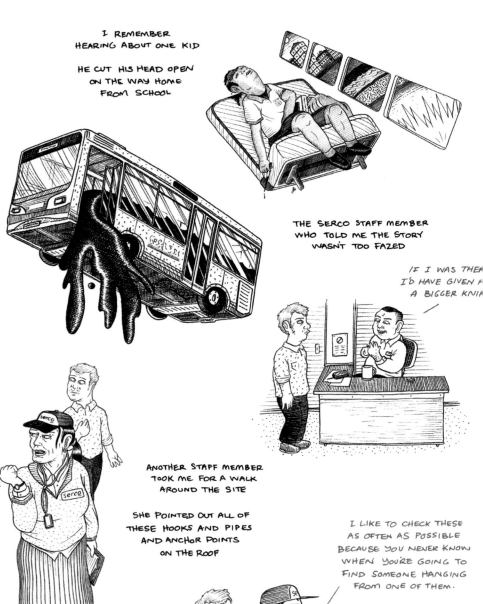

THE SERCO STAFF MEMBER
WHO TOLD ME THE STORY
WASN'T TOO FAZED

IF I WAS THE
I'D HAVE GIVEN
A BIGGER KNIF

ANOTHER STAFF MEMBER
TOOK ME FOR A WALK
AROUND THE SITE

SHE POINTED OUT ALL OF
THESE HOOKS AND PIPES
AND ANCHOR POINTS
ON THE ROOF

I LIKE TO CHECK THESE
AS OFTEN AS POSSIBLE
BECAUSE YOU NEVER KNOW
WHEN YOU'RE GOING TO
FIND SOMEONE HANGING
FROM ONE OF THEM.

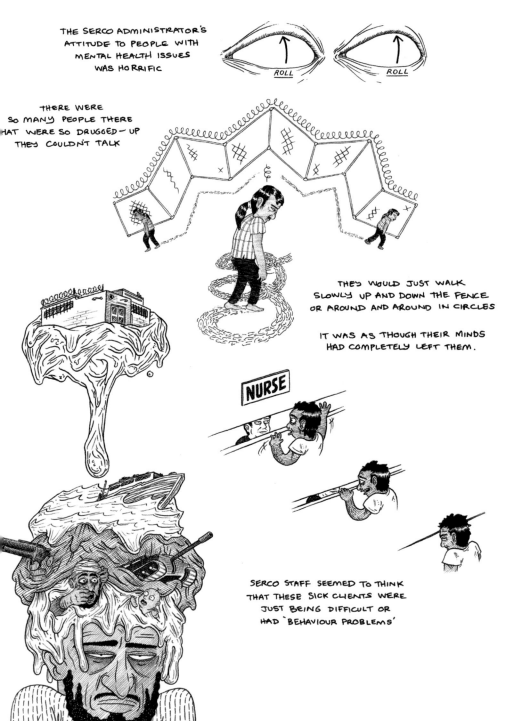

THE SERCO ADMINISTRATOR'S ATTITUDE TO PEOPLE WITH MENTAL HEALTH ISSUES WAS HORRIFIC

ROLL ROLL

THERE WERE SO MANY PEOPLE THERE THAT WERE SO DRUGGED-UP THEY COULDN'T TALK

THEY WOULD JUST WALK SLOWLY UP AND DOWN THE FENCE OR AROUND AND AROUND IN CIRCLES

IT WAS AS THOUGH THEIR MINDS HAD COMPLETELY LEFT THEM.

NURSE

SERCO STAFF SEEMED TO THINK THAT THESE SICK CLIENTS WERE JUST BEING DIFFICULT OR HAD 'BEHAVIOUR PROBLEMS'

I WONDERED ABOUT WHAT THEY HAD BEEN THROUGH BEFORE THEY ARRIVED HERE.

YOU KNOW, WAR, TORTURE, TRAUMA AND I WONDERED WHETHER WE WEREN'T JUST MAKING THINGS WORSE.

THINGS WEREN'T SO GREAT FOR ME AT HOME EITHER.

I WAS STARTING TO ARGUE WITH MY PARTNER

ONE NIGHT, AFTER A FIGHT, I COULDN'T STOP CRYING

I WENT INTO THE KITCHEN AND PULLED A KNIFE OUT OF THE DRAWER

I THOUGHT
"MAYBE IF I CUT MYSELF I CAN UNDERSTAND WHY THEY DO IT"

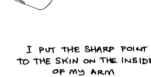
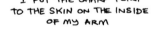
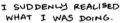

I PUT THE SHARP POINT TO THE SKIN ON THE INSIDE OF MY ARM

I SUDDENLY REALISED WHAT I WAS DOING.

I THREW THE KNIFE AWAY, AND WENT OUTSIDE FOR A CIGARETTE.

I STOPPED SLEEPING AT NIGHT

MY PARTNER AND I FOUGHT MORE AND MORE

THIS IS THAT

NO THIS IS THAT

EVENTUALLY WE BROKE UP

THINGS WERE REALLY SHITTY BUT I KEPT GOING IN TO WORK AT SERCO.

IF ALL THOSE GUYS COULD STAY ALIVE IN THERE, THE LEAST I COULD DO WAS BE STRONG ENOUGH TO TURN UP EVERY DAY TO LISTEN TO THEM.

I'VE GOT A LOT OF RESPECT FOR THE PEOPLE THAT WERE STUCK IN THOSE PLACES.

THE THING WAS, NO MATTER HOW BAD THINGS GOT IN THERE, THEY LOOKED OUT FOR EACH OTHER.

THEY HAD A SENSE OF MUTUAL SUPPORT AND COMMUNITY WHICH I REALLY RESPECTED.

SOMETHING I DON'T SEE VERY OFTEN ON THE OUTSIDE.

BUT EVENTUALLY I GAVE UP MY JOB AT SERC. THE STRESS WAS TOO MUCH.

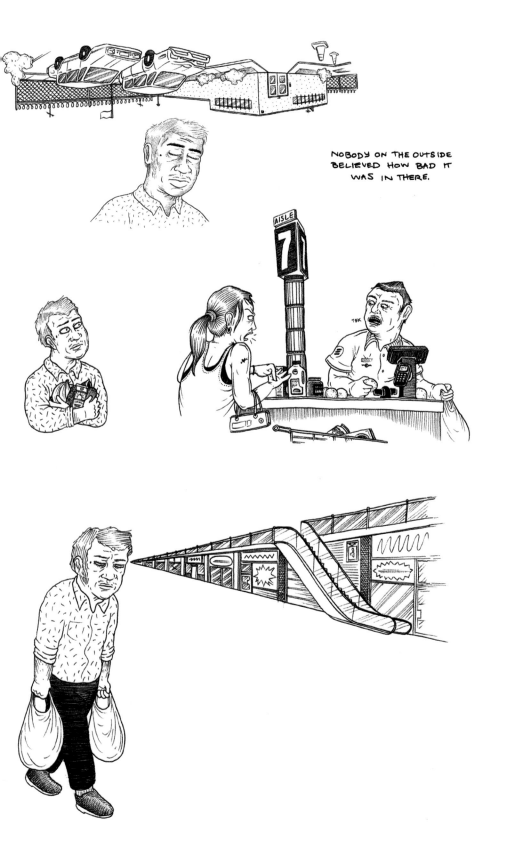

NOBODY ON THE OUTSIDE BELIEVED HOW BAD IT WAS IN THERE.

III

Complex Industries/
Industrial Complexes

The Military and Security Industry: Promoting Europe's Refugee Regime

Mark Akkerman

Building on long-standing policies, the European Union (EU) has escalated its militarization of border security since the start of the so-called refugee crisis, in April 2015.[1] While EU border and migration policy developments have had horrific consequences for refugees, they have meant more profit opportunities for the military and security industry. Large European companies are the big winners.

Since 2015, the use of military means and/or personnel for border security has skyrocketed. Several EU member states—including Austria, Bulgaria, Croatia, Hungary, Macedonia, the Netherlands, and Slovenia—have deployed armed forces at their borders to assist in border control and security. Austria, Bulgaria, Estonia, Greece, Hungary, Lithuania, Macedonia, Slovakia, Slovenia, Spain, Turkey, and Ukraine have each built border security fences adorned with all kinds of detection and surveillance technology.

Frontex, the European Border and Coast Guard Agency, has continued and sometimes intensified its military border security missions in the Mediterranean, which include Poseidon (Greece), Themis (Italy, a follow-up to Triton), and Hera, Indalo, and Minerva (Spain). The EU has also launched Operation Sophia, its own military-run European Union Naval Force Mediterranean (EUNAVFOR MED) operation on the Libyan coast, intended to stop refugees from attempting to cross the Mediterranean. Sophia is the first overtly militaristic response to refugees on an EU level. In June 2016, the operation mandate was extended to include the training of members of the Libyan Coast Guard and navy personnel.[2] Standing maritime NATO missions in the Mediterranean assist Operation Sophia and other border patrols in the Aegean Sea.[3]

The importance the EU attaches to security at its external borders is reflected in the financial support it provides to its member states and third countries to strengthen border security and control. This funding flows largely through three mechanisms: the Schengen Facility, the External Borders Fund, and the Internal Security Fund—Borders and Visa. Through these programs, some €4.5 billion will have been dispersed to EU member states from 2004 to 2020.[4] These funds have backed a wide array of activities and purchases, including vessels, vehicles, helicopters, IT systems, and surveillance equipment.

In September 2016, the British think tank Overseas Development Institute made a "conservative estimate . . . that at the very least, €1.7 billion was committed to measures inside Europe from 2014 to 2016 in an effort to reduce [migration] flows." The report added that this figure "presents only a partial picture of the true cost." Furthermore, "in an attempt to deter refugees from setting off on their journeys . . . since December 2014, €15.3 billion has been spent" in third countries. Again, the quoted figure represents "a very conservative estimate."[5]

Such policies cause shifts in migration routes: when one route is almost closed off due to increased securitization, refugees are forced to look for other, often more dangerous, routes into Europe. Since the November 2015 EU migration deal with Turkey, for example, the predominant migration route to Europe became the sea crossing between Libya and Italy. This is known to be a hazardous route, and a much higher proportion of refugees died during attempted crossings subsequent to the deal than had perished in previous years.[6]

The militarization of border security is not limited to EU borders. Through "externalization of borders" initiatives, the EU uses third countries as forward border posts to stop refugees on their way toward Europe. Hence EU assistance to third countries, mainly in Africa, includes donations of military, security, and biometric equipment. Such support strengthens authoritarian regimes and often leads to more violence against refugees, while also undermining economic development and stability in the affected countries.

The EU's border externalization priorities are evident in the increasingly central role migration plays in its civil-military (CSDP) missions in Mali and Niger.[7] The prioritization of border management within these missions, through training and capacity building, was recognized in the 2016 annual report of the Sahel Regional Action Plan, which concluded that "the three CSDP missions in the Sahel have been adapted to the political priorities of the EU, notably following the EU mobilization against irregular migration."[8]

Year	Irregular arrivals in Europe via Mediterranean	Recorded deaths/ disappearances (Mediterranean)	Ratio recorded deaths/ disappearances : arrivals
2015	1,012,179	3,783	1:268 (0.37%)
2016	363,581	5,143	1:71 (1.41%)
2017	173,712	3,139	1:55 (1.81%)
2018	119,570	2,299	1:52 (1.92%)

Table 11.1: Migrant arrivals and deaths: Europe via the Mediterranean

Industry Shapes Policies

The arms industry plays a significant role in formulating the EU's foreign and security policy agenda. According to Martin Lemberg-Pedersen of the University of Copenhagen's Centre for Advanced Migration Studies, arms companies "establish themselves as experts on border security, and use this position to frame immigration to Europe as leading to ever more security threats in need of ever more [private security company] products"—the very products that these companies sell.[9]

Large European arms companies have their own lobbyists working in Brussels, while also cooperating with the European Organisation for Security (EOS), the lobbying group of the European security industry. Its primary objective is the development of a harmonized European security market. EOS has identified "border security" as one of the main areas of concern in the field of European security. It has issued papers with recommendations and organized several meetings between industry and EU politicians and officials, including European Commissioners. Military companies—including Airbus, Leonardo, Thales, and Indra—play a leading role in EOS, including in its work on border security and control.

Lobbying—both by the EOS and by individual companies—has been highly successful, foremost, in framing migration as a security problem rather than a political and/or humanitarian concern and, secondarily, in promoting military means as the solution. Concrete proposals with roots in industrial lobbying, such as the establishment of a European border guard and of the EU-wide border monitoring system EUROSUR, eventually found their way into EU policy.[10]

Industrial influence on EU policy can also be seen in EU security research funding decisions.[11] In 2004, for example, the European Commission followed the proposal of a Group of Personalities (GoP) to integrate security research into a large seven-year European Research and Technology (R&T) project, the so-called Framework Programmes.[12] This particular GoP was initiated by the European Commission, and eight of its twenty-seven members were representatives of large European military companies and research institutions—many of which turned out to be among the biggest beneficiaries of the new funding.

Company	Country	Number of projects	Coordinated projects	EU funding granted
Airbus	Pan-European	12	2	€9,784,181
Indra	Spain	7	2	€8,106,544
Leonardo	Italy	16	3	€8,091,407
Ingeniería de Sistemas para la Defensa de España (ISDEFE)	Spain	6	0	€8,055,257
Thales	France	18	5	€6,966,736

Table 11.2: Major industrial profiteers of EU-funded border security R&D projects, 2002–2016. Companies sometimes have two or more subsidiaries participating in a single project. For example, Airbus companies had a total of thirty-two participations in twelve projects.
(Source: Community Research and Development Information Service)

Profiteers: Making a Killing

Consultancy company Visiongain estimated that the global border security market was worth $18.9 billion in 2016, up from $15 billion in 2015—a 26 percent growth within one year.[13] Market Research Future predicts continued market growth, at a rate of 8 percent per year until 2023.[14] European arms and technology companies are the major profiteers of the EU segment in this market,[15] with Airbus, Leonardo, Thales, Indra, and IDEMIA standing out as the big winners of the refugee tragedy. Cynically enough, Airbus, Thales, and Leonardo are also large exporters of arms to the Middle East and North Africa, feeding and profiting from the very chaos, war, human rights abuses, and repression that fuel forced migration.[16]

Company	Country	Top 100 arms producing companies rank Europe (world)	Arms sales (US$)	Total sales (US$)	Arms sales as % of total sales
BAE Systems	UK	1 (6)	21.2 billion	22.4 billion	95
Airbus	Pan-European	2 (7)	11.7 billion	75.2 billion	15
Leonardo	Italy	3 (8)	9.8 billion	14.4 billion	68
Thales	France	4 (10)	9.5 billion	18.8 billion	50

Table 11.3: Profits and revenues of Europe's largest arms producing companies, 2018

EU border policies, which are focusing ever more on security and militarization, will be a key driver for the anticipated border security market growth. As of October 2016, Frontex has been able to buy its own equipment (rather than using equipment made available by EU member states) and to instruct EU member states on how to strengthen their border security, presenting a further boost for the border security market.[17] Since 2017, the EU has also financed military research outright, starting with pilot projects and integrating this research as a new priority in funding cycles from 2021.[18] Border security will likely remain an important area of interest.

Recent shifts of attention to the African market is another notable development: with EU pressure and financial encouragement to African countries to strengthen border security, the region is becoming a bigger target for military and security companies. Both Airbus and Thales have explicitly stated that they expect Africa to be the most promising market in the near future, particularly in the field of border security.[19]

The "Border Security" Profiteers

Airbus

Founded: 2000 as European Aeronautic Defence and Space Company (EADS), merger of DaimlerChrysler Aerospace (DASA), Construcciones Aeronáuticas, and Aérospatiale-Matra; renamed Airbus in 2014

Headquarters: Leiden, Netherlands; **Corporate Headquarters:** Toulouse, France

Arms producing companies ranking (2018): seventh (world), second (Europe)[20]

Shareholders: France (11.1 percent), Germany (11.0 percent), Spain (4.2 percent), others (73.6 percent)[21]

Employees (2019): 133,671[22]

Lobbying in Brussels (2018): budget €1,750,000–1,999,999 (approximately US$1,893,000–2,163,000), 11 lobbyists (4.75 full-time equivalent [fte])[23]

Meetings with European Commission officials, November 12, 2014– February 11, 2020: 176[24]

- Headquartered in Netherlands for tax reasons, most of Airbus's production takes place in France, Germany, and Spain. Its border security products range from helicopters via communication systems to radar.

- European border guards using Airbus helicopters include Bulgaria, Finland, Germany, Lithuania, Romania, Ukraine, and Slovenia. The purchases by Finland and Romania were EU-funded.

- In 2004, Romania awarded the company a contract for a "Integrated System for Border Security," bought to meet EU border security requirements before becoming an EU member in 2007. The deal, worth €734 million (approximately US$1 billion), prompted a corruption investigation by the Romanian National Anticorruption Directorate when allegations of bribes paid to Romanian officials surfaced.[25]

- Signalis, a joint venture of Airbus and Atlas Elektronik (Germany), has also sold border security systems to France, Spain, and Bulgaria.

- The German government purchased an array of Airbus equipment to donate to Tunisia for border control purposes.[26]

- In 2017, Airbus sold its DS Electronics and Border Security division to the American private equity firm KKR & Co. for approximately €1.1 billion (approximately US$1.25 billion), maintaining a 25.1 percent minority stake for "a limited number of years post-closing."[27] This division continues to operate under the new name Hensoldt.

Leonardo

Founded: 1948, as Finmeccanica; renamed Leonardo-Finmeccanica (2016–2017), and then Leonardo
Headquarters: Rome, Italy
Arms producing companies ranking (2018): eighth (world), third (Europe)[28]
Shareholders: Italy (30.2 percent), others (69.8 percent)[29]
Employees (2019): 46,462[30]
Lobbying in Brussels (2018): budget €300,000–399,999 (approximately US$354,000–472,000), 3 lobbyists (3 fte)[31]
Meetings with European Commission officials, March 25, 2015–January 27, 2020: 41[32]

- Italian aerospace and defense company that, like Airbus, supplies helicopters to European border guard agencies. Purchases by Bulgaria, Croatia, Cyprus, Estonia, Italy, Latvia, and Malta were funded by the EU. Other customers include Finland and Slovenia. Its 2016 delivery of two AW139 helicopters to Croatia for border surveillance cost the EU over €30 million (approximately US$33 million).
- In 2005, Poland awarded the Leonardo subsidiary Selex a €30 million contract (approximately US$35.7 million) to build a coastal surveillance system (ZSRN) for the Polish border guard. The company also installed radar on maritime patrol aircraft of the Finnish border guard.
- In 2009, Italy and Libya concluded a deal wherein Leonardo was contracted to build a border surveillance system for Libya. The deal stipulated that Italy and the EU would each pay half of the €300 million (approximately US$417 million) involved. The project was halted when the civil war broke out, but talks about reviving it have been ongoing since 2011.
- Supplies ground stations and drone communications technology to the Alliance Ground Surveillance (AGS) for NATO.[33] US arms producer Northrop Grumman is the main contractor for AGS. Assistance in border control is one of the main aims of this system, which was intended to be in use by 2018 at the Italian Naval Air Station Sigonella, in Sicily.
- In June 2017, Leonardo announced a partnership with Heli Protection Europe (HPE), another Italian company, to provide surveillance and reconnaissance services via drones, including to monitor migration.[34]
- In 2018, Leonardo was awarded a contract by Frontex for three hundred hours of drone surveillance flights over the Mediterranean.[35]

Thales

Founded: 1968 as Thomson CSF following the merger of Thomson-Brandt companies with Compagnie Générale de Télégraphie Sans Fil; renamed Thales in 2000
Headquarters: La Défense, France
Arms producing companies ranking (2018): tenth (world), fourth (Europe)[36]
Shareholders: France (25.8 percent), Dassault Aviation (24.7 percent), others (49.5 percent)[37]
Employees (2019): 66,135[38]
Lobbying in Brussels (2019): budget €300,000–399,999 (approximately US$336,000–447,000), 7 lobbyists (2.75 fte)[39]
Meetings with European Commission officials, March 6, 2015–July 12, 2029: 24[40]

- French arms and technology company that has deployed a complete integrated system for border security at the Eastern Latvian border, featuring command and control software and optronics, sensors, and a communication network. Supplied the Spanish Guardia Civil (police force) with two mobile thermal units integrated into 4x4 vehicles and a fixed surveillance thermal optronics system intended for border surveillance.
- Supplied surveillance and access control system, as well as its Spy Copters (military drones), for use in Calais, France—the port city from where many refugees try to cross to the UK.
- In 2015, the Dutch government granted Thales Netherlands a permit to export radar equipment to Egypt, to be built into French corvettes, despite an EU arms embargo against the country. The Dutch government cited the Egyptian navy's role in European border security as justification for its decision.
- Thales radar is used on many (para)military ships around the world, including those used for border patrols.
- Thales produces electronic ID-management systems, which it has sold to France, and to Britain for the encryption of biometric and biographic data for Biometric Residence Permit (BRP) cards for non-EU foreigners in the UK.
- In 2017, Thales acquired Gemalto, a digital security company with a strong presence on the international border security market, providing, for example, biometric passports to Algeria, Côte d'Ivoire, Lebanon, Moldova, Morocco, Nigeria, and Turkey.

IDEMIA

Founded: 2017 as OT Morpho and Safran Identity & Security, following the merger of Morpho (former subsidiary of Safran, founded in 2007) and Oberthur Technologies (founded in 1984); renamed IDEMIA in 2017[41]
Headquarters: Issy-les-Moulineaux, France
Arms producing companies ranking: N/A (not classed an arms producer)
Ownership: Advent International, Bpifrance
Employees (2019): 13,000[42]
Lobbying in Brussels (2019): budget less than €9,999 (approximately US$11,200), 2 lobbyists (0.5 fte)[43]
Meetings: none registered

- An important provider of biometric identity products and services—such as multibiometric facial and fingerprint recognition, identity documents, and Advanced Passenger Information technology—to EU member states, including the UK, France, Slovakia, Finland, Albania, Netherlands, Estonia, and Lithuania (the latter two cofinanced by the EU).
- In February 2013, the European Commission awarded Morpho, in a consortium with Accenture and HP, a contract of up to €70 million (approximately US$93 million) for the maintenance of the European Vision Information System, the system used to store and exchange (biometric) data relating to the visa applications of third-country citizens.[44]
- IDEMIA also profits from EU border externalization. In 2010, it signed a contract with Mauritania to produce secure biometric-based ID documents and implement the Mauritania Visit border control system. For Egypt, it produces national electronic ID (eID) cards in cooperation with AOI Electronics, a military company owned by the Egyptian state, and built an identity management system to ensure their secure issuance.[45]
- In 2016, IDEMIA won a ten-year contract from the government of Mali to provide a complete system for issuing biometrics-based electronic passports.[46] It also provides passports to Uzbekistan, where it implemented an "end-to-end" ID system that also covers border control[47]—a project for which it subcontracted Thales to supply biometric data acquisition stations.[48]

Indra

Founded: 1993

Headquarters: Alcobendas (Madrid), Spain

Arms producing companies ranking: not in global top 100 as of 2018

Ownership: Spain (18.7 percent), Corporación Financiera Alba (10.5 percent), others (70.8 percent)[49]

Employees (2019): 49,000[50]

Lobbying in Brussels (2017): budget €900,000–999,999 (approximately US$1,000,000–1,130,000), 6 lobbyists (6 fte)[51]

Meetings with European Commission officials, January 7, 2015–September 27, 2018: 11[52]

- Spanish technology and consultancy company that developed the Integrated Vigilance System (SIVE), the Spanish maritime border security system, combining maritime traffic control, monitoring, and surveillance. The SIVE system was later exported to Romania, Latvia, and Portugal.
- In 2010, the Spanish Ministry of the Interior awarded Indra a €1.4 million (approximately US$1.9 million) contract to include Morocco, The Gambia, and Guinea Bissau in the Sea Horse Network cooperation program, a project to connect border surveillance capacities across Mediterranean countries.
- In 2016, Frontex contracted Indra to incorporate its Maritime Reconnaissance Intelligence (MRI) aircraft into Operation Triton, to track vessels with migrants on their way to Italy.
- Indra also supplies biometrics-based automated border control (ABC) systems for airports and ports as part of Spain's expanding Smart Border program, which is partly funded by the EU.

Conclusion

Through effective lobbying, the military and security industry shapes EU border and migration policies—particularly regarding the securitization of migration and border militarization—then profits from the markets that ensue. In Europe, a border security industrial complex has emerged, wherein the interests of European security actors and the profits of military and security companies are increasingly aligned. Across and beyond Europe, the main winners often profit further by exporting arms to the regions from which refugees are fleeing.

Refugees carry the burden of these policies and practices. They are stopped at EU borders or earlier on their journey toward Europe and frequently held against their will in inhumane conditions in transit countries. If they reach their destination, many end up in detention or in a permanent state of illegality. Numerous people are forcibly returned to their countries of origin, often by private security companies' employees. Despite severe criticism of its border and migration policies from the UN and countless human rights and refugee support organizations, there are few signs the EU will alter its course—much to the pleasure of the military and security industries, which see opportunities for profit in the border security market for years to come.

Mark Akkerman is a researcher at Stop Wapenhandel (the Dutch campaign against the arms trade) and for the Transnational Institute, specializing in European border militarization and externalization. They live in Amsterdam, Netherlands.

Notes

1   Some of the source data for this chapter has been published previously in Mark Akkerman, *Border Wars: The Arms Dealers Profiting from Europe's Refugee Tragedy* (Amsterdam, NL: Transnational Institute/Stoppen Wapenhandel, 2016), accessed March 23, 2020, https://www.tni.org/files/publication-downloads/border-wars-report-web1207.pdf; Mark Akkerman, *Border Wars II: An Update on the Arms Dealers Profiting from Europe's Refugee Tragedy* (Amsterdam, NL: Transnational Institute/Stop Wapenhandel, 2016), accessed March 23, 2020, https://reliefweb.int/sites/reliefweb.int/files/resources/borderwars-issuebrief-web.pdf; Mark Akkerman, *Expanding the Fortress: The Policies, the Profiteers and the People Shaped by EU's Border Externalisation Programme* (Amsterdam, NL: Transnational Institute/Stop Wapenhandel, 2018), accessed March 23, 2020, https://www.tni.org/files/publication-downloads/expanding_the_fortress_-_1.6_may_11.pdf.

2   "EUNAVFOR MED Operation Sophia: Mandate Extended by One Year, Two New Tasks Added" (press release), Council of the European Union, June 20, 2016, accessed March 23, 2020, https://www.consilium.europa.eu/en/press/press-releases/2016/06/20/fac-eunavfor-med-sophia.

3   Mark Akkerman, "NATO and EU Border Security in the Mediterranean," Stop Wapenhandel, May 2017, accessed March 23, 2020, http://www.stopwapenhandel.org/sites/stopwapenhandel.org/files/NATO-and-bordersecurity-Mediterranean.pdf.

4   Akkerman, "Border Wars: The Arms Dealers Profiting from Europe's Refugee tragedy."

5   John Cosgrave, Karen Hargrave, Marta Foresti, and Isabella Massa, with Justin Beresford, Helen Dempster, and Joanna Rea, *Europe's Refugees and Migrants: Hidden Flows, Tightened Borders and Spiralling Costs* (London: Overseas Development Institute, 2016), accessed March 23, 2020, https://www.odi.org/

publications/10558-europe-s-refugees-and-migrants-hidden-flows-tightened-borders-and-spiralling-costs.

6   "Deaths Recorded in the Mediterranean," Missing Migrants, accessed April 22, 2020, https://missingmigrants.iom.int/region/mediterranean.

7   "Council Conclusions on the Sahel Regional Action Plan 2015–2020" (press release), Council of the European Union, April 20, 2015, accessed March 23, 2020, https://www.consilium.europa.eu/en/press/press-releases/2015/04/20/council-conclusions-sahel-regional-plan.

8   European Commission and the High Representative of the Union for Foreign Affairs and Security Policy, "Joint Staff Working Document: Annual Report on the Sahel Regional Action Plan SWD(2016) 482 final," Council of the European Union: European Commission, December 23, 2016, accessed March 23, 2020, http://data.consilium.europa.eu/doc/document/ST-5009-2017-INIT/en/pdf.

9   Martin Lemberg-Pedersen, "Private Security Companies and the EU Borders," in Thomas Gammeltoft-Hansen and Ninna Nyberg Sørensen, eds., *The Migration Industry and the Commercialization of International Migration* (London: Routledge, 2013), 163.

10 Ben Hayes, *NeoConOpticon: The EU Security-Industrial Complex* (London: Transnational Institute/Statewatch, 2009), accessed March 23, 2020, https://www.statewatch.org/analyses/neoconopticon-report.pdf.

11 Ibid.; Chris Jones, *Market Forces: The Development of the EU Security-Industrial Complex* (London: Transnational Institute/Statewatch, 2017), accessed March 23, 2020, https://www.tni.org/files/publication-downloads/marketforces-report-tni-statewatch.pdf.

12 *Research for a Secure Europe: Report of the Group of Personalities in the Field of Security Research* (Luxembourg: Office for Official Publications of the European Communities, 2004), accessed March 23, 2020, https://ec.europa.eu/home-affairs/sites/homeaffairs/files/e-library/documents/policies/security/pdf/gop_en.pdf.

13 *Border Security Market Report 2017–2027* (London: Visiongain, 2017).

14 Market Research Future, *Border Security Market Research Report: Forecast to 2025* (Maharashtra, IN: WantStats Research and Media Pvt. Ltd., May 2019).

15 For a general overview of the major profiteers in the border security business in recent years, see Akkerman, *Border Wars I and II.*

16 Aude Fleurant, Alexandra Kuimova, Diego Lopes Da Silva, Nan Tian, Pieter D. Wezeman, and Siemon T. Wezeman, "The SIPRI Top 100 Arms-Producing and Military Service Companies 2018," SIPRI Fact Sheet, December 2019, accessed April 22, 2020, https://www.sipri.org/sites/default/files/2019-12/1912_fs_top_100_2018_0.pdf.

17 Regulation (EU) 2016/1624 of the European Parliament and of the Council of 14 September 2016 on the European Border and Coast Guard and Amending Regulation (EU) 2016/399 of the European Parliament and of the Council and Repealing Regulation (EC) No 863/2007 of the European Parliament and of the Council, Council Regulation (EC) No 2007/2004 and Council Decision 2005/267/EC," *Official Journal of the European Union*, September 16, 2016, L251/1–76,

accessed March 23, 2020, https://eur-lex.europa.eu/legal-content/EN/TXT/
PDF/?uri=CELEX:32016R1624&from=EN.

18   European Commission, "A European Defence Fund: €5.5 Billion per Year to Boost
     Europe's Defence Capabilities" (press release), June 7, 2017, accessed March 23,
     2020, https://ec.europa.eu/commission/presscorner/detail/en/IP_17_1508.

19   Guy Martin, "Mali and Egypt to Receive C295s This Year," defenceWeb, June
     23, 2016, accessed March 23, 2020, https://www.defenceweb.co.za/aerospace/
     aerospace-aerospace/mali-and-egypt-to-receive-c295s-this-year; "Africa
     Entering Growth Period with Defense and Security Opportunities," *African
     Defense*, September 1, 2016, accessed March 23, 2020, https://issuu.com/
     jeffmckaughan/docs/african_defense_september; "Why Africa Is a Land of
     Opportunity for ADS," African Aerospace Online News Service, November
     18, 2016, accessed March 23, 2020, https://www.africanaerospace.aero/why-
     africa-is-a-land-of-opportunity-for-ads.html.

20   "SIPRI Arms industry Database," SIPRI, accessed April 22, 2020, https://www.
     sipri.org/databases/armsindustry.

21   "Share Price & Information," Airbus, accessed March 23, 2020, https://www.
     airbus.com/investors/share-price-and-information.html.

22   "Airbus," *Forbes*, accessed April 22, 2020, https://www.forbes.com/companies/
     airbus/#781f9fe469c1; accurate on May 15, 2019.

23   "Airbus," LobbyFacts.eu, accessed April 22, 2020, https://lobbyfacts.eu/repre
     sentative/5b926291742246faae579d445c5d41a2/airbus.

24   Ibid.

25   Romania Insider, "Investigation into Romania's EUR 734 Mln Border Security
     Contract with EADS," Romania-Insider.com, July 11, 2014, accessed March
     23, 2020, https://www.romania-insider.com/investigation-into-romanias-
     eur-734-mln-border-security-contract-with-eads.

26   Hauke Friederichs and Caterina Lobenstein, "Die Gekaufte Grenze," *Zeit*,
     October 29, 2016, accessed March 23, 2020, https://www.zeit.de/2016/45/
     fluechtlinge-grenze-schutz-tunesien-ueberwachungstechnik.

27   "Airbus Completes Divestment of Its Defence Electronics Unit to KKR," Airbus,
     March 1, 2017, accessed March 23, 2020, https://www.airbus.com/newsroom/
     press-releases/en/2017/03/airbus-completes-divestment-of-its-defence-
     electronics-unit-to-kkr.html.

28   "SIPRI Arms industry Database."

29   "Leonardo," Market Screener, accessed March 23, 2020, http://www.4-traders.
     com/LEONARDO-162001/company.

30   "Leonardo," *Forbes*, accessed April 22, 2020, https://www.forbes.com/
     companies/leonardo/#12f2e33c1fff. Accurate as of May 15, 2019.

31   "Leonardo," LobbyFacts.eu, accessed April 9, 2020, https://lobbyfacts.eu/
     representative/ab715c79da934a01821ed36ba8dbfcaa/leonardo-s-p-a.

32   Ibid.

33   Leonardo-Finmeccanica, "Leonardo-Finmeccanica at Warsaw NATO Summit
     with NATO AGS System," defense-aerospace.com, July 8, 2016, accessed March
     23, 2020, http://www.defense-aerospace.com/articles-view/release/3/175302/
     leonardo_finmeccanica-takes-nato-ags-system-to-warsaw-summit.html.

34 "Leonardo to Provide 'Drones as a Service' Surveillance for Civilian Missions," Leonardo, June 20, 2017, accessed March 23, 2020, https://www.leonardocompany.com/en/-/drones-as-service.

35 "Leonardo Deploys Its Falco EVO Remotely-Piloted Air System for Drone-Based Maritime Surveillance as Part of the Frontex Test Programme," Leonardo, December 6, 2018, accessed March 24, 2020, https://www.leonardocompany.com/en/-/falco-drone-frontex-sensori-guardia-finanza.

36 "SIPRI Arms industry Database."

37 "Thales," Market Screener, accessed March 23, 2020, http://www.4-traders.com/THALES-4715/company.

38 "Thales," *Forbes*, accessed April 22, 2020, https://www.forbes.com/companies/thales/#1a7b5b0e3759; accurate on May 15, 2019.

39 "Thales," LobbyFacts.eu, accessed April 22, 2020, https://lobbyfacts.eu/representative/032d0ce7adbe4a2794c1ffd571dc675d/thales.

40 Ibid.

41 "Advent International and Bpifrance Complete the Acquisition of Safran Identity & Security (Morpho) and Create OT-MORPHO, a World Leader in Identification and Digital Security Technologies," Advent International, May 31, 2017, accessed March 24, 2020, https://bit.ly/2znVTcw.

42 IDEMIA, *Our Journey* (Paris: IDEMIA, 2019), 13, accessed April 22, 2020, https://www.idemia.com/sites/corporate/files/about-us/download/idemia-corporate-brochure-201911_0.pdf.

43 "Indemia," LobbyFacts.eu, accessed April 22, 2020, https://lobbyfacts.eu/representative/4bd8429a3c3b439c9bc2449b3c6dbad8/idemia.

44 "European Commission Selects Consortium of Accenture, Morpho and HP to Maintain U Visa Information and Biometric Matching Systems," Accenture, February 20, 2013, accessed March 24, 2020, https://accntu.re/2VsNayk.

45 "Morpho Signs Contract with AOI Electronics to Locally Produce National eID Cards for Egypt," Safran, November 28, 2014, accessed March 24, 2020, https://www.safran-group.com/media/20141128_morpho-signs-contract-aoi-electronics-locally-produce-national-eid-cards-egypt. "Mauritania Used Biometrics to Revamp ID Document System," Planet Biometrics, September 6, 2010, accessed August 10, 2020, https://www.planetbiometrics.com/article-details/i/248.

46 "The Republic of Mali Chooses OT to Supply Its Latest Generation Electronic Passport," IDEMIA, July 20, 2016, accessed March 24, 2020, https://www.idemia.com/news/republic-mali-chooses-ot-supply-its-latest-generation-electronic-passport-2016-07-20.

47 Oberthur Technologies, "Oberthur Technologies Successfully Delivered an End-to-End ePassport Solution in Uzbekistan" (press release), MarketWatch, May 13, 2013, accessed March 24, 2020, https://www.marketwatch.com/press-release/oberthur-technologies-successfully-delivered-an-end-to-end-epassport-solution-in-uzbekistan-2013-05-13.

48 Thales Contact Solutions, "Thales Delivers e-Passport Management System in Uzbekistan," Security Infowatch.com, June 5, 2013, accessed March 24 2020, https://www.securityinfowatch.com/cybersecurity/information-security/

press-release/10957917/thales-contact-solutions-thales-delivers-epassport-management-system-in-uzbekistan.

49 "Indra-Sistemas," Market Screener, accessed March 24, 2020, http://www.4-traders.com/INDRA-SISTEMAS-413470/company.

50 "Sobre Indra," Indra, accessed April 22, 2020, https://www.indracompany.com/es/indra.

51 "Indra," LobbyFacts.eu, accessed April 22, 2020, https://lobbyfacts.eu/represe ntative/31fda6ac0716406a8b2591fb33377144/indra.

52 Ibid.

Making a Refugee Market in the Republic of Nauru

Julia Morris

It's another sunny day on the equator, which draws even more contrast to the long-sleeved gathering convening outside the small prefab building. The blinding light ricochets off its metallic walls, intensified by the limestone pinnacle outcrops in the distant haze of the sea. I make a sharp turn, veering my bike over to the steadily accumulating group. The rusted wheels make it difficult to maneuver around potholes, but I can still manage the coconut-fringed drive, which curves around the back of the Republic of Nauru's government buildings. I've spotted a few familiar faces. A friend, a government lawyer, excitedly waves; one of a steady stream of Fijian legal professionals brought over to develop the small coral atoll's Justice Department. He beckons me to the gleaming structure, which forms the gathering's focal point.

Over the last few months, I haven't failed to notice rapid developments on the small plot of land. "Canstruct"-emblazoned dump trucks have been hard at work, plying up and down Topside, the island's central mound, each full to the brim with crushed limestone: a by-product of phosphate extraction. Phosphate, the lucrative fertilizer component, remains Nauru's main export commodity, still contributing to the country's slowly resurging economy. But few phosphate workers are to be seen here today. Instead, the event signals the country's move from a scientific export to a new legal import commodity.

Balloons flap in the sea breeze, secured tightly to the building's gleaming metallic walls. The usual post-event feast is being ferried in through one of the six doors. Troughs of meat, a roast piglet, head lolling to one side, shiny and thick with grease, metallic trays heaving with rice and chow mein. Inside another door, people have started taking their seats on the rows of reverential pews. Clipped Fijian accents converge with Australian twangs punctuated with a smattering of Nauruan phrases. Conversations trace familiar paths.

"What's your next fly-out rotation? Six weeks on, two weeks off?"

"So you must be on the Menen's east face? I hear the sunset view is unbeatable."

I recognize some faces: Nauru Hash House Harriers regulars, the country's expat walking group, Nauru's two consular representatives, the Australian and Taiwanese commissioners, Australian immigration authorities, a few social workers, a refugee lawyer. Apart from the walking regulars, there are Nauru's minister of finance, a landowner lobbyist, seconded Australian government employees, and several rugged-looking Canstruct workers.

A chauffeured black Cadillac crunches to a halt on the crushed rock alongside the entrance. The Nauruan flag flutters on its hood. Hushed silence falls and the crowd rises to their feet as President Baron Waqa enters, taking his seat at the front. The officiating minister is immediately called forth, still wearing the garb of his day job: striped tie, white-collar shirt threaded with Lady Justice scales, a pen tucked neatly in the pocket, "Judicial Department Nauru" stenciled in blue underneath. Shuffling his transcript into order, he coughs and, with a booming voice, launches in:

> Heavenly father, most merciful and loving God, we thank you for this fruitful day, as we are gathered here to officially inaugurate this new courthouse building. We pray that you bless this gathering. Bless this new building, as it represents law and order, to uphold justice and peace in Nauru. And, most gracious God, we also pray for the Government of Australia, who funded this new building, and you will continue to bless them all and its people and our friends at the RPC [Regional Processing Center]. We commit this building into your hands. Let your will be done, we pray through the mighty name of Jesus. Amen.

Everyone joins in solemn ascent. Baron Waqa wipes some sweat from his brow, pulling at the top of his starched collar. Several iPhone camera clicks, a few flashes: Australian personnel keen to preserve the moment, or maybe circulate it back to Canberra. The photos usually elicit a few staff giggles and interoffice forwards, I've been told.

After a round of applause, the president moves to the front, outweighing the other speakers in girth and charisma. Like most of Nauru's middle-aged population, President Waqa was schooled in Australia and Fiji. He climbed the presidential ladder through careers in high school teaching and as education minister. His way with words is always evident, not least in his occasional Australian newspaper opinion pieces, responding to media attacks levelled at Nauru.

Hands clasped in front, he gives a broad open smile, launching into the inaugural speech:

> Speaker of parliament, honorable members, cabinet ministers, members of the diplomatic core, and our friends from the RPC, DIBP [Australian Department of Immigration and Border Protection], ladies and gentlemen. I just wanted to say a few words before opening this building. I'd like to thank the judiciary, especially CJ [the Chief Justice] and all his staff. The judiciary has been crying out for a long, long time for a building, an extension of the courthouse of some sort, and here we are at this juncture. I'd like to take this opportunity to thank the government of Australia for their continued support to the government of Nauru, as well as the, ahh, numerous requests and needs that we put through to the Australian government, in our, ahh . . . [a barely audible chuckle] . . . very much needed, development. And one of them is the development of our judiciary. The court building will serve us very, very well, and the people of Nauru. There are a lot of cases that are coming through the courts over the last two years, in particular. And now, we'll see hopefully a much more robust, quicker, and easier system. Without further ado, I know that CJ and his staff would like to move in very quickly and start working, so if I may take this honor, and most humbly declare this building open for the public, for Nauru, for Nauruans, for all under this judiciary system of Nauru. *Meta waqa.*

—Field notes: Republic of Nauru Courthouse Opening, Government Buildings, Yaren District. July 17, 2015.

***

The courthouse opening was just one of many incidents I witnessed that are testimony to the major legal and institutional changes taking place in the Republic of Nauru. Nauru is the world's smallest island state at just eight square miles, located in Micronesia—200 miles east of its nearest neighbor, the Kiribati island of Banaba. Under the 2001 Pacific Solution, Nauru, like Papua New Guinea, agreed to house Australia's "irregular maritime arrivals" in exchange for development aid packages and an economic sector for business and employment (the latter at the Manus Island Regional Processing Centre). Australia put the program on hiatus in 2008, when the Kevin Rudd–led Labor government temporarily closed both facilities. However, the decision was exploited by opposition parties, which claimed it had created a border weakness. Pressured by the Liberal Coalition's harder-line campaign and eager to present a clear deterrence strategy during the next election cycle, new Labor leader Julia Gillard reopened Nauru and Manus in 2012 with the validation of her party's Expert Panel Report.[1] The two countries again agreed to become the sites of Australia's maritime asylum operations. The deal was combined with a substantial increase in coast guard and border enforcement cooperation across the Asia Pacific region.

Since 2012, anyone who makes their way by boat and claims to be a refugee in Australian territorial (now excised) waters is "offshored" to Nauru or Papua New Guinea's Manus Island for refugee processing and resettlement. The majority of people arrive by boat from Indonesia or Sri Lanka, although provenances span Iran, Iraq, Afghanistan, Vietnam, Myanmar, and beyond. Histrionic debates about national security, coupled with a deep history of selective nation-building, constitute some of the political currency of offshoring refugee operations for Australia.[2]

This chapter looks more particularly at the legal and financial architecture that coalesces around Nauru, examining how an industrialized regime in refugee law and management has been created and maintained. The opening of the new refugee courthouse in Nauru—built for the third stage of refugee appeal hearings—signals something of the vast capital that revolves around refugees as Nauru's latest commodity. That same morning, I had been at a primary school prize ceremony where the scheduled government ministers were notably not in attendance, all instead at RPC-related events. In their absence, parents handed out awards to expectant young faces.

With the island economically devastated following over a century of phosphate extraction,[3] consecutive Nauruan presidents René Harris and Sprent Dabwido leaped on board with the refugee project from the outset, agreeing to the Australian government's proposals in 2001 and 2012. But prior to the offshore processing project, the country had no history of refugee legislation or refugee settlement. Nauru was not a signatory to the Refugee Convention nor did it have its own state asylum procedures.[4] Indeed, among many in government, there was little understanding of what an asylum system entailed. Yet Nauru took seriously the building of an administrative system for refugee processing and resettlement, primarily guided by a firm belief in the tenets of international law. As a result, the government required extensive international and Australian intervention to administer its newest industrial operation, processing asylum seekers into refugees.[5]

Refugee Capita

The building of Nauru as an offshore refugee site was easy to achieve. Determining and managing refugees has grown into a vast neoliberal regime.[6] From a budget of US$300,000 and thirty-four staff members in 1950, the UN refugee agency, the United Nations High Commissioner for Refugees (UNHCR), is now a bureaucratic leviathan with more than 9,300 staff worldwide and an annual budget of over US$7 billion.[7] IKEA is its partner in Better Shelter refugee flat-pack construction, and Angelina Jolie its special envoy for refugee issues. Lawyers, clinicians, educators, social workers, bureaucrats, and more coalesce around refugee wealth. Some determine if individuals are refugees or help present them as such; others contractually care for asylum seekers and refugees; others still return those with rejected asylum applications to their countries of origin from camps, processing centers, and other geographical localities.[8] Refugee studies centers, programs, and policy institutes proliferate, from Oxford to Toronto, Bangalore to Cairo, Sydney, Dar-es-Salaam, and beyond.[9]

As elsewhere, UNHCR's legal and humanitarian structures frame Nauru's refugee project, resulting in an outgrowth of actors that assist in refugee processing and care. International human rights organizations, together with a range of nongovernmental and commercial contractors, have been central to this project. Over only a few years, Nauru was transformed into a bustling refugee company town with locals trained in refugee determination and resource governance. This bore a striking resemblance, I found, to Nauru's yesteryear, when the country's economic and social life revolved around phosphate, with locals trained in phosphate determination, management, and care.[10] When I arrived in Nauru to conduct my fieldwork in 2015, tied into Nauru's University of the South Pacific as a research student, visiting dignitaries were taken on tours of both the refugee processing and phosphate processing operations. Balloons fluttered in the sea breeze to proud fanfare at the opening of the new refugee courthouse, as scientific modernity was replaced by legal progress and industry. From refugee legal claims and settlement services to child welfare and medical support, numerous organizations buoy the UNHCR's developmental practice in the country.

Phosphate meets the refugee industry: pickups carrying refugee workers (left) and phosphate workers (right).
(Photos by Julia Morris, 2015)

Nauru is prominent on the global media stage. Across the summer of 2016, the small sovereign state found itself at the center of another global media frenzy, with the *Guardian* newspaper's Nauru files leaks. With a catalogue of over two thousand filed incident reports, Nauru's offshore refugee operations were characterized as an exceptionality, a "gulag archipelago,"[11] "a dark, wretched Truman Show without the cameras" rife with "horrible mistreatment," "squalor," "trauma and self-harm."[12] Media outlets and spokespeople around the world took up this narrative, stressing the brutal conditions for refugees through humanitarian tropes of suffering, persecution, and vulnerability. Other commentators continue to level anti-civilizational accusations on Nauruans as savages, claiming that the country is outside the rule of law and international oversight, with Nauruans chasing refugees through the streets with machetes. "Regular—we're not talking several incidents. Regular, systematic attacks from local population. People are hacked with machetes," said Amnesty International's Anna Neistat in an interview on National Public Radio (NPR) on August 11, 2016, after flying to Nauru on a three-day "refugee mission." She continued: "Every single woman I spoke to told me that they cannot go out because now they're absolutely at the mercy of the locals."[13] Headlines such as "Nauru, Refugees and Australia's 'Torture Complex'"[14] and "Island of Despair" are commonplace.[15] Academic press is replete with titles like "Repeating Despair on Nauru: The Impacts of Offshore Processing on Asylum Seekers" and *Offshore: Behind the Wire on Manus and Nauru*.[16] There are documentaries and books like *Chasing Asylum*,[17] *Freedom or Death*,[18] *The Undesirables: Inside Nauru*,[19] and *Yearning to Breathe Free: Seeking Asylum in Australia*.[20]

This chapter is part of a wider research project that seeks to bring Nauru's two resource sectors into conversation, as a way of reifying the ecological consequences in mineral and migrant extractive industries.[21] My purpose here is to take up the problem of transferability: what, in the offshore oil and gas industry, Hannah Appel calls "modularity."[22] What does the ease with which Nauru surged into existence as a processing state reveal about the standardization process through which new outsourced refugee sites come into being? What do the moral values that revolve around the refugee—as evidenced in Nauru's anti-politics—tell us about the industry's replicability?

Based on fifteen months of fieldwork in 2014 and 2015 spanning Geneva, Australia, Fiji, and the Republic of Nauru, I argue that the problem is located in the development regime of the refugee and asylum industry. Paradoxically, the strength of "the refugee" as a subject of humanitarianism propels this enterprise, belying the power and capital that underlie its rationalities. This logic advances an inherently demeaning and politically fraught regime, while dissolving the refugee into lucrative market networks. This is not to say that migrants are not involved as active players in the refugee industry.[23] Throughout, I promote a critical approach to the study of the "refugee economy," a term I use to describe the circulation of capital around "the refugee" as political, economic, and moral in nature. I integrate refugee claimants as labor industrialists working to insert themselves into state economies within a geographical landscape of deep structural imbalance.

In the next section, I move on to the problem of industrial replication, discussing the institutional regime of Nauru's refugee industry, which lies within the hegemony of the UNHCR's development frame. My analysis reveals an institutionalization that expands on many studies of, for example, technologies of state and non-state actors,[24] the refugee complex,[25] and biopolitical practice[26]—or the demands of truth-telling and refugee performativity.[27] It reveals the capital that is central to the industry's expansion and its replicability to new localities—in this case, the development of an entire system in refugee determination and managerialism. I close with a consideration of the problem of transferability, arguing that moving beyond the "suffering subject" and reframing the refugee narrative to one of global (im)mobility might provide a more productive frame.[28] Given the increase in extraterritorial processing,[29] this approach opens a new direction for an empirical study of the shifting geographies of territorial controls.

A Transferable Industry

Resources have come up enormously, so liquified natural gas has gone through an enormous boom in Australia. And the Japanese, Koreans, and Chinese buy our gas because of our proximity to them. Now it's starting to taper off, and that has an effect on our industry. Then you've got iron ore, which is a massive industry in Australia. Australia produces more iron ore than any industry in the world, but that's starting to finish off now. Coal, obviously, that's slowed down enormously, so that's come to a stop. So resources are coming off, but it's about constantly changing and reinventing yourself and making yourself relevant to your customer. Because if you're relevant to your customer, then your customer's relevant to you.
—engineering firm CEO, operating in Nauru, personal interview, 2015

It's like any commercial enterprise. You set up a business, and let's say you're selling bread, you have to price it, because you don't have a guarantee that every day the same people will be coming to buy your bread, so you need to factor that into your price. Factor in that some days you might have less bread, and some days you might have a whole bunch.
—NGO counseling services CEO, operating in Nauru, personal interview, 2015

Like the majority of Australia's once public-led services, most of which were privatized under the Hawke and Keating Labor governments in the 1990s, the efficiency of markets at finding low-cost solutions are the main rubric of Australian immigration and refugee resettlement policies. As Nauru has become the principal destination for Australia's maritime refugee processing project, a range of organizations have been contracted to create the institutional support for a legal administrative and welfare project. When I arrived in Nauru in 2015, the number of "fly-in, fly-out" workers was astounding. Firms that specialize in remote environments, from offshore mining services to supplying aid to isolated communities and catering to vulnerable populations—sometimes with historical legacies of aboriginal assimilation and mission containment, as with the Brisbane Catholic Education Services—all came together in the offshore asylum market. Because immigration and refugee management services are thoroughly institutionalized industrial sectors, many—such as the newly formed Australian NGO consortium Connect Settlement Services, made up of Melbourne's Australian Multicultural Education Services and the Brisbane-based Multicultural Development Association—already have certified refugee sector expertise. Some of these organizations have close political ties and are commonly elicited as key government providers—including Craddock Murray Neuman, the Sydney-based legal firm contracted to provide legal assistance in Nauru to those seeking asylum. Others have a history in Pacific commerce—such as Transfield Services, already active in the offshore oil and gas sector but now focused on the offshore refugee industry—easily expanding their geographical and institutional fabric into Nauru's offshore human extractive world.

By the time I conducted my fieldwork, Nauru had also become a site of intense international interest. Counter to dominant global media narratives, the assistance of international refugee law experts, intergovernmental agencies, and nongovernment agencies helped establish a refugee determination system that, in the words of one of its Australian legal architects, is "truly world class"—as much as it is morally dubious. As Susanne Freidberg shows in press-sensitive food supply chains, corporate-level anxiety about the "tarnish" of bad press has led to an ethical turn within supply chains.[30] I also found that the level of regulation in Nauru's morally dubious operations verged on the extreme. Médecins Sans Frontières, British legal academics, and Australian clinicians all made an appearance during my fieldwork. Fly-in, fly-out factory inspectorates of Comcare health and safety personnel, Commonwealth Ombudsman, the Jesuit Refugee Service, the International Committee of the Red Cross, the Office of the United Nations High Commission for Human Rights, the Australian Red Cross, the UNHCR, the UN Sub-Committee on the Prevention of Torture, and more were firm fixtures around the company town district.

Moral values did structure some of the involvement of the major institutional players in the offshore refugee processing industry. After signing a much criticized refugee processing contract for asylum seekers from the Tampa boat in 2001, the UNHCR—as one prominent industry player—refused the same contractual involvement in the country's reinvigorated refugee enterprise. Instead, the UNHCR staff took a backstage system advisory role but publicly critiqued the viability of importing asylum seekers to Nauru long-term. Other industry professionals developed separate consortiums or changed names to evade reputational damage from their involvement.

In Nauru, I was frequently handed literature on the oft-cited humanitarian paradox by Australian social workers and lawyers, who lamented the crux of supporting the offshore refugee industry, adding the words "better us, not them." But rather than think of apologist frictions in Nauru's capitalist production, these actions illuminate more how institutionalized refugees have become within industrial practice. It is here where we see quite how explicitly the figure of the refugee has dissolved as a commodity, upheld through the work of trained refugee studies graduates, well-versed in humanitarian and post-developmental critique. The operations, of course, are hardly without their fault lines. Nevertheless, that refugee processing is able to move on to Libya (where the British government has created a similar operation to stop migrants before arrival), to Mexico (through a similar United States government plan), and to Turkey (on the basis of European Union projects), shows how easily template forms are facilitated separate from the specificities of place.[31]

Biopolitical Norms

The biopoliticality of the refugee as a human commodity form is equally important. For many, it has become incredibly hard to move elsewhere. Refugee certification is one, albeit often demeaning, means of moving across borders, laced with ideologies of Western salvation from Third World poverty and state tyranny.[32] In one instance down at Nauru's boat harbor, I spoke with Jamal, from Iran, recently certified as a refugee in the country. His backstory was horrific; he had been beaten and assaulted along his long and arduous journey to an Indonesian port to board a boat to Australia, where he hoped to eventually rebuild his life. But, ultimately, so much of the horror he encountered was exacerbated by his inability to move across borders—restricted in his movement by virtue of his Iranian citizenship. The victimizing frame of refugee suffering obscures the structural reasons that account for Jamal's situation.

However, it is also the biopoliticality of presenting oneself as a refugee that makes it hard to de-fetishize the processes that go into the production of migrants as refugees. Jamal, like so many other people I spoke with in Nauru, was reliant on the refugee frame, trapped in what Annelise Riles terms the Weberian "iron cage of legalism."[33] He was figured and figured himself through a refugee identity,[34] which is how he sought to move elsewhere, unable to obtain a visa by other means. This is not to say that many people, like Jamal, have not been through incredibly difficult and at times unthinkable experiences that should legally make them refugees. But increased border securitization for particular populations places individuals in a position where proving suffering is the prevailing mode of border entry over accusations of economic migrancy. Freedom of movement is permitted for some but not for others. Populations are treated differently on the basis of citizenship, class, and other ethnoracial and gendered differences. The highly skilled, elite, young, healthy, and those with familial ties are more desirable and risk-free for consumer economies, in contrast to the less skilled, low-class, and detached unable to fit within these categories.[35]

For some in Nauru, such as contracted industry workers, the notion of refugees as suffering victims provided clear advantage. In sheer desperation, one strategy that some of Nauru's refugees adopted—in tandem with refugee activist groups in Australia—was to use the discourse of refugee suffering to shed light on their situations. A few took photos of others who had self-harmed and posted them on locally maintained websites like Offshore Processing Centre Voice and the Facebook group Nauru's Refugees' News. On several occasions, I encountered some of Nauru's more vehement campaigners on the phone with Australia's refugee activists or with high-profile refugee and human rights lawyers. Several months prior, I had been in interviews with activists and legal teams in Australia, who were also on calls with or texting refugees in Nauru. Many refugees I met in Nauru did not agree with these moves,

A refugee protest at Nibok resettlement housing compound
(Photo by Julia Morris, 2015)

which led to constant internal tensions. Unfortunately, as I have argued, contrary to scholarship that depicts networked activism in apolitical terms,[36] these narratives only provide more moral capital to the overall refugee industry contracted to carry out the tasks of refugee determination and management in refugee camps and outsourced extraction zones like Nauru. It is the promotion and industry marketing campaigns behind making/accepting more "refugees" that makes possible the creation of strange new refugee worlds replete with devastating toxicities, as I have shown elsewhere.[37]

A Never-Ending Parthenogenesis

I will close this chapter by returning to the problem of transferability. How do we push back against the creation of outsourced, offshored, far-flung refugee extractive worlds? An enormous amount of capital is invested in the figure of the refugee. The analysis I have presented here shows the ways in which capital circulates in, through, and from the migrant body, as institutional actors look to create a sensationalized refugee product identity to attract the attention of publics who will invest in or support the refugee industry's growth. This makes it all the more difficult to reframe the narrative in terms of human (im)mobility, when "helping refugees" makes us feel as if we are bettering people's lives.[38] In discussing the sociocultural entanglements of the oil industry, Stephanie LeMenager calls this dynamic "petromelancholia": a failure to imagine an alternative to a fossil fueled capitalist modernity.[39] Even when faced with intense processes of extraction and precarious future reserves, the affective and embodied routines of living oil produce an "amnesia" that screens the consequences of extraction and consumption. So too, impassioned "refugee suffering" campaigns have become enveloped by brick walls. My industry and activist interlocutors used terms like "refugee compassion" and "refugee empowerment." As a result, we so often fail to "get behind the veil, the fetishism of the market and the commodity, in order to tell the full story of social reproduction."[40] It is the notion of people as refugees buoyed by a mega-industry that makes possible the creation of dystopian refugee worlds like Nauru's new company town—or wherever the next booming industrial sites are to be found.

The near-global move toward policies that deregulate national economies and liberalize trade and investment have given rise to profit-making capacities that define resource extraction worldwide, from mineral to new migrant commodity forms. Concurrently, ever-growing networks of advocacy groups, NGOs, watchdog organizations, and engaged citizens have emerged to monitor forms of resource governance that impact people's lives. My central concerns are to understand what meaning the refugee identity holds for the actors who are promoting it and to pay attention to the negatives of refugee promotion, including the discursive practices that make outsourced supply chains possible. It is important to underline how and why people are made into refugees in order to redirect energies toward the uneven points of production and hazardous determination cycles. Just as the inequalities of capitalism push people to search for better lives, capitalism guides militarization and resource extraction that results in extreme dispossession. In turn, the movement of people becomes the site of the creation of brand-new markets tied to migrants and refugees.

Yet, promoting the refugee trope of "Third World" persecution and "First World" salvationism can legitimize the increase in military interventions that drives the refugee cycle. Rather than calling for an increase in refugee import quotas or an increase in industry funding in the West, we would do better to decrease the militarization and border frontiering that drive human displacement so as to work toward more equitable futures. Insofar as people are ever more integrated into capital as an accumulation strategy, the necessity of a broad political response becomes increasingly urgent. But what kind of social power will this take? There is a great need for research into the geographies of migration governance to include experiences of exploitation, environmental destruction, and the risks that come with globalized refugee production, as well as the forms of colonial power and economic dependency that sustains them.

Julia Morris is assistant professor of international studies at the University of North Carolina Wilmington.

Notes

1   See "Report of the Expert Panel on Asylum Seekers," Australian Government, August 2012, accessed March 25, 2020, https://www.kaldorcentre.unsw.edu.au/sites/default/files/expert-panel-report.pdf.
2   David Marr and Marian Wilkinson, *Dark Victory* (Crows Nest, AU: Allen & Unwin, 2003).
3   Nancy Viviani, *Nauru: Phosphate and Political Progress* (Canberra: Australian National University Press, 1970).
4   For the Refugee Convention, see Convention and Protocol Relating to the Status of Refugees, UNHCR, accessed March 29, 2020, https://www.unhcr.org/protection/basic/3b66c2aa10/convention-protocol-relating-status-refugees.html.
5   Julia Morris, "Refugee Extractivism: Law and Mining a Human Commodity in the Republic of Nauru," *Saint Louis University Law Journal* 64, no. 1 (May 2020).
6   Julia Morris, "Power, Capital and Immigration Detention Rights: Making Networked Markets in Global Detention Governance at UNHCR," *Global Networks* 17, no. 3 (April 2017): 400–22.
7   "History of UNHCR," UNHCR USA, accessed March 25, 2020, http://www.unhcr.org/en-us/history-of-unhcr.html.
8   Dominique Moran, Nick Gill, and Deirdre Conlon, eds., *Carceral Spaces: Mobility and Agency in Imprisonment and Migrant Detention* (Aldershot, UK: Ashgate Publishing Ltd., 2013).
9   B.S. Chimni, "The Birth of a 'Discipline': From Refugee to Forced Migration Studies," *Journal of Refugee Studies* 22, no. 1 (March 2009): 11–29; Liisa H. Malkki, "Refugees and Exile: From 'Refugee Studies' to the National Order of Things," *Annual Review of Anthropology* 24 (1995): 495–523, accessed March 25, 2020, https://is.cuni.cz/studium/predmety/index.php?do=download&did=85562&kod=JMM664.
10 Maslyn Williams and Barrie Macdonald, *The Phosphateers: A History of the British Phosphate Commissioners and the Christmas Island Phosphate Commission* (Melbourne: Melbourne University Press, 1985).
11 Julia Baird, "Australia's Gulag Archipelago," *New York Times*, August 30, 2016, accessed March 25, 2020, https://www.nytimes.com/2016/08/31/opinion/australias-gulag-archipelago.html.

12 Paul Farrell, Nick Evershed, and Helen Davidson, "The Nauru Files: Cache of 2,000 Leaked Reports Reveal Scale of Abuse of Children in Australian Offshore Detention," *Guardian*, August 10, 2016, accessed March 25, 2020, https://www.theguardian.com/australia-news/2016/aug/10/the-nauru-files-2000-leaked-reports-reveal-scale-of-abuse-of-children-in-australian-offshore-detention.

13 "Claims Probed of Brutal Conditions for Refugees on Island of Nauru," NPR, August 11, 2016, accessed March 25, 2020, https://www.npr.org/2016/08/11/489584342/claims-probed-of-brutal-conditions-for-refugees-on-island-of-nauru.

14 Tom Nightingale, "Nauru Rule of Law 'Nonexistent,' Former Magistrate Says', Australian Broadcasting Corporation: The World Today, July 10, 2015, accessed March 25, 2020, https://www.abc.net.au/radio/programs/worldtoday/nauru-rule-of-law-nonexistent-former-magistrate/6610610.

15 Michael Koziol, "'Island of Despair': Australia Intentionally Torturing Refugees on Nauru, Says Major Amnesty International Report," *The Sydney Morning Herald*, October 17, 2016, accessed April 10, 2020, https://www.smh.com.au/politics/federal/island-of-despair-australia-intentionally-torturing-refugees-on-nauru-says-major-amnesty-international-report-20161017-gs3sm4.html.

16 Caroline Fleay, "Repeating Despair on Nauru: The Impacts of Offshore Processing on Asylum Seekers," Curtin University Centre for Human Rights Education, September 2012, accessed March 25, 2020, https://www.academia.edu/7200024/Repeating_Despair_on_Nauru_The_Impacts_of_Offshore_Processing_on_Asylum_Seekers; Madeline Gleeson, *Offshore: Behind the Wire on Manus and Nauru* (Sydney, AU: NewSouth Publishing, 2016).

17 Eva Orner, dir., *Chasing Asylum* (Melbourne: Nerdy Girl Films, 2016).

18 Elliot Spencer, dir., *Freedom or Death* (Brisbane, AU: Autonomous Productions, 2009).

19 Mark Isaacs, *The Undesirables: Inside Nauru* (Sydney: Hardie Grant Books, 2014).

20 Dean Lusher and Nick Haslam, eds., *Yearning to Breathe Free: Seeking Asylum in Australia* (Sydney: Federation Press, 2007).

21 Julia Morris, "Violence and Extraction of a Human Commodity: From Phosphate to Refugees in the Republic of Nauru," *Extractive Industries and Society* 6, no. 4 (November 2019): 1122–33.

22 Hannah Appel, "Offshore Work: Oil, Modularity, and the How of Capitalism in Equatorial Guinea," *American Ethnologist* 39, no. 4 (November 2012): 692–709, accessed March 25, 2020, https://www.sv.uio.no/sai/english/research/projects/anthropos-and-the-material/Intranet/economic-practices/reading-group/texts/appel-offshore-work.pdf.

23 To destabilize the "asylum seeker" construct, which has become fixed with a great deal of ideological baggage over the years, including ideas of "welfare scrounging" and/or humanitarian suffering, I use the word "migrant" to refer to anyone making an asylum claim. Using the term "migrant" places emphasis on the human movement and immobility impediments that ultimately lie

behind people's claims, even as "the migrant" also comes with racialized and class-based connotations.

24 Malkki, "Refugees and Exile."

25 Alexander Betts, "The Refugee Regime Complex," *Refugee Survey Quarterly* 29, no. 1 (August 2010): 12–37.

26 Aihwa Ong, *Buddha Is Hiding: Refugees, Citizenship, the New America* (Berkeley: University of California Press, 2003).

27 Melanie Griffiths, "'Vile Liars and Truth Distorters': Truth, Trust and the Asylum System," *Anthropology Today* 28, no. 5 (October 2012): 8–12, accessed March 25, 2020, https://righttoremain.org.uk/vile-liars-and-truth-distorters-truth-trust-and-the-asylum-system.

28 Joel Robbins, "Beyond the Suffering Subject: Toward an Anthropology of the Good," *Journal of the Royal Anthropological Institute* 19, no. 3 (September 2013): 447–62.

29 Julia Morris, "Extractive Landscapes: The Case of the Jordan Refugee Compact," *Refuge: Canada's Journal on Refugees* 37, no. 2 (May 2020): 87–96.

30 Susanne Freidberg, "Cleaning Up Down South: Supermarkets, Ethical Trade, and African Horticulture," *Social and Cultural Geography* 4, no. 1 (March 2003): 27–43, accessed March 25, 2020, https://www.researchgate.net/publication/249005893_Cleaning_Up_Down_South_Supermarkets_Ethical_Trade_and_African_Horticulture.

31 Appel, "Offshore Work."

32 Gil Loescher and John A. Scanlan, *Calculated Kindness: Refugees and America's Half-Open Door, 1945 to the Present* (New York: Free Press, 1986).

33 Annelise Riles, "Anthropology, Human Rights, and Legal Knowledge: Culture in the Iron Cage," *American Anthropologist* 108, no. 1 (March 2006): 52–65, accessed March 31, 2020, https://scholarship.law.cornell.edu/cgi/viewcontent.cgi?article=1741&context=facpub.

34 Liisa H. Malkki, *Purity and Exile: Violence, Memory, and National Cosmology among Hutu Refugees in Tanzania* (Chicago: University of Chicago Press, 1995); Ong, *Buddha is Hiding*.

35 Matthew B. Sparke, "A Neoliberal Nexus: Economy, Security and the Biopolitics of Citizenship on the Border," *Political Geography* 25, no. 2 (February 2006): 151–80.

36 Margaret E. Keck and Kathryn Sikkink, *Activists beyond Borders: Advocacy Networks in International Politics* (Ithaca, NY: Cornell University Press, 1998).

37 Morris, "Violence and Extraction."

38 Miriam Ticktin, "What's Wrong with Innocence," Society for Cultural Anthropology, June 28, 2016, accessed March 25, 2020, https://culanth.org/fieldsights/whats-wrong-with-innocence.

39 Stephanie LeMenager, *Living Oil: Petroleum Culture in the American Century* (Oxford: Oxford University Press, 2014).

40 David Harvey, "Between Space and Time: Reflections on the Geographical Imagination," *Annals of the Association of American Geographers* 80, no. 3 (September 1990): 423, accessed March 25, 2020, http://appliedmapping.fiu.edu/readings/harvey2.pdf.

The Cost of Freedom

Marzena Zukowska

In 2018, Guinean asylum seeker Aboubacar Soumah was presented with an opportunity to get out of immigration detention under the United States immigration bail bond system. The opportunity came with a price tag of $15,000. With "only $59 to his name" and no network of friends or relatives in the country, Soumah was forced to remain in detention indefinitely.[1]

Soumah's case is not unique. As in the US criminal justice system, an immigration bond can be offered to a person in detention at the discretion of a judge as a way of securing their release while their case is pending. Officially, bonds are intended to guarantee that the person will attend future court hearings, and the bond amount paid to Immigration and Customs Enforcement (ICE) should be refunded once the case is resolved. Few judges grant bail, however, and those who do often set exorbitantly high amounts. Those able to pay can spend years trying to get their money back, if they manage to do so at all.[2] Those who cannot pay face an impossible choice: remain in jail (possibly indefinitely) awaiting backlogged courts to hear their case or go into significant debt to come up with the bail money.

This criminalization of poverty is part of a wider trend: the increasing extraction of profit from immigrant communities by corporate interests in the United States.[3] The ways that private companies profit from detaining immigrants are well established.[4] Less is known about the money being made from setting them "free."

The Bond System: Penalizing the Poor

Proponents of immigration bonds argue that they effectively function as collateral to ensure people do not abscond post-release. Immigrant rights activists contest this claim, citing the Department of Justice's own data that the majority of immigrants attend mandatory court hearings.[5] Criminal justice statistics reveal a similar trend. Washington, DC, nearly eliminated its criminal bail system in 1992. Assessing the impact of that ruling in 2016, DC Superior Court Judge Truman Morrison concluded: "There is no evidence you need money to get people back to court. It's irrational, ineffective, unsafe, and profoundly unfair."[6]

An increasing number of states are considering abolishing bail for criminal cases.[7] In the meantime, thousands of criminal court defendants are forced to accept guilty plea deals to secure release from jail, simply because they cannot afford bail. The overwhelming majority are Black people and other people of color.[8] Asylum seekers in immigration detention, who are unlikely to have much if any financial capital in the United States, often have no choice but to remain imprisoned—potentially for years—while their claim is considered.[9] The for-profit private detention estate gladly accepts $134 per person per day from the federal government to keep them there.[10]

Both the criminal and immigration incarceration systems are rooted in racism and function to financially exploit the already poor. Criminal court judges are at least required by law to consider a defendant's financial circumstances when setting a bail amount and to accept partial payments. No such requirements exist for immigration cases, with people usually expected to pay the full cash amount before release.[11] Although $1,500 is the the legal minimum for immigration bail, 40 percent of bonds were above $10,000 in 2018,[12] and some can be as high as $60,000.[13]

Jamila Hammami, founding executive director of Queer Detainee Empowerment Project (QDEP), which crowdsources bail money for those unable to pay, says a lack of clarity leads to wildly different amounts being set. Hammami explains, "There are constant issues with judges believing that ICE should determine bond amounts, with ICE stating that it's to the judges' discretion." Few actually get the "opportunity" to break the bank and post bail. While the number of bonds granted varies wildly by jurisdiction, on average one in four detained immigrants was given the option between 2014 and 2018.[14]

Immigration judges regularly deny bail to those they deem to be "a flight risk" or a "danger to public or national security"—language marked by racialized bias.[15] Historically, these characterizations have tended not to apply to people seeking asylum. In the current political context, however, all immigrants are criminalized. Government agencies have been actively discrediting the validity of asylum seekers via social media.[16] Meanwhile, they are erecting barriers to those legally eligible to claim asylum, rushing them through processing, limiting access to attorneys, and spreading misinformation.[17] Constructing asylum seekers as dangerous and criminal immigrants is a means to denying them their legal rights—and further reducing the likelihood that they will be offered bail.

For those who do manage to obtain bail, securing a refund can take years. If they do not have a lawyer or English proficiency, some never see their money again. As of July 31, 2018, ICE held a staggering $204 million in unreturned bond money.[18] This pot had increased by 40 percent since 2014, when the Obama administration imprisoned thousands of immigrant families fleeing violence, in large part due to US economic and political intervention in Central America.[19] These people, whom the US government refused to recognize as refugees despite United Nations directives naming them as such,[20] filled ICE coffers, while their rights, ostensibly guaranteed under international law, were ignored.

The subsequent government set out to extract profits from immigrants along a different track. "The Trump administration has successfully expanded how they criminalize immigrant communities so that everyone has become a target," explains Gabriela Marquez-Benitez, membership director at Detention Watch Network (DWN), a national coalition fighting to end immigrant detention. "While President Obama's administration solidified the detention infrastructure, the Trump administration has made it clear that they intend to expand on that infrastructure to detain upward of sixty thousand people per day as of fiscal year 2020."[21] The proposed increase is astronomical: in fiscal year 2019, ICE held a daily average of forty-two thousand people in detention. Most were housed in for-profit prisons run by corporations like GEO Group and CoreCivic.[22] Those companies' stock prices have skyrocketed since Trump signed his first set of executive orders on immigration in January 2017.[23]

To meet these new detention targets, the Trump administration began foreclosing access to bail. In April 2019, US Attorney General William Barr struck down a decades-old policy that granted asylum seekers the right to request bond, making asylum seekers wholly reliant on ICE to grant them parole (a waiver to leave detention, albeit under strict government supervision).[24] By that point, the frequency of parole granted to asylum seekers had already dropped to near zero in some ICE field offices, down from 92 percent in just five years.[25] Barr's ruling prompted an immediate challenge from immigrant rights groups. It was eventually overturned by a federal appeals court in March 2020, with the government ordered to resume bond hearings.[26]

Despite the discriminatory nature of immigration bonds, Barr's attempt to revoke them reveals that a perversely more profitable human disaster and further expansion of the indefinite detention regime remain possible. Currently, even the option of "voluntary departure"—the chance to effectively self-deport without being automatically barred from legally returning at a later date—carries a bond of at least $500. Given the high costs—both human and financial—of seeking asylum in the United States, it's understandable why some people make this "choice."

There Is No "Alternative"

Private detention and bond money are just two elements of this profiteering equation—monetizing surveillance is a notable other. "Not only is bond money going straight back to the pockets of Department of Homeland Security (DHS), but we're seeing a rise in groups that disguise themselves as nonprofits to gain from the bond system," said Marquez-Benitez.

Companies like Libre by Nexus (Libre) sell private services that get people out of detention—at a price. As immigration judges are more likely to grant bail when the individual is not deemed to be a "flight risk," Libre "helps" (the US federal government, its stakeholders, and ostensibly its clients) by offering to monitor a client's location through an electronic GPS ankle bracelet, while providing bail money loans. While cheaper for the state than housing someone in detention, the move shifts an increased cost burden onto immigrants and their communities. At 2019 rates, a Libre client pays an initial $620 service fee before "renting" an ankle monitor from the company for $420 per month. They also pay Libre a one-time, nonrefundable 20 percent premium on the bond amount covered by the loan.[27] Only if the client puts down more than 80 percent of the bond, and pays the rest in installments, will the ankle bracelet be removed. These devices require the wearer to spend hours next to an electric outlet to charge, and can cause sores, bruising, and occasional burning. For lost or damaged monitors, clients can incur costs of up to $3,950.[28]

Libre has seen its bottom line surge since 2013. Longer processing times for asylum claims and impossibly high bond amounts have forced more people to look to private companies for help getting out of detention.[29] Libre founder Mike Donovan calls the scheme "an opportunity" for immigrants. Meanwhile, human rights activists are battling against misleading contracts, predatory sales pitches, and the exorbitant fees that keep immigrants and their families in cycles of debt.[30] "I've even heard of cases where [a client] not paying back the money on time can mean Libre gets to press criminal charges," says Marquez-Benitez.

The company has faced a series of investigative probes, both from the federal Consumer Financial Protection Bureau and statewide from attorney generals in Virginia, New York, and Washington State.[31] Libre aggressively denies allegations of wrongdoing, even suing Buzzfeed for defamation in 2017.[32] While Buzzfeed was ultimately left unscathed by the legal action, investigations into Libre have since been closed with no illegal activity found.[33] Community groups, however, remain skeptical that Libre's $30 million annual revenue is anything more than rapacious profit from a system rooted in racism and xenophobia.[34]

For Marquez-Benitez, privatized bond loan and monitoring schemes are "an extension of detention, not an alternative," causing "trauma that extends to immigrants' communities and families." Marquez-Benitez is referring to the popular terminology used to describe outsourced services as an "alternative to detention" (ATD). The connotations of ATD have shifted over the past decade: once promoted by the United Nations High Commissioner for Refugees (UNHCR), activists, and community groups as a pathway to ending detention through the use of community-based, humane models, ATD has become yet another source of private gain.[35]

"I used to really believe in alternatives to detention, but when ICE co-opted the language, and began utilizing shackles as an 'alternative,' my view really shifted," says Hammami. "These ploys by the state are nothing more than another form of surveillance of migrant community members—they are absolute schemes."

Southwest Key, another major ATD player, markets its network of immigrant youth shelters as keeping young people safe until they can be reunited with family members. In 2018, the company held federal contracts valued at $626 million—and for over a decade has operated with little to no government oversight.[36] Activists have equated such detention facilities to "cages" and "internment camps" with abysmal health and safety conditions. Its Casa Padre location in Brownsville, Texas—a former Walmart— had been under immense scrutiny over sexual abuse allegations dating back to 2017.[37] In April 2019, Juan de León Gutiérrez, a sixteen-year-old boy from Guatemala, died while being held in Casa Padre.[38] He is one of six immigrant children known to have died in government custody over just six months between December 2018 and May 2019.[39] A lack of oversight, overcrowding, and abysmal conditions are characteristic of privately run immigration facilities, often including those regarded as ATD. Without public scrutiny, these conditions would go unchecked; only after the *New York Times* reported on Southwest Key's mismanagement in 2018 did the Justice Department open its own investigation.[40]

Reform and/or Revolution

Profit extraction from—and surveillance of—immigrant communities is not going away. For fiscal year 2020, the Trump administration demanded a massive funding increase for the DHS, in addition to its proposed $5 billion wall at the US-Mexico border.[41] The same corporate industry giants investing in detention and ATD programs are set to profit from this "border securitization," whatever form it eventually takes.[42] Within this daunting reality, immigrant rights activists continue to grapple with reformist versus revolutionary approaches to social justice organizing.

Legal organizations like the American Civil Liberties Union (ACLU)— in collaboration with grassroots groups—have litigated against the bond system on multiple fronts. In 2016, the ACLU Foundation of Southern California sued the federal government for setting "unreasonable bonds for detained immigrants, including asylum seekers, by failing to consider immigrants' financial resources or ability to pay."[43] Its goal was to reform immigration bail in line with the federal criminal justice bond system, which safeguards against people remaining in jail indefinitely because of poverty. In 2018, the ACLU sued ICE and the DHS for issuing blanket parole denial to asylum seekers,[44] then the following year mounted a legal challenge to the Trump administration's decision to detain asylum seekers indefinitely without bond.[45] While successful in their efforts to protect the rights of thousands of immigrants currently and yet to be detained, bringing these cases has put huge strain on ACLU and its partners' resources.

Meanwhile, grassroots organizations like QDEP use crowdfunding—pooling money from a large number of small donations—to raise bonds for people without sufficient resources or wealthy personal connections. "It takes an entire community to come together and raise a bond for someone," explains Hammami. "Supporting one another's campaigns through digital outreach and social media is imperative. Bonds aren't going away any time soon, so it's important for it to be a collaborative effort across the community." To date, QDEP has raised tens of thousands of dollars this way, focusing on supporting queer and trans immigrants.[46] Other long-standing nonprofits like the National Bail Fund Network—which has traditionally focused on raising criminal justice system bonds—are creatively expanding their funding pools to either partially or fully cover immigration bond costs. This eases the burden of fundraising on families and individuals, helping them to avoid schemes like Libre by Nexus.

Many organizers, however, agree that community bail-raising is a temporary intervention not a long-term solution. "The detention system is clearly designed where, unfortunately, every time we raise funds for a family member, we know we are providing the same system with money for more detention," says Marquez-Benitez. Hammami concurs, explaining the importance of a multipronged activism: "We have to recognize that if we don't get a person out of immigration prison, they will suffer, so we must feed into the system. But organizing against immigration prisons and bond is also an imperative piece of the work. It's a challenge to juggle the two but absolutely paramount to do so." Hammami, a resolute abolitionist, advocates a "reform-to-revolution" approach.

Revolutionary change—abolishing the current system and its sustaining ideology of carceral punishment—will require many strategies, including cutting off the monetary bloodline of the prison industrial complex and targeting institutions with links to the prison industry. Both QDEP and DWN are part of the Prison Industry Divestment Movement, working alongside other multiracial organizing groups like the Black Alliance for Just Immigration and Freedom to Thrive.[47] To date, the campaign has successfully pressured universities, churches, philanthropic institutions, and local governments to divest hundreds of millions of dollars from corporations such as GEO Group and CoreCivic.[48] This money is often invested through banks like Wells Fargo and BlackRock, unbeknown to account holders. Financial institutions' investment portfolios include over one million shares in private prison corporations—a 60 percent stake in the industry.[49] Encouraging institutions and individuals to move their money can lead to large-scale divestment—meaning less access to capital, fewer contracts, weaker lobbying power for these corporations, and, ultimately, less incentive to build prisons.

Without radical social change, corporate interests will continue to find ways to monetize every aspect of the immigration process. As both Hammami and Marquez-Benitez argue, change requires dismantling the shared physical infrastructure of and the ideological justification for detention centers and jails. Without interrogating how xenophobia, racism, anti-Black, and anti-poor sentiments drive the lucrative activity of incarceration—one that at its core exploits those already living at the economic margins—"freedom" will continue to come with a price tag.

Marzena Zukowska is a London-based writer, researcher, and community organizer. She cofounded Polish Migrants Organise for Change (POMOC) and is on the leadership team of the Radical Communicators Network. Born in Poland, she grew up undocumented in the United States.

Notes

1   Mallory Moench, "Too Poor to Be Free: High Bond Keeps Asylum-Seekers Behind Bars," WNYC News, February 7, 2018, accessed March 25, 2020, https://www.wnyc.org/story/too-poor-be-free-high-bond-keeps-asylum-seekers-behind-bars.

2   Meagan Flynn, "ICE Is Holding $204 Million in Bond Money, and Some Immigrants Might Never Get It Back," *Washington Post*, April 26, 2019, accessed March 25, 2020, https://www.washingtonpost.com/immigration/ice-is-holding-204-million-in-bond-money-and-some-immigrants-might-never-get-it-back/2019/04/26/dcaa69a0-5709-11e9-9136-f8e636f1f6df_story.html.

3   Denise Gilman and Luis A. Romero, "Immigration Detention, Inc.," *Journal on Migration and Human Society* 6, no. 2 (January 2018): 145–147, accessed March 25, 2020, https://journals.sagepub.com/doi/full/10.1177/2311502418765414.

4   See Louise Tassin, "From Paris to Lampedusa: The New Business of Migrant Detention in Europe," this volume, 79–93; Mark Akkerman, "The Military and Security Industry: Promoting Europe's Refugee Regime," this volume, 149–63.

5   John Kruzel, "Majority of Undocumented Immigrants Show Up for Court, Data Shows," PolitiFact, June 26, 2018, accessed March 25, 2020, https://www.politifact.com/punditfact/statements/2018/jun/26/wolf-blitzer/majority-undocumented-immigrants-show-court-data-s.

6   Ann E. Marimow, "When It Comes to Pretrial Release, Few Other Jurisdictions Do It D.C.'s Way," *Washington Post*, July 4, 2016, accessed March 25, 2020, https://wapo.st/2RY58Xe.

7   Marimow, "When It Comes to Pretrial Release."

8   Sari Aviv, "Re-making Bail," CBS News, June 2, 2019, accessed March 25, 2020, https://www.cbsnews.com/news/re-making-bail.

9   Gaby Del Valle, "Most Criminal Cases End in Plea Bargains, Not Trials," Outline, August 7, 2017, accessed March 25, 2020, https://theoutline.com/post/2066/most-criminal-cases-end-in-plea-bargains-not-trials.

10 Department of Homeland Security and US Immigration Customs and Enforcement, *Budget Overview: Fiscal Year 2018*, ICE-14, accessed March 25, 2020, https://www.dhs.gov/sites/default/files/publications/ICE%20FY18%20Budget.pdf.

11 Moench, "Too Poor to Be Free."

12 "Three-Fold Difference in Immigration Bond Amounts by Court Location," TRACImmigration, accessed March 25, 2020, https://trac.syr.edu/immigration/reports/519.

13 Jamila Hammami, email correspondence, April 14, 2019.

14 Especially in a rapidly changing policy climate, with records split between multiple agencies and often not tracked at all, it is incredibly difficult to ascertain precise numbers; see "Three-fold Difference in Immigration Bond Amounts by Court Location."

15 Alejandro Fernández Sanabria, Inti Pachezo, and Antonio Cucho, "Costly Bonds: For Undocumented Immigrants, Bail Depends on a Judge's Subjectivity," UnivisionNEWS, February 28, 2018, accessed March 25, 2020, https://www.univision.com/univision-news/immigration/costly-bonds-for-undocumented-immigrants-freedom-depends-on-a-judges-subjectivity; Spencer Ackerman, "TSA Screening Program Risks Racial Profiling Amid Shaky Science—Study," *Guardian*, February 8, 2017, accessed March 25, 2020, https://www.theguardian.com/us-news/2017/feb/08/tsa-screening-racial-religious-profiling-aclu-study.

16 Kennji Kizuka (@KennjiKizuka), "This notice is to inform you that your 'fact sheet' on asylum seekers has been rejected for the reasons below," Twitter, May 13, 2019, accessed March 25, 2020, https://twitter.com/KennjiKizuka/status/1127946771060133888.

17 Samantha Balaban, Sophia Alvarez Boyd, and Lulu Garcia-Navarro, "Without a Lawyer, Asylum-Seekers Struggle with Confusing Legal Processes," NPR, February 25, 2018, accessed March 25, 2020, https://www.npr.org/2018/02/25/588646667/without-a-lawyer-asylum-seekers-struggle-with-confusing-legal-processes.

18 Flynn, "ICE Is Holding $204 Million in Bond Money."

19 Cristina Parker, Judy Greene, Bob Libal, and Alexis Mazón, *For-Profit Family Detention: Meet the Private Prison Corporations Making Millions by Locking Up Refugee Families* (Austin, TX: Grassroots Leadership/Justice Strategies, 2014), accessed March 25, 2020, https://grassrootsleadership.org/sites/default/files/uploads/For-Profit%20Family%20Detention.pdf.

20 United Nations High Commissioner for Refugees, *Women on the Run: First-Hand Accounts of Refugees Fleeing El Salvador, Guatemala, Honduras, and Mexico* (Geneva: UNHCR, 2015), accessed March 25, 2020, https://www.unhcr.org/5630f24c6.html.

21 Gabriela Marquez-Benitez, phone interview, April 23, 2019; memo referenced by Marquez-Benitez: *A Budget for a Better America: Promises Kept. Taxpayers First: Fiscal Year 2020 Budget of the U.S. Government* (Washington, DC: US Government Publishing Office, 2019), accessed March 25, 2020, https://www.whitehouse.gov/wp-content/uploads/2019/03/budget-fy2020.pdf.

22 Geneva Sands, "This Year Saw the Most People in Immigration Detention Since 2001," CNN, November 12, 2018, accessed March 25, 2020, https://www.cnn.com/2018/11/12/politics/ice-detention/index.html.

23 Zusha Elinson, "Trump's Immigrant-Detention Plans Benefit Private Prison Operators," *Wall Street Journal*, July 2, 2018, accessed March 25, 2020, https://www.wsj.com/articles/trumps-immigrant-detention-plans-benefit-these-companies-1530523800.

24 Kristina Cooke, "Rights Groups Sue Over U.S. Decision to Hold Asylum Seekers without Bond," Reuters, May 2, 2019, accessed March 25, 2020, https://www.reuters.com/article/us-usa-immigration-bond/rights-groups-sue-over-us-decision-to-hold-asylum-seekers-without-bond-idUSKCN1S9047.

25 American Civil Liberties Union, Center for Gender & Refugee Studies, and Human Rights First, "Practice Advisory: *Damus v. Nielsen* Parole of Arriving Asylum Seekers Who Have Passed Credible Fear," ACLU, July 30, 2018, accessed March 25, 2020, https://www.aclu.org/legal-document/damus-parole-advisory.

26 Priscilla Alvarez and Geneva Sand, "Appeals Court Blocks Administration Policy Denying Bond to Asylum Seekers," CNN, March 27, 2020, accessed April 22, 2020, https://edition.cnn.com/2020/03/27/politics/appeals-court-blocks-policy-bond-asylum-seekers/index.html.

27 Adolfo Flores, "Immigrants Desperate to Get Out of U.S. Detention Can Get Trapped by Debt," Buzzfeed News, July 23, 2016, accessed March 25, 2020, https://www.buzzfeednews.com/article/adolfoflores/immigrant-detainees-and-bail-bond-terms.

28 Steve Fisher, "Getting Immigrants Out of Detention Is Very Profitable," *Mother Jones*, September–October 2016, accessed March 25, 2020, https://www.motherjones.com/politics/2016/09/immigration-detainees-bond-ankle-monitors-libre.

29 Ibid.

30 Flores, "Immigrants Desperate to Get Out of U.S. Detention Can Get Trapped by Debt."

31 Michael E. Miller, "Firm Accused of Preying on Detained Immigrants Faces Widening Investigations," *Washington Post*, April 21, 2018, https://www.washingtonpost.com/local/investigations-expand-into-company-accused-of-preying-on-detained-immigrants/2018/04/20/e31329d8-44a6-11e8-8569-26fda6b404c7_story.html.

32 Tim Ryan, "Immigration Bond Company Sues BuzzFeed for $5 Million," *Courthouse News Service*, July 25, 2017, accessed March 25, 2020, https://www.courthousenews.com/immigration-bond-company-sues-buzzfeed-5-million.

33 Brad Kutner, "Buzzfeed a Step Closer to Defeating Bail Company's Defamation Claim," *Courthouse News Service*, May 17, 2018, accessed March 25, 2020,

https://www.courthousenews.com/judge-takes-issue-with-bail-companys-buzzfeed-defamation-claim.

34 Michael E. Miller, "This Company Is Making Millions from America's Broken Immigration System," *Washington Post*, March 9, 2017, https://wapo.st/3aw5qM4.

35 "Global Roundtable on Alternatives to Detention of Asylum-Seekers, Refugees, Migrants and Stateless Persons," UNHCR, May 11–12, 2011, accessed March 25, 2020, https://www.unhcr.org/protection/expert/536a00576/global-roundtable-alternatives-detention-asylum-seekers-refugees-migrants.html.

36 Kim Barker and Nicholas Kulish, "Inquiry into Migrant Shelters Poses Dilemma: What Happens to the Children?" *New York Times*, January 5, 2019, accessed March 25, 2020, https://www.nytimes.com/2019/01/05/us/southwest-key-migrant-shelters.html.

37 Jess Morales Rocketto (@JessLivMo), "American detention centers for migrant families are internment camps," Twitter, June 7, 2019, accessed March 25, 2020 https://twitter.com/JessLivMo/status/1137033318585786370.

38 Hamed Aleaziz and Adolfo Flores, "A 16-Year-Old Unaccompanied Immigrant Boy Has Died in US Government Custody," Buzzfeed News, May 3, 2019, accessed March 25, 2020, https://www.buzzfeednews.com/article/hamedaleaziz/unaccompanied-immigrant-boy-dies-us-custody.

39 Patricia Sulbarán Lovera, "How Did Six Migrant Children Die on the US Border?" BBC News, May 23, 2019, accessed March 25, 2020, https://www.bbc.com/news/world-us-canada-48346228.

40 Barker and Kulish, "Inquiry into Migrant Shelters Poses Dilemma."

41 *A Budget for a Better America.*

42 Jaden Urbi, "Here's Who's Making Money from Immigration Enforcement," CNBC, June 29, 2018, accessed March 25, 2020, https://www.cnbc.com/2018/06/28/companies-profiting-immigration-enforcement-private-sector-prison-tech.html.

43 "Civil Rights Groups Sue the Federal Government Seeking Bond Reform in Immigration System," ACLU of Southern California, April 6, 2016, accessed March 25, 2020, https://www.aclusocal.org/en/press-releases/civil-rights-groups-sue-federal-government-seeking-bond-reform-immigration-system.

44 "US Judge Orders Quicker Bond Hearings for Asylum Seekers," Associated Press, April 5, 2019, accessed March 25, 2020, https://www.apnews.com/e97c6 2318dc0423aab05eb5a0a6fe21b.

45 Cooke, "Rights Groups Sue over U.S. Decision."

46 "Trans/Queer Migrant Freedom Bond Fund," Queer Detainee Empowerment Project, accessed March 25, 2020, http://www.qdep.org/tqmff.

47 "Campaign Partners," Prison Industry Divestment Movement, accessed March 25, 2020, https://prisondivest.com/home/campaign-partners.

48 Ibid.

49 "Million Shares Club," Prison Industry Divestment Movement, accessed March 25, 2020, https://prisondivest.com/why-divestment/million-shares-club.

Making Profits in Hostile Environments: Asylum Accommodation Markets in the UK and Ireland

John Grayson

The UK Immigration and Asylum Act 1999 defined reception policies for asylum seekers that remain in place up to the present day. The act introduced a new regime of detention centers and the dispersal of housing for asylum seekers from cities to declining and often hostile "rust belt" areas across the country. The new policies also deprived asylum seekers of any existing tenants' rights under UK common law or legislation. The introduction of the Direct Provision (DP) system in Ireland, in 2000, was based on the then-new UK model. DP similarly dispersed asylum seekers, including whole families, to remote, often racist, rural and coastal areas, placing them in disused holiday camps, hotels, and convents. Liz Fekete of the UK Institute for Race Relations described the processes in both countries as "the dispersal of xenophobia."[1]

Since then, reception policies in both the UK and Ireland have been designed to "deter" inflows of asylum seekers and have been framed within discourses that demonize and marginalize refugees as "bogus asylum seekers,"[2] who take advantage of an overly generous, "soft touch" state.[3] In September 2009, for example, a senior UK Home Office civil servant was asked by the chair of the Parliamentary Home Affairs Committee: "Why are children detained under the immigration system, they have not done anything wrong, have they?" The civil servant replied that ending the detention of children "would act as a significant magnet and pull to families from abroad."[4] By 2012, then UK Home Secretary Theresa May openly pledged to introduce a "hostile reception" for migrants and refugees.[5] These infamous words prefigured a calculated—and heavily

racialized—set of policies that further demonized immigrants, while subjecting thousands of people to raids, indefinite detention, the denial of
rights and services, and unlawful deportations during May's tenures as
home secretary and later prime minister.[6]

A similar rhetoric—that intolerable living conditions will deter
asylum seekers from coming to the UK and Ireland—appears to have
informed the governments' shared attitude toward housing those not
held in detention. My research and field work in the UK (2012–2017)
and in Ireland (2016) shed light on the distinctive place of housing and
accommodation provision to asylum seekers in the deterrent reception policies of the two nations. These case studies are indicative of the
European Migration Industrial Complex[7]—in particular the neoliberal
asylum markets expanding across Northern Europe.[8] The outsourcing
and privatization of asylum accommodation is now firmly embedded in
the neoliberal economies of the UK and Ireland. While asylum seekers are
increasingly made destitute, corporate coffers continue to swell.

Poor Housing and Bare Subsistence

As of 2018, asylum seekers in the UK are provided with furnished housing
and £5.40 (US$6.90) a day for food, clothing, transport, and all other
essentials. In Ireland, where accommodation and meals are provided in
DP centers, the weekly allowance for adults was fixed in 2000 at €19.10
(approximately US$21.80) and remained unchanged for seventeen years.
In August 2017, it increased by just €2.50 (approximately US$2.85). In both
the UK and Ireland, asylum seekers are banned from working to support
themselves, except in very limited cases. In the UK, asylum seekers are
regularly imprisoned if caught working with forged or incorrect documents.[9] These policies force many into the paradoxical position of being
wholly reliant on support from governments determined to provide only
a deeply unappealing quality of service. The poor condition of UK housing
for asylum seekers and of DP centers in Ireland has been extensively documented. Unsurprisingly, evidence presented in Westminster parliamentary inquiries, in Irish Oireachtas (parliamentary) committees, and in
debates in the Dáil (Irish assembly) have all been met with scant concern.

Ireland's Direct Provision, Two Decades On

The Irish asylum market, created in 2000, was the first European example
of state-funded outsourcing of all asylum accommodation. As of 2017,

according to the *Irish Times,* "Direct Provision is a multimillion-euro industry."[10] DP centers house around 4,300 asylum seekers, almost half of whom are under eighteen.[11] In 2016, the Irish government paid private contractors €60.3 million (approximately US$68.7 million) to provide catering to the centers, including €5 million (approximately US$5.7 million) to US food corporation Aramark, which is infamous for labor abuses,[12] as well as €7 million (approximately US$8 million) to the Canadian corporation East Coast Catering.[13]

There is no limit to the length of time families can be forced to live in DP centers as they await a case decision. Decade-long stays are not uncommon. In 2016, Naomi, an accountant from Nigeria and volunteer worker in the Johnston Marina DP center in Tralee, Ireland, told me: "One family from Nigeria, with four children, had been in the center for nine years; children had been born here and attended local schools." Despite this, Naomi explained, "The government said that they 'had shown little evidence of making efforts to integrate into local community life.'" The family was deported.

No cooking is allowed in the vast majority of DP centers, with food provided by catering corporations. Christine, from Zimbabwe, told me of her seven years in the Tralee DP center: "We are not allowed to cook or even do our own washing. My clothes are ruined in the industrial washers they use in there. I am hungry most of the time. I am vegetarian, but they will not cook me food I can eat." In 2015, the Irish government commissioned a survey of 110 children who had lived in DP centers. Survey respondents described the food as "always the same" and "has no taste," with many expressing the wish that their mothers could cook for them.[14]

Hostility and Profitability in UK Asylum Seeker Housing

In 2012, UK asylum housing—provided for around forty thousand asylum seekers awaiting outcomes of their claims—was outsourced on a five-year, £1.7 billion (approximately US$2.2 billion) Home Office Commercial and Operational Managers Procuring Asylum Support Services (COMPASS) contract. The contracts were awarded to international security companies G4S and Serco and to a smaller security company, Reliance. G4S is the largest private security company in the world, with around six hundred thousand employees.

Five years of COMPASS asylum housing contracts have rewarded private companies at huge emotional and physical cost to asylum seekers.

The UK Home Affairs Select Committee report on Asylum Accommodation, published in January 2017, found multiple cases of "children living with infestations of mice, rats or bed bugs, lack of health care for pregnant women" in G4S and Serco contracted housing.[15] My own research—conducted with lone mothers and their young children in G4S-contracted "mother and baby hostels" from 2012 to 2017 in northern England—revealed similarly unhealthy and dangerous properties.[16]

In October 2012, for example, I visited a G4S-run hostel in Stockton-on-Tees that housed around thirty lone mothers with children under three years old. In 2016, Jomast, the property development company that provided the hostel to G4S, described it as "an exemplary product" in their portfolio. The women I interviewed there took a different view, describing their rooms as "cells," with no floor space for their children to play. One resident, Diane, told me, "I was dumped in [the hostel] weeks after giving birth." Another, Louise, said, "They simply want to make profits out of us. They show us no respect. We are just numbers for them in making a profit." Despite repeated complaints and reported failings, the hostel was subsequently expanded to provide around ninety places for mothers and toddlers.

In February 2015, I visited a large suburban villa in Leeds that had been turned into asylum seeker housing after sitting abandoned for years. It was in such poor condition that to make it habitable the new residents—twelve mothers with young babies—had to clean the place themselves upon their arrival, including buying cleaning materials. Currently, G4S receives £8.42 per night, per resident—around £70,000 (approximately US$92,000) a year—for running the building. The same company is paid £51,600 (approximately US$67,000) per year to maintain another notorious hostel in Halifax, which was referred to as "death trap" by neighbors when I visited in 2017. At that time, the residence housed six families with nine children between them, most of whom were babies and toddlers. Flooding was a recurrent problem—water was streaming through light sockets on my visit in June 2017. The building's fire alarms were defective and escape routes were blocked by strollers, as there was nowhere else to store them.

Asylum "Management": A Global Industry
The market for asylum seeker "management" shows no sign of abating—and industry leaders are well-placed to ensure the future growth of the sector internationally, within broader neoliberal trends of public service

privatization. Rupert Soames, CEO of Serco (and grandson of Winston Churchill), told BBC Radio in June 2015 that new global outsourcing markets, "make Britain now to public service provision what Silicon Valley is to IT."[17]

Indeed, in the first three months of 2016 alone, 65 percent of all new UK public sector contracts—worth a combined £1.35 billion (approximately US$1.8 billion)—were outsourced to private companies. These companies provide well-paid positions to former politicians and other prominent public figures. In 2009, for example, John Reid, a former Labour Party home secretary and defence secretary, took a £45,000-a-year (approximately US$70,650) "consultancy" role at G4S, while still a serving member of parliament.[18] High-profile G4S board members have included Lord Condon, former commissioner of the London Metropolitan Police, and Adam Crozier, head of Independent Television. Company and subsidiary shareholders are doing well; in 2017, Stuart Monk, owner of G4S contractor Jomast, had a reported net worth of £185 million (approximately US$240 million).[19]

As housing and service providers race to the bottom globally, contracts and ownerships—and therefore profits and liabilities—regularly change hands. Asylum seekers suffer the consequences of cost-cutting measures (with increasingly murky recourse to justice), while vulture and private equity funds gain. For example, the Westbourne DP center in Limerick, Ireland, was owned and run from 2001 to 2014 by property development company Kenny Commercial Holdings. When Kenny went into receivership in 2010, its unpaid loans were taken over by the Irish government's National Asset Management Agency (NAMA)—though remarkably the government's Reception and Integration Agency continued to tender contracts for housing asylum seekers in the Westbourne Centre, effectively to Kenny Commercial Holdings, for six more years. The Kenny loans were eventually sold by NAMA, in July 2016, to OCM EmRu Debtco DAC, a subsidiary of Oaktree Capital Management—a multibillion dollar "vulture fund" that acquires "distressed assets" to sell at a profit. Shortly after the Irish government handed over the center, it was shut down due to health and safety concerns, following repeated failures to carry out urgent maintenance work. Over sixty asylum seekers received notices of eviction.[20]

The Swiss company ORS Service—which owns state contracts for reception centers and asylum camps in Switzerland, Austria, and Germany—is another prime example. ORS has been sold to private equity companies three times since 2005, including to London-based private equity firm Equistone Partners Europe Ltd., in 2013, for an undisclosed sum. Equistone, part of Barclays Bank until 2011, currently controls two buyout funds worth close to US$4 billion. Its 2013 annual report touted its acquisition of asylum seeker management services as a new opportunity with "promising organic and acquisitive growth potential."[21] Its 2014 publication noted further investments in the area, reporting: "The business has won several new mandates and has penetrated the market further."[22]

Between 2007 and 2014, ORS revenues rose threefold, from US$33 million to US$99 million. When the so-called European refugee crisis took hold in 2014, ORS was primed to take on more lucrative contracts.[23] Following a damning UN report that described conditions at one ORS facility as "beneath human dignity," independent researcher Antony Loewenstein concluded: "[A] growing number of corporations [are] seeing financial opportunity in the most vulnerable people. Refugees become numbers to be processed; the profit motive is paramount in the minds of many multinationals. . . . ORS Service has thrived on Europe's inability to cope with the refugee crisis."[24]

Resistance to the Asylum Market

Asylum seekers have not passively accepted the commodification of housing provision. Coalitional and community-based groups campaign continuously against marketization of services, including Movement of Asylum Seekers in Ireland (MASI) and my own organization, the South Yorkshire Migration and Asylum Action Group (SYMAAG). Researching and documenting conditions and naming and shaming unscrupulous companies are among our core tactics. In January 2018, the UK Home Office announced that G4S—one of the world's major outsourced security companies—had lost all of its bids to provide asylum housing contracts under the new ten-year £4 billion (approximately US$5.3 billion) scheme set to launch in 2019. Asylum tenants and campaigning organizations celebrated the victory and are determined to continue the fight.

John Grayson is an adult educator and independent activist researcher with South Yorkshire Migration and Asylum Action Group (SYMAAG), a British asylum rights organization. He is based in Barnsley, UK, and writes for openDemocracy (www.opendemocracy.net) and the Institute of Race Relations News Service (www.irr.org.uk).

Notes

1   Liz Fekete, "The Dispersal of Xenophobia," Institute of Race Relations News Service, August 16, 2000, accessed March 25, 2020, http://www.irr.org.uk/news/the-dispersal-of-xenophobia-a-new-report-from-the-irr.

2   Imogen Tyler, *Revolting Subjects: Social Abjection and Resistance in Neoliberal Britain* (London: Zed Books, 2013).

3   This terminology has been popular especially in the right-wing press; see, e.g., Tom Kelly, "Soft-Touch Britain, the Asylum Seeker Capital of Europe," *Daily Mail*, June 22, 2012, accessed March 25, 2020, https://www.dailymail.co.uk/news/article-2166738/Soft-touch-Britain-asylum-seeker-capital-Europe-Welet-year.html.

4   Dave Wood, "Evidence of Dave Wood to UK Parliamentary Home Affairs Select Committee, September 16, 2009, Examination of Witnesses (Questions 24–39)," accessed March 25, 2020, https://publications.parliament.uk/pa/cm200809/cmselect/cmhaff/970/09091604.htm.

5   James Kirkup and Robert Winnett, "Theresa May Interview: 'We're Going to Give Illegal Migrants a Really Hostile Reception,'" *Telegraph*, May 25, 2012, accessed March 25, 2020, http://www.telegraph.co.uk/news/uknews/immigration/9291483/Theresa-May-interview-Were-going-to-give-illegal-migrants-a-really-hostile-reception.html.

6   "A Guide to the Hostile Environment: The Border Controls Dividing Our Communities—and How We Can Bring Them Down," Liberty, April 2018, accessed March 31, 2020, https://www.libertyhumanrights.org.uk/issue/report-a-guide-to-the-hostile-environment; Jamie Grierson, "Hostile Environment: Anatomy of a Policy Disaster," *Guardian*, August 27, 2018, accessed March 25, 2020, https://www.theguardian.com/uk-news/2018/aug/27/hostile-environment-anatomy-of-a-policy-disaster.

7   Daniel Trilling, "Europe's Migration Industrial Complex," *Foreign Policy*, June 18, 2015, accessed March 25, 2020, http://foreignpolicy.com/2015/06/18/immigration-privatization-britain-italy-syria.

8   Georg Menz, "The Neo-Liberal State and the Growth of the Migration Industry," in Thomas Gammeltoft-Hansen and Ninna Nyberg Sørensen, eds., *The Migration Industry and the Commercialization of International Migration*, (London: Routledge, 2013), 108–27; John Grayson, "The Corporate Greed of Strangers," Institute of Race Relations News Service, February 25, 2015, accessed March 25, 2020, http://www.irr.org.uk/news/the-corporate-greed-of-strangers; also see Mark Akkerman, "The Military and Security Industry: Promoting Europe's Refugee Regime," this volume, 149–63.

9   See, e.g., Evening Standard Staff Writer, "Asylum Seeker on Fake Passport Worked for Immigration Service for a Year," *Evening Standard*, January 18, 2008, accessed March 25, 2020, https://www.standard.co.uk/news/asylum-seeker-on-fake-passport-worked-for-immigration-service-for-a-year-6682589.html; Coventry Live, "Asylum Seeker Jailed Over False ID," *Coventry Telegraph*, April 9, 2008, accessed March 25, 2020, https://www.coventrytelegraph.net/news/coventry-news/asylum-seeker-jailed-over-fake-3098869; Neil Atkinson, "Asylum Seeker Who Used Fake Passport to Be Deported After

Jail Sentence," *Huddersfield Examiner*, August 13, 2015, accessed March 25, 2020, https://www.examinerlive.co.uk/news/west-yorkshire-news/asylum-seeker-who-used-fake-9852227.

10 Una Mullally, "Who Benefits from the System of Direct Provision?" *Irish Times*, February 8, 2016, accessed March 25, 2020, https://www.irishtimes.com/opinion/una-mullally-who-benefits-from-the-system-of-direct-provision-1.2525821.

11 Statistics on Ireland are drawn from Annual Reports of the Reception and Integration Agency, part of the Ministry of Justice that is responsible for contracts and payments for DP centers.

12 Philip Mattera, "Aramark," First Corporate Research Project, last updated August 19, 2016, accessed March 25, 2020, https://www.corp-research.org/aramark.

13 Gordon Deegan, "State Paid €43.5m to Eight Direct Provision Operators in 2016," *Irish Times*, February 23, 2017, accessed March 25, 2020, https://www.irishtimes.com/news/social-affairs/state-paid-43-5m-to-eight-direct-provision-operators-in-2016-1.2987004.

14 Department of Children and Youth Affairs, *Report of DCYA Consultations with Children and Young People Living in Direct Provision*" (Dublin: DCYA, 2015), accessed March 26, 2020, https://bit.ly/34OIlyG. The findings of the survey were not published until the *Irish Times* submitted a FOI request in July 2017.

15 UK Home Affairs Committee, "Asylum Accommodation Is a Disgrace," January 31, 2017, accessed March 25, 2020, https://bit.ly/3dGp6PH.

16 See, e.g., John Grayson, "G4S, Jomast Stockton Hostel and the Mother-and-Baby-Market," October 24, 2012, accessed March 26, 2020, http://www.irr.org.uk/news/g4s-jomast-stockton-hostel-and-the-mother-and-baby-market; John Grayson, "One Bath for 12 Women and 11 Babies: UK Asylum Housing by G4S," openDemocracy, March 7, 2015, accessed March 26, 2020, https://www.opendemocracy.net/en/shine-a-light/one-bath-for-12-women-and-11-babies-uk-asylum-housing-by-g4s; John Grayson, "'How Do We Get Out if There's a Fire?' In Yorkshire, G4S Tenants Live in Fear," openDemocracy, June 26, 2017, accessed March 26, 2020, https://www.opendemocracy.net/shinelight/john-grayson/how-do-we-get-out-if-there-s-fire-in-yorkshire-g4s-tenants-live. Detailed references in activist research articles can be found at https://www.opendemocracy.net/author/john-grayson and at www.irr.org.uk, both accessed March 26, 2020.

17 "Outsourcing," BBC Radio 4: The Bottom Line, June 18, 2015, accessed March 26, 2020, https://www.bbc.co.uk/programmes/b05zyyhx.

18 Rajeev Syal, "Ex-Home Secretary Reid has Private Security Job," *Guardian*, January 11, 2009, accessed March 26, 2020, https://www.theguardian.com/politics/2009/jan/11/john-reid-g4s.

19 "The Sunday Times Rich List 2017: The Richest in the Northeast," *Sunday Times*, May 5, 2017, accessed March 26, 2020, https://www.thetimes.co.uk/article/the-sunday-times-rich-list-2017-the-richest-in-the-northeast-lb0ssh8l3.

20 David Raleigh, "Direct Provision Centre Shut Over 'Safety Fears' Was Paid €12.7 Million by the State," *Journal*, January 27, 2017, accessed March 26, 2020, https://www.thejournal.ie/direct-provision-centre-closed-3206637-Jan2017.

21 *Equistone: 2013 Annual Review* (London: Equistone, 2013), 26, accessed March 26, 2020, https://www.equistonepe.com/website/sites/EN/uploads/documents/annualreviews/2013-Equistone-Annual-Review.pdf.

22 *Equistone: 2014 Annual Review* (London: Equistone, 2014), 10–11, accessed March 26, 2020, https://www.equistonepe.com/website/sites/EN/uploads/documents/annualreviews/2014-Equistone-Annual-Review.pdf.

23 Anton Troianovski, Manuela Mesco, and Simon Clark, "The Growth of Refugee Inc. In Europe, Small Shopkeepers to Private Equity Find Ways to Profit from Migrant Flood," *Wall Street Journal*, September 15, 2015, accessed March 26, 2020, https://www.wsj.com/articles/in-european-refugee-crisis-an-industry-evolves-1442252165.

24 Antony Loewenstein, "How Private Companies Are Exploiting the Refugee Crisis for Profit," *Independent*, October 23 2015, accessed March 26, 2020, https://www.independent.co.uk/voices/how-companies-have-been-exploiting-the-refugee-crisis-for-profit-a6706587.html.

An "Expert" View of the Asylum Industry

Adrienne Pine

For the past fifteen years, I have worked in US federal asylum courts as a country conditions expert for Honduran asylum seekers. In this chapter, I draw on two similar cases with different outcomes—those of José López (a pseudonym) and Jenny Artola. I did not serve as an expert in either of these specific cases, so I am not bound by confidentiality rules. I was acquainted with both José and Jenny before they left Honduras, and I followed their cases through my networks. With their consent, I use their cases here to help illustrate some of the many painful internal contradictions of state-based asylum practice framed by capitalist and imperialist logics that I have seen in my capacity as "expert."

José and Jenny

I interviewed José, and we worked together to summarize the story of his asylum, which is published in this volume.[1] José is a highly educated, English-speaking Honduran political activist, small business owner, and gay man, who came to the United States seeking safety after being violently attacked and threatened. The confusing and contradictory legal advice he received from immigration-focused nonprofits and his difficulty finding affordable legal help led him to make the decision to file an asylum claim on his own.

José risked his life to briefly return to Honduras to put his legal and business affairs in order, not realizing that doing so would harm his case, and was jailed in the infamous Atlanta City Detention Center upon his return. After three months, José made the painful decision to withdraw his asylum case and accept deportation to Honduras. He did this despite presenting what his immigration court judge described as "the best pro se application he had seen in his seventeen years working on immigration cases,"[2] because he feared the jail's violence even more than he feared Honduras. Shortly after his humiliating deportation, he left for Barcelona, where he again sought asylum. He lost his business and lives with crippling debt as a result of the experience, and for years carried the stigma of being an asylum seeker.

I met Jenny Artola once in 2014 with her mom, my friend Sandra Zambrano, shortly after Jenny had been kidnapped and tortured in retaliation for Sandra's activism. Her mother had been fighting against the institutionalized homophobic and transphobic violence that increased dramatically following the 2009 US-supported coup. I remember Jenny as a bored but good-humored young teenager, sighing loudly (prompting giggles from her mom) as she waited for Sandra to finish up work in her office. By June 2019, Jenny was a twenty-two-year-old university student and prominent lesbian activist herself, when—despite possessing a valid tourist visa—she was detained on arrival to Miami International Airport, accused by a migration officer of coming to the United States with plans to illegally remain in the country. Jenny had, in fact, come to the country for a "cooling off" period after receiving death threats at home but did not arrive with a specific plan to request asylum. After telling the officer she feared for her life should she be deported to Honduras, Jenny was sent briefly to the Krome Service Processing Center, a detention center in Miami, then transferred to the Broward Transitional Center in Pompano Beach, Florida. She spent four long months there, with a brief transfer to the squalid Baker County Facility detention center during Hurricane Dorian. Jenny—in part due to the constant advocacy of her anguished mother, who had numerous connections (including me) with experience of the US asylum process—ended up getting pro bono representation and winning the asylum case she had been obligated to file. She is currently living with family and trying to heal from the trauma of her imprisonment, now unable to return to Honduras.

Cherry-Picking

When I began expert work in the mid-aughts, I received one or two requests per month. Following the 2009 coup in Honduras, those numbers increased to three or four per month. Today, with the exodus of Hondurans fleeing northward to survive the US-installed Juan Orlando Hernández narco-dictatorship, I receive four or five requests a week, sometimes several in one day. I can accept around one in twenty of the requests I receive.

In my career to date, I don't recall having been approached to serve as an expert by a pro se asylum applicant. This matters, because—according to a *University of Pennsylvania Law Review* article examining data from over 1.2 million deportation cases decided between 2007 and 2012—only 37 percent of all immigrants and 14 percent of detained immigrants managed to secure representation.[3] The same study found that only 2 percent of asylum seekers in deportation proceedings obtained pro bono represen-tation from nonprofit organizations, law school clinics, or large law firm volunteer programs. Today, with asylum seekers prevented from even entering the country or—worse—being deported to "safe third countries" (absurdly, including Honduras), even more people are being blocked from seeking asylum and obtaining legal representation. While I am occasion-ally asked by private attorneys to help with cases for asylum seekers paying out of pocket for legal representation, the vast majority of the cases I am asked to assist with are receiving pro bono representation from corporate law firms or nonprofits. Therefore, the cases I work on come mostly from among that privileged 2 percent of clients who—like Jenny—manage to secure free legal representation.

José and Jenny—unlike a majority of Honduran migrant detain-ees—come from backgrounds of relative privilege. Like most Honduran migrant detainees, however, both were imprisoned without opportunity for parole or release on bond. There are regional differences across the United States in detained migrants' chances of receiving parole once they've passed their credible fear interview. A lawyer with whom I've collaborated from the Immigrant Legal Aid Center (ILAC, a pseudonym) told me during an interview that this has to do primarily with the profit-based logics of the prison industrial complex: "The decision [to release someone] is made based on how much bed space is available. When we've seen them release people is when they're running out of beds. In practice, of course, they never say that is why."

Having interviewed both José and Jenny at length about their expe-riences at various points from 2016 (when José was detained) to late 2019 (when Jenny was released), I believe they both had strong cases for asylum, but only Jenny managed to secure representation. When detained asylum seekers manage to get representation, it is usually through the intervention of nonprofit organizations. I frequently collaborate with ILAC, one such nonprofit in the area where I live. ILAC finds most of its clients through a triage process in regional prisons where migrants are detained pending their asylum or withholding from removal cases. ILAC staff travel at least once every two weeks to these detention centers, with which they work hard to maintain good relationships—including refraining from criticizing abuses in public (since ILAC's access could be cut at any time). During their visits, ILAC staff and trained volunteers conduct interviews with up to three hundred imprisoned migrants per day, categorizing each asylum seeker according to the strength of their case. Given the volume of new prisoners on each visit, ILAC's sorting of applicants into a hierarchy of legally legitimate suffering is based on interviews of no more than five minutes each.

In about 95 percent of the cases for which I have served as an expert, the applicants have been granted asylum (or withholding from removal),[4] compared to an overall (2018) acceptance rate of 31.3 percent for Honduran asylum applicants in US federal courts.[5] As much as I'd like to attribute this apparent "success rate" to my argumentational genius or courtroom flair, it has relatively little to do with me. As Siobhán McGuirk has eloquently argued, asylum statistics are particularly deceptive. By the time an asylum case reaches my hands, it has usually been cherry-picked by a nonprofit immigrant aid organization for its "sexiness" and winnability (not to be confused with deservingness) and often invested in heavily by large corporate law firms seeking out relatively low-stakes opportunities for less experienced associates to cut their teeth in the courtroom.[6]

One clear result of this asylum industry devil's bargain is that countless people who may have had a good chance at asylum based on the facts of their case will not have legal representation, since they fail in five minutes to disclose to a stranger experiences that are hard to recount. In many cases, the first person to interview an asylum applicant is a uniformed officer not unlike those many such applicants are fleeing in their home countries. ILAC staff and volunteers have told me that prisoners are also often wary of them, and that they themselves often come to embody and articulate as trauma and "burnout" the profound structural impotence resulting from the barriers to effective communication and advocacy within the prison setting. I have worked on cases with Honduran asylum applicants who only divulged key details for their legal cases months, or even years, after they had initially been prompted—details like being raped by a Honduran military officer as an act of political torture. I have also seen applicants neglect to tell stories that are inconsequential from their perspective—like the gang member shooting of an asylum applicant's beloved puppy that didn't come up in dozens of hours of interviews but played a key role in the dog-loving judge's affirmative decision when the applicant mentioned it for the first time in his hearing.

In addition to their efforts to pair asylum applicants with pro bono attorneys, ILAC staff have fought to move toward a public defender model for detained asylum seekers.[7] And they have made some progress, in collaboration with other regional immigration advocacy organizations and the Vera Institute of Justice, which advocates for public representation on a nationwide scale. One of the most important achievements toward institutionalizing a right to representation for detained asylum seekers in the past decade was the 2013 adoption of a nationwide policy providing government-funded representation for detainees with "serious mental disorders or conditions that may render them mentally incompetent to represent themselves in immigration proceedings," following the *Franco-Gonzales v. Holder* litigation.[8]

Building on that victory, ILAC also successfully lobbied two large local counties to pay for the organization's legal services when representing incarcerated asylum seekers (regardless of competency) and created a lottery system for inmates to access those services. Such mechanisms enable ILAC attorneys to mitigate the harmful, inequitable effects of the pro bono triage system. And while securing them was a victory, such patchwork solutions—as opposed to a universal right to representation extending to all asylum applicants (or better yet, the abolition of borders)— are contingent on political realities shaped by xenophobia and austerity, key elements in the current context of neoliberal fascism.[9]

In José's case, since he had made the mistake of leaving the country after filing his claim and was not a widely recognized LGBT rights activist, he would not have been high on an immigration nonprofit's list. Additionally, Atlanta judges are known for granting asylum more rarely than most courts throughout the country. Unsurprisingly, he secured neither corporate pro bono nor nonprofit representation. Jenny, on the other hand, had a very well-documented case, including protective measures issued by the Inter-American Human Rights Court, newspaper reports about persecution she had suffered, and a network of people with the knowledge and symbolic capital necessary to give her a leg up. Through the advocacy of Americans for Immigrant Justice (AIJ), a nonprofit Miami law firm that places strong detained asylum seeker cases with local corporate firms seeking pro bono work, Jenny found representation with a Miami-based firm, Drucker and Lazio (DL, a pseudonym). DL, an international corporate law firm that reported a revenue of $1.5 billion in 2018, lists LGBT issues and "immigrants, human rights, and refugee matters" among its top pro bono priorities, so Jenny's case was certainly a good match.

As part of the "corporate social responsibility" programs of large corporate law firms, pro bono work serves important symbolic and public relations functions, helping to whitewash the harm done to democracy and sovereignty in the United States and around the world by such firms' tremendously lucrative legal defense of power. I have worked on cases with a large corporate law firm infamous for its role (and subsequent censure) in a major financial scandal, a firm from which one associate subsequently resigned to work for the Trump administration, famously arguing in federal court that providing soap for detained children presented an excessive cost to taxpayers, and numerous firms that have defended international war and corporate criminals.

The Pro Bono Conundrum

Jenny had nothing but praise for her attorney at DL, who—she said—had already come to an agreement with the government attorney prior to Jenny's asylum hearing. Jenny told me that the government attorney didn't even ask her any questions at the hearing itself. The only potential stumbling block that came up at her hearing was the judge pointing out that she was eligible for dual citizenship in Nicaragua. But—she told me—he continued, "I know what the situation is like in Nicaragua, and I can't send you to a country that is the same as or worse than Honduras." (While this assertion is perfectly in line with official US policy toward Nicaragua, it's important to note here that it has no basis in fact.) DL lost no time in publicizing Jenny's asylum win by issuing a press release that AIJ had named her attorney a "Pro Bono Hero."

Yet the fact that a DL associate helped Jenny obtain asylum provides an example of the bitter irony involved in asylum in the US and capitalist contexts in general: one of DL's most prominent former associates, former New York City mayor and international crime control consultant Rudolph Giuliani, bears direct responsibility for the development of Zero Tolerance policies in Honduras that led to the targeted assassination of tens of thousands of activists and young people and put at great risk the lives of people who—like Jenny and José—fought for social justice there.[10] And while DL's chairman bristled at Giuliani's public statements and pushed him to resign after he joined Donald Trump's legal team in early 2018, a late-night October 16, 2019, butt dial to an NBC reporter revealed that Giuliani was still working closely with at least one DL associate to uncover information harmful to Trump presidential rival Joe Biden (whose policies as Obama's vice president, including the Biden Plan for Central America, were also disastrous for Hondurans and fueled the current Great Migration).[11] DL is consistently one of the top law firms contributing to federal candidates, with support for Democrats and Republicans almost evenly split.

It is beyond the scope of this short essay to enumerate all the ways DL and its associates have actively harmed Honduran prospects for sovereignty, democracy, and security—and in so doing fueled the asylum crisis. But two key additional examples paint a troubling picture. Just prior to joining DL, the firm's former and now retired senior director for global trade and investment served as chief US negotiator for the 2005 Central American Free Trade Agreement, which barred citizens in Central America and the Dominican Republic from participating in sovereign decisions about their protections and rights, thus dramatically weakening them.[12] Her work on CAFTA was touted in her DL bio and other materials as an asset to business clients working in Central America. And the DL government affairs director (at the time) billed a wealthy Miami businessman, Oscar M. Cerna, tens of thousands of dollars for lobbying that impacted Honduran sovereignty. DL's work for Cerna included organizing a Congressional hearing I attended in March 2010, to increase support for the regime installed by the 2009 Honduran military coup and call for the return to Cerna of cement company CEMAR, which Cerna claimed had been illegally expropriated during the administration of the ousted, democratically elected president Manuel Zelaya.[13]

Meanwhile, in the United States, DL has played a key role in expanding prison privatization through clients like Pride Enterprises, which runs "prison industry" programs. Scholars and abolitionists have denounced such programs as slave labor, designed to increase corporations' profit margins by replacing decently paid, and in many cases unionized, workers.[14] DL has also lobbied directly on behalf of Koch Industries, which has spent decades working to stack the judiciary with deeply conservative judges to ensure that increasingly criminalized vulnerable populations like immigrants are denied access to adequate legal representation (and, in the case of citizens, disenfranchised as well).[15]

So while DL has indeed provided desperately needed services for detained immigrants (and advertised relentlessly about doing so), those services are so desperately needed because DL, directly and indirectly, has profited from: a) creating the conditions causing hundreds of thousands of Hondurans to seek asylum in the United States; b) privatizing prisons to ensure their profitability and supporting the increase in migrant incarceration; c) representing actors who have made it more difficult for asylum applicants to get access to representation or to win their cases even when they do.

Of course, DL is no worse than any other big corporate law firm doing pro bono work; a simple internet search is enough to find that nearly any such firm is complicit in producing the structural conditions that created the need for its pro bono work (asylum-related or otherwise) in the first place. For example, Walmart offers its foreign-born "associates" dubiously effective "citizenship services," while selling ICE baseball caps and paying its workers sub-survival wages;[16] Amazon sells technology to support ICE and congratulates itself for spending scant millions on homeless shelters, while paying no taxes toward publicly run and accountable services on its billion-dollar revenue[17]—and its CEO can spend another fraction of those tax-free profits to buy one of the most politically influential newspapers in the country that has never met a Latin American coup it didn't like ("Democracy Dies in Darkness"!);[18] and the Koch Institute funds pop-up art exhibits extolling the benefits of migration,[19] while spending millions to criminalize immigrants and make them even more vulnerable.[20]

Corporate social responsibility is at best a public relations tool, doing minimal good on a micro scale. At worst, it is a tool for whitewashing and reinforcing extreme structural violence in this era of (neoliberal) regressive taxation. In such a system, even cause lawyers taking on asylum cases in the nonprofit sector are doomed to a practice that is merely reactive to the interlocked state and the imperial and corporate structural violence causing people to seek asylum.

No amount of asylum representation—not even the full coverage public defender model advocated for by ILAC—could suffice to fill the demand that the agents of capitalism have created. And that "demand"— described adequately—is trauma.

Experting

Trauma only has value in the asylum industry, however, if it's the right *kind* of trauma. Convincing the judge that an applicant's trauma is worthy is where I come in.

As an expert, my role is fairly mundane. I am brought on as a "country conditions expert," which means that I should be able to credibly vouch on paper and possibly by phone or in person in court that the situation an asylum applicant describes in their own narrative (itself carefully crafted by lawyers and/or others familiar with the required format out of the applicant's messier, meandering life story) is plausible, and that they would most likely face persecution or death based on very specific categories should they be deported. I do mean very specific categories, one example being "deeply religious family members of a person killed by a gang who hold a public wake for their relative knowing that doing so will be seen as an act of defiance to the gang that killed him." And while the first few paragraphs of each ten- to twenty-page document always focus on my decades of experience of research in and writing about Honduras, in fact, nearly any Honduran I know living in the country could convincingly (if not "credibly") vouch for and describe the conditions they face daily—if perhaps not craft the sometimes counterintuitive arguments that win asylum cases in US courts. It is my symbolic capital as a tenured academic with a particular research background, my familiarity with the asylum process (which many corporate pro bono lawyers themselves lack), my familiarity with the language and format of written affidavits—and with the embodied, arrogant performance of "expertise" in court—that makes me valuable.

I rarely accept remuneration from noncorporate clients but charge far more than I ever expected to earn per hour for corporate firms doing pro bono (public relations) work that comes out of their profits from representing clients that are often complicit in creating the economic and social conditions that produce refugees. I am usually not given the chance to speak with the person seeking asylum, which sometimes has to do with my working at a distance or their being incarcerated for attempting to exercise their ostensible human right to seek asylum.

Of course, each case requires some research. I have found myself digging into mid-level drug dealers' Facebook posts for evidence of money laundering, have paid Honduran friends to go morgue hopping, and have often called friends living in an applicant's home region to figure out what search terms I should be using to find dirt on local criminal networks. It's not work I expected to do when I sought to become an anthropologist, and it's troubling to me that I actually find it quite fun. Because in enjoying (and in some cases profiting from) the work, I participate in the fetishization of the asylum applicant's trauma as capital within a system that offers no hope for changing the roots of that trauma.

Symbolic Capital

As my anthropological career progressed and I got older, my expertise is less frequently interrogated in court. That said, one question I am often asked by government attorneys in an attempt to decrease my value as "expert" is whether I have ever turned down a case because I didn't think it worthy of asylum or didn't believe the applicant's story. And while the latter has, in fact, happened (thrice in fifteen years), the question itself is a trick. Given the abovementioned cherry-picking that happens prior to most requests reaching my inbox, most cases that reach me have a great chance of winning and thus creating PR value for corporate law firms and/or helping immigration nonprofits attract more funding. I do not make this point in court.

The asylum applicant's embodied performance of trauma (criminalized, shackled, and via video for many incarcerated applicants) and my embodied performance of expertise are only two of the various types of symbolic capital circulating in the courtroom. Within the US legal profession, one's alma mater is one of the most important forms of capital there is. The vast majority of lawyers who represent the government in asylum cases come from second- or third-tier law schools. For lawyers who graduate from such schools with tremendous debt and have an interest in immigration law and few prospects for employment at a large corporate firm, government work is a much better and more stable option for their own economic survival than nonprofit or private practice. And while some government attorneys are decidedly hostile to all asylum applicants to the point of being xenophobic, many enter the profession hoping to do good from within the system—a structurally complicated proposition. In contrast, many of the corporate attorneys taking on pro bono cases with tremendous resources at their disposal (including funds to pay for experts like me) are graduates of Harvard, Yale, Stanford, and other top-tier schools. As such, an asylum courtroom hierarchy (always with the judge on top, of course) is often established from the start.

Judges, meanwhile, confront quotas implemented in 2018, "part of a broader effort to speed up deportations and reduce a massive backlog of immigration cases."[21] The National Association of Immigration Judges (their union) has strongly opposed the new requirement, arguing that it erodes due process for immigrants and undermines judicial independence, likening the proposed model to an assembly line. Dozens and often hundreds of total hours of remunerated and volunteer labor go into preparing hundreds of pages of documents (including country conditions reports—in José's pro se case compiled by himself, and in Jenny's pro bono case written by a contracted expert) for each case. Yet judges must hear three cases per day to comply with their mandate. Within an already discriminatory system, the lack of sufficient judicial personnel (including judges and both government and asylum attorneys) to provide a marginally fair process has been weaponized to justify neoliberal labor restructuring within the judiciary that increases structural violence against asylum seekers. Given that it is virtually impossible for a judge to read all the materials submitted in any given case, the performance of various forms of symbolic capital rooted in economic capital (including formal expertise) take on the utmost importance in the courtroom.

As for the claimants, Jenny and other Hondurans granted asylum to the United States with the support of an expert face the combined trauma for which they originally sought asylum and the trauma inflicted by the asylum process itself—trauma that is intimately related to the economic and symbolic capital created through the process. When I take into account that asylum applicants generally consider the trauma of the asylum process preferable to the trauma of deportation, the expert work I do sometimes seems worth it. But cases like José's remind me that that is not always the case. Experting within a US system driven by capitalist logics may be necessary work to ensure that certain individuals can have a chance at leading safe and dignified lives, but it is a vastly insufficient and perhaps even counterproductive tool for fixing the problem.

Adrienne Pine (editor) is associate professor of anthropology at American University, Washington, DC. She has published on embodied imperialist violence in Honduras, the dangers of health information technologies (HIT) to nurses and other humans, and the importance of somatic solidarity in an era of neoliberal fascism.

Notes

1   José López, "On Seeking Refuge from an Undeclared War," this volume, 21–28.
2   Ibid.
3   Ingrid V. Eagley and Steven Shafer, "A National Study of Access to Counsel in Immigration Court," *University of Pennsylvania Law Review* 164, no. 1 (December 2015), accessed March 26, 2020, https://scholarship.law.upenn.edu/cgi/viewcontent.cgi?article=9502&context=penn_law_review.
4   I am including relief granted under the Convention against Torture (CAT) here, a form of withholding of removal granted by an immigration judge if they deem a person is more likely than not to be tortured if deported to their country of origin; see the Convention against Torture and Other Cruel, Inhuman or Degrading Treatment or Punishment, United Nations Human Rights Office of the High Commissioner, December 10, 1984, accessed March 31, 2020, https://www.ohchr.org/en/professionalinterest/pages/cat.aspx.
5   "Asylum Applications and Refugees from Honduras," WorldData.info, accessed March 31, 2020, https://www.worlddata.info/america/honduras/asylum.php.
6   Siobhán McGuirk, "(In)credible Subjects: NGOs, Attorneys, and Permissible LGBT Asylum Seeker Identities," *Political and Legal Anthropology Review* 41, no. S1 (September 2018): 4–18.
7   For an analysis of the public defender model in the context of the United Kingdom, see Jo Wilding, "The Marketization of Asylum Justice in the UK," this volume, 231–39.
8   United States Department of Justice, "Department of Justice and the Department of Homeland Security Announce Safeguards for Unrepresented Immigration Detainees with Serious Mental Disorders or Conditions," April 22, 2013, accessed May 31, 2020, https://www.justice.gov/eoir/pr/department-justice-and-department-homeland-security-announce-safeguards-unrepresented; Caleb Korngold, Kristen Ochoa, Talia Inlender, Dale McNiel, and Renée Binder,"Mental Health and Immigrant Detainees in the United States: Competency and Self-Representation,"*Journal of the American Academy of Psychiatry and the Law* 43, no. 3 (September 2015): 277–81, accessed May 31, 2020, http://jaapl.org/content/43/3/277.
9   Adrienne Pine, "Forging an Anthropology of Neoliberal Fascism," *Public Anthropologist* 1, no. 1 (January 2019): 20–40.
10 Adrienne Pine, *Working Hard, Drinking Hard: On Violence and Survival in Honduras* (Berkeley: University of California Press, 2008), 25–84.
11 Max Blumenthal, "How Joe Biden's Privatization Plans Helped Doom Latin America and Fuel the Migration Crisis," *Grayzone*, July 28, 2019, accessed March 26, 2020, https://thegrayzone.com/2019/07/28/biden-privatization-plan-colombia-honduras-migration.
12 For example, allowing wealthy US and Canadian companies to sue for not being issued mining concessions, denying access to affordable healthcare by blocking the sale of generic drugs, etc.

13 See "Ambassador Meeting with Trade Minister Cerrato," November 28, 2008, Wikileaks, accessed March 26, 2020, https://wikileaks.org/plusd/cables/08TEGUCIGALPA1071_a.html.

14 See, e.g., Sarah Shemkus, "Beyond Cheap Labor: Can Prison Work Programs Benefit Inmates?" *Guardian*, December 9, 2015, accessed March 31, 2020, https://www.theguardian.com/sustainable-business/2015/dec/09/prison-work-program-ohsa-whole-foods-inmate-labor-incarceration; Rob Goyanes, "The Secret History of Florida Prison Labor," New Tropic, January 4, 2016, accessed March 31, 2020, https://thenewtropic.com/prison-labor-florida.

15 Lobbying Report filed with Secretary of the Senate, February 13, 2003; held on file by author.

16 "I.C.E. Immigration and Customs Enforcement," Walmart, product listing, accessed March 31, 2020, https://www.walmart.com/ip/I-C-E-Immigration-Customs-Enforcement/520707670; "Citizenship Resources," OneWalmart, accessed March 31, 2020, https://one.walmart.com/content/usone/en_us/company/community/citizenship-resources.html; Clare O'Connor, "Report: Walmart Workers Cost Taxpayers $6.2 Billion in Public Assistance," *Forbes*, April 15, 2014, accessed March 31, 2020, https://www.forbes.com/sites/clareoconnor/2014/04/15/report-walmart-workers-cost-taxpayers-6-2-billion-in-public-assistance.

17 Kari Paul, "Protesters Demand Amazon Break Ties with Ice and Homeland Security," *Guardian*, July 11, 2019, accessed March 31, 2020, https://www.theguardian.com/us-news/2019/jul/11/amazon-ice-protest-immigrant-tech; Jessica Stillman, "Amazon Is Opening a Homeless Shelter at Its HQ a Year After Killing a Tax to Help the Homeless," Inc., November 12, 2019, accessed March 31, 2020, https://www.inc.com/jessica-stillman/amazon-is-opening-a-homeless-shelter-at-its-hq-a-year-after-killing-a-tax-to-help-homeless.html?cid=sf01001.

18 Democracy Dies in Darkness is the slogan adopted by the *Washington Times* in 2017. Amazon CEO Jeff Bezos has owned the *Washington Post* since 2013.

19 Rafael Bernal, "Koch Groups Take Immigration Art Exhibit to DC Ahead of DACA Hearing at Supreme Court," *Hill*, November 4, 2009, accessed March 26, 2020, https://thehill.com/latino/468810-koch-groups-take-immigration-art-exhibit-to-dc-ahead-of-daca-hearing-at-supreme-court.

20 Alex Kotch, "The Kochs Have Professed Concern for Immigrants—but Their Spending Tells a Different Story," Rewire.News, March 9, 2018, accessed March 26, 2020, https://rewire.news/article/2018/03/09/kochs-professed-concern-immigrants-spending-tells-different-story.

21 Joel Rose, "Justice Department Rolls Out Quotas for Immigration Judges," NPR, April 3, 2018, accessed March 26, 2020, https://www.npr.org/2018/04/03/599158232/justice-department-rolls-out-quotas-for-immigration-judges.

IV

"Nonprofit"/ "Nongovernmental"

In the Best Interest of Whom? Professional Humanitarians and Selfie Samaritans in the Danish Asylum Industry

Annika Lindberg

> I don't know if it's a Scandinavian understanding of the state. When I'm in Red Cross offices in other countries, they are critical of the fact that the Danish Red Cross works for the state and accepts state money. But maybe it's a Northern European thing to believe that we can have a contract with authorities and solve issues with them, without that jeopardizing our independence.[1]

Bente, a Red Cross (RC) professional working at the organization's headquarters in Denmark, paints a relatively uncomplicated image of cooperation between the state and civil society.[2] I interviewed Bente in April 2016, as I was interested in the expanding role of the RC in the Danish asylum industry. For decades, it has been the main operator of the country's asylum centers, but its role had expanded in recent years, with RC staff also contracted to run health clinics and "activation programs" in deportation centers and to offer so-called voluntary return advice, all on a salaried basis. Their increasing professional involvement occurred at a time when the situation was becoming more precarious for people seeking asylum in Denmark, as the right-leaning governing coalition adopted a record number of restrictive policy changes with the aim of deterring, excluding, and "making life intolerable" for migrants who were—in the government's view—unwanted in Denmark.[3] Hence, while the RC was claiming to work in the best interests of people seeking asylum, its employees were inevitably taking an active part in enforcing a dehumanizing policy regime.

What is at stake when humanitarian organizations become complicit in enforcing repressive state policies? For me, this question first arose during a conversation with Akelio, a friend who came to Denmark as a refugee in recent years. When he fled violence in his country of origin, he had been sheltered and aided by the RC. He initially felt relieved when he arrived in Denmark and was accommodated in a RC camp—in his experience, the organization had been there to protect him. But after spending years being shuffled around different RC asylum centers, during a long and exhausting asylum claim process that ended with a deportation order, he concluded: "Over there, the RC saved lives, but here, they help [in] killing us slowly."

Akelio's remark significantly differs from Bente's portrayal of an uncomplicated relationship between the state and civil society. At a point where humanitarian organizations have become professional enforcers of state policies, can they really claim to work in the best interest of refugees? In this chapter, I address the ambivalent role of the self-proclaimed humanitarians of the Danish asylum industry and argue that their increasingly professionalized engagement depoliticizes and even legitimizes an increasingly repressive asylum system. I conclude that the RC, in their quest for government funding and for a moral high ground within the asylum industry, effectively puts the state's interests before the interests of refugees. As a result, the role of the asylum system itself in producing suffering is obscured.[4]

The Growth of the Rescue Industry

Investments in migration and border control have generated a highly productive industry, attracting a variety of actors that provide mechanisms of migrant control, facilitation, care, and rescue.[5] Researchers have shown how this industry produces more of the outcomes it claims to curtail, namely migrant "illegality" and border deaths.[6] Yet the industry remains financially and morally productive, as it provides opportunities for both security agencies and humanitarian actors to compete for state contracts and funding and to establish themselves as professionalized service providers. While these third-party actors function both "as agents for the state and assisting migrants to circumvent the state,"[7] their engagement is unlikely to challenge state policies. Indeed, in their scramble for government funding and with increasing professionalization, the role of NGOs such as the RC is depoliticized; as noted by Kalir and Wissink, state agencies tasked with enforcing border and migration control and civil society actors claiming to be the defenders of human rights operate alongside rather than in opposition to each other.[8] As a result, humanitarianism can also be utilized as a cloak for repressive practices; for instance, when the EU argues that its lethal border policies prevent migrant deaths in the Mediterranean.[9] It appears, then, as if the rescue industry mainly serves the purpose of commodifying human life, its misery, and its safety.[10]

Yet this depoliticization can still generate dilemmas for those actors tasked with alleviating human suffering, notably when the policies they are complicit in enforcing are designed to do the contrary. Large NGOs, such as the RC, may have secured material resources from the state, but their role in the moral economy of "do-gooders" is challenged by grassroots movements that take a more explicit stand against the state. In what follows, I will explore how self-proclaimed humanitarians of the Danish asylum industry justify their role and how they compete for material and social capital and assess the consequential opportunities created for challenging state policies. My analysis is based on ethnographic field notes and interviews carried out at an RC asylum camp in Denmark during summer 2016.

The Ambivalent Humanitarians of the Danish Asylum Industry

> Field notes, July 20, 2016: When I arrive in the Red Cross camp on my first day of fieldwork, I am told that the Red Cross runs the camps in the "best interest of asylum seekers" and see themselves as a "counterbalance" to the immigration service. Moreover, they should be distinguished from their main contenders for state contracts in the asylum reception field: the municipalities, who are "just in it for the money," and the prison and probation service, who "put the state interest first." Camp workers hope—and expect—that I will be able to notice this difference. I am given a Red Cross vest, which I am told to wear at all times in the camp. When I hesitate, I am told that the Red Cross vest symbolizes "neutrality" in the asylum system, so I should not be concerned to wear it.

Neutrality is indeed one of the proclaimed core values and principles of the RC. On the charter nailed onto the wall in the reception area in the asylum center, "neutrality" appears next to "humanity, impartiality, and independence."[11] But is there such a thing as a neutral position within an asylum system designed to control, deter, and expel people that the government has categorized as unwanted? The RC has been contracted by the Danish state to run asylum centers since 1984 and is a well-established actor in the national asylum industry. Katrine Syppli-Kohl has elaborated on the dilemmas embedded in the Danish camp system, which is supposed to "ensur(e) the welfare of the asylum seeker while simultaneously defending society against unwanted integration."[12] Yet salaried RC workers' justification for this position seemed to me, at first, uncomplicated and straightforward. Sasja, an RC staff member, tried to assure me that being part of the system elsewhere might be a problem—but not in Denmark: "I could never work as part of the system in, say, Hungary, but in Denmark we have a humane system. We can also bend the rules in favor of asylum seekers. We're like a humane watchdog of the asylum system." The red vests worn by Sasja and colleagues at all times in the center allegedly functioned as both a symbol of their "humanity" and as an identifier. Yet the vests serve an additional, important function: much like in declared "crisis" zones in Europe and globally, where humanitarian organizations also compete for funding, such branded clothing constitutes part of the marketization of humanitarian relief.[13]

Critical scholars have highlighted that far from a politically "neutral" position, humanitarianism reifies exclusionary policies. For instance, Liisa Malkki, Katerina Rozakou, and Miriam Ticktin have each argued that humanitarianism should not be seen as a response to a condition of suffering but as an approach that *produces* its own objects of protection. The people to be rescued only exist in the form of a strictly apolitical "naked" humanity.[14] Rather than an expression of solidarity, humanitarianism maintains and reproduces unequal power relations between caring and suffering subjects. However, along with its alleged neutrality, the RC's self-ascribed "helping" role was vital for the organization's salaried workers. Many staff working in the asylum camp, including social workers and security guards, were trained professionals. Yet others worked in the center as a side job while finishing their studies. When I asked how they ended up working in the asylum field, they all assured me that they had been motivated by the possibility to "help people" and emphasized that if they had been interested in earning money they certainly would not have ended up working there, as salaries were better anywhere else. In fact, there are two types of capital at stake for the humanitarian professionals of the asylum industry: one material, the other the social capital awarded to "do-gooders."

Some staff members admitted that working for the state did not necessarily equal "doing good" and sometimes entailed compromising their personal values and principles. Micha, whom I interviewed in July 2016, said:

> Personally, I trust the immigration service and the police that are handling the cases.[15] I trust the system, and that they make the right decisions . . . from their objective judgement of what is and what is not asylum. And then I stand on the other side, and I see some people and can say that this is completely unreasonable, how can they not be permitted to stay? But I have to shut out these feelings and tell myself that I cannot do anything about it.

Micha's colleagues voiced similar concerns, while also acknowledging that working "for the system" required them to ignore some aspects of the reality they were witnessing—be they perceived unfair outcomes of asylum procedures or the deteriorating well-being of asylum center residents awaiting decisions on their claims.[16] Reports have confirmed that uncertainty and waiting in asylum centers have a detrimental effect on asylum seekers' well-being, notably in the case of children. There are even examples of asylum seekers whose mental health deteriorated so much during their stay in the Danish asylum centers that they were eventually granted humanitarian residence permits on those grounds.[17] As Micha's quote above indicates, it requires either a profound conviction that the system produces fair outcomes or a well-developed cognitive dissonance for RC workers to bridge the gap between their self-understanding as "helpers" and the realities they observe on the ground.

Professional Humanitarians versus Selfie Samaritans?

The "helping" industry requires—and helps to sustain—suffering among its target population. Indeed, while the pragmatism of the RC enables it to secure material capital for its operation, RC staff are regularly challenged by volunteers engaging in various grassroots movements, who assert their *social* capital in support for people seeking asylum. Indeed, the RC's role as the "humane face" of the asylum system has repeatedly been questioned by grassroots movements and refugee solidarity networks that more openly criticize state policies. In the past few years, such grassroots movements have gained momentum. For instance, Venligboerne (Friendly Neighbors) has launched initiatives to address shortcomings in the asylum system and to end the forced isolation of people in asylum centers across Denmark. As a grassroots initiative with no reliance on state funding, Venligboerne is free to publicly criticize government policies that the RC is complicit in enforcing. Much like solidarity movements elsewhere in Europe, other initiatives, such as Welcome to Denmark, Refugees Welcome, and Medmenneskesmuglerne (Humane Smugglers), have gone even further in challenging the legitimacy of migration and border regimes by engaging in civil disobedience to contest the forced isolation and immobilization of people seeking asylum.[18]

While RC center staff had nothing in principle against grassroots initiatives, they remained skeptical of what they perceived as the naive interventions of "selfie Samaritans," a term that RC workers—and state officials—used to describe what they regarded as the superficial engagement of citizens who saw the arrival of refugees as an opportunity to be seen as "doing good." Scholars have debated the selfie as a means to exploit the suffering of refugees in order to assert the moral position of the "helper." Rather than demonstrating solidarity, argues Anja Karlsson Franck, selfies "place the refugee body at the center of value extraction processes."[19] The term "selfie Samaritan" is not limited to individuals who literally take such pictures but is used to dismiss a broader group of people. State and NGO workers' use of this critique is somewhat ironic, however; corporate humanitarian organizations also use images of refugee bodies to attract funding, and a similar neoliberal and exploitative approach is to some degree visible in the smaller charity organizations' collection of images that verify their own identity as "do-gooders"—and therefore enhance their social capital.

Henriette, a salaried RC staff member of the asylum center, was critical of the ad hoc engagement of individuals she labeled selfie Samaritans. In 2015, for instance, a steady stream of people had shown up at the RC center gates to "help the refugees."[20] Henriette told me of one incident, in which:

> One man had bought twenty pizzas for the six hundred residents of the center, believing it could serve as emergency relief. They think this is emergency aid; but it's not what happens in Sweden, Norway, Denmark, or Germany. Here, they always get accommodation and food in the first place. . . . I think when people hear about refugees, they think they need food and water—so hurry up and get them food

and water! Sometimes it's been difficult to handle, a lot of people want to make a difference, but, again, we have to focus on the fact that these are people with good hearts who would love to make a difference, even though we may sometimes feel like, phew . . . it would be better if they donated money to the Red Cross instead.

During the period when I was conducting fieldwork, the perception of a "refugee crisis" incentivized new actors to partake in and act upon the "border spectacle,"[21] where many seemed compelled to join a competitive field for the moral high ground of refugee reception and its subsequent rewards—both in terms of financial resources and social capital. While Henriette acknowledged the "good intention" of people rushing to the aid of refugees, she stressed that this "aid" was not necessarily in the interest of people seeking asylum. This perspective was also at the core of Henriette's critique of grassroots activists' engagement. Asserting her own "professional" position as a helper, she deemed the ad hoc support of grassroots movements to be largely unnecessary, indicating that the RC would be better suited to provide support—and to handle the money. Underlying this line of argument was the assumption that salaried work holds more value, not only in material terms but also in the moral economy of refugee reception. For most RC workers, it was inconceivable that anybody other than those working within "the system"—meaning the state and its agents—should provide services and support to people seeking asylum and, by extension, that only the state and its agents knew what was best for them. Some workers would, however, acknowledge that the system was no less self-interested than grassroots movements. Kai, who had worked in the asylum center for over a decade, told me:

> Nowadays, it's just about management. We went from having more socially oriented work to just management. . . . It's all about the money. The volunteers run all social activities—although I don't think they should outsource responsibility for these things to volunteers, it should be provided by the system. Meanwhile, the Red Cross makes big money from the asylum centers! People say refugees are so expensive, but, in fact, all these businesses make lots of money from them.[22]

Kai readily admits that the RC is just as much a business participating in the asylum industry for profit and self-interest rather than in the best interests of people seeking asylum. Instead of providing care and support, Kai felt that his role as a humanitarian worker had been reduced to monitoring the distribution of scarce resources in the asylum center, for example, controlling the number of fruit items each resident took from the canteen or making sure nobody received more cups of coffee than anyone else. At the same time, the "humane" aspects of his work were gradually eroding. Under such conditions, it becomes ever more pressing to ask: What is it that makes RC staff "professional" helpers, who are they assisting, and to what end?

Humanitarianism in the Best Interest of Whom?

Let us return to Akelio's reflection on the complicity of humanitarian actors like the RC in enforcing exclusionary and even harmful migration and border policies. This role is justified by the assumption, as vocalized by RC staff member Sasja, quoted above, that the Danish state is humane and trustworthy in contrast to other states. Yet given Denmark's active participation in the European race to the bottom in asylum and migration policy and the government's promise to make life intolerable for unwelcome migrants, there are good reasons to question this assumption. Akelio's remark that the Danish asylum system is "killing slowly" those who came to ask for its protection echoes criticism voiced by refugees in camps across Denmark and elsewhere in Europe.[23] Given these developments, any insistence on the neutrality of the RC or denial of their complicity in the politics of "killing slowly" risks depoliticizing and downplaying the tensions that exist between the "best interests" of people seeking asylum and those of the state. This is precisely the concern voiced by critical scholars who highlight how humanitarians, in their quest for funding from governments, put the state's interest and logic before the interest of the people they claim to help. Professionalized civil society engagement does not challenge these exclusionary practices; quite the contrary, it runs the risk of undermining possibilities for structural change by legitimating the rules of the game as set by the state.[24]

For organizations like the RC, however, playing along with state rules turns out to be economically profitable and morally productive. In exchange for lending the asylum system a "humane" face, salaried humanitarian workers continue to receive government funding. Whether their engagement really benefits the asylum seekers placed under their care is doubtful at best, because, as noted by Syppli-Kohl,[25] this "care" is necessarily performed under conditions that reinforce the social and political exclusion of people seeking asylum. While the interventions of grassroots movements and activists does to some extent challenge this top-down, essentially exclusionary, humanitarian-security consensus, they may also be said to profit from those same exclusionary policies.[26] The scramble for material and social capital in the asylum industry further risks depoliticizing and silencing the voices of people seeking protection and comes at a human cost—as Akelio's reflection illustrates.

While the Danish state—like many of its European counterparts—turns its back on people seeking protection, those who claim to act in the "best interest of asylum seekers" must once again make political claims against the state. This entails acknowledging the potency of solidarity action outside the "national order of things" rather than reducing people to commodified subjects whose suffering fuels the moral and material economy of a growing asylum industry.[27]

Annika Lindberg is a visiting postdoctoral researcher at AMIS, University of Copenhagen. Her research focuses on state violence, bureaucracy, migration control, and deportation.

Notes

1   Interview, Copenhagen, April 2016. All interviewees have been given pseudonyms.

2   Liv Egholm Feldt and Mathias Hein Jessen, "Producing Civil Society: Practices, Concepts and the Common Good: Denmark 1900–2016"; paper prepared for the forty-first annual conference of the Social Science History Association, Chicago, Illinois, 2016.

3   "Europe's Race to the Bottom: Denmark Turns Its Back to Refugees," ECRE: European Council on Refugees and Exiles, January 29, 2016, accessed March 26, 2020, https://www.ecre.org/europes-race-to-the-bottom-denmark-turns-its-back-to-refugees.

4   Ruben Andersson, "Europe's Failed 'Fight' against Irregular Migration: Ethnographic Notes on a Counterproductive Industry," *Journal of Ethnic and Migration Studies* 42, no. 7 (January 2016): 1055–75, accessed March 26, 2020, https://www.tandfonline.com/doi/full/10.1080/1369183X.2016.1139446; Nicholas Gill, "New State-Theoretic Approaches to Asylum and Refugee Geographies," *Progress in Human Geography* 34, no. 5 (September 2010): 626–45, accessed August 10, 2020, https://ore.exeter.ac.uk/repository/handle/10871/11408; William Walters, "Foucault and Frontiers: Notes on the Birth of the Humanitarian Border," in Ulrich Bröckling, Susanne Krasmann, and Thomas Lemke eds., *Governmentality: Current Issues and Future Challenges* (New York: Routledge, 2011).

5   Thomas Gammeltoft-Hansen and Ninna Nyberg Sørensen, *The Migration Industry and the Commercialization of International Migration* (London: Routledge, 2013).

6   Andersson, "Europe's Failed 'Fight' against Irregular Migration."

7   Sophie Cranston, Joris Schapendonk, and Ernst Spaan, "New Directions in Exploring the Migration Industries: Introduction to Special Issue," *Journal of Ethnic and Migration Studies* 44, no. 4 (March 2018): 556, accessed March 26, 2020, https://www.tandfonline.com/doi/full/10.1080/1369183X.2017.1315504.

8   Barak Kalir and Lieke Wissink, "The Deportation Continuum: Convergences between State Agents and NGO Workers in the Dutch Deportation Field," *Citizenship Studies* 20, no. 1 (November 2015): 34–49, accessed March 26, 2020, https://www.researchgate.net/publication/283848447_The_deportation_continuum_convergences_between_state_agents_and_NGO_workers_in_the_Dutch_deportation_field/link/58dd3785458515add9f6cb32/download.

9   Greg Feldman, "Europe's Border Control with a Humanitarian Face," *Middle East Research and Information Project* 261 (Winter 2011), accessed March 26, 2020, https://merip.org/2011/11/europes-border-control-with-a-humanitarian-face; Katerina Rozakou, "The Biopolitics of Hospitality in Greece: Humanitarianism and the Management of Refugees," *American Ethnologist* 39, no. 3 (August 2012): 562–77; also see Alva, Uyi, and Madi, "The Business of Selling Life: Reflections from a Rescue Ship in the Mediterranean Sea," this volume, 29–39.

10   Andersson, "Europe's Failed 'Fight' against Irregular Migration."

11   Also see "The Seven Fundamental Principles," International Federation of the Red Cross and Red Crescent Societies, accessed March 26, 2020, http://www.ifrc.org/en/who-we-are/vision-and-mission/the-seven-fundamental-principles.

12   Katrine Syppli-Kohl, "Asylaktivering og Ambivalens: Forvaltningen af asylan-søgere på asylcentre" (PhD diss., University of Copenhagen, 2015), 235.

13   Anja Karlsson Franck, "The Lesvos Refugee Crisis as Disaster Capitalism," *Peace Review* 30, no. 2 (April–June 2018): 199–205, accessed March 26, 2020, https://www.tandfonline.com/doi/full/10.1080/10402659.2018.1458951; Rozakou, "The Biopolitics of Hospitality in Greece."

14   Liisa Malkki, "Speechless Emissaries: Refugees, Humanitarianism, and Dehistoricization," *Cultural Anthropology* 11, no. 3 (August 1996): 377–404; Rozakou, "The Biopolitics of Hospitality in Greece"; Miriam Ticktin, "Thinking beyond Humanitarian Borders," *Social Research: An International Quarterly* 83, no. 2 (Summer 2016): 255–71, accessed March 26, 2020, https://muse.jhu.edu/article/631162.

15   In Denmark, the national immigration police are in charge of registering asylum seekers and of their eventual deportation. The Immigration Service processes asylum applications and make decisions on applicants' right to remain.

16   Field notes, August 2016; also see Syppli-Kohl, "Asylaktivering og Ambivalens," 117.

17   Michala Clante-Bendixen, *Asylcenter Limbo: En rapport om udsendelseshin-dringer* (Copenhagen: Refugees Welcome Denmark, 2011), 10.

18 Annastiina Kallius, Daniel Monterescu, and Prem Kumar Rajaram, "Immobilizing Mobility: Border Ethnography, Illiberal Democracy, and the Politics of the 'Refugee Crisis' in Hungary," *American Ethnologist* 43, no. 1 (February 2016): 1–13, accessed March 26, 2020, https://www.academia. edu/20386757/Immobilizing_Mobility_Border_Ethnography_Illiberal_ Democracy_and_the_Politics_of_the_Refugee_Crisis_in_Hungary_American_ Ethnologist_43_1_1-12_.

19 Karlsson Franck, "The Lesvos Refugee Crisis as Disaster Capitalism."

20 Field notes, July 29, 2016.

21 Andersson, "Europe's Failed 'Fight' against Irregular Migration."

22 Field notes, July 20, 2016.

23 Julia Suarez-Krabbe, José Arce, and Annika Lindberg, *Stop Killing Us Slowly: A Research Report on the Motivation Enhancement Measures and the Criminalisation of Rejected Asylum Seekers in Denmark* (Copenhagen: Roskilde University, 2018).

24 Kalir and Wissink, "The Deportation Continuum."

25 Syppli-Kohl, *Asylaktivering og Ambivalems.*

26 Gill, "New State-Theoretic Approaches to Asylum and Refugee Geographies"; Karlsson Franck, "The Lesvos Refugee Crisis as Disaster Capitalism."

27 Kallius et al., "Immobilizing Mobility"; Malkki, "Speechless Emissaries."

The Marketization of Asylum Justice in the UK

Jo Wilding

Legal aid in the United Kingdom means the provision of legal advice and representation, for certain types of cases, paid for by the government. All asylum seekers are entitled to legal aid for their asylum claims and any appeals if they do not have money or assets above a certain value and their appeal has at least a 50 percent chance of success, as estimated by the lawyer. Prior to the 1990s, and unlike health or education services, which the state provides directly, legal aid was delivered under the "judicare" model—by private firms and practitioners working for clients and then billing the state for their work. In that respect, legal aid services were always part of a market system. But reforms since the 1990s, and particularly since 2006, have intentionally made legal aid services more closely resemble a competitive market, with quality to be maintained at the lowest possible cost.

In such a market, one might expect lawyers to profit from providing legal services within the asylum industry: the more asylum applications, the more profit. But my research suggests that lawyers who are "doing it properly" make at best a slim profit; generally they subsidize their legal aid asylum work from other income streams and seek ways of minimizing financial losses. Faced with an explicit conflict between doing good work and maintaining financial viability, some lawyers compromise quality for profit or survival, while others go out of business or withdraw from legal aid work altogether. The (peer-recognized) best lawyers, firms, and nonprofits continue doing unprofitable work almost in the role of activists, pushing forward strategic cases—which seek to overturn harsh government policies and unfair asylum procedures—at the same time as protecting individual clients. The marketized regime for providing legal aid, especially the fee cuts, creates tensions between quality and financial viability that are extremely difficult for providers to reconcile. It also threatens asylum seekers' access to adequate legal assistance in an extremely hostile asylum system.

A Brief History of Asylum Legal Aid in the UK

There was no systematic immigration control in the UK until the Aliens Act 1905,[1] which mainly aimed at limiting entry by Jews fleeing Tsarist Russia. After that, immigration controls became increasingly complex, as the 1951 Refugee Convention created new state obligations to refugees,[2] postwar labor migration gave rise to conflicting demands, and the disintegration of the British Empire changed notions of citizenship and the right to enter the UK.[3] This more complex control system led the government to create rights of appeal against immigration officers' decisions. Since appeals were adversarial, both state and migrant were entitled to be legally represented.[4]

State-funded legal aid in the UK began in 1948. Eligibility was means-tested, but the threshold was high enough that that not only the very poor but also those of moderate means were entitled. As explained above, most services were provided by private practitioners. In 1969, for the new immigration appeal system, the UK government set up the Immigration Advisory Service (UKIAS) to provide advice and representation. Unlike all other free legal services, this was a state-funded, salaried, or "welfare" model of legal aid.

UKIAS set up its specialist Refugee Unit in 1976, which became a separate charity called the Refugee Legal Centre (RLC) in 1992. At that time, the number of people seeking asylum in the UK was increasing, and the British authorities were refusing refugee status in far more cases than previously. RLC lawyers from that period describe having an ethos of commitment to their clients and to the Refugee Convention, to challenging policies and practices that were unfair, and to pushing forward legal cases that would establish the most expansive or protective interpretations of the law.

A system called the Green Form scheme allowed for a certain amount of advice work to be done by a private firm of solicitors and billed to the legal aid fund, but, until 1998, there was no legal aid for private firms to represent in asylum appeals. The vast majority were done by the RLC—then a single office in London—and a network of Law Centres around the UK, which were not-for-profit legal advice centers focused on social welfare issues. In a sense, the extension of legal aid to cover asylum and immigration appeals created the first competitive market for providing representation in asylum appeals.

In 2000, the UK began "dispersing" asylum seekers across the country, to areas with cheap, vacant housing. By that time, policy changes had already excluded asylum seekers from mainstream welfare benefits and social housing, with accommodation and subsistence payments supplied through the National Asylum Support scheme.[5] At the same time, increasing numbers of asylum seekers were being detained. In addition to the first dedicated immigration detention center, Harmondsworth, which had opened in 1970, the UK government opened new centers in 1993 and 1996, followed by two more each year from 2000 to 2002. These were run by private companies under contract to the government.

These policy changes created demand for legal services in areas across the UK where they had not previously existed. The RLC opened three new offices, including one in Oakington detention center. During this period, RLC lawyers also mounted a legal challenge to the detention center asylum procedure, arguing that it was unfair. Had the challenge been successful, RLC staff would have lost their jobs. Clearly, profit was not the core motivation driving RLC lawyers.

RLC lawyers referred to the period from 1992 to 2004 as "the best of times," when they were funded by a block grant with minimal bureaucracy, leaving caseworkers free to focus on the needs of clients. In 2004, however, the RLC was brought within the remit of the Legal Services Commission, the arm's-length government agency that was then responsible for administering legal aid. Instead of a block grant, it was funded case by case in the same way as private firms, initially at hourly rates and later at a fixed fee. In that period, the UK government drastically and systematically defunded legal aid. Rates did not increase for fifteen years from 1998, when they were first set for appeals on initial asylum decisions. This real terms cut of 34 percent was followed by a further 10 percent cut in 2011.[6]

Marketization of Asylum Legal Services

In 2004, cuts to legal aid placed strict limits on the number of hours of work that the government would fund at each stage of an asylum application or appeal, including a cap of just five hours on an asylum case up to the point when the Home Office decided whether or not to grant refugee status.[7] Advisers were no longer paid to attend the asylum interview with their clients. Further changes in 2005 meant representatives had do certain work "at risk," receiving payment only if the application was successful. These cuts created dilemmas for lawyers who believed their work could not be done to an adequate standard within the funding constraints.[8]

A voluntary franchising scheme for law firms and nonprofits, which started in 1994, became mandatory in 2000, with controversial compulsory contracts limiting the number of cases, or "matter starts," each provider could open. In 2006, the Legal Services Commission imposed a contractual requirement to maintain a 40 percent success rate in appeals for immigration and asylum providers. This wholly flawed proxy measure of "quality" led some providers to drop complex cases at the appeal stage, claiming there were insufficient prospects of success, rather than risk lowering their success rate. When the Asylum Appellate Project reviewed such decisions, it found that in 84 percent of cases the prospects of success were, in fact, adequate, and that legal aid funding should have been granted to appeal the decision (and, indeed, was granted following the Project's intervention). The contractual requirement for a success rate had the effect of restricting access to legal aid for people with some of the most difficult cases.[9]

The number of providers of legal aid immigration and asylum services fell by 40 percent between 2004 (380 providers) and 2006 (234), as a result of compulsory franchising and rate cuts.[10] Yet the UK government-commissioned review of legal aid procurement, published in July 2006 by Lord Carter of Coles, advocated a move to an expressly market-based system for providing legal aid services.[11] Carter's proposals included competitive price tendering for block contracts, underpinned by quality control through peer review—only firms achieving the top two levels (of five) would be eligible for contracts. The quality criteria, however, were diluted so that level three became acceptable for a contract. At this level, the provider need not even "add value" to the case. In the 2007 tender, virtually every bidder received a contract for one hundred matter starts—too few for many organizations to remain viable—without any attempt to differentiate on grounds of quality, an obvious distortion of the market since the lowest-quality providers were guaranteed as many clients as the highest, so long as demand equaled or exceeded supply.

The government imposed fixed fees to replace hourly rates for the majority of immigration and asylum cases. These remain in place today but have been reduced.[12] When the work done on the file amounts to three times the fixed fee, it may "escape" the fixed-fee scheme and be paid at an hourly rate. Providers I interviewed said cases commonly cost two to two-and-a-half times the fixed fee—requiring substantial unpaid work.

The Legal Aid Agency assesses files claimed at "escape fee" and, according to providers, frequently knocks money off them.[13] Assessors argue, for example, that letters should take twelve minutes to write, not eighteen, or that witness statements should be drafted in three hours, rather than four. Providers usually succeed in obtaining payment eventually for most of their billable hours but only after appealing the Legal Aid Agency's initial assessment. This process itself takes up a lot of time—time which cannot be billed and that would otherwise have been spent on casework. Under the current scheme, conscientious providers either lose large sums of money by working to a high standard on each case or spend extra time fighting for their clients to escape the fixed-fee scheme.

Other firms are less tenacious about appealing assessments and instead give up on billing at escape fee rates, choosing to work as close to fixed-fee hours as possible. Caseworkers I interviewed recalled working at firms that deliberately capped the amount of work done to stay within fixed-fee payments, a practice that in turn allowed the government to argue that adequate services could be provided within fixed-fee hours. One solicitor had worked in a firm that opened files for clients and effectively did no work at all until they received a Home Office decision but nevertheless claimed full fixed fees for each case. This anecdotal claim is supported by a report which found that 29 percent of contract holders had made more than 20 percent profit in fixed-fee work (in breach of the contract) and 73 percent had earned more on fixed fees than they would have earned on hourly rates in 2009.[14] The practice appears to be based on a business model that holds that there is no point doing the work when they can claim the fee without doing it. Interviewees also thought some caseworkers simply did not know how to do a good job, due to poor training and supervision.

The Beginning of Market Failure?

Meanwhile, from 2006 to 2008, the RLC had expanded again, opening eight new offices in "advice deserts." This move helped the Legal Services Commission to fulfil its remit of providing for underserved areas but inevitably increased RLC's own overheads. Although it had started to seek charitable grants to subsidize its casework, the RLC was unable to manage its overheads on the new fixed-fee payment scheme and went into administration in June 2010. Thousands of people lost their representatives in a single week. Some suffered the same fate again when the Immigration Advisory Service collapsed a year later.

The involvement of charities in the legal services market had been expressly part of the LSC's strategy for meeting legal need. They were considered to provide a more holistic and client focused service than private law firms and to provide equally good or even better-quality services.[15] Yet it was becoming clear that charities like RLC, IAS, and the Law Centres could not provide legal services on the same contract terms as the private firms, which were allowed into the legal aid asylum market from 1998. Without access to bank loans for working capital and without private paying clients, charities could not survive on the very tight margins for casework.

The loss of the two biggest providers of legal aid services in the UK brings the role of profit in the legal aid sector into sharp focus. While caseworkers explain that the bureaucracy of billing and auditing is "a distraction from casework and doing everything to help your client," without it, the organization ceases to exist and cannot help any clients at all. The best of the immigration legal profession is characterized by commitment to the client group against "the enemy," namely the Home Office. It does vast amounts of pro bono work. Its professional network engages in lobbying and policy work on behalf of migrants, funded by the members. There is a collegiate and supportive relationship between legal professionals, even those in rival firms and organizations. The sector, therefore, had to find ways to resolve the tension between quality and financial viability without compromising the commitment to clients.

Interviewees in four organizations I studied—including private firms and nonprofits—managed to reconcile the tension between quality and financial viability by prioritizing those cases still paid at hourly rates. This included work for unaccompanied children seeking asylum and cases where the client was in detention. It also included judicial review work, for which they risked not being paid at all but, if successful, would have their costs paid at private (rather than legal aid) rates by the losing party— i.e., the Home Office. This approach meant lawyers could do high-quality work and bill for most of it, albeit likely with long delays and reductions in payment.

However, prioritizing hourly rate work meant declining fixed-fee work. These organizations were turning away numerous clients, because they did not have capacity to take on more cases, yet it was uneconomical to expand to meet the demand. Even when subsidizing their legal aid work from private paid work or charity money, each organization sought to cap its losses by minimizing the least profitable work. Where providers could reconcile quality and financial viability, it appeared that they must do so at the expense of access.

Another firm I researched had given up its legal aid contract, because it had lost money, even while keeping casework hours within fixed-fee limits. More significantly for the partners, they found the bureaucracy attached to holding a contract so burdensome and stressful that they decided not to continue. In particular, audits involved frequent inspections of their files and punitive sanctions for relatively minor administrative oversights, like failing to tick a box on a form. The firm had a poor reputation locally, but its withdrawal from legal aid reduced access to services in the region by two-thirds. Clearly, there is an irreconcilable tension between financial viability, quality, and access.

Conclusion

Given that legal aid has always been administered by private firms paid from public funds, it could be said that there was a market in providing legal services for asylum seekers long before the Carter reforms introduced a market-driven procurement system. The intention of those reforms was that a competitive market would ensure quality services at the lowest possible price. Yet, ironically, these reforms have deformed the market that previously existed. Serial cuts to remuneration rates, alongside an ever-tightening regime of audits and surveillance, have driven many of the better-quality legal aid providers out of the sector and allowed some of the least scrupulous to flourish. Clients have no means of assessing the respective quality of providers before choosing one—if they have a choice in the local area (and they cannot go out of the area unless the local provider is unable to take them on). If they discover that the adviser is of poor quality, it is next to impossible to change providers once legal aid has been granted.

This process, typical of neoliberalized public services in the UK, has left a dysfunctional field populated only by those committed activist lawyers who are willing and able to cross-subsidize their legal aid work and those content to provide a lower-quality "rump" service on the truncated funding available. The "marketization" process has left the state funded legal services market unable to ensure quality and access for asylum clients and should be reversed.

Jo Wilding is a postdoctoral researcher at the University of Brighton and a barrister at Garden Court Chambers.

Notes

1   Aliens Act, 1905, accessed April 23, 2020, http://www.uniset.ca/naty/aliensact1905.pdf.

2   For the Refugee Convention, see Convention and Protocol Relating to the Status of Refugees, UNHCR, accessed March 29, 2020, https://www.unhcr.org/protection/basic/3b66c2aa10/convention-protocol-relating-status-refugees.html.

3   For a more detailed discussion, see Ann Dummett and Andrew Nicol, *Subjects, Citizens, Aliens and Others: Nationality and Immigration Law* (London: Weidenfeld and Nicolson, 1990); Sarah Spencer, *The Migration Debate* (Cambridge: Policy Press, 2011).

4   Geoffrey Care, *Migrants and the Courts: A Century of Trial and Error?* (Aldershot, UK: Ashgate, 2013).

5   For more, see Vaughan Robinson, Roger Andersson, and Sako Musterd, *Spreading the "Burden"? A Review of Policies to Disperse Asylum Seekers and Refugees* (Cambridge: Policy Press, 2003).

6   House of Commons Committee of Public Accounts , "Committee of Public Accounts, Implementing Reforms to Civil Legal Aid: Thirty-Sixth Report of Session 2014–15," House of Commons, February 4, 2015, accessed April 1, 2020, https://www.parliament.uk/documents/commons-committees/public-accounts/HC%20808%20civil%20aid%20final%20(web%20version)%20v2.pdf.

7   Later, it became possible to apply for extensions to the five-hour cap.

8   Anne Singh and Frances Webber, "Excluding Migrants from Justice: The Legal Aid Cuts," Institute of Race Relations, July 1, 2011, accessed March 26, 2020, https://www.bl.uk/collection-items/excluding-migrants-from-justice-the-legal-aid-cuts; Marjorie Mayo, "Providing Access to Justice in Disadvantaged Communities: Commitments to Welfare Revisited in Neo-Liberal Times," *Critical Social Policy* 33, no. 4 (November 2013): 679–99; Deborah James and Evan Killick, "Empathy and Expertise: Case Workers and Immigration/Asylum Applicants in London," *Law & Social Inquiry* 37, no. 2 (Spring 2012): 430–55, accessed March 26, 2020, http://eprints.lse.ac.uk/44027/1/_lse.ac.uk_storage_LIBRARY_Secondary_libfile_shared_repository_Content_James,%20D_Empathy%20and%20expertise_James_Empathy%20expertise_2015.pdf.

9   Devon Law Centre, "Asylum Appellate Project: Second Year Report," June 2009.

10 Grania Langdon-Down, "Knockout Punch?" *Law Society Gazette*, November 2, 2006, accessed March 26, 2020, https://www.lawgazette.co.uk/analysis/knockout-punch/2057.article.

11 Lord Carter of Coles, *Legal Aid: A Market-Based Approach to Reform* (London: House of Lords, 2006), accessed March 26, 2020, https://webarchive. nationalarchives.gov.uk/20081205143452/http:/www.legalaidprocurement review.gov.uk/docs/carter-review-p1.pdf.

12 Fixed fees differ for initial applications and appeals and are difficult to express in terms of hours, but they roughly equate to eight hours of work to prepare an asylum appeal when compared to the hourly rate.

13 The Legal Aid Agency replaced the Legal Services Commission in 2013.

14 Deri Hughes-Roberts, *Rethinking Asylum Legal Representation: Promoting Quality and Innovation at a Time of Austerity* (London: Asylum Aid, 2013).

15 Richard Moorhead, Alan Paterson, and Avrom Sherr, "Contesting Professionalism: Legal Aid and Nonlawyers in England and Wales," *Law & Society Review* 37, no. 4 (December 2003): 765–808.

Free Wireless Network Activism and the Industrial Media Infrastructures of Forced Migration

Tim Schütz and Monic Meisel

From October 2012 to April 2014, several hundred refugees occupied the Oranienplatz square and an empty school in Berlin's Kreuzberg district. In this act of civil disobedience, members of the self-organized OPlatz movement protested for an end to policies that mandated residence in refugee camps, for improved living conditions in those camps, and for access to educational resources.[1] In solidarity with the squatters, participants of the Freifunk (Free Wireless) initiative used routers and antennas to supply the inhabitants with steady internet access. To do this, the participants used equipment running the latest Freifunk firmware—a combination of open-access software and routing protocols that connected devices in a horizontal "mesh network." This in turn allowed the activists to share a private internet uplink with the camp—connecting the school-based occupiers to the already existing city-wide Freifunk backbone infrastructure.

Since then, Freifunk activists have steadily expanded this sociotechnical initiative, supporting over 350 refugee shelters and reception centers across Germany by 2017.[2] Within activist communities, public wiki platforms are particularly important to collectively document shelter locations and the availability of internet access, as well as to contact people.[3] Activists also created the online platform Freifunk Helps: Access Is a Human Right, which explains Freifunk's actions in more general terms and allows people to donate to the project. Further, the website emphasizes that the Freifunk project plans to promote wireless community networks for a host of other social institutions, for example, homeless shelters, youth centers, and public schools.

In this chapter, we reflect collaboratively and critically on these grand aspirations—a decision informed by our shared concern with the long-term goals of the Freifunk project. As network activists, we are troubled by the increasing responsibility placed on volunteers rather than the state to provide basic digital infrastructure. We are also worried that big companies and "social enterprises" are increasingly thriving on problematic media representations of refugees and do not offer a joint critique of digital infrastructure politics in Germany in their activities.

Analytical work based on notions of the "asylum" or "migration" industry have been absent from scholarly and community-based reflections on hacker culture and politics to date.[4] We use this lens to ask how media and communication infrastructures have been configured as part of the "asylum industry" to enable profit-making. We identify three key actors: internet service providers, telecommunication companies, and refugee NGOs. Spatially, we focus on refugee reception centers or shelters and migration offices in two cities, Bremen and Berlin. In terms of practices, we address corporate social responsibility campaigns, the promotion of "niche" markets, and the fundraising efforts of self-organized media infrastructure groups. We ask: How does Freifunk's vision of equal access challenge and reconfigure profit-oriented internet provision for asylum seekers at these sites? Our analysis is based on literature examining "hacktivist" practices in their contemporary context, an ethnographic study on Freifunk installations in Bremen,[5] and Monic's firsthand experience of "doing" Freifunk in Berlin since its inception.

From Subversive DIY Networks to "Humanitarian Hacking"?
Founded in Berlin in the early 2000s, Freifunk is among the largest and longest-standing initiatives in Europe to establish local, community-driven, decentralized, open, uncensored, and uncommercial wireless networks.[6] It does not offer membership; one participates in Freifunk simply by "doing it." Participation could involve maintenance of a private Freifunk "node," for example, or engaging in mailing lists and chat room conversations or attending bi-weekly meetings. Often located in open technology hubs like community-run "maker spaces" (commonly found in schools or libraries), free wireless initiatives form part of a thriving yet (politically) heterogeneous hacker scene.[7]

Though "hacker" is a notoriously fuzzy label,[8] Freifunk can be defined as a hacker collective because of its core practices, which serve to politicize contemporary media technologies and infrastructures (MTI). First of all, Freifunk participants "act on" MTI, since they "tinker with, deconstruct and rearrange existing technologies."[9] In the case of Freifunk, collectively developed routing firmware and protocols invert the idea of traditional networks from centralized to decentralized. Similar to large political hacker organizations like the Chaos Computer Club (CCC),[10] Freifunk participants challenge government policy and corporate regulations and push back against law enforcement in the form of censorship and data surveillance.

Like many free software projects, Freifunk's "hacktivism" works within a normative concept of freedom that, through claims to human rights, seeks to expose those actors who restrict the rights of others.[11] This political imaginary of subversion and reform also underpins other, less technology-focused forms of humanitarianism that local groups organize for refugees in Germany, such as language classes or clothing donations.[12] In the context of the refugee shelters, Freifunk participants aim to turn stationary internet uplinks into wireless networks or use antennas to redirect uplinks from nearby households or businesses to refugee shelters, reception centers, and improvised camps that do not have internet access. In terms of financing, Freifunk generally depends on volunteer labor, donations, and shared equipment on a nonprofit basis. Recently, however, local political parties and municipal governments have started to subsidize this bottom-up approach in order to offer more wireless hotspots. This shift highlights how Freifunk—and the components of hacking—are always intertwined with the interests, strategies, and rhetoric of states and corporations.

Internet Service Providers and Humanitarian Campaigns

When asked about their activities, Freifunk participants usually highlight that the advantage of their activism lies in its spontaneous character and capacity to improvise quickly, which they frame in sharp contrast to service provision by the state, social service providers, or private companies. By making such statements in public and among themselves, Freifunk members highlight the political dimension of internet infrastructures and aim to demonstrate why other actors are too slow to respond to the situation.[13] More specifically, they are critiquing the actions taken by large Internet Service Providers (ISPs) like German Telekom, which include working with municipalities to provide wireless internet access, offering unused company properties to house refugees, creating internship programs for refugees, and even training employees to assist in processing asylum cases at the Federal Ministry for Migration and Refugees.[14]

German Telekom is resistant to civic involvement in such projects. Company employees have publicly stated that municipalities and not individual activists should discuss internet access for refugees with the company.[15] Similarly, all "big four" ISPs ignored Freifunk activists' requests to collaborate. This attitude has prompted Freifunk participants to regard the company's "corporate social responsibility" as more akin to public relations campaigns than humanitarian programs. Comparatively, small ISPs in Berlin and Bremen have agreed to redirect their uplinks to neighboring reception centers and shelters using Freifunk.

Freifunk activists also argue that the initiatives envisioned by large IT infrastructure providers were not only too partial and slow to arrive, but also came with a host of undesired side effects, for instance, the fact that corporate hotspots—both in accommodations and in all public areas— demand user registration. This requirement excludes asylum seekers who do not possess a valid email address or who are wary that registering will lead to unwanted costs or surveillance when accessing the network. Freifunk participants explained that Telekom attempted to solve this issue by distributing premade accounts and passwords to migrants in emergency camps. However, handing out easily lost slips of paper to a constantly fluctuating population of residents proved ineffective. Compared to these "horror stories," Freifunk's practices and the configuration of open networks seem much more efficient, accessible, and unbureaucratic.

Academic Elizabeth Dunn notes that even though commonly associated with order and peace, humanitarian actions often introduce new forms of friction and "chaos."[16] Among the most salient discussions for Freifunk communities was the question of how to direct ownership and responsibility for "free" installations—which includes paying for routing equipment, the installation, and the local network's maintenance—toward professional social service providers. At times, social service providers would offer money to Freifunk participants for the installation and upkeep of infrastructures, which caused internal controversy over whether accepting payment would undermine Freifunk noncommercial values. While fundraising solved some of the monetary needs, an ongoing question within the Freifunk community was how reliable a service supported by donations could be—and could be expected to be—since the network might break down frequently in the course of updates and community experiments.

The controversy around Freifunk for Refugees turning into a "service" revealed further contradictions. Many Freifunk participants believed that the emancipatory and "self-help" dimension of Freifunk would get lost in any contractual engagement with social service providers. As anthropologist Gregers Petersen shows in his ethnographic account of Freifunk workshops in Berlin, mutual aid and exchange are important group values—the violation of which can quickly lead to conflicts of interest.[17] In many instances, the ideal and desired scenario—that either social workers or residents of the accommodations would take the initiative to learn from the community and eventually take over the infrastructure management themselves—rarely materialized. In some cases, this was because equipment was locked away for security reasons, preventing residents from being able to productively tinker with it. In others, Freifunk activists distributed flyers that explained the network features (e.g., that there was no registration required but that connections were not encrypted) in French, Farsi, and Arabic but did not offer the type of tailored workshop that could have explained and taught Freifunk practices more thoroughly to residents and staff.

When such installations were successfully negotiated and internet service was "officially" provided by the reception centers/shelters, the government argued that the provision justified it cutting the monthly stipend it provided to asylum seekers in some parts of Germany. For example, allowances to asylum seekers and refugees in Bavaria were reduced from €145 to €109 (approximately US$160 to US$120) once a regular free wireless uplink was in place.[18] Therefore, to circumvent cuts in the budget, the only solution open to Freifunk was to unofficially provide uplinks—which again inevitably placed responsibility for figuring out and maintaining the installation on activists and volunteers.

Mobile Internet Access and Marketing to Migrants

Refugees and asylum seekers are heavily reliant on mobile technologies like smartphones and tablets for Skype calls to family and friends, researching legal processes, keeping up with news, and countering the boredom of detention with music and movies.[19] As Vassilis Tsianos argues, while on the move, migrants navigate uneven "accessibility" to digital infrastructures,[20] including the high cost of data-intensive services.

Therefore, commercial actors shape mobile communication in and around the asylum industry—an industry in which Freifunk, through its interventions, is also entangled.

The County Office for Health and Social Affairs (LAGeSo), a key actor in regulating migration, provides an illustrative example that touches on the central role of mobile access. LAGeSo is where refugees and asylum seekers start their procedure and paperwork. During winter 2015, thousands of people had to endure harsh, inclement weather while waiting outside the Berlin office for their number to be called and their papers to be processed. Again, Freifunk participants redirected an internet uplink from the local service provider ("IN-Berlin e.V.") to enable access on the street in front of the building. In this case, Freifunk became one more feature of a rapidly evolving "service economy" around the office, where posters for nearby language schools appeared next to local kiosks selling snacks, which also increasingly advertised cheap international mobile phone cards.[21]

Even though Freifunk managed to provide connectivity on one particular street, this practice cannot solve the problems that refugees encounter with commercial mobile internet providers. First, data packages produce high costs when used for data-intensive services. Second, following recent legislation requiring that SIM card buyers show legal identification, asylum seekers have reported difficulties getting SIM cards with their provisional documents.[22] This situation should provide Freifunk activists leeway to continue to advocate for networks that are cost-free and require no registration. In other instances, employees of the company Lycamobile distributed free SIM cards to newly arrived migrants at train stations. Similarly, the German company yourfone partnered with social service providers Red Cross and Caritas to donate fifty thousand SIM cards. These remained exceptional acts due to backlash from commentators who either criticized this as "an unethical business practice" or questioned whether refugees deserved such "gifts."[23]

Although the Freifunk initiative provides a different type of service— wireless not mobile internet access—participants might usefully expand their aims of inverting existing infrastructures to provide alternatives to the emerging mobile service business targeting migrants. For example, before cooperating with the In-Berlin e.V. provider, activists approached the LAGeSo office to ask permission to share the LAGeSo network via Freifunk. The request was refused for "security reasons." While Monic stresses that such fears are unfounded, she highlights that it always takes skill to "find the right person" within an organization who can be convinced to participate in Freifunk. Consequently, people without papers are frequently constrained to certain localities, such as shelters and reception centers, beyond which they have no option but to rely on mostly industry-driven internet access options, which present multiple challenges. In turn, Freifunk's vision of countering such exclusions in the future remains to be fully explored and achieved in practice.

Infrastructural Standards and Funding for Self-Organized Refugee NGOs

Doing Freifunk in the asylum industry also entails intensified engage-ment with traditional party politics and nongovernmental organizations (NGOs), because Freifunk activists problematize the standards in refugee reception centers/shelters provided by the state. A 2015 report released by the LAGeSo office lists several "quality requirements," including adequate room size, access to outdoor space, nutrition, and a paragraph-long set of guidelines on "information and communication." The latter requirement states that commonly shared or public spaces must be equipped with a cost-free wireless connection and one laptop or tablet per hundred inhabitants.[24]

For Freifunk, this policy should present another opportunity to shift debate away from the binary question of whether or not access is provided toward questions of the quality and quantity of networks and devices. Criticism regarding the scope of the cited "quality requirements" is articu-lated at all Freifunk meetings and across its forums, as well as within alternative and mainstream media outlets. In practice, however, Freifunk participants increasingly focus on local politicians and administrators who sympathize with forms of civic participation rather than focusing on policy reform. For example, a community manager in Bremen working with refugees argued in an interview that Freifunk-style initiatives are vital for cities that are short on public funding. Similarly, the supervi-sor of a large emergency shelter in a remote part of Bremen argued that, as she is busy ensuring that enough showers are available and media infrastructures are not part of her budget, she depends on volunteers to provide internet access, just as she does for clothing donations or lan-guage classes. Critical scholars might argue that Freifunk for Refugees resembles a "firefighter operation," taking responsibility for a state that has been hollowed out by contemporary neoliberal politics.[25]

Despite taking up tasks usually reserved for humanitarian NGOs, Freifunk activists have also embraced existing projects that combine humanitarian engagement and socially just access to media technologies. In Berlin and Brandenburg, the NGO Refugees Emancipation (RE) has been working on the idea of offering both access to and education about computers in self-governed internet cafés in refugee homes, since 2001. The CCC, Freifunk Berlin, and its registered association Förderverein Freie Netzwerke e.V. have begun to support RE projects, for example, by organizing tech workshops, donating hardware, and running a fundraising campaign that raised over €75,000. By doing this, Freifunk did not directly diverge from its noncommercial stance, since most of the activities rely on the donation of time, hardware, and participants' skills. Nevertheless, because RE offers an expense allowance to system administrators who operate the internet cafés, it demands steady and reliable funding. Therefore, despite its more radical promise, the engagement is drawing Freifunk closer to what Monica Krause describes as characteristic of the humanitarian aid sector: the production of "good projects" and its competitive terrain for funding.[26]

Conclusion

In our analysis, the asylum industry becomes visible as a set of actors, practices, and legal regulations that significantly shape the availability and costs of internet access in key sites of refugee and asylum seekers' lives. The Freifunk initiative's response is threefold. First, Freifunk critiques the inefficient "humanitarian" campaigns of large corporate service providers by framing them as incapable and slow and demonstrating the feasibility of Freifunk's alternative practices. Second, it tries to counter the (un)intended consequences of mobile providers' marketing directed at refugees and asylum seekers in precarious situations. Aside from focusing on wireless networks, Freifunk mostly stays in a "prefigurative" mode of politics, only creating apps and services that provide an alternative to mobile usage.[27] Third, Freifunk positioned and aligned itself in relation to NGOs as an important actor in the asylum industry but has yet to take monitoring and fundraising to a sustainable level. (In comparison to the tens of thousands of euros collected earlier, the fundraising campaign for 2017 brought in only €500 [approximately US$565].)

Many of these emerging tensions and controversies are not only impacting the Freifunk movement but also trouble other groups and initiatives. Among them remains the question of how asymmetric rela-tionships between "supporting" activists and "receiving" refugees can be rethought. For example, one can look to events like the United Neighbors protests in 2014 that partly resulted from the OPlatz occupations. Under this rubric, long-standing Berlin residents and recent migrants demon-strated together against forced evictions and displacement and for more common spaces.[28] It remains to be seen whether similar alliances demand-ing a right to the city can be forged when it comes to the vision of the "network commons" that Freifunk Helps demands.

Further, the controversies and tensions discussed here are subject to rapid change. Migration is again increasingly being managed in so-called hot spots, while reception centers are shutting down, as fewer people seeking asylum arrive in Germany—a consequence of efforts to make Europe more difficult for them to reach. As Freifunk equipment is rolled back, many refugees and asylum seekers are left with expensive SIM cards, internet sticks, and precarious access to public Wi-Fi hotspots. In the meantime, new openly "humanitarian" configurations have started to embrace the field of forced migration and technology, including the international aid initiative "Techfugees." Under the slogan "empowering the displaced with technology," this consortium of renowned NGOs, in partnership with companies like Facebook, Uber, and Microsoft, arranges hackathons and tech support start-ups.[29] On closer inspection, the ini-tiative shares many characteristics with Freifunk, ranging from a focus on digital infrastructure provision to the engagement of volunteers and decentralized organization in regional "chapters." It remains unclear what activist responses to this reshuffling of industry actors will look like beyond the narrow scope of service provision in Germany.

Ultimately, this messy entanglement between industry, state, and the morphing ideology of "free/open software" should be further explored rather than negated in the search for a pure radical position. Calling out blind volunteerism and apolitical humanitarian intervention that lets both state and industries off the hook is certainly important, especially in the context of migration. All the same, it's an opportunity to more closely assess which forms of (entrepreneurial) innovation,[30] participation,[31] and experimental practices Freifunk enables.[32] Our own collaboration, a serendipitous "part-nerdship" between academia and activism built on mutual fascination is only one way to keep Freifunk's political analysis up to speed in neoliberal times.[33]

Tim Schütz is a graduate student and Fulbright Fellow in Medicine, Science and Technology Studies (MSTS) at the University of California Irvine.
Monic Meisel is a Berlin-based senior consultant, who studied digital design and business administration. She is a free networks activist and cofounder of the Freifunk movement, which launched the platform www.freifunk-hilft.de.

Notes

1   Napuli Langa, "About the Refugee Movement in Kreuzberg/Berlin," *Movements: Journal for Critical Migration and Border Regime Studies* 1, no. 2 (2015), accessed March 26, 2020, http://movements-journal.org/issues/02.kaempfe/08.langa–refugee-movement-kreuzberg-berlin.html.

2   Inga Schröder, "Freifunk Hilft," in Werner Schiffauer, Anne Eilert, and Marlene Rudloff, eds., *So schaffen wir das-eine Zivilgesellschaft im Aufbruch: 90 wegweisende Projekte mit Geflüchteten* (Bielefeld: transcript, 2017), 181–83.

3   See, e.g., "Berlin: Refugees," friefunk.net, accessed March 26, 2020, https://wiki.freifunk.net/Berlin:Refugees.

4   Sophie Cranston, Joris Schapendonk, and Ernst Spaan, "New Directions in Exploring the Migration Industries: Introduction to Special Issue," *Journal of Ethnic and Migration Studies* 44, no. 4 (March 2018): 543–57, accessed March 26, 2020, https://www.tandfonline.com/doi/full/10.1080/1369183X.2017.1315504.

5   Sebastian Kubitschko and Tim Schütz, "Humanitarian Media Intervention: Infrastructuring in Times of Forced Migration," *spheres: Journal for Digital Cultures* no. 3 (May 2017): 1–14, accessed March 26, 2020, http://spheres-journal.org/humanitarian-media-intervention-infrastructuring-in-times-of-forced-migration.

6   Gregers Petersen, "Freifunk: When Technology and Politics Assemble into Subversion," in James Leach and Lee Wilson, eds., *Subversion, Conversion, Development: Cross-Cultural Knowledge Exchange and the Politics of Design* (Cambridge, MA: MIT Press, 2014), 39–56.

7   Sebastian Kubitschko, Annika Richterich, and Karin Wenz, "'There Simply Is No Unified Hacker Movement.' Why We Should Consider the Plurality of Hacker and Maker Cultures," *Digital Culture & Society* 3, no. 1 (2017): 185–95, accessed April 1, 2020, https://www.mediarep.org/bitstream/handle/doc/3181/DIGITAL-CULTURE-AND-SOCIETY_3_1_2017_185-195_Kubitschko_Conversation_.pdf?sequence=4&isAllowed=y.

8   Luis Felipe R. Murillo and Christopher M. Kelty, "Hackers and Hacking," in Gertraud Koch, ed., *Digitisation: Theories and Concepts for Empirical Cultural Research* (New York: Routledge, 2017), 95–116.

9   Sebastian Kubitschko, "Acting on Media Technologies and Infrastructures: Expanding the Media as Practice Approach," *Media, Culture & Society* 40, no. 4 (May 2018): 632.

10 Founded in 1981 in Germany, the Chaos Computer Club (CCC) is one of the largest hacker organizations in Europe, advocating for technology issues related to privacy and security. For its political significance, see Sebastian Kubitschko, "The Role of Hackers in Countering Surveillance and Promoting Democracy,"

Media and Communication 3, no. 2 (September 2015): 77–87, accessed March 27, 2020, https://www.cogitatiopress.com/mediaandcommunication/article/view/281/281.

11   Christopher M. Kelty, "The Fog of Freedom," in Tarleton Gillespie, Pablo J. Boczkowski, and Kirsten A. Foot, eds., *Media Technologies: Essays on Communication, Materiality, and Society* (Cambridge, MA: MIT Press, 2014), 202.

12   Elizabeth C. Dunn, "Vernacular #Humanitarianism, Adhocracy, and the Problem of Emotion," Allegra Lab, September 26, 2017, accessed March 27, 2020, http://allegralaboratory.net/vernacular-humanitarianism-adhocracy-and-the-problem-of-emotion.

13   Kubitschko, "The Role of Hackers in Countering Surveillance and Promoting Democracy."

14   "Telekom sagt Hilfe bei Unterstützung von Flüchtlingen zu," *Telekom*, September 8, 2015, accessed March 27, 2020, https://www.telekom.com/de/medien/medieninformationen/detail/telekom-sagt-hilfe-bei-unterstuetzung-von-fluechtlingen-zu-349232.

15   "Internet für Flüchtlinge," *Telekom*, November 24, 2015, accessed March 27, 2020, https://telekomhilft.telekom.de/t5/Sonstiges/Internet-fuer-Fluechtlinge/m-p/1568511#M221719.

16   Elizabeth C. Dunn, "The Chaos of Humanitarian Aid: Adhocracy in the Republic of Georgia," *Humanity* 3, no. 1 (Spring 2012): 1–23, accessed March 27, 2020, https://static1.squarespace.com/static/55f7642be4b07229ccbb16e7/t/5665d7e9a976af1373134002/1449514985868/Dunn-2012-Chaos+of+Humanitarian+Aid_Adhocracy.pdf.

17   Petersen, "Freifunk," 50.

18   "Gratis-Wlan für Flüchtlinge: Stadt Nürnberg will kämpfen," *Nürnberger Nachrichten*, March 16, 2016, accessed March 27, 2020, www.nordbayern.de/region/nuernberg/gratis-wlan-fur-fluchtlinge-stadt-nurnberg-will-kampfen-1.5061354.

19   Fritz Habekuß and Stefan Schmitt, "Why Do You Need a Mobile Phone?" *Zeit*, October 1, 2015, accessed March 27, 2020, https://www.zeit.de/gesellschaft/zeitgeschehen/2015-09/smartphones-mobil-phones-refugees-help; Maria Ullrich, "Media Use During Escape—A Contribution to Refugees' Collective Agency," *spheres: Journal for Digital Cultures*, 4 (June 2017): 1–11, accessed March 27, 2020, http://spheres-journal.org/media-use-during-escape-a-contribution-to-refugees-collective-agency.

20   Vassilis Tsianos in conversation with Peter Ott and Ute Holl, "Feldforschung in den 'Mobile Commons,'" *Zeitschrift für Medienwissenschaft* no. 12 (2015): 115–25, accessed March 27, 2020, https://mediarep.org/bitstream/handle/doc/2535/ZfM_12_115-125_Tsianos_et_al_Feldforschung_mobile_commons_.pdf?sequence=4.

21   Elisa Hänel, Stefanie Kofnyt, and Charlotte Seiler, "Smartphones und Sonnenblumenkerne: Die Rolle der digitalen Medien in der Freiwilligenarbeit vor dem LaGeSo in Berlin," in Gökce Yurdakul, Regina Römhild, Anja Schwanhäußer, Birgit zur Nieden, Aleksandra Lakic, and Serhat Karakayali,

eds., *E-Book Project of Humboldt-University Students: Witnessing the Transition: Refugees, Asylum-Seekers and Migrants in Transnational Perspective* (Berlin: Humboldt-Universität zu Berlin, 2016).

22 Tracy, "Aldi-Talk: Refugees Can Not Activate SIM Card," cblog, August 30, 2017, accessed March 27, 2020, http://blog.cubot.net/2017/08/13829.html.

23 See Hilke Fischer, "Migration Widens Niche Mobile Markets," *Deutsche Welle*, March 29, 2016, accessed March 27, 2020, http://www.dw.com/en/migration-widens-niche-mobile-markets/a-19147807.

24 "Berliner Unterbringungsleitstelle, Anlage 2—Qualitätsanforderungen," Landesamt für Gesundheit und Soziales, accessed March 27, 2020, http://www.fluechtlingsinfo-berlin.de/fr/pdf/Qualitaetsanforderungen_LAgeSo_Juni2015.pdf.

25 Wendy Brown, *Undoing the Demos: Neoliberalism's Stealth Revolution* (Cambridge, MA: MIT Press, 2015).

26 Monica Krause, *The Good Project: Humanitarian Relief NGOs and the Fragmentation of Reason* (Chicago: University of Chicago Press, 2014).

27 Michael Hardt and Antonio Negri, *Assembly* (Oxford: Oxford University Press, 2017), 288.

28 Chandra-Milena Danielzik and Daniel Bendix, "Neighbours Welcome! Die Willkommenskultur, die Geflüchteten-Bewegung und die Suche nach Gemeinsamkeiten der Kämpfe um Rechte," in Sabine Hess, Bernd Kasparek, Stefanie Kron, Mathias Rodatz, Maria Schwertl, and Simon Sontowski, eds., *Der lange Sommer der Migration* (Berlin: Assoziation A, 2016), 196–206.

29 "Where We Operate," Techfugees, accessed March 27, 2020, https://techfugees.com/chapters.

30 Lilly Irani, *Chasing Innovation: Making Entrepreneurial Citizens in Modern India* (Princeton, NJ: Princeton University Press, 2019).

31 Christopher M. Kelty, "Too Much Democracy in All the Wrong Places: Toward a Grammar of Participation," *Current Anthropology* 58, no. S15 (February 2017): S77–S90, accessed March 27, 2020, https://www.journals.uchicago.edu/doi/pdfplus/10.1086/688705.

32 Dimitris Papadopoulos, *Experimental Practice: Technoscience, Alterontologies, and More-Than-Social Movements* (Durham, NC: Duke University Press, 2018).

33 John Postill, *The Rise of Nerd Politics: Digital Activism and Political Change* (London: Pluto Press, 2018), 183.

Surmounting the Hostile Environment: Reflections on Social Work Activism without Borders

Lynn King, Bridget Ng'andu, and Lauren Wroe

Social Workers Without Borders (SWWB) is a voluntary organization founded in March 2016, following the unprecedented movement of asylum seekers across Europe in 2015. At that time, an estimated 6,000 people were living in a migrant camp in Calais, France, near the sea crossing to England, including approximately 1,600 unaccompanied asylum-seeking children (UASC). As social workers, we were appalled at the lack of a clear strategy from both the British and French governments for supporting these young people.

SWWB focused initial attention on Calais, conducting needs and best interests assessments with UASC and other residents in support of their legal claims to be reunited with family in the UK. Our work quickly evolved into three distinctive strands: direct work in support of refugees, social work education in the UK, and campaigning for an end to the inhumane immigration policies that harm adults and children alike.

In this chapter, we reflect on the context, contours, and challenges of SWWB's work. First, we explore the relationship between social work and the state, focusing our analysis on shifting ideologies and service provisions for asylum seekers, refugees, and migrants in the UK. Second, we explore our response to the so-called migrant crisis of 2015, read against the backdrop of processes of neoliberalization affecting social work practice more broadly. Third, we explain the challenges faced and aspirations held by SWWB volunteers working within these contexts. We conclude by restating our commitment to social justice and solidarity, without legitimizing states' abdication of their responsibilities.

Social Work in Times of Austerity and Hostility

Social work is underpinned by a set of principles, including human rights, social justice, and equality.[1] While most states (via their founding and official statements and representatives) also claim to respect these principles, underlying tensions between political economic interests of governments and the vocational advocacy of social workers often lead to conflict. The relationship between the British state and professional social workers has seen its share of fallout, especially with regard to asylum seekers and refugees. Discussions of social work provisions for those populations has long been obscured by "the noise and heat of political opinions and policy debates,"[2] even as the rhetoric around asylum seekers and refugees has varied according to the ruling ideology of the day.

In the UK, people seeking asylum are eligible for subsistence and housing support under special provisions outlined in the Immigration and Asylum Act 1999.[3] However, this act also institutionalized the exclusion of asylum seekers from access to mainstream welfare programs and some migrants from other forms of public funds. While exclusion from "public funds" does not incorporate social services, this is a (purposefully) complicated area of legislation that often leads to confusion about what individuals and families are entitled to.

Despite this long-standing exclusion of asylum seekers and many migrants from access to public funds, discussions of state provisions to asylum seekers in the United Kingdom have been framed—since the 2010 election of a Conservative Party–led coalition government—by "austerity" policies aimed at reducing the national deficit through spending cuts, tax increases, or a combination of both.[4] The squeeze on funding for public services has fueled anti-immigrant sentiment within government and across society.

The government's embrace of austerity has seen public services spending in the UK severely slashed yearly for a decade.[5] To restructure the social work profession into a tool to implement these measures, local government authorities implemented workforce changes. The first cuts to services were aimed at social workers themselves, creating job losses and insecurity. Subsequent cuts forced social workers to wield the austerity axe on those most in need of support as services were rolled back across the country. Coupled with persistent tabloid attacks on the profession, which have increased public hostility toward social workers,[6] this strategy has effectively neutralized social work organizations' attempts to challenge oppression and advocate for social justice.

Concurrent to its austerity agenda, the Conservative government adopted a "tougher stance" on immigration, reflected in its Immigration Acts of 2014 and 2016.[7] These policies were explicitly designed to make life difficult for asylum seekers (and other immigrants) through the creation of a "hostile environment"—by instructing doctors, landlords, bank staff, and even driving instructors to adopt immigration enforcement roles.[8] As Europe experienced an unprecedented rate of people moving across its borders in 2015, then prime minister David Cameron disparagingly referred to asylum seekers in the Calais camp as a "swarm of migrants."[9] The aim of these Immigration Acts, backed by their creators' rhetoric, was to deter people from seeking asylum in the UK and to discourage those deemed by the state to be in the UK without appropriate legal status from accessing state support.

The right-wing press has avidly echoed these anti-immigrant, pro-austerity positions. It has also sought—as is common during economic downturns, in this case, following the 2008 global financial crisis—to blame poverty on the poor. With society's weakest members shouldering the blame for the banking sector's greed, the brunt of welfare cuts fell largely unopposed by those in a position to challenge such injustice.[10] In this context, asylum seekers and refugees were routinely framed as "drains" on the taxpayer and dangerous to society.[11] Photos of young people arriving from Calais were splashed across front pages under headlines that questioned their "real" ages, fueling suspicion that these asylum seekers were not actually children but adults seeking "easy" access to the welfare system by submitting "bogus" claims.[12]

By the time the "refugee crisis" had reached global prominence, public sympathy was heavily reduced. Though UK citizens and longer-term residents may not have advocated for refugees to be subjected to appalling circumstances, fears for their own socioeconomic conditions created an uncomfortable dissonance for many. The dominant Europe-wide political narrative of delegitimizing refugees by rhetorically reducing them to "economic migrants" provided a convenient escape route—erasing the violent neoliberal and military policies (including of the UK) that are largely responsible for mass migration. While austerity policies similarly impacted citizens and immigrants, scapegoating asylum seekers again proved easier than confronting structural realities.

Austerity also made it more difficult for overstretched and job-insecure social workers in local authorities to challenge the government's shifting stance on asylum seekers' rights. Social workers are increasingly placed in the morally compromising position of being expected to act as the "eyes" and "ears" of the government. In some cases, social workers have removed children from their asylum-seeking parents, whose inability to support their children cannot be understood outside of their state-approved criminalization and marginalization.[13] Immigration officials have been posted to work alongside social work teams in some local authorities. Participating in such forms of surveillance directly contradicts the ethics of most social workers, who tend to take quite seriously those advocacy obligations—despite the tenuous balance between state employment and advocating for victims of capitalist and state violence.[14] Such monitoring practices further suggest the state suspects social workers are prioritizing the human needs of asylum seekers over their newer neoliberal professional obligations.

SWWB: Foundations in Calais

The formation of SWWB came against a backdrop of pent-up anger within the social work profession, caused largely by factors outlined above. Facing the limitations of our statutory practice to address concerns about the so-called refugee crisis, our founding members sought a return to the core principles of ethical social work: to challenge social injustice and to work in solidarity with the oppressed.[15] As an organization of volunteer social workers, SWWB navigates a grey area between a traditional statutory social work model, conducting needs assessments to access state funded services and legal protections, and volunteer activism. Since our inception, we have had to negotiate a number of practical and legal issues in this new terrain.

Our early work took us to Calais. We had been asked by a UK law firm to conduct "best interests" assessments in the unofficial refugee camp to support the asylum applications of forty-one unaccompanied asylum-seeking children. Before agreeing, we sought advice from our professional membership organization regarding our ability to conduct voluntary social work assessments outside of the UK. In response, it told us we were "trailblazing"—and advised us to seek legal advice, as there was no legal or organizational precedent for this type of work.

There was a total absence of formal provision for the people in Calais; the British and French governments had failed to meet the basic needs of individuals in the camp. The safeguarding of people seeking refuge had fallen to a coalition of professional and voluntary service provision organizations. Consequently, there was no adequate statutory approach for protecting the children in the camp, preventing human trafficking or child sexual exploitation, or providing safe passage routes or access to legal representation in France. This is despite the fact that both the UK and France have ratified the Convention on the Rights of the Child (UN General Assembly, 1989),[16] committing them to protecting the civil, political, economic, social, health, and cultural rights of children and young people in their territories.

The notable absence of the state fit within an agenda of deterrence that became brutally visible in 2017, when the French government made it a crime to assist undocumented persons and the UK government retracted an amendment to the Immigration Act 2016 allowing safe passage to the UK for refugee children in Europe.[17] While the British and French states made their agenda clear in Calais, the people were not deterred. As Somali-British writer Warsan Shire poignantly reminds us: "No one puts their children in a boat unless the water is safer than the land."[18]

As thousands of people arrived in Calais hoping to seek refuge in the UK, similar numbers of volunteers arrived to cocreate infrastructure and provision, including schools, cafés, mosques, legal shelters, and food and clothing distribution points. The show of solidarity was a direct challenge to the UK's "hostile environment" agenda and the hegemonic politic of racism and exclusion toward migrants across Europe. Such action is essential for building movements that challenge racist political agendas and practice solidarity and resistance. Practical and ideological tensions have also arisen, however.

We encountered unexpected initial difficulties in Calais. Independent volunteers, who had provided first response services in the camp—food, clothing, shelter, and social support—were suspicious of social workers, even though we were aligned with neither the UK nor French governments and considered ourselves "radical." Their mistrust may have been influenced by the long-standing demonization of social workers in the UK media—the hostility we encountered was not from refugees themselves but from volunteers, who, like us, came ostensibly to help.

Another challenge SWWB encountered related to the specialist language we had been trained to use. We soon became acutely aware that "assessment," "therapeutic interventions," "empowerment," and so on were incomprehensible and/or reminiscent of state "refugee management" terminology. We also realized that our reliance on such terms—established in academic contexts or under the rhetoric of a marketization agenda—was preventing us from really thinking about what we were doing and why. Having to think outside of these conceptual constraints was exciting and liberating and forced us to design and word assessments according to the needs of those we supported rather than as gatekeepers of services. For example, we did not use terms such as "strengths-based" or "outcome-focused"—the latest incarnations of rebranded austerity-driven social work—instead speaking straightforwardly and empathetically, aiming to convey support and solidarity.

By April 2016, only a few months after our formation, SWWB was growing rapidly. During the critical weeks leading up to the Calais camp being dismantled by state officials—with no discernible plan for French and UK authorities to safeguard the 1,500 unaccompanied child refugees who were then living in the camp—we contacted government agencies and several well-known charities, offering them the service of hundreds of volunteer social workers in the UK, who could properly assess the needs of the unaccompanied children, so that they might be suitability accommodated in the UK or France. We were met with silence and disinterest. Following the October 2016 destruction of the camp, we established ourselves as a registered UK charity. Though not our original intention, we decided this was a necessary means to gain status, without which we would continue to be marginalized by governments and large charities.

SWWB: Reflections and Aspirations

Central to the development of our work model and the reflexive process that has accompanied it is the question: How can we demonstrate solidarity as professionals without legitimizing the state's abdication of its responsibility to children and families? SWWB volunteers now largely work in the UK, conducting assessments of the impact of family separations through detention or deportation to support appeals based on the European Convention on Human Rights.[19] We conduct "needs assessments" to advocate for access to services where local authorities have denied provision based on immigration or asylum status. We take case referrals from lawyers and organizations in the UK, such as Bail for Immigration Detainees and Kids in Need of Defence, and conduct this work in line with our professional code of ethics and legislation outlining the duties of the local authorities in the case of both adults and children.[20] We carry out assessments where legal aid funding for expert reports is lacking or decisions have been made following poor practice by local authorities—which are often quick to deny access to services to individuals and families with no recourse to public funds (NRPF).[21] SWWB subverts the NRPF status by providing free advocacy and expert assessments and by challenging local authority and Home Office decisions to deny care or legal protections.

The issue for organizations such as ours, in positioning ourselves as volunteer professionals, is that our solidarity occurs against the backdrop of the rapid neoliberalizing of the welfare state: an ideological dismantling of public services and the social safety net that instead promotes the withdrawal of government responsibility for citizen welfare and the marketization of the care sector, emphasizing volunteerism, self-sustainability, individual choice, and responsibility.

As public sector workers—in a feminized and insecure care sector, with increasingly dangerous working conditions brought about by high caseloads and lack of resources—we risk legitimizing this retracting of state responsibility by rearranging our family responsibilities and laboring outside of work hours to fill gaps in state provision. We must therefore control the narrative and work to undermine the antisocial values that are simultaneously dismantling our workplaces and necessary societal support structures. In the words of 1970s Queensland Aboriginal activists: "If you have come here to help me, you are wasting your time. But if you have come because your liberation is bound up with mine, then let us work together."[22] It is through this process of identifying our common struggle and forming collective responses that communities of resistance can be created.

Contrary to the antisocial neoliberal values of competition, marketization, and consumerism that plague the care sector,[23] our profession's *social* values promote solidarity, equality, and social and economic justice for *all*. As such, an essential part of SWWB's work is visibly embedding these values in our professional labor and engaging further in solidarity actions. Through our website, newsletters, social media accounts, and collaborations we campaign for social care for all, regardless of race, nationality, or immigration status. We have developed and delivered trainings for students at universities and other institutions promoting understanding and solidarity with refugees, asylum seekers, and others made vulnerable by border regimes. In our actions, we promote principles of social justice and liberation from oppressive state practices and ideologies—put simply, that "another social work is possible."

An intervention carried out by SWWB in 2017 demonstrates how the three facets of our work (campaigning, education, and solidarity) intersect:

> In June 2017, a legal firm in Calais asked SWWB to review the case of a young man who had applied to enter the UK from France. When "Ahmed" arrived in the UK, the Home Office assessed him as eighteen years old and placed him in adult accommodation for asylum seekers, even though he had been represented in France as a minor—based on a SWWB assessment outlining his needs as a sixteen-year-old child.
>
> Ria, the volunteer who had assessed Ahmed in Calais, became his advocate in the UK, with SWWB network support. In the UK, local authorities can disregard the age provided by the Home Office and make their own assessments, in order to meet the needs of those they assess as being children. So Ria made a referral to Children and Family Services (CFS), explaining the situation and requesting they complete a new age assessment for Ahmed. CFS initially declined the referral. Following sustained advocacy, including solicitor letters outlining local authorities' legal duties, CFS eventually changed its stance. The social worker assigned to the case, Katherine, called on SWWB for advice. We explained our role and case findings in Calais—including that Ahmed's rights had been repeatedly undermined by the total absence of care for children crossing Europe. Ahmed was reassessed and placed in the care of the local authority as a sixteen-year-old. Outraged by the lack of care shown to him by the authorities, Katherine collected further clothes and donations from colleagues to ensure Ahmed could settle in to his new home.
>
> SWWB shared this case study with our trade union, which reissued its guidance to social workers that age assessment should not be used as a gatekeeping tactic. We also shared it with our professional networks, reminding colleagues that social workers need not be complicit with the Home Office's deterrence systems—and that a network of professionals exists to support them in their commitment to social justice.

As this case study emphasizes, SWWB can demonstrate solidarity as professionals without legitimizing the state's abdication of responsibility to children and families through a combination of direct work, education, and campaigning. Working alongside Ahmed, we ensured his rights as a child were respected and that his material conditions were improved. Partnership with the local authority social worker facilitated a dialogue that politicized Ahmed's exclusion and mitigated the gatekeeping administrative routine of local authority social work. Finally, we tackled the manifestation of the government's "hostile environment" agenda in social care, by engaging in a campaign strategy to highlight the misuse of age assessment and by encouraging social workers to interrogate the role they are asked to play not only in gatekeeping (a symptom of the ideological shift away from the welfare state) but in policing borders.

We must continue to question the government's approach to the needs of asylum seekers. Our role as social workers obligates us to adhere to our legal duties and responsibilities, including accordance with the European Convention on Human Rights.[24] We must continue to critically analyze the relationship between the state and social work practice. Most importantly, we must continue to challenge state institutions when they do not adhere to—or indeed actively violate—the human rights principles they purport to uphold.

Postscript

In 2018, SWWB withdrew from the Social Worker of the Year (SWOTY) Award shortlist after discovering the event would be sponsored by the outsourcing company Capita. This is an abridged version of the statement SWWB published announcing its decision:

> Capita is a key player in the neoliberalization of the welfare state and the encroaching securitization of public spaces and public services . . . and the creation of a hostile environment for migrant and non-migrant individuals and families alike. SWWB cannot accept an award that is funded by a company whose ethics are antithetical to and violently undermine those of the social work profession.
>
> Capita has had several lucrative contracts with the Home Office to trace and administrate the removal of "overstayers." Most recently, Capita has been a major player in the attacks on the Windrush generation—threatening individuals who have resided in the UK since

childhood with removal, sometimes via text message and with little explanation. Earlier this year, Capita was offered substantial financial "bonuses" in its Home Office contract for hitting and exceeding targets to remove individuals from the UK. Put simply: Capita profits from the racist targeting of individuals and families for removal from the UK. Its contracts lead to the detention of individuals in detentions centers, from which it also profits: a subsidiary of Capita, Tascor, runs multiple residential short-term holding facilities used to detain—often for administrative purposes and often in error—immigration detainees...

Capita's treatment of asylum seekers in removal centers and on removal flights is of grave concern. In May this year, an Inspectorate of Prisons report concluded that Tascor had used excessive restraint on asylum-seeking individuals on a removal flight, and its staff had used degrading language to intimidate and mock detainees. The risks of excessive restraint are incredibly high, and can be fatal (as was the case with the murder of Jimmy Mubenga by G4S staff in a similarly disproportionate use of force in 2010). This work, alongside Capita's appalling behavior in other areas of social care (such as offering bonuses to staff for cutting care packages in Southampton Council) is a threat to our professional values and ethics, and to the individuals and families we work alongside. Capita's work is an attack on social work as it is an attack on migrants across the UK.

We thank all of those who voted to put us forward for this award, and for our social work volunteers who work tirelessly outside of their 9–5 jobs to deliver our assessment, campaigning, and education work. We call on the Social Work Awards to re-consider collusion with organizations such as Capita: social workers across the country are fighting the privatization of services, funding cuts, and the demonization and marginalization of the families with which we work. In short, we must fight the encroaching of Capita into our profession.

We dedicate our nomination to all those who fight the hostile environment on a daily basis, out of necessity or conviction.
In solidarity,
Social Workers Without Borders.

Shortly after publication of this statement, Capita withdrew its sponsorship of the event, and SWOTY announced the establishment of a new ethics panel for future event sponsorship, which it invited SWWB to join. Despite its withdrawal from the Award, the SWOTY judging panel presented SWWB with the Championing Social Work Values prize. SWWB accepted the award, "in recognition of those we support and the amazing work and dedication of all our network members."

Lynn King is one of the founders of Social Workers Without Borders and is a qualified social worker and the Practice Development Lead for Adult Social Work in Kent, UK.
Bridget Ng'andu is a qualified social worker and a lecturer at the University of Kent, UK. She is a member of Social Workers Without Borders and is interested in social work activism.
Lauren Wroe is a social worker, social work academic, and activist interested in repositioning social work as a social justice profession and challenging borders in social work theory and practice.

Notes

1 Sarah Banks, "Ethics," in Iain Ferguson and Michael Lavalette eds., *Critical and Radical Debates in Social Work* (Bristol: Policy Press, 2014); International Federation of Social Workers, "Global Social Work Statement of Ethical Principles," IFSW, July 2, 2018, accessed March 27, 2020, http://ifsw.org/policies/statement-of-ethical-principles.

2 Ravi Kohli and Fiona Mitchell, *Working with Unaccompanied Asylum Seekers: Issues for Policy and Practice* (Basingstoke: Palgrave, 2007), x.

3 Immigration and Asylum Act 1999, legislation.gov.uk, accessed March 27, 2020, http://www.legislation.gov.uk/ukpga/1999/33/contents.

4 Pete Alcock, *Social Policy in Britain* (London: Palgrave Macmillan, 2014).

5 Ann Pettifor, "A Triumph for George Osbourne's Austerity Plan? Not When Our Social Fabric Is in Tatters," *Guardian*, March 4, 2018, accessed March 27, 2020, www.theguardian.com/commentisfree/2018/mar/04/george-osborne-eliminating-current-deficit-austerity-terrible-cost-hubris.

6 Simon Brody, "Social Workers Deserve Better Treatment by the Press," Journalism.co.uk, March 11, 2009, accessed March 27, 2020, https://www.journalism.co.uk/news-commentary/-social-workers-deserve-better-treatment-by-the-press-/s6/a533768.

7 Immigration Act 2014, legislation.gov.uk, accessed March 27, 2020, http://www.legislation.gov.uk/ukpga/2014/22/contents/enacted; Immigration Act 2016, legislation.gov.uk, accessed March 27, 2020, http://www.legislation.gov.uk/ukpga/2016/19/contents/enacted.

8 "Briefing: What Is the Hostile Environment, Where Does It Come from, Who Does It Affect?" Free Movement, accessed April 1, 2020, https://www.

freemovement.org.uk/briefing-what-is-the-hostile-environment-where-does-it-come-from-who-does-it-affect.

9   Jessica Elgot, "How David Cameron's Language on Refugees Has Provoked Anger," *Guardian,* January 27, 2016, accessed March 27, 2020, https://www.theguardian.com/uk-news/2016/jan/27/david-camerons-bunch-of-migrants-quip-is-latest-of-several-such-comments.

10 Michael Lavalette and Vasilios Loakimidis, "International Social Work or Social Work Internationalism? Radical Social Work in Global Perspective," in Michael Lavalette, ed., *Radical Social Work Today, Social Work at the Crossroads,* (Bristol: Polity Press, 2011).

11 Liz Gerard, "The Press and Immigration: Reporting the News or Fanning the Flames of Hatred," *SubScribe,* September 3, 2016, accessed March 27, 2020, http://www.sub-scribe.co.uk/2016/09/the-press-and-immigration-reporting.html.

12 Carly McLaughlin, "'They Don't Look Like Children': Child Asylum-Seekers, the Dubs Amendment and the Politics of Childhood," *Journal of Ethnic and Migration Studies* 44, no. 11 (August 2018): 1757–73, accessed March 27, 2020, https://www.tandfonline.com/doi/full/10.1080/1369183X.2017.1417027.

13 Evidence gathered by UK advocacy projects uncovered frequent instances of children being removed from destitute asylum-seeking parents. This is in direct contradiction to UK legislation (The Children's Act 1989, legislation.gov.uk, accessed March 27, 2020, http://www.legislation.gov.uk/ukpga/1989/41/contents), which states that social services have a responsibly to protect children "by supporting the family as a whole." The destitution of parent(s) must be understood within the context of their state-directed marginalization, underpinned by neoliberalist ideologies and the resultant racist and xenophobic policies required to maintain this hegemony.

14 Chris Smethhurst, "Class and Inequality," in Kish Bhatti-Sinclair and Chris Smethurst, eds., *Diversity, Difference and Professional Dilemmas: Developing Skills in Challenging Times* (London: Open University Press/McGraw Hill, 2017).

15 Linda Briskman and Sarah Cemlyn, "Reclaiming Humanity for Asylum-Seekers," *International Social Work* 48, no. 6 (November 2005): 714–24.

16 Convention on the Rights of the Child, November 20, 1989, United Nations Human Rights Office of the High Commissioner, accessed March 27, 2020, https://www.ohchr.org/en/professionalinterest/pages/crc.aspx.

17 In 2016, the UK government was forced to accept the "Dubs Amendment" to its Immigration Act, which required the UK to resettle "an unspecified amount" of UASC from France, Italy, and Greece—so worded to avoid setting an upper limit but expected to prompt resettlement of around 3,000 young people. Following a series of controversially announced "limits" on the number of places available—first of 350, then of 480—a 2018 investigation found just 20 children resettled in the UK under the scheme were unaccompanied; see Mark Townsend, "UK Admits Only 20 Unaccompanied Child Refugees in Two Years," *Guardian,* November 3, 2018, accessed April 1, 2020 https://www.theguardian.com/world/2018/nov/03/uk-admits-only-20-unaccompanied-child-refugees-in-two-years.

18 Warsan Shire, "Home," SeekersGuidance: The Global Islamic Seminary, September 2, 2015, accessed April 1, 2020, https://www.seekershub.org/blog/2015/09/home-warsan-shire.

19 Specifically, article 8 of the European Convention on Human Rights, which covers the right to respect for private and family life.

20 "The Code of Ethics for Social Work," British Association of Social Workers, last updated October 2014, accessed March 27, 2020, https://www.basw.co.uk/about-basw/code-ethics; Care Act 2014, legislation.gov.uk, accessed March 27, 2020, http://www.legislation.gov.uk/ukpga/2014/23/contents/enacted; Children's Act 1989, legislation.gov.uk, accessed March 27, 2020, https://www.legislation.gov.uk/ukpga/1989/41.

21 NRPF guidelines, introduced in 1999, limit access to mainstream welfare and housing benefits for certain immigrant populations, although they retain some access to state support. They are, however, often misinterpreted by local authorities; see Natalia Jane Farmer, "'No Recourse to Public Funds', Insecure Immigration Status and Destitution: The Role of Social Work?" *Critical and Radical Social Work* 5, no. 3 (November 2017): 11, accessed March 27, 2020, https://researchonline.gcu.ac.uk/ws/portalfiles/portal/26605608/CRSW_S_17_00028.pdf.

22 Reni Eddo-Lodge, "Episode 9: The Big Question" (podcast), About Race, May 16, 2018, accessed March 27, 2020, https://www.aboutracepodcast.com/9-the-big-question. This quote is often attributed to Lilla Watson, a member of the 1970s coalition of Aboriginal activists that together originated the phrase. Watson has repeatedly requested attribution to the broader group.

23 Aditya Chakraborty, "These Councils Smashed Themselves to Bits: Who Will Pick up the Pieces?" *Guardian*, August 13, 2018, accessed March 27, 2020, https://www.theguardian.com/commentisfree/2018/aug/13/councils-austerity-outsourcing-northamptonshire-barnet.

24 European Convention on Human Rights, European Court of Human Rights, accessed March 27, 2020, https://www.echr.coe.int/Documents/Convention_ENG.pdf.

Neoliberalism and LGBT Asylum: A Play in Five Acts

Siobhán McGuirk

Act I

A small US organization boasts a signature appearance in regional Pride parades.[1] Under a banner reading, "Still hiding in 75 countries. Please help. Donate online," a group of people march with paper bags over their heads, blocky brown visages disturbed only by peep holes. They are intended to represent Lesbian, Gay, Bisexual, and/or Transgender (LGBT) asylum seekers.[2]

The spectacle is organized by a local church-affiliated group, set up over a decade ago to provide material support specifically and only to LGBT asylum seekers. In the early years, the people wearing bags at Pride mostly fit that description; they were people receiving organizational support. Five years in, at a pre-Pride planning meeting, new arrival Mariah asked if she could wear a rainbow mask instead of the bag. Mariah explained that, while she didn't want to risk a stray viral photograph outing her to people back home, she still wanted to "celebrate Pride" by wearing something joyful. Mariah privately told me she found the bag demeaning but thought it would be wise to adopt a conciliatory tone at the meeting. It was a prudent approach.

The organization leader, Jennifer—who walked every year unmasked, very much the public face of the group—did not appreciate Mariah's suggestion or the enthusiastic response it prompted among other asylum seekers at the meeting. Jennifer, a white US citizen who felt called by her faith to help LGBT asylum seekers, said rainbow masks would water down the organization's message—a hard truth that the public "needed to

267

hear." Jennifer recapped the facts as she saw them for those present: LGBT asylum seekers have to hide their identities, because their own immigrant communities are not safe; many do not feel proud and suffer from internalized shame; the organization relies on donations to continue its lifesaving work. She concluded with her catchphrase: "Pulling on heartstrings opens purse strings." An uneasy compromise was reached: each person marching, except, of course, Jennifer, could choose to wear either a bag or a mask.

In the event, none of the LGBT asylum seekers or asylees marching in Pride wanted to wear a bag. Fretful that their signature message would be lost, Jennifer asked volunteers to don the paper bags. A surreal performance ensued: under the same somber banner, half a dozen white US citizens marched in silence, their faces mostly covered by brown paper bags, projecting an image of dejected, defenseless LGBT asylum seekers. Meanwhile, actual LGBT asylum seekers danced and posed for photos, wide smiles visible below facial features obscured by glitter. A few wore the flags of their home countries around their shoulders, a self-determined and politically potent assertion of national and personal pride.

After the march, Jennifer told Beyoncé, a trans asylum seeker from Trinidad, that her "provocative" dancing had "sent the wrong message." If she wanted to do that in the future, Jennifer explained, she should join another Pride parade contingent. Reliant on the organization for housing and financial support while she awaited a decision on her asylum claim— or a work permit, if that arrived first—Beyoncé understood Jennifer's warning.

Act II

A variety of organizations work specifically with LGBT asylum seekers in the United States, from small, local, all-volunteer groups to national nonprofits with salaried staff and million-dollar turnovers. The messaging these groups promote is more or less refined, depending on PR budget. It is also more or less the same: LGBT asylum seekers are among the "most vulnerable" immigrants,[3] "voiceless,"[4] and "living in the shadows,"[5] until they are granted "safety" and "freedom in the United States."[6] They are shunned by their families and immigrant communities, which are inherently homophobic.[7] They are "innocent" victims,[8] persecuted for "who they love"[9]—their political agency at most a secondary issue. They are reliant on donations and aid from their US "brothers and sisters" but are eager to contribute to US society,[10] as indicated by their professional credentials, admirable work ethic, and desire for monogamous marriage.[11]

At least, this is what I have gleaned from the hundreds of fundraising emails, flyers, videos, newspaper articles, and social media campaigns I have studied over the past decade. Taken together, they solidify limited imaginings of who an LGBT asylum seeker is or can be—and of who they are not. Asylum adjudicators working for the state rely on stereotypes to grant or deny claims.[12] Nongovernmental organizations (NGOs), ostensibly resisting these constructions, paradoxically create new ones, embedded in wider homonationalist discourses that promote a clear victim/savior binary—and frame the United States itself as a benevolent protector of (deserving liberal) subjects.[13]

NGO staff and volunteers told me that this rhetoric "works" for their organizations, prompting donations and media attention. It rarely "works" for individual LGBT asylum seekers—at least not beyond the context of their asylum claim. After receiving a decision on their case, most of my interlocutors disavowed the identity as swiftly as possible, eager not to be associated with neediness, abjection, or an uncritical embrace of a rainbow flag. Not incidentally, most organizations' service provision ceases at the same juncture.

Reticence to be known as an "LGBT asylum seeker" can prove challenging for NGOs reliant on willing participants to tell their stories—to "pull on heartstrings." Some people do embrace the identity categorization, of course, or agree to speak at events as a way to "give back" to organizations that have helped them. Others see it as a politically important position from which they might highlight anti-LGBT persecution back home or promote immigrant rights in the United States. Perceptions and narratives are difficult to control, however.

Mikel was repeatedly invited to speak at events organized by think tanks, NGOs, and local government offices, contacted through the small LGBT asylum support group that provided him with a monthly stipend. Mikel had founded an important human rights organization back in his home country and had grown accustomed to "invited expert" status. He was, therefore, irked whenever his US event bio simply read: "LGBT asylee." He told me he stopped talking at events, because: "Nobody ever saw me as me." Audiences wanted to hear his trauma—not his analyses. Mikel was also frustrated with the lack of compensation provided for his time or contributions. While other invited speakers received honorariums or counted their time as salaried work hours, Mikel was offered only platitudes about "making a difference" and "promoting the support group."

At the time, Mikel worked a minimum-wage job. He had applied for positions at various LGBT organizations, his CV full of relevant (over-seas) experience. He was not invited to any interviews. His friend Joni, a prominent African trans rights activist, applied for an unpaid internship at the high-profile LGBT asylum legal specialist organization that had sup-ported his claim a year prior. NGO staff had talked effusively about Joni's expertise when courting him to appear (unpaid) in a promotional video, so Joni was confident in his application. The rejection email said he was "not the right fit." Victims cannot take saviors' jobs.

Act III

I got involved with the LGBT Freedom and Asylum Network (LGBT-FAN) in 2012. The group was founded by people affiliated with faith organiza-tions but soon grew to include a broader cross-section, including more asylum seekers and asylees. I joined because I saw it as an entry point for interrupting dominant narratives.

We organized a congressional briefing in early 2014, with LGBT-FAN's leadership deciding to prioritize policy change and lobbying efforts. Our speakers advocated for a rollback in detention and investments in alterna-tives to detention (ATD),[14] a ban on shackles in immigration hearings, the right to legal representation in asylum hearings, an end to the one-year filing deadline, better competency training on LGBT experience for immi-gration officers, and quicker access to welfare services and employment permits for asylum seekers.

Important issues all, but ones more established organizations were already making—and to far larger audiences. We were a small, unfunded network lacking sufficient resources to support or create high-profile policy action. Some members aspired toward one day becoming an influ-ential NGO. Others—myself included—felt LGBT-FAN should sidestep the trappings and traps of the nonprofit industrial complex and focus on simpler goals: connecting existing groups spread across the country; organizing horizontally with people seeking asylum; sharing news, infor-mation, advice, questions, referrals, campaigns, etc. As we put more energy into this low-profile work, the makeup of LGBT-FAN members changed; reformist voices drifted away as more radical actors signed up.

This shift was precipitated by another internal debate: "How could we disrupt those limited, dominant narratives?" At least, that was the conversation we aspired toward. In reality, many people attracted to LGBT asylum seeker support networks did not want to disrupt those discourses. They were motivated by them.

At one LGBT-FAN affiliate meeting, for example, attendees balked at calls to support a policy proposal that would allow undocumented people to obtain a driver's license. One person exclaimed, "I don't think of asylum seekers as 'immigrants'!" At events, we were frequently asked, "What can we do about people pretending to be gay to get asylum?" These statements and concerns were antithetical to our published aims but dominated popular imaginaries. At our own meetings, we spent as much time correcting stereotypes as developing new projects.

We set out to do both with our 2015 publication *Stronger Together: A Best Practices Guide to Supporting LGBT Asylum Seekers in the United States*.[15] Its foremost purpose was to elevate LGBT asylum seekers and asylees as the best source of advice and knowledge about their own experiences and needs. It was further designed to provide accurate information about the asylum process in plain language for a broad audience, to encourage service providers to embrace sustainable and ethical practices, and to promote collaboration—not competition—between organizations.

In producing the publication, we wanted to put politics into practice: individuals with direct experience of seeking asylum were credited as they chose to be and recognized as experts throughout. Our modest funding was split evenly between four author-researchers, regardless of their titles or immigration status. The research process itself facilitated connection-building across organizations, allowing us to create a directory of service providers, expand our email listserv, and create forums where challenging but necessary and productive conversations have played out, including between radical queer no-borders activists, liberal NGO staff, unfunded ministry-based organization volunteers, and people with diametrically different experiences of seeking asylum.

Working with two high-profile NGO funders was instructive: our budget was as small as the hours dedicated to discussing logo sizes and placements were long. Undoubtedly, we depended on these backers for resources and visibility. The actual content of our project appeared of little concern to them, however; one of the NGO's in-house magazines included the xenophobic broadside in its article on *Stronger Together*: "All too often, they cannot find refuge with . . . others who have resettled in this country; anti-LGBT attitudes abound in many of those communities."

LGBT-FAN ran out of steam in 2017. We lacked the continuous funding and volunteer time needed to maintain up-to-date resources and manage websites, inboxes, and social media accounts. Moreover, the advent of Trump prompted many of our members to reevaluate their priorities. LGBT-FAN did important work but was a product of its time. Times change.

Act IV

In 2014, two Ivy League undergraduate students contacted LGBT-FAN about a website and smartphone app they were developing, intended to connect LGBT asylum seekers with suitable service providers. They invited us to be the "established partner" required to enter a $100,000, university-sponsored enterprise competition. LGBT-FAN agreed in principle, but the proposal was not prizewinning.

A few months later, one of the now graduates contacted us from an .org email tied to the heavily branded, already launched website of ASLink.[16] The email asked for all our data on New York service providers and introductions to LGBT asylum seekers. Concerned that ASLink was plowing ahead (and soliciting donations) despite little apparent knowledge of, or even contact with, its target population, we declined.

Venture funders, social innovation accelerators, and a few foundations responded otherwise, and ASLink's profile has grown slowly but steadily in subsequent years. Its team members seem well-intentioned. Its listings have likely helped people find resources. In its current guise, however, it promotes a deeply distorted image of LGBT asylum seekers (and adjacent populations). It perpetuates savior/victim tropes, asserts elite-led technological solutions to sociopolitical problems, and erases the work and realities of immigrant-led, solidarity-focused advocacy and service provision.

It's the same old story—with a modern twist.

ASLink publicity materials say it is a "lifesaving resource." It does not, however, provide direct services or informed referrals. It simply catalogues already existing companies and organizations that ASLink volunteers either locate online or that request inclusion in the database. For-profit businesses seeking paying clients are welcome to self-nominate.

"Verification" that a resource is "LGBTQ+ and immigrant-friendly" involves: "researching and often directly communicating with each resource." Volunteer data managers are responsible for this task. Requirements for the data management intern position include having "obtained or pursuing a bachelor's or graduate degree" and being able to work, unpaid, 10:00 a.m.–5:00 p.m., Monday–Friday for three months. An extraordinarily privileged few people fit this profile. Neither Mikel nor Joni, despite their relevant experience, would qualify.

While ASLink interns remotely e-verify resources, low-profile organizations and networks continue to provide vital everyday support to LGBT asylum seekers and adjacent populations regardless of immigration status. These groups do not always advertise and rarely with search engine optimization in mind. They establish reputations over time and through word of mouth. While some announce that they are (read: aim to be) "LGBT-friendly," others let it be known through tacit, coded, colloquial, or non-English terminology. Low-maintenance Facebook pages, increasingly popular in place of websites, are made and named for local community members—not ASLink data managers. The ASLink "verification process" thus privileges those private businesses and large NGOs with the time, staff, and savvy to maintain attractive websites and answer cold calls and emails with tick box questions.

For already overstretched groups, answering non-pressing emails is a markedly low priority. One queer immigrant group leader told me they had received but not replied to ASLink emails, explaining: "They kept trying to talk to me 'before we can list your organization' but I was legit too busy—I was running multiple campaigns and at immigration prisons at the time.... They were very entitled. They didn't know enough about the actual infrastructure or lived experience of asylum seekers but posed like they did."

Unsurprisingly, the ASLink catalogue disclaimer reads: "We make no representations regarding the viability or capabilities of any such providers.... Asylum seekers who contact any providers do so at their own risk." That's the small print. A recent press release more boldly asserts: "Without [ASLink's] information on where it is safe to go for help, LGBT asylum seekers face increased risk of homelessness, homophobic or transphobic service providers, or no option besides giving up on their asylum claim and facing deportation."

Framing the population it designs to help as incapable, unresourceful, and wholly reliant on its own digital catalogue for survival justifies ASLink's existence. It also erases long-standing resource creation, information-sharing, and community-building projects led by LGBT asylum seekers and other queer immigrants. Without such work there would be little to catalogue.

ASLink recently announced plans for a new "product": a forum for people seeking asylum to share information and advice. It states that this will be an "online safe space" but does not explain how the safety of users—people ASLink itself defines as "vulnerable"—will be ensured. Elsewhere in the United States, immigrant rights advocates are issuing stern warnings about digital security culture,[17] while Immigrations and Customs Enforcement (ICE) officers are creating puppet accounts specifically to "infiltrate" digital spaces.[18] Such realities do not appear to trouble ASLink.

Its announcement emphasizes that it is the message board infrastructure—not the anticipated contributions of LGBT asylum seeker users—that is "invaluable." "Without [our forum]" the announcement boasts, two hypothetical Mexican trans women living in San Francisco "would likely never meet." It's a bizarre claim, given San Francisco's renowned—albeit under threat—Latinx communities, resources, networks, and spaces. Moreover, there are already apps for that: LGBT immigrants (like millions of others) already use established social networking platforms to share information and advice—and to build trust on their own terms.[19]

Following a tech start-up model wherein web presence signifies existence and success is measured in "growth," "unique visitors," and "reach," ASLink has forgone ground-level research and long-standing network-building in favor of rapid geographical expansion.[20] Convinced of their project's utility and their own positionality as lifesavers, a leadership team well-versed in social enterprise marketing has attracted high-profile support by leveraging cultural capital—whiteness, citizenship, family name, alma mater—that is beyond the reach of many small immigrant-led projects, especially those prioritizing political action over large NGO- and social enterprise–led "solutions."

In the niche of the LGBT asylum seekers' rights movement, there should be space for complementary high- and low-tech resources, for recognition of mainstream and grassroots projects, and for multivocal and collaborative work. In a competitive funding environment, however, the neoliberal NGO imperative to be "the first," "the only," "the biggest," etc. consumes that space.[21] Its leaders refuse to acknowledge the shoulders upon which they stand—and appear content to stamp down. ASLink has sought to corner the market through such branding. In doing so, it has elevated its visibility far beyond its capability.

Notably few people with direct experience of seeking asylum remain involved in ASLink. Its #YouBelong social media campaign uses stock photos as stand-ins for LGBT asylum seekers ostensibly endorsing the project. None of the four people featured have publicly identified as LGBT; three of them live outside the United States.[22] Their faces have been commodified without their consent or knowledge to provide a dubious sheen of diversity and "authenticity" to ASLink, an action with profound ethical implications and racist overtones.[23]

A white, elite-educated, nonimmigrant director is (once again) very much the public face of the project. She is steadily building her profile as "a social entrepreneur and LGBT advocate"—increasingly cited as an "informed" voice on LGBT asylum and racking up personal achievement awards. For financial year 2018–2019, the ASLink fundraising priority was an executive director salary. When the job advert goes live, Mikel and Joni need not apply.

Act V

Academics are quick to critique—too slow to self-reflect.

I am a queer woman legally protected against discrimination where I live and work. I am a white British citizen. Given my family ties, I face a relatively smooth—if expensive—pathway to legal residency in either the United States or a European Union member state. This is not mere privilege. It is luxury. My own cultural and professional capital has been fortified by LGBT asylum seekers (among many others) letting me into their lives and allowing me to write about their insights and experiences. Through this, I too have become an "expert" voice.

It is reassuring to think that I am a different sort of anthropologist; a different sort of NGO volunteer; a different sort of writer. Or that my words jam the gears of rhetorical juggernauts promoting and justifying colonial, racist, xenophobic, elitist, homonormative, neoliberal norms. But I also recognize: I have been complicit in every act.

Siobhán McGuirk (editor) is a postdoctoral researcher in anthropology at Goldsmiths, University of London. She also works as a filmmaker and curator and is an editor of *Red Pepper* magazine (www.redpepper.org.uk). Her work addresses gender, sexuality, migration, structures of social injustice, and arts-based activism.

Notes

1   These reflections are based on extensive ethnographic fieldwork carried out in sites across the United States from 2012 to 2018. I use pseudonyms and have omitted identifying information throughout, with the exception of LGBT-FAN, an organization to which my name is publicly tied. The views contained within this chapter are entirely my own and are not representative of LGBT-FAN or any other organization with which I am or have been affiliated.

2   I use "LGBT" here for consistency, while recognizing the importance of more inclusive acronyms that include queer (Q), non-binary (NB), asexual (A) and more (+) non-normative sexual and/or gender identities. The majority of organizations herein discussed either have used in the past or continue to use "LGBT."

3   Andre Banks, "Urgent: Get Her to Safety," September 28, 2015, email sent to All Out public listserv in New York.

4   *Rainbow Bridges: A Community Guide to Rebuilding the Lives of LGBTI Refugees and Asylees* (San Francisco, CA: Organization for Refuge, Asylum, and Migration, 2012), accessed March 27, 2020, https://www.refworld.org/docid/524d3e9d4.html.

5   Crosby Burns, Ann Garcia, and Philip E. Wolgin, "Living in Dual Shadows: LGBT Undocumented Immigrants," Center for American Progress, March 8, 2013, accessed March 27, 2020, https://www.americanprogress.org/issues/immigration/reports/2013/03/08/55674/living-in-dual-shadows.

6   Gene Robinson, "LGBT Asylum Seekers Need America More Than Ever," *Daily Beast*, June 29, 2014, accessed March 27, 2020, https://www.thedailybeast.com/lgbt-asylum-seekers-need-america-more-than-ever; the same article was also published by the *Daily Beast* under the headline "A Harrowing Escape from Anti-Gay Africa."

7   Aaron Nicodemus, "Beatings, Persecution Fuel Bids for Residency," *Worcester Telegram*, July 21, 2009, accessed March 27, 2020, https://www.telegram.com/article/20090721/NEWS/907210416.

8   Fern Remedi-Brown, "Boston Pride Still Not Safe," *Guardian Liberty Voice*, June 15, 2014, accessed March 27, 2020, https://guardianlv.com/2014/06/boston-pride-still-not-safe.

9   Maria Inés Taracena, "LGBT Global Persecution Leads to Asylum Seekers in Southern AZ," *Arizona Public Media*, May 27, 2014, accessed March 27, 2020, azpm.org/s/19678-headline.

10 *Rainbow Bridges.*

11 Caroline Dessert, "Tamara's Journey: A Story of Hope," December 15, 2015, email sent to Immigration Equality public listserv in New York.

12 Michael Kimmel and Cheryl Llewellyn, "Homosexuality, Gender Nonconformity, and the Neoliberal State," *Journal of Homosexuality* 59, no. 7 (August 2012): 1087–94; Deborah A. Morgan, "Not Gay Enough for the Government: Racial and Sexual Stereotypes in Sexual Orientation Asylum Cases," *Law & Sexuality* 15 (2006): 135–61.

13 Siobhán McGuirk, "(In)credible Subjects: NGOs, Attorneys, and Permissible LGBT Asylum Seeker Identities," *Political and Legal Anthropology Review (PoLAR)* 41, no. S1: (September 2018): 4–18.

14 As noted by Marzena Zukowska, "ATD" programs and terminology emerged from grassroots community-based initiatives to find alternatives to mass incarceration for asylum seekers and others facing immigration prisons but has in recent years been co-opted by both for-profit companies and a federal government invested in expanding the prison infrastructure; see Marzena Zukowska, "The Cost of Freedom," this volume, 181–91.

15 Siobhán McGuirk, Max Niedzwiecki, Temitope Oke, and Anastasia Volkova, *Stronger Together: A Guide to Supporting LGBT Asylum Seekers* (Washington, DC: LGBT Freedom and Asylum Network, 2015), accessed March 27, 2020, https://assets2.hrc.org/files/assets/resources/LGBT_Asylum_Seekers_FINAL.pdf.

16 ASLink is a pseudonym. Unless otherwise noted, attributed quotes are taken from the organization's publications and promotional materials.

17 Malkia Cyril, "Fed Up with Facebook, Activists Find New Ways to Defend Their Movements," Tech Crunch, April 10, 2018, accessed March 27, 2020, https://techcrunch.com/2018/04/10/fed-up-with-facebook-activists-find-new-ways-to-defend-their-movements.

18 Amanda Holpuch, "Facebook Urged to Tackle Spread of Fake Profiles Used by US Police," *Guardian*, April 22, 2019, accessed March 27, 2020, https://www.theguardian.com/technology/2019/apr/22/facebook-law-enforcement-fake-profiles-ice; Rachel Levinson-Waldman, "How ICE and Other DHS Agencies Mine Social Media in the Name of National Security," Common Dreams, June 5, 2019, accessed April 1, 2020, https://www.commondreams.org/views/2019/06/05/how-ice-and-other-dhs-agencies-mine-social-media-name-national-security.

19 Multiple sources within immigrant rights movements have informed me that WhatsApp (or Signal) is preferred for messaging, due to its end-to-end encryption, and that Facebook remains the go-to site for finding networks and sharing information.

20 In private conversation, an activist who identifies as undocuqueer described ASLink's "expansion" into Mexico as "nonprofit imperialism."

21 Lori A. Brainard and Patricia D. Siplon, "Toward Nonprofit Organization Reform in the Voluntary Spirit: Lessons from the Internet," *Nonprofit and Voluntary Sector Quarterly* 33, no. 3 (September 2004): 439, accessed March 28, 2020, http://citeseerx.ist.psu.edu/viewdoc/download?doi=10.1.1.615.4234&rep=rep1&type=pdf.

22 Using a reverse image search and contacting the credited photographers, I found that the people featured in the ASLink #YouBelong campaign are: a Muslim mother of three living in Italy photographed by a local "street photographer"; a Dutch model whose portfolio images frequently appear in "Hottest Men's Haircuts" articles; a university student posing for her aspiring photographer friend in the US Midwest; an unnamed man in Lima, Peru. These faces are now all coded online as LGBT asylum seekers living in the United States.

23 Nancy Leong, "Racial Capitalism," *Harvard Law Review* 126, no. 8 (June 2013): 2151–2226, accessed March 28, 2020, https://harvardlawreview.org/wp-content/uploads/pdfs/vol126_leong.pdf.

V
Aftermaths?

Border Militarization in a Warming World: Climate Adaptation for the Rich and Powerful

Todd Miller

A few days after the earthquake in January 2010, a US Air Force cargo plane circled the devastated country of Haiti for five hours as part of one of the first aid missions. Over and over again the plane broadcasted the loud, prerecorded voice of Haiti's ambassador to the United States, Raymond Joseph, in Kreyol:

> Listen, don't rush on boats to leave the country. If you do that, we'll all have even worse problems. Because I'll be honest with you: If you think you will reach the US and all the doors will be wide open to you, that's not at all the case. And they will intercept you right on the water and send you back home to where you came from.[1]

The disembodied voice from the sky addressed a still stunned population scrambling in the rubble of an earthquake that killed approximately 316,000 people and left one million homeless. In a way, the announcement was a clear message not only for the Haitian people in that moment but also for anyone across the globe facing such a catastrophe: you will be physically blockaded if you even dare to try to enter the United States.

In Haiti's case, the US border had already arrived at its shores in the form of sixteen coast guard cutters. The private company GEO Group had also cleared a six-hundred-bed space at the infamous US base in Guantanamo Bay, Cuba, to incarcerate these would-be asylum seekers.

This scenario of environmental destruction gives a glimpse of what is in store for this planet in an era of accelerated global warming. While there may not be a clear connection between earthquakes and climate change, there are strong forecasts for other dire situations, such as crops wilting in widespread droughts, rising seas inundating coastal megacities, and powerful super storms devastating huge swaths of territory, like the island of Barbuda, which was declared "extinguished" after Hurricane Irma in September 2017.[2] The Internal Displacement Monitoring Centre reports that between 2008 and 2016 more than 21.5 million people per year were displaced due to "climate-related hazards."[3] The numbers are larger than those displaced by war and do not include those impacted by drought.

Future projections of people on the move due to climate upheavals range widely from 150 million to one billion people by 2050. There are vigorous debates around these projections. Regardless, according to the report *In Search of Shelter: Mapping the Effects of Climate Change on Human Migration and Displacement*, the displacements will be "staggering" and "the scope and scale could vastly exceed anything that has occurred before."[4]

If things continue in this fashion, and if emissions continue business as usual, asylum seekers will triple by the year 2100, according to a report by Columbia University and the London School of Economics.[5] Although researchers made these calculations based on data captured in Europe between 2000 and 2014, similar trends could very well occur across the globe, including in the United States.

However, there is no legal framework—neither internationally nor in any country (though New Zealand may soon be the one exception)—that offers status to people on the move due to environmental destruction, as seen so clearly in the above Haiti example. Instead, there will be border walls in every sense of the word.

More Walls

As sociologist Christian Parenti puts it, climate change is the "catastrophic convergence" of political, economic, and ecological crises compounding in places like Haiti in the Global South.[6] Migration forced by catastrophic climate change is nowhere recognized as grounds for asylum, however. Keeping it off the table has become a sort of dual investment for international elites. First, it has not only enhanced but has ensured the continued spectacular growth of the homeland security industry, most specifically in terms of global border fortifications. Second, such border controls become part of a climate adaptation for the rich and powerful, engineered to manage the blowbacks of climate change—i.e., the very people it displaces, who would be seeking asylum if they could.

When the Berlin Wall fell in 1989, there were fifteen border walls across the globe. By 2018, there were seventy-seven, two-thirds of which were constructed post-9/11. These walls are only one part of an increasingly sophisticated and expanding enforcement and exclusion apparatus that hardly stays put on international boundary lines. In the United States, for example, there are one hundred-mile border jurisdiction zones that are and can be further filled with roving patrols of agents, checkpoints, and surveillance hardware. The US border and other borders across the globe have become high-tech surveillance zones, reinforced by super cameras, biometric systems, motion sensors, and drones—as a few examples—produced by private companies for an industry that by all forecasts will continue to grow for the foreseeable future.[7] The denial of asylum fuels this industry.

In 2016, the global security market grew at an 8.3 percent clip valued at $658 billion. The biometric submarket, or Big Brother, if you prefer, is forecast to triple between 2015 and 2022, rising from $10.74 billion to $32.73 billion—a more than 16 percent per year growth rate. Biometrics include facial, voice, and iris recognition, and large database systems of the sort that might have been described in a tech-fetishizing sci-fi novel not too long ago. Also forecast is a world with three times more drones, if that market indeed triples as forecast, from $6 billion in 2015 to $22 billion in 2022.

A good portion of those security industry billions is being poured into the jagged dividing lines between the Global North and South. Instead of asylum for the climate-displaced who dare to cross international borders—many do not—border zones will be one of the places where future battlefields of the Capitalocene take shape.[8] And the more such "battles" happen, the more profitable border surveillance and "security" zones will be for companies like Lockheed Martin, Raytheon, and Elbit Systems—whose border systems are deployed worldwide—and private prison corporations like Core Civic (formerly Corrections Corporations of America) and the GEO Group, which make, at least in the United States, around $124 per day per bed used in immigration detention.[9]

More Threats

Governments and the corporations that benefit from their contracts are treating climate change, as it is framed by the Pentagon and other military institutions across the world, as a "threat multiplier." From this point of view, the actual weather event is secondary to the people most impacted by the event. More of a threat than the drought itself is the farmer fleeing the drought. The fisher folk on the coast are more dangerous to "stability" than the actual hurricane and storm surge that displaces them. More dangerous than the inundations themselves are the people who live in the flooded homes, especially if they are poor.

More dangerous than the earthquakes and hurricanes that have so impacted his country is Samuel, who I met in Mexico at the Nogales port of entry where he had been camping with other Haitians for several days. Samuel was with a group that arrived at the US border from Brazil, where many had been living since the 2010 earthquake, until employment dried up after the 2016 Summer Olympics.

One of the first things that Samuel told me that day in October 2016, near the line where people waited to enter the United States, was that it would be difficult to return to Haiti, because Hurricane Matthew had devastated 50 to 60 percent of the country. Indeed, the category four storm destroyed approximately two hundred thousand houses and left 1.4 million people in need of humanitarian aid. Samuel's family, including his six- and two-year-old children, were okay, but there was simply no way to make a living in the wreckage. The catastrophic convergence in Haiti was in full effect; the free market capitalist economic model—which had long ago devastated Haiti's small rice farmers—left the country with one of the highest levels of poverty in the world. This wretched economic situation was compounded by a volatile political situation historically defined by a series of US-instigated coups and ironfisted dictators. Now, there was not only the 2010 earthquake; the country was in the throes of global warming.

According to Michael Gerrard, the director of Columbia University's Sabin Center on Climate Change Law, if the world were to treat the coming ecological displacements fairly,[10] the countries responsible for the highest level of greenhouse gas emissions would take in the highest numbers of refugees. For example, since the United States is responsible for 27 percent of emissions from 1850 to 2011, if there were a hundred million climate displaced by 2050 (a low estimate), the United States would take in twenty-seven million of them, a gigantic jump up from the current, increasingly restricted number of people it already accepts.

Precisely the opposite is happening: the countries with the largest emissions are the ones fortifying their borders.

As Samuel talked about Hurricane Matthew, behind him stood the imposing US border wall, the $4 million per mile barrier that he was up against as he petitioned for asylum. Somewhere behind that wall were the lucrative detention centers of Immigration and Customs Enforcement, where he would likely be incarcerated and then deported like thousands of other Haitians (and thousands and thousands of people from across the world). That day, Samuel might as well have been hearing the US Air Force jumbo jet flying over Haiti after the 2010 earthquake: "If you think you will reach the US and all the doors will be wide open to you, that's not at all the case." In our twenty-first century, this border enforcement is as predictable as are the droughts and the super storms, unless changes start to happen now.

Todd Miller is a journalist and author based in Tucson, Arizona. His books include *Empire of Borders: The Expansion of the U.S. Border around the World* (Verso, 2019) and *Storming the Wall: Climate Change, Migration, and Homeland Security* (City Lights, 2017).

Notes

1   James C McKinley Jr., "Homeless Haitians Told Not to Flee to U.S.," *New York Times*, January 18, 2010, accessed March 28, 2020, http://www.nytimes.com/2010/01/19/us/19refugee.html.

2   T.J. Raphael, "Barbuda Needs the World's Help Right Now," PRI, September 13, 2017, accessed March 28, 2020, https://www.pri.org/stories/2017-09-13/barbuda-needs-worlds-help-right-now.

3   "2016 Global Report on Internal Displacement (Grid 2016)," Internal Displacement Monitoring Centre, accessed March 28, 2020, https://www.internal-displacement.org/publications/2016-global-report-on-internal-displacement-grid-2016.

4   Koko Warner, Charles Ehrhart, Alex de Sherbinin, Susana Admo, and Tricia Chai-Onn, *In Search of Shelter: Mapping the Effects of Climate Change on Human Migration and Displacement* (Geneva: Cooperative for Assistance and Relief Everywhere, Inc. [CARE], 2009), accessed March 28, 2020, https://www.ciesin.columbia.edu/documents/clim-migr-report-june09_final.pdf.

5   Anouch Missirian and Wolfram Schlenker, "Asylum Applications Respond to Temperature Fluctuations," *Science* 358, no. 6370 (December 2017): 1610–14, accessed March 28, 2020, https://science.sciencemag.org/content/358/6370/1610.

6   Christian Parenti, *Tropic of Chaos: Climate Change and the New Geography of Violence* (New York: Nation Books, 2011).

7   See Mark Akkerman, "The Military and Security Industry: Promoting Europe's Refugee Regime," this volume, 149–63.

8   Jason W. Moore, ed., *Anthropocene or Capitalocene? Nature, History, and the Crisis of Capitalism* (Oakland: PM Press, 2016).

9   see Marzena Zukowska, "The Cost of Freedom," this volume, 181–91.

10   Michael B. Gerrard, "America Is the Worst Polluter in the History of the World. We Should Let Climate Change Refugees Resettle Here," *Washington Post*, June 25, 2015, accessed March 28, 2020, https://www.washingtonpost.com/opinions/america-is-the-worst-polluter-in-the-history-of-the-world-we-should-let-climate-change-refugees-resettle-here/2015/06/25/28a55238-1a9c-11e5-ab92-c75ae6ab94b5_story.html.

Beds, Masks, and Prayers: Mexican Migrants, the Immigration Regime, and Investments in Social Exclusion in Canada

Paloma E. Villegas

Discussions about Mexicans' migration routes do not regularly conjure Canada. However, the number of Mexican migrants (with varying immigration statuses) to Canada has increased since the mid-1990s. There are several reasons for this. First, growing insecuritization in Mexico, stemming from actions related to organized crime and the "War on Drugs," as well as government policies to keep working-class Mexicans in precarious livelihoods, has led Mexicans to seek security abroad. Second, migration to the United States, the primary destination for Mexicans, has become more difficult. Security measures at points of entry, as well as within US borders, have intensified in the last few decades, with particularly punitive rhetoric and actions after the 2016 presidential election. Third, until 2009 (and once again after December 2016), Mexicans did not need a visa to enter Canada.[1]

While the Canadian immigration system is often depicted as more accessible than that of the United States, Mexicans in Canada face significant difficulties accessing permanent residence unless they fit into skilled worker immigration streams or are eligible for a narrow conception of family reunification. Those excluded from such applications fall into what Goldring, Berinstein, and Bernhard term precarious immigration status, an umbrella category that includes temporary foreign workers, international students, spouses undergoing the sponsorship process, undocumented migrants, and refugee/asylum claimants.[2]

The process of applying for refugee/asylum status in Canada is difficult to navigate.[3] Applicants must outline their case and provide evidence in support of it. This process involves investment of time, energy, and money (lawyers, translation fees, and shipping costs for documents), as well as the emotional labor needed to relive trauma and to perform it in a way that is palatable and legible to immigration authorities. Sometimes those investments are not enough. Approval rates for Mexican refugee/asylum claimants have ranged between 8 and 28 percent in recent years (see figure 22.1).[4]

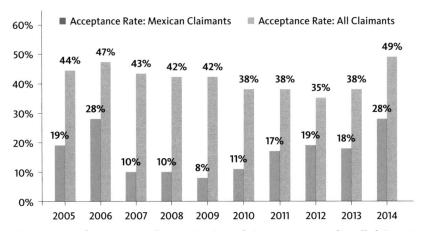

Figure 22.1: Refugee approval rates: Mexican claimants compared to all claimants
(Data source: Citizenship and Immigration Canada)

To contextualize this shift, refugee/asylum applications from Mexican nationals prior to 2009 made it a top source country (see figure 22.2).[5] The Canadian government's response to the high number of applications was to identify Mexican claimants as "bogus"—using the low acceptance rate as evidence to support their rhetoric. This maneuver positioned Mexican claimants as undeserving of protection and legitimized a 2009 policy that required Mexican nationals traveling to Canada to have an entry visa.[6] Additionally, in 2013, the Canadian government identified Mexico as a "safe country" for the purposes of refugee determination, making it more difficult for Mexicans to successfully apply for protection.[7]

As a Mexican migrant in Canada, an immigration scholar, and an artist, I analyze the case of Mexican precarious-status migrants in Canada using three art pieces.[8] Each piece draws from my research findings and personal experience. I arrived in Canada in 2006, after having lived in the US undocumented for almost fifteen years. In 2009 and 2010 and again in 2014 and 2015, I conducted research with Mexican precarious-status migrants in Toronto, interviewing a total of twenty-one participants.[9]

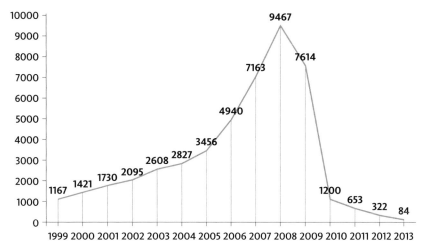

Figure 22.2: Number of claims by Mexican nationals
(Data source: Citizenship and Immigration Canada)

I propose that Mexican precarious-status migrants in Canada, particularly refugee/asylum claimants and undocumented persons, experience what Menjívar and Abrego term "legal violence": explicit and implicit violence enacted by the government and its legal systems on non-citizens.[10] In this case, the barriers produced by the immigration system through limited access to refugee protection and permanent residence lead to violent encounters in terms of employment, access to social services, and the navigation of everyday life. For Mexican refugee/asylum claimants, one way legal violence operates is through low acceptance rates and the reasons provided for those decisions: Mexico is "safe," and Mexicans can relocate to internal flight alternatives (IFAs)—urban areas or far-off sites within the country—if they feel unsafe in a particular region. Low acceptance rates send a message to potential applicants that they should not apply for protection, because the likelihood of approval will be low. This violence renders refugee/asylum seekers vulnerable to detention and deportation, the day-to-day operations of which are often outsourced by the state to private companies.[11] Their vulnerability in turn creates profitable opportunities (linked to further violence) for individuals and companies offering informal employment and services outside the public sector, as well as entities profiting from the immigration industrial complex.

In this context, legal violence involves at least three types of investments. First is an ideological investment in a Canadian national narrative that depicts its systems as fair and generous, ignoring the outcomes of its immigration policy. Second is an investment in fiscal responsibility and austerity that portrays Mexican refugee/asylum claimants as "abusing" the system by applying for protection and accessing social goods during that process.[12] During the application process, claimants have access to ESL courses, health care services, social assistance, including some legal aid, and can apply for a work permit. Given the high rate of unsuccessful refugee/asylum claims, the third investment involves maintaining precarious-status migrants in an exploitable existence by refusing to recognize migrants' claims or by preventing migrants from making claims. This process, as noted above, allows the Canadian nation-state and economy to profit from the labor of precarious-status migrants, who have difficulty exerting their rights, given the possibility of being deported. This is particularly salient when considering the unsafe working conditions inherent in the jobs available for such migrants. They often experience an interlocking of difficult physical work conditions and psychological abuse, with women migrants also facing the possibility of sexual violence.

Pleading at the Border depicts the relationship that refugee claimants are often assumed to have with the nation-states they apply to for protection: seeking sanctuary from a benevolent entity. The border in the painting can be imagined in two ways: a port of entry and an internal border. At the port of entry, migrants are asked about their intent to stay in Canada, often in a humiliating manner.[13] Sometimes those who apply for protection are held in detention centers, marked as "flight risks." The painting illustrates the yearning for security that many migrants experience and the violence and investments (in terms of immensely expensive walls, fences, and technologies of interdiction and detention) that nation-states enact to manage migration. Once migrants enter a nation-state, they face internal borders that create wealth for others while inhibiting their chances for survival—barriers that curtail their ability to access social services and work and limit their freedom to move around the city, particularly if their refugee/asylum claim is refused. Yet migrants engage in resistance to the xenophobic capitalist state. This is illustrated through the brick that has been dislodged from the border onto the floor.

Borders also have a temporal aspect.[14] For those able to apply for protection, awaiting the resolution of their case can be stressful. *I Can't Even Buy a Bed Because I Don't Know if I'll be Able to Stay* references Berenice,[15] a Mexican woman I interviewed in 2009, who explained her inability to

Pleading at the Border, by Paloma E. Villegas

purchase material goods, because her refugee claim might be refused. Berenice's account demonstrates the temporal, spatial, and economic limbo that refugee/asylum claimants are placed in as they await the res- olution of their applications or the opportunity to apply under a new application. This process can often take years and greatly exacerbate the financial insecurity migrants experience as a result of their liminal status. While it does not prevent the possibility of making plans for the future, it

I Can't Even Buy a Bed Because I Don't Know if I'll be Able to Stay, by Paloma E. Villegas

can greatly curtail them as a result of multiple insecurities. The bed, while representing an everyday household item, also signals a location of rest, something that is hard to come by with the continued threat of detention and deportation. The painting facilitates a discussion about the types of investments governments make to exclude precarious-status migrants from Canada's territory and institutions. For Mexican refugee/asylum claimants, one way this legal violence operates is the establishment of a low acceptance rate (explained above), which can increase migrants' experiences of a legal limbo.

Finally, borders are also racialized, another aspect of legal violence. *Gringo Mask* references Teresa, whom I interviewed in 2010, and who proposed wearing a mask to look like a gringo (a white North American) to pass as having secure immigration status. However, as the painting demonstrates, because of a person's features, skin color, and accent, as well as lack of documentation, wearing a mask is futile. That is, the different markings of the body can betray the mask shown to the world. The mask also signals the way Canada operates according to an ongoing white settler

Gringo Mask, by Paloma E. Villegas

identity, while at the same time marketing itself as multicultural and inclusionary.[16] Henry and Tator define this type of democratic racism as:

> an ideology that permits and justifies the maintenance of two apparently conflicting sets of values. One set consists of a commitment to a democratic society motivated by egalitarian values of fairness, justice and equality. In conflict with these liberal values, a second set of attitudes and behaviors includes negative feelings about people of color that carry the potential for differential treatment or discrimination.[17]

Democratic racism produces the mirage of a "color-blind" society and ignores the ways immigration status and racialization intersect to identify migrants of color as detainable and deportable. It also demonstrates the investment in identifying Mexicans as "bogus" to facilitate the rejection of their refugee/asylum claims and uphold the idea that the Canadian refugee determination system is fair.

Ideological and economic investments influence the violence migrants experience when they have a precarious immigration status. While Canada's system of immigrant detention is not officially a for-profit enterprise, there are numerous sites of profit-making that depend on the existence and vulnerability of precarious-status migrants. Ideologically, Canada's reputation profits from a global identification as an immigrant-friendly country, a process that makes invisible the racism and xeno-phobia that exists in its immigration policy and promotes an ever-ready reserve army of precarious labor.[18] While Canada's migration system for "skilled" workers touts itself as "color-blind," focusing instead on human capital—education, work experience, and the "soft" skills required to navi-gate working at Canadian firms (what is often referred to as "Canadian experience")—this class-based system obscures racist forms of exclusion involved in evaluating the "quality" of applicants' skills.[19] Furthermore, wealthy applicants (in need of protection or not) can bypass many appli-cation requirements if they invest a certain amount of money in Canada.[20] A second profit-making process occurs through labor exploitation, par-ticularly because precarious-status migrants receive minimal protec-tions. This makes them vulnerable to violence at the hands of state officials, employers who engage in wage theft and other violations, and health care providers whose fees for uninsured patients are unregulated.[21] Third, profit-making occurs through application and other fees. For instance, approved refugees (those whose refugee/asylum claims were deemed "legitimate") have to pay processing fees to apply for permanent residence, which provides them with a more secure immigration status.[22] Claimants might also be asked to pay legal, translation, and other fees if they are deemed ineligible for legal assistance. These investments intersect to uphold a legal violence that denies precarious-status migrants security by maintaining insecure living conditions and the threat of deportation—in turn creating profit opportunities for others.

Paloma E. Villegas is an interdisciplinary artist and assistant professor of sociology at California State University San Bernardino. Her research examines the production of migrant illegalization and its intersections with race, gender, and class.

Notes

1   "Canada Imposes a Visa on Mexico," TFO Canada, July 14, 2009, accessed March 28, 2020, http://www.cic.gc.ca/english/department/media/releases/2009/2009-07-13; Kathleen Harris, "John McCallum Says Mexican Visa Could Be 'Reimposed' if Refugee Claims Spike," CBC News, November 15, 2016, accessed March 28, 2020, http://www.cbc.ca/news/politics/mexico-visa-refugee-canada-trump-1.3851904.

2   Luin Goldring, Carolina Berinstein, and Judith Bernhard, "Institutionalizing Precarious Migratory Status in Canada," *Citizenship Studies* 13, no. 3 (June 2009): 3–27, accessed March 28, 2020, https://escholarship.org/uc/item/8jm4x7pw.

3   There are two avenues to apply for refugee protection in Canada. The first involves an application for resettlement from abroad (often from refugee camps) alongside a referral from an organization like the United Nations High Commissioner for Refugees (UNHCR). The second, for which Mexicans are eligible, can only occur inside Canada. Applicants apply at the border or at an immigration office, are evaluated in terms of eligibility to apply, and then must provide specific evidence to prove that their need for protection aligns with the criteria outlined in the Immigration and Refugee Protection Act (IRPA).

4   Citizenship and Immigration Canada, "Backgrounder: The Visa Requirement for Mexico," July 13, 2009, accessed August 25, 2009, http://www.cic.gc.ca/english/department/media/backgrounders/2009/2009-07-13.asp; Citizenship and Immigration Canada, "Facts and Figures 2013: Immigration Overview: Temporary Residents," December 31, 2014, accessed January 15, 2016, http://www.cic.gc.ca/english/resources/statistics/facts2013/temporary/index.asp; Citizenship and Immigration Canada, "Facts and Figures 2014: Immigration Overview: Permanent Residents," August 1, 2015, accessed January 15, 2016, http://www.cic.gc.ca/english/resources/statistics/facts2014/index.asp.

5   Citizenship and Immigration Canada, "Backgrounder: The Visa Requirement"; "Facts and Figures 2013"; "Facts and Figures 2014."

6   "Canada Defends Visa Change for Mexicans, Czechs," CBC News, July 14, 2009, accessed August 3, 2010, http://www.cbc.ca/world/story/2009/07/14/czech-visas-mexico.html; Liette Gilbert, "Canada's Visa Requirement for Mexicans and Its Political Rationalities," *Norteamérica* 8, no. 1 (January–June 2013): 139–61, accessed March 28, 2020, https://bit.ly/2X2mMww; Paloma .E. Villegas, "Assembling a Visa Requirement against the Mexican 'Wave': Migrant Illegalization, Policy and Affective 'Crises' in Canada," *Ethnic and Racial Studies* 36, no. 12 (December 2013).

7   Citizenship and Immigration Canada, "Designated Countries of Origin," June 17, 2013, accessed March 28, 2020, http://www.cic.gc.ca/english/refugees/reform-safe.asp.

8   As Goldring and Landolt argue, it is important to think about these different statuses, because migrants experience "legal status transitions" in their immigration status trajectories; Luin Goldring and Patricia Landolt, "The Conditionality of Legal Status and Rights: Conceptualizing Precarious Non-Citizenship in Canada," in Luin Goldring and Patricia Landolt, eds., *Producing and Negotiating Non-Citizenship: Precarious Legal Status in Canada* (Toronto: University of Toronto Press, 2013), 3–28.

9   P.E. Villegas, "Assembling and (Re)Marking Migrant Illegalization: Mexican Migrants with Precarious Status in Toronto" (PhD diss., OISE/University of Toronto, 2012).

10 Cecilia Menjívar and Leisy J. Abrego, "Legal Violence: Immigration Law and the Lives of Central American Immigrants," *American Journal of Sociology* 117, no. 5 (March 2012): 1380–1421.

11   "Immigration Detention in Canada," Global Detention Project, June 2018, accessed March 28, 2020, https://www.globaldetentionproject.org/countries/americas/canada#_ftn114.

12   "Jason Kenney, Minister of Citizenship, Immigration and Multiculturalism," Frontier Centre for Public Policy, June 8, 2012, accessed March 28, 2020, https://fcpp.org/2012/06/08/jason-kenney-minister-of-citizenship-immigration-and-multiculturalism.

13   Paloma E. Villegas, "Moments of Humiliation, Intimidation and Implied 'Illegality': Encounters with Immigration Officials at the Border and the Performance of Sovereignty," *Journal of Ethnic and Migration Studies* 41, no. 14 (August 2015): 2357–75.

14   Paloma E. Villegas, "'I Can't Even Buy a Bed Because I Don't Know If I'll Have to Leave Tomorrow': Temporal Orientations among Mexican Precarious Status Migrants in Toronto," *Citizenship Studies* 18, no. 3–4 (May 2014): 277–91.

15   Pseudonym chosen by participant.

16   Himani Bannerji, *The Dark Side of the Nation: Essays on Multiculturalism, Nationalism and Gender* (Toronto: Canadian Scholars' Press, 2000); Nandita Sharma, "Canadian Multiculturalism and Its Nationalisms," in May Chazan, Lisa Helps, Anna Stanley, and Sonali Thakkar, eds., *Home and Native Land: Unsettling Multiculturalism in Canada* (Toronto: Between the Lines, 2011), 85–101.

17   Frances Henry and Carol Tator, "The Ideology of Racism: Democratic Racism," *Canadian Ethnic Studies* 26, no. 2 (1994): 1–14.

18   Peter S. Li, "The Racial Subtext in Canada's Immigration Discourse," *Journal of International Migration and Integration* 2, no. 1 (Winter 2001): 77–97, accessed March 28, 2020, https://refugeeresearch.net/wp-content/uploads/2016/11/Li-2001-The-Racial-subtext-in-Canadas-immigration-discourse.pdf.

19   Rupaleem Bhuyan, Daphne Jeyapal, Jane Ku, Izumi Sakamoto, and Elena Chou, "Branding 'Canadian Experience' in Immigration Policy: Nation Building in a Neoliberal Era," *Journal of International Migration and Integration* 18, no. 1 (February 2017): 47–62.

20   "Investor Program," Immigration, Francisation et Intégration Québec, February 28, 2018, accessed March 28, 2020, http://www.immigration-quebec.gouv.qc.ca/en/immigrate-settle/businesspeople/applying-business-immigrant/three-programs/investors/index.html.

21   Paloma E. Villegas, "Negotiating the Boundaries of Membership: Health Care Providers, Access to Social Goods and Immigration Status," in Luin Goldring and Patricia Landolt, eds., *Producing and Negotiating Non-Citizenship*, 221–37.

22   "Fee List," October 19, 2017, Immigration and Citizenship Canada, accessed March 28, 2020, http://www.cic.gc.ca/english/information/fees/fees.asp.

Contesting Profit Structures:
Rejected Asylum Seekers between
Modern Slavery and Autonomy

Jorinde Bijl and Sarah Nimführ

> Malta is a big problem. I've paid my taxes for nearly ten years but still no benefit. Ten years in Malta and no passport. But they always keep me working.
> —Tayeb Kashif, nondeportable rejected asylum seeker.[1]

Precarious ways of living are on the rise, shaped by an "endemic uncertainty" that is the result of efforts upon efforts to deregularize,[2] make flexible, and rationalize the economy. This uncertainty is reflected in the increase of atypical, temporary employments, "working poor syndromes,"[3] and ever-widening gaps in social welfare. Especially for refugees,[4] employment continues to be an issue of serious concern. Unique about Malta is that not only are asylum seekers and recognized refugees allowed to work, but rejected asylum seekers can also obtain a permit to work pending their deportation.[5] This regulation was adopted to avoid rejected asylum seekers becoming destitute. In practice, however, our study shows that most people in this position are not able to obtain a secure social position.[6] The permit does not legalize their presence in Malta, and few employers are willing to employ them formally. According to sociologist Robert Castel, the expansion of uncertain employment relationships is entwined with social disintegration. Precarization has demoralizing effects on people; it is "like a virus, which penetrates the everyday life, dissolves social relations and undermines psychic structures of individuals."[7]

In this chapter, we analyze the impact of the "asylum industry" on nondeportable rejected asylum seekers' pathways to inclusion in the asylum arena,[8] focusing on the small island state of Malta. This arena consists of different actors—state agencies, companies, NGOs, refugees, and the islanders—negotiating access to society and its civil rights on an everyday and practical level. Drawing on fieldwork and qualitative interviews conducted in Malta from 2015 to 2018, we consider how the permit to work regulation functions and how Malta's asylum industry profits from it.

First, we provide a brief overview of the Maltese context. Then we point out how the work permit policy and its practices create an "endemic uncertainty" for refugees living in a limbo.[9] Next, we illustrate strategies that refugees use to handle constraints and increase their well-being in the Maltese social and economic system. Here, we also refer to an earlier attempt by institutional actors to regularize the stay of nondeportable refugees. To conclude, we link our findings to Castel's "zones of precariousness,"[10] which constitute new forms of modern slavery.

Malta: Small Island, Big Movements

Malta is a Southern European island state located in the center of the Mediterranean Sea between Libya and Italy that has become a central spot for migratory movements to Europe.[11] Between 2004, the year Malta joined the European Union (EU), and 2017, nearly sixteen thousand asylum seekers arrived on the island by boat.[12] The majority were sub-Saharan Africans, presumably departing from Libya.[13] During that period, Malta received the highest number of asylum seekers in the world relative to its size and population.[14] After 2015, the number of boat arrivals decreased, while air arrivals rose.[15] According to the Armed Forces of Malta, the falling number of boat arrivals was the result of smugglers changing routes in response to rescue operations. Representatives of NGOs, however, trace the decrease to a secretive "migrant deal" struck between Malta and Italy.[16] Until 2016, all asylum seekers were detained for up to eighteen months after their arrival. Now, unregulated arriving refugees are accommodated at an Initial Reception Center for a vulnerability assessment,[17] after which they are either accommodated in an open center—a form of accommodation where refugees can live after being released from detention—or detained for a maximum of nine months.

From 2004 to 2014, only 3 percent of all asylum applicants obtained refugee status. Fifty-six percent held Subsidiary Protection status, 5 percent were issued Temporary Humanitarian Protection status, and 31 percent received a notice of rejection.[18] Usually, a notice of rejection is followed by deportation. However, there is a clear gap between the number of notices of returns issued and the number of effective deportations. This disparity is called the "deportation gap" and is caused by various legal and practical factors,[19] for example, the refusal of a country of origin or transit to issue requisite travel documents.[20] Individuals caught in this gap become "nondeportable." Even though the length of this status is unknowable, no financial or social safety nets exist for those within it. Hence, nondeportable refugees live in a permanent temporary state, which Zygmunt Bauman calls the "nowhere-land of non-humanity."[21] Stripped of legal entitlements, they often end up in precarious work relationships in both the formal and informal sector.

Avoiding Destitution?

To understand precarious work, it is necessary to explain Malta's contemporary context of employment law. Since entering the EU in 2004, Malta's formal economic indicators have improved, reflected in its low unemployment rate of 4 percent against an EU average rate of 10.1 percent, in June 2016.[22] However, the unemployment rate among asylum seekers in Malta at that time was, according to an NGO-sponsored study, 45.8 percent.[23]

Ostensibly so that rejected asylum seekers might avoid destitution, the government adopted a policy of providing permits for "regular work." This is a remarkable initiative, as Maltese asylum status agent Fabio Marjani explained during an interview in April 2016: "Somebody with rejected status, legally, should not work. That's European law. Should not work, because he should leave the country." As this policy is not legally enforced, it confers a status not covered by labor laws. Marjani clarified: "[The rejected asylum seeker] won't get a work permit, but he will get a permit to work, which is different."

Even though the official aim of the permit to work is to help nondeportable rejected asylum seekers avoid destitution, the reality differs. First, it is a license valid only pending deportation and does not regularize their legal status. Second, although they contribute to national insurance and pay taxes via their paychecks, holders do not have access to health insurance, unemployment benefits, sickness benefits, child allowance, or pension.[24] Human rights lawyer Katy Benello summarized the situation in a July 2015 interview:

A very limited set of rights in itself brings about an amount of insecurity... that your quality of life is very poor, and... your well-being
is very precarious.... Even those who are doing well, it's extremely
precarious because [if] you lose your job, everything goes. You get
sick, so you can't work anymore? Everything goes. In one minute,
everything collapses.

Nondeportable rejected asylum seekers' labor is effectively funding
services they don't have access to, challenging the common xenophobic
rhetoric of asylum seekers costing the "taxpayer"—a term widely understood as "citizen," despite asylum seekers' equivalent tax contributions.

A third pernicious reality is that these permits to work are not bound
to minimum-wage laws, which automatically exacerbates nondeportable
refugees' place in a "zone of precariousness."[25] According to Eurofound,
migrants in Malta are particularly vulnerable to being classified as
"working poor."[26] Many refugees report that their employers refused to
officially request a permit, provide a contract, or pay a fair salary.[27] We
found that their wages were also lower compared to Maltese citizens
doing the same work. In short, the permits do not protect refugees from
exploitative practices.

Fourth, permits to work are only issued for up to three months and
renewal costs €34 (approximately US$37), a fee paid generally by the
permit holder.[28] The very limited duration of these permits may be one
factor in employers refusing contracts, preferring employees with protected status so, in the words of Benello: "they don't have to go through
the hassle of applying for a permit which needs to be renewed every three
months." Furthermore, the permit does not allow holders to register at
the job and training center, making it difficult to establish contact with
potential employers.[29]

The Permit to Work in Practice
To obtain a permit to work, the employer applies in the name of the
worker (the rejected asylum seeker). As a result, the permit holder can
only work for that employer, stimulating an unequal power relationship
in which the employee is dependent on the employer. Ebrima Jawara,
a rejected asylum seeker, summarized his situation working without
papers as a mechanical assistant for one of Malta's biggest cruise companies: "More than one year my boss promises to give me a contract. Each

time I ask when this will happen, he said, 'Don't complain; be thankful that you are allowed to work at all.'... That's like Babylon"—a reference to "Babylon System," a Bob Marley song that condemns systems that oppress or discriminate.

Paul Keller, the vice executive director of a local NGO, acknowledged that nondeportable refugees are particularly vulnerable to abuse in low-skilled jobs with poor working conditions. He explained: "The policies allow for a broad scope of exploitations by potential employers. Particularly for rejected cases ... because they need an approval of the future employer to obtain their employment license." The informal sector is also characterized by different facets of exploitation. "Many people are waiting as day laborers at the roadside. I've heard of people who were working a whole day for a bottle of coke and a *ftira* [Maltese bread]," Keller added, noting that people accept these circumstances as they look desperately for jobs: "This is the first possibility to get out of the open centers and live independently." Musa Rahim, a young Senegalese refugee, told us in June 2015 about a friend who had agreed to be paid €30 (approximately US$33) for a day's construction work. At the end of the day, he only received 30 cents. "What was he to do? Where was he to go?" he asked us, rhetorically. No institutions exist to address such abuses.

Benello pointed out that female rejected asylum seekers in particular often end up in bad work relationships, which are further characterized by unequal gender power relations: "As soon as you are in this situation, you are really vulnerable ... finding yourself in relationships you would not normally enter." Florence Gbeho, the founder of a local NGO, also explained that accessing stable employment has continued to be a problem for many female refugees, who often find jobs in kitchens or hotels or as domestic workers:

> [If a refugee woman] decides to leave the house of the employer because of abuse, she mostly ends up without a contract.... After six months working hard, she realizes that the others [colleagues] are getting paid €720.... She started bargaining with him [because she was] getting only €500.... She told the employer, "Look, you have to give me €720; this is the minimum." And the employer says, "Okay, I will increase you to €550 but no more."... And then she says, "I want to leave. I cannot take this abuse. I don't want to report you; I just want to leave." He agrees.

Gbeho explained that in cases such as this, the employer has to write a termination letter for the employee to show at the job center to get another permit. But if the past employer alleges that the woman broke the contract, she will be blacklisted and barred from applying for other jobs—in which case, Gbeho explained, "She is going to the illegal economy."

What can be seen from these empirical insights is that the permit to work system does not prevent the permit holder from becoming destitute. In Malta, the transition from informal labor to precarious labor within the assumed formal economy is fluent, while uncertainty is constant. It seems that the policy was implemented primarily for employers to benefit from refugees' labor supply and "as a means of monitoring the rejected asylum seeker population in the event of forced return."[30] Additionally, as these permits are only valid for a short time and renewal costs are charged to the applicant, the government also gains financially from the system. The major benefit, however, is the accumulation of taxes from the asylum seekers without the requirement to provide service to them.

Strategies to Survive

Fear of entering a prolonged battle prevents many nondeportable refugees from fighting for their labor rights via the courts. Yet some have formed activist groups and migrant organizations to arrange demonstrations and solidarity walks.[31] "We are slaves for the economy of Malta," read one protester's poster at a July 2015 demonstration. They express the feeling of being deprived of their rights relative to Maltese citizens, as well as to recognized refugees.

In 2016, in response to the restriction on rejected asylum seekers registering for the job and training center, a migrant organization created an online skills register that "interviews . . . migrants, and records their skills with the intention of creating useful resource for potential employers . . . and to give the migrants an opportunity to work."[32] As part of this pilot project, the organization also offered free workshops in cooperation with various institutions.[33] As of 2018, the project remained unfunded, but the organization was still trying to support refugees through its register. Demand is high, particularly from women. Our research has shown that most female refugees did not have any professional training or education beyond compulsory schooling in their country of origin. Many did not have any schooling at all. Illiteracy and lack of language knowledge are further obstacles to work for many women. Muslim women experience further prejudice and discrimination, especially if they wear a veil.

In 2017, Malta passed its first integration policy. Previously, the Maltese government did not seek to invest in structured integration measures.[34] Free English language courses were offered in the open centers, but by volunteers not staff. Alice Zammit, an employee of a governmental agency, told us in 2015: "We also have independent volunteers who come here. . . . It would be a waste if the state would offer that." Zammit added, "It is very obvious that no asylum seeker . . . wants to stay in Malta. And I think the more we are making people stay . . . by integration, the more we are doing harm to these people." Her words reveal that sustaining barriers to access education and work are economic choices; the government does not want to "waste" money on integration for people who are going to leave and who better serve the state's interest if they are unable to participate fully in society. Furthermore, although complimentary language courses are offered by NGOs or volunteers, they are mainly reserved for refugees with protected status. EU grant funds are also tied to protected status, creating a hierarchy of deservingness: nondeportable refugees are framed as "undeserving" and denied the legal and social means by which they might join the "deserving." As a result, refugees often offer reciprocal translation services in exchange for payment or equivalent services.[35]

The government previously dealt with nondeportable refugees through a national non-asylum linked form of protection, the Temporary Humanitarian Protection New (THPN).[36] Since 2010, THPN has been issued to persons with a notice of rejection if they had been in Malta for at least five years "living in a private residence . . . and keeping a clean police conduct."[37] When a new asylum status agent took office at the end of 2016, THPN was, however, suspended pending a review process.[38] Mohammed Sangaré, a young Malian who had been living in Malta since 2003 with a notice of rejection, was a THPN holder. He managed to set up his own business, as THPN allowed him to hold a one-year work permit, and even to recruit employees.[39] Due to the policy suspension, Sangaré was unable to continue operating without breaking the law. Left without any form of documentation, he was forced to close his business. The withdrawal of THPN led to uncertainty for beneficiaries like Sangaré and can be understood as "disintegrating the integrated."[40] The retraction seemed to be guided by opportunistic politics rather than thoughtful policy, as it plunged refugees into destitution and pushed them to survive in the informal economy without any protection.[41]

Conclusion

We have argued that Malta's policy of providing temporary work permits to nondeportable rejected asylum seekers does not help them to avoid destitution, despite its stated intention. Instead, the policy engenders dependencies between the employer and the employee and does not protect the workers from exploitation. Employees often end up in precarious relationships, with little agency to ensure the stable income required to shape their own lives. Precarious workers, who are forced by circumstances into the least valued and lowest paid jobs, also find it difficult to earn social recognition. In that sense, Castel's hypothesis of disintegration applies to our research partners, none of whom found that the permit to work and its associated practices provided a stable basis upon which to plan their future. In the case of formally employed refugees like Mohammed Sangaré, efforts to build long-term financial security were only rarely successful and easily thwarted by changing policies. The apparent impossibility of securing social stability often fueled feelings of uncertainty, shame, anger, and resignation among refugees.

The limitations of the permit to work policy have led to the emergence of an informal sector similarly marked by uncertainty and inequality. Some of our research partners consider their current precarious informal work status as a stepping-stone to ordinary employment, hoping for a "sticking effect" from their work. As shown by the case of Ebrima Jawara, their chances are low. Indeed, this outlook might routinize a problematic informal sector; in trying to convince Maltese citizens of their contributions to the country, many nondeportable rejected asylum seekers strategically use narratives of being "hardworking" and "self-sufficient" in an effort to obtain more rights and social inclusion, downplaying narratives that note their experiences of discrimination, exploitation, and marginalization. Others have given up hope for formal employment and are instead organizing among themselves to live without state support, relying on their own informal structures and integration mechanisms.

Following Castel, we argue that the current policy promotes both structural and cultural disintegration instead of enabling inclusion. Moreover, it can be seen as "organized disintegration,"[42] as integration in the sense of holding a reputable social position—particularly apparent in the field of employment—is not possible for those ostensibly permitted to work. Instead, without access to social security, refugees are officially used to meet employer demand. At the same time, their distinctive legal vulnerability facilitates a high degree of exploitation, as "their labor is regularized, but their bodies aren't."[43]

Theoretically, nondeportable refugees are free, yet bound to a particularly pernicious model of labor relations, which can be described as a "new face of slavery."[44] While this exclusion and exploitation generates further inequalities, refugees attempt to counteract the effects of such policies with new forms of political activism. Refugees are not outside but are part of the asylum arena in which they actively intervene. Acting as "activist citizens,"[45] they challenge the binary status/non-status that causes their precarious situation. They form solidarity networks, organize (political) mobilizations, and help each other by sharing skills, information, and contacts. Through community support, the negative effects of their precarious situation can be mitigated for a certain time and to a certain extent. Nevertheless, nondeportable refugees are embedded in a multi-actor framework, in which their agency is circumscribed by the interests and practices of others. As such, their lives are confronted by a sense of substantial uncertainty, which is reproduced by law.

Jorinde Bijl is a cultural anthropologist with a Masters in International Development Studies (Wageningen University) and founder of the Education Gives Hope Foundation, supporting young people in Sierra Leone. She is based in Rotterdam, Netherlands. **Sarah Nimführ** is a cultural anthropologist and critical migration scholar holding a PhD in European Ethnology from the University of Vienna.

Notes

1   Interviewed July 2015. For anonymity, we use pseudonyms for all research partners and interviewees.
2   Zygmunt Bauman, *In Search of Politics* (Cambridge: Polity Press, 1999); Zygmunt Bauman, *Liquid Times: Living in an Age of Uncertainty* (Cambridge: Polity Press, 2007).
3   David K. Shipler, *The Working Poor: Invisible in America* (New York: Knopf, 2008).
4   Our use of the term "refugee" is not equivalent with the legal definition. We use it here to refer to the experience, the process, and the involuntariness of the migrated individual. We refer to people who have been granted asylum under the Geneva Convention as "legally recognized refugees."
5   Maria Pisani, "There's an Elephant in the Room and She's 'Rejected' and Black: Observations on Rejected Female Asylum Seekers from Sub-Saharan Africa in Malta," *Open Citizenship* 2 (Spring 2011): 24–51, accessed March 28, 2020, https://www.academia.edu/934092/Theres_an_elephant_in_the_room_and_shes_

rejected_and_black_Observations_on_rejected_female_asylum_seekers_from_ sub-Saharan_Africa_in_Malta.

6   This article is based on empirical data collected in Malta in 2015–2018. Jorinde Bijl spent nine months conducting research in the field, three months of which she spent as a volunteer with a local NGO. For her PhD thesis, Sarah Nimführ conducted a research project with nondeportable rejected asylum seekers, both in Malta and Italy. For this article we examined our respective data in view of the asylum industry context and collated the findings.

7   Robert Castel, *Die Stärkung des Sozialen: Leben im neuen Wohlfahrtsstaat*, (Hamburg: Hamburger Edition, 2005), 38; translated from German by the authors.

8   We first heard the term "asylum industry" used by the NGO founder and academic Isabella Pagona, interviewed February 2015.

9   Bauman, *In Search of Politics.*

10 Robert Castel, *Die Metamorphosen der sozialen Frage: Eine Chronik der Lohnarbeit* (Konstanz: UVK, 2000).

11 Sarah Nimführ, Laura Otto, and Gabriel Samateh, "Gerettet, aber nicht angekommen: Von Geflüchteten in Malta," in Sabine Hess, Bernd Kasparek, Stefanie Kron, Mathias Rodatz, and Maria Schwertl, eds., *Der lange Sommer der Migration: Grenzregime III* (Berlin: Assoziation A, 2017), 137–50.

12 "World Refugee Day: June 2017" (press release), National Statistics Office Malta, accessed March 28, 2020, https://nso.gov.mt/en/News_Releases/View_by_Unit/ Unit_C5/Population_and_Migration_Statistics/Documents/2017/News2017_098. pdf.

13 Pisani, "There's an Elephant in the Room and She's 'Rejected' and Black," 27.

14 *UNHCR Asylum Trends 2013: Levels and Trends in Industrialized Countries*, (Geneva: UNHCR, 2014), 15, accessed March 28, 2020, http://www.unhcr.org/ 5329b15a9.pdf.

15 "Malta Asylum Trends 2014," UNHCR, accessed March 28, 2020, https://www. unhcr.org/mt/wp-content/uploads/sites/54/2018/05/7_2014_malta_asylum_ trends.pdf.

16 In 2016, the home affairs minister of Malta stated that there was an informal agreement between Malta and Italy regarding the reception of rescued refugees—commonly known as the "migrant deal"—but later he retracted the statement, saying there was only "close collaboration"; see Kevin Schembri Orland, "Malta-Italy Migration 'Secret Deal' Resurfaces in the International Media," *Malta Independent*, September 4, 2016, accessed March 28, 2020, http://www. independent.com.mt/articles/2016-04-09/local-news/Malta-Italy-migration- secret-deal-resurfaces-in-the-international-media-6736156026; also see Sarah Nimführ, "Living in Liminality: Ethnological Insights into the Life Situation of Non-Deportable Refugees in Malta," *Österreichische Zeitschrift für Volkskunde* 70, no. 119 (January 2016): 256.

17 According to the 1951 Geneva Convention (see Convention and Protocol Relating to the Status of Refugees, UNHCR, accessed March 29, 2020, https:// www.unhcr.org/protection/basic/3b66c2aa10/convention-protocol-relating- status-refugees.html), compulsory migration does not require a "regular

entry." To avoid criminalization of forced migration, the term "unregulated" is used. The term "undocumented" is problematic here, as it can mean either refugees who have been documented or refugees without documents; in Malta, an individual is documented upon applying for asylum. In cases of an infeasible deportation, rejected asylum seekers are registered with the Immigration Police. There may, however, also be cases where they are "undocumented."

18 "Malta Asylum Trends 2004–2014." The remaining 5 percent consist of closed cases, when individuals withdraw their claim. Note: subsidiary protection (SP) is an international form of protection. Holders obtain personal documents and a renewable one-year residence permit. Temporary Humanitarian Protection (THP) is a form of national protection. It is granted to persons whose application for international protection has been rejected, but who should not be deported on medical or other humanitarian grounds. Holders of an SP or THP have access to employment and to core social welfare benefits. Their employment license is applied for by and issued to the refugee.

19 Matthew J. Gibney, "Asylum and the Expansion of Deportation in the United Kingdom," *Government & Opposition* 43, no. 2 (Spring 2008): 149.

20 Maria Pisani and Anna Giustiani, "Programmes and Strategies in Malta Fostering Assisted Return to and Reintegration in Third Countries," European Migration Network, 2009, accessed December 12, 2018, https://homeaffairs.gov.mt/en/MHASInformation/EMN/Documents/EMN%20Assisted%20Return%20Study.pdf.

21 Bauman, *Liquid Times*.

22 "June 2016: Unemployment Rates, Seasonally Adjusted" (press release), Eurostat, July 29, 2016, accessed April 14, 2020, https://ec.europa.eu/eurostat/documents/2995521/7572550/3-29072016-AP-EN.pdf/73014d16-b7c9-44a7-86b7-78bd9c9d6e95.

23 Julian Caruana, *Struggling to Survive: An Investigation into the Risk of Poverty among Asylum Seekers in Malta* (Malta: Jesuit Refugee Service Malta and Aditus Foundation, 2016), 38, accessed March 28, 2020, http://www.asylumineurope.org/sites/default/files/resources/strugglingtosurvive.pdf; note: the research population includes rejected asylum seekers and refugees with various protection statuses.

24 Nondeportable asylum seekers are only provided emergency health care services.

25 Castel, *Die Metamorphosen der sozialen Frage*; note: the "zone of precariousness" includes employment relationships that do not provide a permanent livelihood, e.g., low paid jobs, temporary work, etc.

26 "Working Poor in Europe–Malta," Eurofound, April 5, 2010, accessed March 28, 2020, http://www.eurofound.europa.eu/observatories/eurwork/comparative-information/national-contributions/malta/working-poor-in-europe-malta.

27 To obtain a permit to work, the employer has to apply in the name of the employee.

28 Caruana, *Struggling to Survive*, 46.

29 Pisani, "There's an Elephant in the Room and She's 'Rejected' and Black," 44.

30 Ibid.

31 Nimführ, Otto, and Samateh, "Gerettet, aber nicht angekommen," 147f.

32 The Skilled Migrant, a project of the migrant organization referenced, was funded by the Small Initiatives Support Scheme (SIS) and managed by the Malta Council for the Voluntary Sector (MCVS).

33 Migrant organization, "Roots of Education are bitter, but the fruit is sweet," Facebook, December 16, 2016.

34 Sarah Nimführ, Laura Otto, and Gabriel Samateh, "Denying, While Demanding Integration," in Sophie Hinger and Reinhard Schweitzer, eds., *Regimes of Dis-Integration* (Switzerland: Springer Open, 2020), 161–81.

35 Nimführ, "Living in Liminality."

36 THPN is different from THP, which cannot be granted to individuals who have received a final rejection decision.

37 "Humanitarian Protection," integration.gov.mt, accessed March 28, 2020, https://integration.gov.mt/en/ResidenceAndVisas/Pages/Humanitarian-Other-Reasons.aspx.

38 Ministry for Home Affairs and National Security, "Strategy for the Reception of Asylum Seekers and Irregular Migrants," meae.gov.mt, accessed March 28, 2020, https://meae.gov.mt/en/Public_Consultations/MHAS/Pages/Consultations/2015StrategyReceptionAsylumSeekersIrregularImmigrants.aspx.

39 THPN holders also had access to core social welfare benefits.

40 "Disintegrating the Integrated: A Joint Editorial by *Malta Today*, *Times of Malta*, the *Malta Independent*," *Malta Today*, February 1, 2017, accessed March 28, 2020, https://www.maltatoday.com.mt/comment/editorial/74000/disintegrating_the_integrated#.Xjx7hi10cWo.

41 The THPN was replaced at the end of November 2018: "[E]ligible applicants are able to apply for a two-year renewable residence permit as part of a new Specific Residence Authorisation policy." The conditions of eligibility for application are "subject to the fulfillment of a number of integration measures"; see Denise Grech, "Rejected Asylum Seekers Will Not Need Annual Certificate to Remain in Malta," *Times of Malta*, November 15, 2018, https://www.timesofmalta.com/articles/view/20181115/local/rejected-asylum-seekers-will-not-need-annual-certificate-to-remain-in.694391.

42 Vicki Täubig, *Totale Institution Asyl: Empirische Befunde zu alltäglichen Lebensführungen in der organisierten Desintegration* (Wiesbaden: Juventa, 2009).

43 Nicholas De Genova, "The Production of Culprits: From Deportability to Detainability in the Aftermath of Homeland Security," *Citizenship Studies* 11, no. 5, (2007): 426.

44 Gilles Reckinger, *Bittere Orangen: Ein neues Gesicht der Sklaverei* (Wuppertal: Peter Hammer Verlag, 2018).

45 Engin F. Isin, "Citizenship in Flux: The Figure of the Activist Citizen," *Subjectivity* 29, no. 1 (October 2009): 367–88.

Grounded: Power, Profit, and the Deportation Industrial Complex

Ruth Potts and Jo Ram

On March 28, 2017, fifteen activists from End Deportations, Lesbians and Gays Support the Migrants, and Plane Stupid lay on the tarmac at London's Stansted Airport, blocking a Titan Airways Boeing 767 plane chartered by the United Kingdom Home Office from rolling out of a remote parking bay. Wearing pink hi-vis jackets and sweatshirts bearing the words "no-one is illegal" and "mass deportations kill," four people locked themselves around the front wheel of the plane and ten locked themselves around a tripod to the side of the plane. The tripod, which had one person perched on top, carried a bright pink banner emblazoned: "no-one is illegal." The flight had been chartered to remove sixty people to Nigeria, Ghana, and Sierra Leone. The action prevented takeoff, becoming the first grounding of a mass deportation flight in the UK. The activists, later collectively known as "the Stansted 15," were arrested and charged under terrorism-related laws. On December 10, 2018, following a ten-week trial, all were found guilty of "endangering an airport" under the Aviation and Maritime Security Act 1990.[1] They were sentenced on February 6, 2019. At the time of press, they were all appealing the conviction. Here, we, two of the fifteen, explain why we did it—and what it cost:

> It's dawn. There's a thump at your door. You're forcibly and violently removed from your home and taken to a detention center, perhaps hundreds of miles away.

You arrive at a training event your bosses have told you is obligatory. It's a trap, set by immigration enforcement, aided and abetted by your employers.

You apply for asylum because your sexuality is "illegal" in the country of your citizenship. British state agencies claim you've faked your relationship.

Your mother and young sister are granted asylum. They're allowed to stay. You are not.

You're held in a detention center—for "administrative" purposes. With up to 650 others. It feels like a prison. It looks like a prison. It's surrounded by barbed wire. You're abused—verbally and physically—by other inmates and guards. The food is appalling. You're denied access to medical care. You're not told how long you're being held for. The uncertainty is unbearable.

You're served papers informing you that you are being deported. Or that you're on the "reserve list." You might be forced onto a plane. You might not. Perhaps you navigate the complexities of the asylum appeal process. Maybe you are one of the very few people who manages to contact an immigration lawyer. There is no time. You're told you can continue your appeal once you've been removed—a near-impossible process that has never been successful.

You're handcuffed. Two, possibly three, security guards accompany you. They work long hours for low pay. They have no training in restraint in confined spaces. They have been recorded using threatening racist and sexist language—and that was when the Chief Inspector of Prisons was on the plane.

Mass deportations, operating from the UK since 2001, connect the institutional racism of the British state with the violence of the prison industrial complex, legacies of colonialism (including homophobia), the racism of climate change, and a political class and press eager to engage in divisive and destructive populist political spectacles. From 2010 to 2016, the UK Home Office oversaw the implementation of some of the most draconian immigration legislation for decades. Under Home Secretary Theresa May, the department defended immigration detention centers against criticism and renewed contracts with the private contractor Serco, despite reports of inhumane conditions and sexual violence.[2] As of 2019, the UK had the largest immigration detention estate in Europe, controlled and run by private security firms. It is an extension of what Angela Davis describes as the prison industrial complex, and it is a big business.[3] This is where states pay private contractors to disappear people, like magic. This is where there's money to be made.

The extraction of large amounts of profit takes place at almost every stage of the detention and deportation regime. The security guards who break down doors: private contract. The deportation centers people are incarcerated in, often indefinitely: private contract. The unpaid or barely remunerated work people are forced to do there: private profit. Carlson Wagonlit Travel, a broker for charter flight deportations: private contract. The two security guards accompanying each person deported: private contract. The coaches that transport them all to the airport: private contract. Management of the "processing zone" they pass through, as far as possible from public gaze: private contract. The Titan plane: private contract. The prison wing in Nigeria, paid for by the UK government so they can transfer people there: private contract.[4] The money that the UK pays other governments to ensure that it can deport people: state-to-state treaty (which enables millions more to be made within the deportation industrial complex).[5] According to security company Mitie, which took over the "escort and travel services" contract from Tascor in May 2018 in a ten-year deal with the UK government, the forcible removal of people from the UK is worth over £50 million a year (approximately US$66.5 million in 2018).[6] And that's just one aspect of the deportation process.

This particular new frontier of private profit has been opened up by successive UK governments since 2001. By 2016, policies designed to create a "hostile environment" brought Britain's borders—long de-territorialized and re-territorialized in airports and other transit points—into schools, playgrounds, hospitals, workplaces, and into the streets, where homelessness charities began collaborating with the police in immigration raids.[7] The message was clear: if you have sought asylum in the UK, not only are you unwanted, you will be questioned at every turn. From hospital visits to work training events, everyday activity could lead to indefinite incarceration and forced removal.

Up to thirty thousand people are incarcerated in immigration detention centers each year in the UK, where there is currently no time limit on how long a person can be detained. The Home Office justifies this by citing administrative purposes.[8] Observers have described conditions as worse than prison.[9] The government deports people through both "voluntary" returns and enforced removals—though the former have been described by campaigners as coercive, with people put under extreme pressure by the Home Office to "voluntarily" return, often in exchange for release from indefinite detention. In 2017, the "voluntary" return option was accepted by 19,896 people, and 12,229 people were subject to "enforced removal," either on passenger or charter flights. According to Corporate Watch, each 2017 chartered deportation flight cost £5,345.56 (approximately US$6,895.77) per person on board.[10]

Data collection, surveillance, indeterminate detention, and arbitrary removal on mass deportation flights all mean that to be "other" in the United Kingdom is to be at risk, and that violent borders are everywhere. Nowhere was this clearer than with the now infamous 2013 Home Office Operation Vaken, which sent mobile billboards mounted on the back of vans into areas with high levels of immigration, emblazoned with the words: "In the UK illegally? GO HOME OR FACE ARREST." These "go home vans" were widely mocked, swiftly withdrawn, and failed in their direct aim of encouraging people to leave "voluntarily."[11] They did, however, successfully set the scene for the increasingly toxic public debate on immigration that has followed—the greatest impact of Operation Vaken was not measurable in policy effectiveness but in the hate crimes its rhetoric catalyzed (and legitimized). It was a precursor for widespread anti-immigration sentiment, flamed by both sides of the 2016 "Brexit" referendum campaign. Trump threatened to build a wall; the British political establishment drove one through the heart of our communities: from 2013 to 2018, hate crimes in the United Kingdom doubled. This is the impact of state racism, emboldened by the politics of fear, enflamed by the right-wing press, made possible by the erosion of community and everyday uncertainty created by an economic system that has failed all but the richest. Cultivation of this noxious cultural terrain may have been driven by the right, but many on the left have given credence to and thus helped legitimize a racist anti-immigrant agenda. As Gary Younge wrote in 2002, responding to Labour Party "pandering" to anti-immigrant sentiment: "Every step you make in the direction of a racist agenda does not 'neutralise' racists but emboldens them."[12]

Mass deportations are a cornerstone of an increasingly hostile, xenophobic environment. They take place under the cover of night, using private security services on privately contracted planes, primarily traveling to Britain's former colonies[13]—sites of historic extraction that built the wealth of an empire—or sites of British military intervention, such as Pakistan, Nigeria, and Afghanistan. People are rounded up based on their perceived nationality in the interests of filling the plane, sometimes without an opportunity to lodge or resolve a legal claim and often fearing for their lives.[14] To justify the cost of the flight, every seat on the plane must be occupied. The practice of "taking reserves"—people taken to the airport who do not discover until the last minute whether or not they will be on the flight—continues, despite the Home Affairs Select Committee demanding an end to the "inhumane" practice in 2013.[15]

An increasingly dystopian and doggedly intransigent Home Office that lurches from crisis to crisis presides over deportations, grudgingly expressing "regrets" over abuses exposed but never fundamentally changing its practices. For the very few cases that receive media or public attention—usually because the individual's social capital renders them visible or because a friend or relative has somehow managed to find a journalist willing to take up the story—a deportation order may be magically overturned and "right to remain" granted. Meanwhile, systemic failures to assess claims or treat people with anything other than the most abject cruelty continues unabated. Repeat scandals prove that this is not accidental. In 2010, the Home Office destroyed files that proved Windrush generation members' right to remain in the UK, leaving thousands destitute and many dead.[16] In 2014, Home Office officials were given shopping vouchers as "rewards" for ensuring rejected asylum claims were upheld at tribunals.[17] Argos vouchers—purchased by the government from the retailer—were gifted in return for lives shattered and lives endangered: the banality of evil in the deportation industrial complex.

Mass deportations are not about "controlling immigration." They are about sowing fear and division. They are racist and homophobic. In an effort to reject claims, the Home Office subjects LGBTQ+ asylum seekers to intrusive Home Office investigations and offensive allegations of fabricated relationships.[18] Once forcibly deported, LGBTQ+ people frequently face criminalization, persecution, or death because of their sexuality. Homosexuality is a criminal offence in forty Commonwealth nations as a direct consequence of British colonial penal codes. This legacy should demand that the UK government work to decriminalize homosexuality worldwide and explore ways of addressing the historical debts of colonialism. Instead, it provides "financial aid" to countries boasting anti-sodomy laws specifically to build new prisons.[19]

When we stopped the mass deportation flight to Nigeria and Ghana, we knew that one of the women on board had been threatened by her abusive ex-husband from a forced marriage. He said he would kill her when she returned and had "reported" her sexuality to the police, putting her at extreme risk of state violence. Another passenger, who had lived in the UK for eighteen years, had threatened to kill himself if sent to Ghana. Another had been told by the Home Office to make his own way from Ghana to the Ivory Coast—his home country, where he had been tortured by the state. By choice, the UK government does not track what happens to the people it removes.[20]

Following our direct action, Stansted Airport refused to facilitate deportation flights to Nigeria or Jamaica. For a time, the government suspended flights to Jamaica completely and ordered that flights to Nigeria depart from Brize Norton, a military base where the army promised to treat any protestors as "enemy forces." Such flights were later ordered to depart from other airports distributed around the country. On February 6, 2019, the day we were sentenced, mass deportation flights to Jamaica resumed. Although public outrage over the treatment of the Windrush generation had halted the flights temporarily, it doesn't take long to return to business as usual in the deportation industrial complex, and the state will go to huge lengths to keep the wheels turning. In charging human rights protestors with terrorism-related offences, the UK government showed that it is prepared to use its full force to maintain its system of oppression, fear, and racist and arbitrary expulsion.

The decision to evoke terrorism-related rather than civil disobedience charges necessitated a ten-week Crown Court trial, with all the costs that entails: teams of lawyers, a jury, Home Office barristers, the police officers that populated the front row of the public gallery, and months of work carried out by the Crown Prosecution Service. The full force of state apparatus is expensive, but states around the world are increasingly prepared to pay such costs: since 2014, over 250 people across fourteen European countries have been arrested, charged, or investigated for helping migrants under a range of laws.[21]

This is where we draw the line. This must stop. We can and we must expose these practices to public scrutiny. Doing this must mean both countering divisive partisanship on the left and opposing the xenophobic right: we must reject the false divisions between "good" and "bad" migrants, "deserving" and "undeserving poor," "white working class" and "immigrant" that emasculate our power. We must not accept these capitalist logics. This means acting in solidarity. This means refusing our consent to state cruelty. This is where we come together to say: this is not us. We demand an immediate end to these brutal flights and an end to the "hostile environment." A movement is growing. Join us.

Take action: @edeportations/Detainedvoices.com/@lgsmigrants

Ruth Potts is an academic, journalist, and cofounder of bread, print & roses (www.breadprintandroses.org). She lectures on social change and alternative economics at Schumacher College, Devon, and is interested in the politics of utopia and the spaces where change happens.

Jo Ram is an academic, a cofounder of Community Reinvest, and an environmental justice campaigner with Platform and the Art Not Oil Coalition. She lectures on social action and climate change at the Bartlett School of Planning, University College London.

Notes

1 Aviation and Maritime Security Act 1990, legislation.gov.uk, accessed March 28, 2020, https://www.legislation.gov.uk/ukpga/1990/31/contents.

2 Mark Townsend, "Serco, the Observer, and a Hunt for the Truth about Yarl's Wood Asylum Centre," *Guardian*, May 17, 2014, accessed March 28, 2020, https://www.theguardian.com/uk-news/2014/may/17/serco-yarls-wood-asylum-centre.

3 Angela Y. Davis, "The Prison Industrial Complex" (speech), Colorado College, Colorado, May 5, 1997.

4 On March 7, 2018, UK Foreign Secretary Boris Johnson announced the UK government's intention to build a prison wing at Kirikiri Maximum Security Prison in Apapa, Lagos State, Nigeria, to enable the deportation of prisoners from the UK to Nigeria. The British state signed a Prisoner Transfer Agreement in 2014 with Nigeria but had been legally unable to deport people there because of the substandard conditions of Nigeria's prisons.

5 For example, the UK government pays the Nigerian High Commission the £70 fee for the emergency travel documents required to deport people without necessary documentation, including their passport application fee; see Immigration Enforcement Freedom of Information & Parliamentary Question Team, Freedom of Information—40842, Home Office, accessed March 28, 2020, https://www.whatdotheyknow.com/request/353835/response/871490/attach/html/3/FOI%2040842%20Smith.pdf.html.

6 "Mitie Awarded Contract with the Home Office" (press release), Mitie, December 14, 2017, accessed March 28, 2020, http://news.mitie.com/pressreleases/mitie-awarded-contract-with-the-home-office-2329956.

7   See John Grayson, "Making Profits in Hostile Environments: Asylum Accommodation Markers in the UK and Ireland," this volume, 193–201; Jo Wilding, "The Marketization of Asylum Justice in the UK," this volume, 231–39; Tim Schütz and Monic Meisel, "Surmounting the Hostile Environment: Reflections on Social Work Activism without Borders," this volume, 241–52.

8   See Immigration Minister Caroline Nokes's comments in Joint Committee on Human Rights, Oral Evidence: Immigration Detention, HC 1484, Houses of Parliament, December 5, 2018, accessed March 28, 2020, http://data.parliament. uk/writtenevidence/committeeevidence.svc/evidencedocument/human-rights-committee/immigration-detention/oral/93664.pdf.

9   Catrin Nye, "UK Immigration Removal Centres 'Worse than Prison,'" BBC News, August 19, 2014, accessed March 28, 2020, https://www.bbc.com/news/av/uk-28852351/uk-immigration-removal-centres-worse-than-prison.

10 "Deportation Charter Flights: Updated Report 2018," Corporate Watch, July 2, 2018, accessed May 19, 2020, https://corporatewatch.org/deportation-charter-flights-updated-report-2018.

11 Jeremy Bernhaut, "One Year on from the 'Go Home Vans' Flop: Has the Home Office Learned Anything?" openDemocracy, August 5, 2014, accessed March 28, 2020, https://www.opendemocracy.net/en/5050/one-year-on-from-go-home-vans-flop-has-home-office-learned-anything.

12 Gary Younge, "Appeasing Racists Won't See Them Off," Guardian, April 25, 2002, accessed March 28, 2020, https://www.theguardian.com/politics/2002/apr/25/thefarright.labour.

13 The political scandal surrounding the deportation of people who were born British subjects and had arrived in the UK before 1973 became known as the Windrush scandal, named after the Empire Windrush, the ship that brought the first group of West Indian migrants to the UK in 1948. The scandal, which erupted in 2018 following a campaign by Caribbean diplomats in the UK, concerned people who were wrongly detained, denied legal rights, threatened with deportation, and, in at least eighty-three cases, wrongly deported from the UK by the Home Office. An unknown number of people were wrongly detained, lost their jobs or homes, or were denied the benefits or medical care to which they were entitled. A number of long-term UK residents were wrongly refused reentry to the UK, and a larger number were threatened with immediate deportation by the Home Office.

14 Phil Miller and Shiar Youssef, Collective Expulsion: The Case against Britain's Mass Deportation Charter Flights (London: Corporate Watch, 2013).

15 Ibid.

16 Rob Merrick, "Home Office under Theresa May Destroyed Evidence Able to Spare Windrush Generation from Deportation," Independent, April 17, 2018, accessed March 28, 2020, https://www.independent.co.uk/news/uk/politics/windrush-home-office-evidence-deport-theresa-may-david-lammy-a8308936.html.

17 Diane Taylor and Rowena Mason, "Home Office Staff Rewarded with Gift Vouchers for Fighting off Asylum Cases," Guardian, January 14, 2014, accessed

March 28, 2020, https://www.theguardian.com/uk-news/2014/jan/14/home-office-asylum-seekers-gift-vouchers.

18 Chaka L. Bachmann, *No Safe Refuge: Experiences of LGBT Asylum Seekers in Detention* (London: Stonewall, 2016), accessed March 28, 2020, https://www.stonewall.org.uk/system/files/no_safe_refuge.pdf.

19 CWTEMP, "Carceral Colonialism: Britain's Plan to Build a Prison Wing in Nigeria," Corporate Watch, April 17, 2018, accessed March 28, 2020, https://corporatewatch.org/carceral-colonialism-britains-plan-to-build-a-prison-wing-in-nigeria.

20 See "Mini Feature: Post-Deportation Risks and Monitoring," *Forced Migration Review*, February 2017, accessed March 29, 2020, https://www.fmreview.org/resettlement/post-deportation-intro.

21 Nandini Archer, Claudia Torrisi, Claire Provost, Alexander Nabert, and Belen Lobos, "Hundreds of Europeans 'Criminalised' for Helping Migrants—as Far Right Aims to Win Big in European Elections," openDemocracy, May 18, 2019, accessed March 29, 2020, https://www.opendemocracy.net/en/5050/hundreds-of-europeans-criminalised-for-helping-migrants-new-data-shows-as-far-right-aims-to-win-big-in-european-elections.

Kuja Meri?

Joël van Houdt

Despite nearly forty years of war, two decade-long occupations by former Cold War superpowers, and a security vacuum that could engulf the region, the world is turning a blind eye to the fate of Afghanistan's people, especially its refugees.

A spiraling security situation, weak government, and abysmal economic prospects mean Afghans are trying to leave their country in huge numbers. Because it is virtually impossible for Afghans to obtain a visa for a Western country, many are pushed into the hands of smugglers. In Kabul's main money market, countless *hawalas* (informal money transfer systems) are in place to pay traffickers. Often, refugees are only able to pay for part of the journey and get stuck somewhere along the way—traffickers do not provide any information or advice about the journey. With their families at home then forced to raise more money, they often must sell important possessions, including their homes.

If they finally make it to a country where they can apply for asylum, their requests are often rejected. In accepting Afghan refugees, the West would have to confront the fact that the war to "liberate" the country was a failure.

Unlike Syrians, Iraqis, or Eritreans, in 2016, Afghans were excluded from the European Union–Turkey refugee deal.[1] While other nationalities were still allowed to cross EU borders, Afghans found themselves stuck in Serbia and Turkey. Germany sends planeloads of Afghans home. The United Kingdom,[2] Pakistan, and Iran have collectively deported hundreds of thousands of Afghan refugees in the past decade.

I designed the public exhibit "Kuja Meri?"—"Where are you going?" in Dari—with an Afghan audience in mind. To reach this audience, I pasted around fifty billboard-sized photographs on concrete blast walls surrounding the Ministry of Information in the center of Kabul, in October 2017. A selection of those images is shared here.

London, United Kingdom, 2016: Anti-migrant headlines on the front pages of British newspapers sold in a Sainsbury's supermarket, three days after the UK voted to leave the European Union.

Daykundi, Afghanistan, 2017: a shepherd walking his flock home in Nili, the capital of Daykundi Province, passes a billboard paid for by the Australian government to dissuade Afghans from traveling there.

Kabul, Afghanistan, 2013: many brokers at Sarai Shahzada, a currency market in downtown Kabul, are part of a money-transfer system known as hawala, which is often used in the refugee-smuggling business. Afghans leaving their country pay smugglers here in advance. Their funds won't be released to the smugglers until they have reached their destination, likely Europe or Australia. The market is used for many other transactions as well, including converting foreign currency.

Nimruz, Afghanistan, 2016: Afghans ride in a truck with traffickers in Nimruz. They are trying to cross into Pakistan's Baluchistan before continuing on to Iran, where many people hope to find work.

Indian Ocean, between Indonesia and Australia, 2013: a thirty-foot long boat carries fifty-seven asylum seekers, all Iranian aside from one man from Kunduz, Afghanistan, and two Indonesian crew members. Their destination is Christmas Island, an Australian territory, a three-day journey of over two hundred miles across the Indian Ocean. If they make it, they will be taken to the island's detention centers, then flown to Papua New Guinea or the tiny Republic of Nauru. In 2013, to discourage future asylum seekers traveling this route, Australia ruled that people arriving by boat would never be allowed to settle in the country.[3]

Istanbul, Turkey, 2017: Mohebullah, who works shining shoes, talks with an unfriendly Turkish man while waiting for customers in Istanbul's Zeytinburnu district. Mohebullah left his village in the Afghan province of Kunar, close to the border with Pakistan, because of the fighting there. He came to Istanbul with his wife and two children, because "everybody told me there was money in the trees here, but so far I haven't seen any." He says the boats to Greece are too dangerous to try to travel farther.

Belgrade, Serbia, 2016: Afghan men try to forcibly wash Nabikhan, also known as Comando, from Afghanistan's Nangarhar Province. They say he lost his mind after Croatian police hit him on the head and shocked him with electric batons when he tried to cross the EU border. They are trying to find a way to take Nabikhan back to Afghanistan because of his mental illness. An estimated one thousand people live in derelict warehouses behind the central train and bus station in the Serbian capital, in sub-zero temperatures. There are not enough government facilities to process claims, but many also prefer not to apply for asylum in Serbia and try to continue their journey to Northern Europe. Many are stuck here for months while trying to cross the closed borders with Hungary or Croatia.

Lesbos, Greece, 2017: Afghan teenager Mortaza swims in the Aegean Sea in the port of Mitilini. The coast of Turkey, from where he arrived, can be seen in the background. He is staying with other Afghan minors in a house while waiting for the Greek government to decide on his asylum request.

Calais, France, 2016: an Afghan refugee holds his belongings while a fire destroys his tent on the third day of a police operation to demolish a makeshift refugee camp next to the highway leading to the port of Calais. At the time, an estimated eight thousand refugees and migrants trying to reach the UK were living there, often stuck for many months or even years.

Berlin, Germany, 2017: refugees staying in the Tempelhof refugee shelter, a former airport. The shelter houses around five hundred refugees, half of whom are from Afghanistan. Many have been here for over a year.

London, United Kingdom, 2017: Nazir from Afghanistan's Baghlan Province works at a fruit and vegetable stand in Burnt Oak, North London. He works seven days a week, 8:00 a.m. to 8:00 p.m. Nazir arrived in the UK six years ago, traveling via Italy and Calais, where he lived for four "too hard" months before crossing the border in the back of a truck. He had to wait five years to receive his papers.

Kabul, Afghanistan, 2017: Farshid is back in Afghanistan after his asylum claim in Netherlands was rejected. He walks at dusk in Kabul, covering his face. He says he fears reprisals from the criminal group that attacked him before he left, prompting his search for asylum. The claim process took two years before being denied. When he turned eighteen, he was detained by Dutch authorities. He agreed to be sent back to Kabul within a month. He was given antidepressant drugs in detention and says his mind wasn't clear when he returned. He spent around US$10,000 to go to Europe. He hopes to be a singer one day.

Joël van Houdt, born in Netherlands, lived and worked as a photojournalist in Afghanistan from 2010 to 2015. In 2012, he started following Afghans trying to leave their country. He is based in London.

Notes

1   The EU-Turkey refugee deal, signed on March 18, 2016, was designed to send Syrians arriving in Greek territories back to Turkey for asylum claim processing. In exchange, the EU would accept Syrians already granted asylum in Turkey and resettle them in member states. The EU promised Turkey €6 million (approximately US$6.6 million) in foreign aid (half of which was to be spent on services for asylum seekers and refugees) as part of this deal, which only applied to Syrians—not other nationalities; see: BBC, "Migrant Crisis: EU-Turkey Deal Comes into Effect," BBC News, May 20, 2016, accessed March 29, 2020, https://www.bbc.com/news/world-europe-35854413.

2   In 2016, the EU struck a deal with Afghanistan to accept an unlimited number of deportees at the same time as agreeing to provide hundreds of millions of dollars in foreign aid, see Rebecca Hersher, "EU Will Send Afghans Back to an Increasingly Violent Home Country," NPR, October 6, 2016, accessed March 29, 2020, https://www.npr.org/sections/thetwo-way/2016/10/06/496871738/eu-will-send-afghans-back-to-an-increasingly-violent-home-country.

3   See Sara Dehm, "Outsourcing, Responsibility, and Refugee Claim-Making in Australia's Offshore Detention Regime," this volume, 47–65; Behrouz Boochani and Omid Tofighian, "The Poetics of Prison Protest," this volume, 101–11; Julia Morris, "Making a Refugee Market in the Republic of Nauru," this volume, 165–80.

Index

Page numbers in *italic* refer to illustrations. "Passim" (literally "scattered") indicates intermittent discussion of a topic over a cluster of pages.

abduction of women and children: Honduras, 204; Nigeria, 114
Accenture, 157
ACLU. *See* American Civil Liberties Union (ACLU)
administrative detention centers. *See* detention centers
Aegean Sea, 150, 328
Afghan refugees, 319–33 passim, 324–31
Afghanistan, 313, 319–24 passim, 332
Afghan refugees, 319–33 passim, 324–31
Airbus, 151, 152, 153, 154
Algeria, 36, 156
alternatives to detention (ATD), 184–85, 186
Amazon.com, 210
American Civil Liberties Union (ACLU), 186
Americans for Immigration Justice (AIJ), 208
Amnesty International, 31, 58, 109
ankle monitors, 184–85
AOI Electronics, 157
Aramark, 195

arms industry, 151–53 passim
Artola, Jenny, 203–9 passim
asylum seekers, LGBT. *See* LGBT asylum seekers
asylum seekers' housing: Ireland and UK, 193–201, 233
Atlanta: immigration judges, 207
Atlanta City Detention Center, 23–24, 203
Australasian Correctional Services (ACS), 49–50, 60n7
Australia, 9, 47–65, 101–11 passim, 127–45; Aboriginal activists, 259; Afghanistan and, 322, 323; Christmas Island, 325; Dept. of Immigration and Multicultural and Indigenous Affairs (DIMIA), 49, 50, 60n8; Nauru relations, 48, 51, 53, 59, 62n23, 103–9 passim, 166–75 passim; Operation Sovereign Borders, 110
Austria, 197

BAE Systems, 153
bail (criminal justice), 182

bail, immigrant. *See* immigrant bond system
Barbuda, 282
Barclays Bank, 14n4, 198
Barr, William, 183–84
Bauman, Zygmunt, 299
Benello, Katy, 299–300
Berlin, 241–49 passim; refugee shelters, 330
Biden, Joe, 209
biometric technology, 156, 157, 283
Boko Haram, 114–20 passim
Boochani, Behrouz, 48, 58, 59, 101–11 passim
border walls and fences, 41, 79, 149, 186, 282, 283, 285
Brazil, 70, 284
Bremen, 242, 244, 247
Britain. *See* Great Britain
Brize Norton air force base. *See* RAF Brize Norton
Broadspectrum. *See* Transfield/Broadspectrum
Bulgaria, 154, 155
Buzzi, Salvatore, 81, 86–87

Calais, France, 156, 253–60 passim, 329, 331
Cameron, David, 255
Cameroon, 114, 117, 120
camps, Red Cross: Denmark, 220–22 passim, 226
camps, refugee. *See* refugee camps
Canada: East Coast Catering, 195; Mexican asylum seekers and refugees, 287–96
Capita, 261–63
Caritas, 246
Carminati, Massimo, 81, 87
Carlson Wagonlit Travel, 311
Carter, Patrick, Baron Carter of Coles, 234
Casa Padre immigrant youth shelter, Brownsville, Texas, 186
Castel, Robert, 297, 298, 304
CEMAR, 209

Central American Free Trade Movement (CAFTA), 44, 209
Cerna, Oscar M., 209
Chaos Computer Club (CCC), 243, 248, 250n10
child refugees. *See* refugee children
child trafficking, 118
children, abduction of. *See* abduction of women and children
children, detention of, 185–86, 193
children, unaccompanied asylum-seeking. *See* unaccompanied asylum-seeking children (UASC)
children of asylum seekers, 256; Denmark, 223; Ireland, 194; UK, 198, 264n13
Children's Act 1989 (UK), 264n13
China, 43, 73
Christmas Island, 110
class action litigation, 54–55, 207
Cleveland Clinic, 71–72
climate refugees, 281–86
clothing industry: Central America, 44
Cold War, 4–5
Condon, Paul, Baron Condon, 197
Connect Settlement Services, 173
Convention on the Rights of the Child. *See* United Nations: Convention on the Rights of the Child
CoreCivic, 183, 187, 283
Côte d'Ivoire, 156, 314
"credible fear interviews," 23, 205
Croatia, 155, 327
Crozier, Adam, 197
Cyprus, 155

death of detainees, 186, 262
death of migrants, 31, 51, 75, 150, 151, 220, 221
De Genova, Nicholas, 3
De León, Jason, 75
Denmark, 219–29
Department of Homeland Security (DHS). *See* US Department of Homeland Security (DHS)

deportation: of Afghans, 319, 333n2; direct action against, 309, 314; France, 83; Ireland, 195; quotas, 213; to "safe third countries," 205; self-deportation ("voluntary" deportation), 184, 311–12; UK, 262, 309–17; violence during, 80, 262

Detained Voices, 96

detainees, death of. *See* death of detainees

detention center inmates' labor, 96–97, 99, 100

detention centers: Atlanta, 23–24; Australia, 49; Canada, 290; Denmark, 219–29 passim; Florida, 204; France, 80–86; Italy, 80, 81, 86–90; Nauru, 51, 62n23, 103–9 passim, 166–76 passim; Papua New Guinea, 47–65 passim; UK, 95–100, 193, 233, 310–11; Unites States, 206. *See also* immigrant youth shelters

detention of children. *See* children, detention of

Detention Watch Network (DWN), 183, 187

Deutsche Telekom, 243–44

Doctors Without Borders. *See* Médicins Sans Frontières (MSF)

Donovan, Mike, 185

drone surveillance, 155, 283

drownings, 31, 38, 51

Dunn, Elizabeth, 244

East Lorengau Refugee Transit Centre, Papua New Guinea, 47, 57, 64n49

Egypt, 156, 157

electronic monitoring, 184–85

ENGIE, 84

environmental refugees, 282

Equistone Partners Europe, 198

Eritrean refugees, 37, 319

Estonia, 155

European Asylum Support Office (EASO), 88, 89

European Commission, 157

European Convention on Human Rights, 258, 261

European Organization for Security (EOS), 151

European Union, 72, 79–80, 149–63, 221; Afghanistan and, 333n2; Brexit, 312; Frontex, 30, 31, 89, 149, 153, 155, 158; grant funds, 303; Malta in, 298, 299; Operation Sophia, 149–50; transplant trafficking, 73; Turkey refugee deal, 319, 333n1

European Union Naval Force Mediterranean (EUNAVFOR MED), 149

expert witnesses, 203–15

External Borders Fund (EU), 150

Fanon, Frantz, xiv

fatalities, migrant. *See* death of migrants

Federation of Muslim Women's Associations in Nigeria (FOMWAN), 115

Fekete, Liz, 193

fences and walls. *See* border walls and fences

Finland, 154

Fiorenza, Elisabeth Schüssler, 111n9

Florida: detention centers, 204. *See also* Miami

food services and catering, privatized, 24, 84, 195

forced labor, 3, 98, 114, 115

forced marriage, 117, 119

for-profit prisons and detention centers. *See* private prison corporations

France, 264n17; Calais, 156, 253–60 passim, 329, 331; IDEMIA, 157; Thales, 151, 152, 153, 156

Franck, Anna Karlsson, 224

Franco-Gonzales v. Holder, 207

free trade agreements, 41–46 passim

Freidberg, Susanne, 173

Freifunk initiative (Germany), 241–52

Frontex, 30, 31, 89, 149, 153, 155, 158

garment industry. *See* clothing industry
gay asylum seekers. *See* LGBT asylum seekers
Gbeho, Florence, 301–2
Gemalto, 156
Geneva Conventions, 4, 305n4, 306–7n17
GEO Group, 183, 187, 281, 283
GEPSA, 84, 85, 86
German Telekom. *See* Deutsche Telekom
Germany: Airbus and, 154; deportation of Afghans, 319; ORS Service and, 197; Sea-Watch, 31; wireless network activism, 241–52
Gerrard, Michael, 284
G4S, 49–57 passim, 88, 96, 97; UK, 195, 196, 197, 198, 262
Ghana, 309, 314
Gillard, Julia, 50, 168
girls: Nigeria, 113–17 passim, 121, 122
Giuliani, Rudolph, 208–9
global warming, 281–86 passim
Great Britain, 9, 95–100, 231–39, 253–65; Afghan immigrants, 331; air force bases, 314; army, 314; asylum seekers' housing, 193–201 passim; BAE Systems, 153; Brexit, 312, 321; Calais and, 156, 253–60 passim, 329, 331; Children's Act 1989, 264n13; deportation, 309–17, 319; IDEMIA, 157; Immigration Acts of 2014 and 2016, 255; Immigration and Asylum Act (1999), 193, 254; legal aid, 231–39 passim; Thales, 156
Greece, 88, 149, 264n17, 326, 328, 333n1
Grewcock, Michael, 51
GSL, 60n8
Guantanamo Bay, Cuba, 281
Guatemala, 23, 44
Guatemalan refugees, 26, 186
Guinean asylum seekers, 181

Haiti and Haitian asylum seekers, 281, 284–85
Hammami, Jamila, 182, 185, 187, 188
hate crimes: UK, 312
Heli Protection Europe (HPE), 155
Henry, Frances, 293
Hensolsdt, 154
Hernández, Joan Orland, 205
Herwa Community Development Initiative, 115
homophobic and transphobic violence: Honduras, 204
Honduras and Hondurans, 21–28, 44, 203–15
housing, asylum seekers'. *See* asylum seekers' housing
Howard, John, 49, 50
HP Inc., 157
Human Rights Watch, 116
human trafficking: Nigeria, 113–25 passim
Hungary, 327
hunger strikes, 49, 95, 98–99
Hurricane Irma, 282
Hurricane Matthew, 284

ICE. *See* US Immigration and Customs Enforcement (ICE)
IDEMIA, 157
identification-management systems, 156, 157
immigrant detention centers. *See* detention centers
immigrant youth shelters, 185–86
Immigration Acts of 2014 and 2016 (UK), 255, 257, 264n17
Immigration and Asylum Act 1999 (UK), 193, 254
Immigration and Customs Enforcement (ICE). *See* US Immigration and Customs Enforcement (ICE)
Immigration and Refugee Protection Act (Canada), 295n3
immigration bond system, 181–91 passim, 259

immigration judges, 182–83, 207, 212–13
immigration prisons. *See* detention centers
Indian Ocean, 325
Indonesia, 168, 325
Indra, 151, 152, 158
Ingeniería Sistemas para la Defensa de España (ISDEFE), 152
Internal Security Fund—Borders and Visa (EU), 150
internally displaced people (IDPs): Nigeria, 113–25
International Health and Medical Services (IHMS), 108
international law, 15n12, 116, 169, 183
International Organization for Migration, 50–51
internet access, wireless. *See* wireless internet access
Iran, 319, 324
Iranian asylum seekers and refugees, 54, 58, 174–75, 325
Iraqis, 69, 319
Ireland: asylum seekers' housing, 193–201 passim
ISDEFE. *See* Ingeniería Sistemas para la Defensa de España (ISDEFE)
Israelis and transplant trafficking, 67–71 passim, 74, 75n2
Italy, 29–38 passim, 86–90, 149, 150, 264n17, 331; Leonardo, 151, 152, 153, 155; Mafia Capitale scandal, 81, 87; Malta relations, 306n16; Syrian refugees, 72
Ivory Coast. *See* Côte d'Ivoire

Jamaica, 314
Jawara, Ebrima, 300–301, 304
Jomast, 196, 197
judges, immigration. *See* immigration judges

Kabul, 319, 323, 332
Kamasaee, Majid, 54–55
Kashif, Tayeb, 297

Keely, Charles B., 5
Keller, Paul, 301
Kenny Commercial Holdings, 197
kidnapping of women and children. *See* abduction of women and children
kidney trafficking, 67–76 passim
Koch Industries, 209–10
Koch Institute, 210
Kurdish asylum seekers, 57
kyriarchy, 108, 111n9

labor. *See* detention center inmates' labor; forced labor; sweatshop labor; work permits
LAGeSo (Das Landesamt für Gesundheit und Soziales), 246, 247
Lampedusa, 86–90 passim
Latvia, 155, 158
Lebanon, 71, 72, 156
legal advice and representation: pro bono, 3, 25, 204–13 passim, 236; UK, 231–39
Legal Aid Agency (UK), 235
Legal Services Commission, 233, 234, 235–36
Lemberg-Pedersen, Martin, 151
LeMenager, Stephanie, 177
Leonardo (multinational company), 151, 152, 153, 155
lesbian and gay asylum seekers. *See* LGBT asylum seekers
Lesbos, 88, 328
Lewis, Brandon, 98
LGBT asylum seekers, 21–28, 203–7 passim, 267–77, 310, 313
LGBT Freedom and Asylum Network (LGBT-FAN), 270–72
Libre by Nexus, 184–85, 187
Libya, 29–36 passim, 150, 155
Lithuania, 154
litigation, 48, 207; against ICE, 186; torts claims, 54–55
Loewenstein, Antony, 198

Maleknia, Mehdi, 58

Mali, 150, 157
Malian refugees, 35–36, 303
Malkki, Liisa, 6–7, 222
Malta, 155, 297–308
Manus Island Regional Processing
 Centre (RPC), 47–65 passim, 101–11
 passim, 168
Marjani, Fabio, 299
Marquez-Benitez, Gabriela, 183–88
 passim
marriage, forced. *See* forced
 marriage
Marx, Karl, xi, xii
mass deportations, 309–17
Mauritania, 157
May, Teresa, 193, 310
Médicins Sans Frontières (MSF):
 Aquarius (search and rescue ship),
 29–38 passim, 29
Mediterranean refugees, 9, 29–39,
 149–51, 155, 221, 297–308
Mexican migrants, 43–44, 74–75;
 Canada, 287–96
Mexico–United States border. *See*
 United States–Mexico border
Miami, 204, 208, 209
migrant detention centers. *See*
 detention centers
Mitie, 311
Moldova, 156
Monk, Stuart, 197
Morocco, 156
Morpho, 157
Morrison, Scott, 110
Morrison, Truman, 182
Muhamat, Abdul Aziz, 57–58
murder by detention center and
 security guards, 57, 262

NAFTA. *See* North American Free
 Trade Agreement (NAFTA)
Namah, Belden, 55
National Agency for the Prohibition
 of Trafficking in Persons (NAPTIP)
 (Nigeria), 116, 117

National Asset Management Agency
 (NAMA) (Ireland), 197
National Association of Immigration
 Judges, 213
National Bail Fund Network (US), 187
NATO, 150, 155
Nauru, 48, 51, 53, 59, 62n23, 62–63n29,
 103–9 passim, 165–80, 325
Neistat, Anna, 170–71
Netcare Corporation, 70, 73
Netherlands, 154, 156, 332
"neutrality," 221–22
New Zealand, 110, 282
Nicaragua, 208
Niger, 32, 33, 150
Nigeria, 113–25, 156, 309, 311, 313, 314
Nigerian refugees and asylum
 seekers, 31–35, 195
No Business in Abuse, 52
*No Friend but the Mountains: Writings
 from Manus Prison* (Boochani),
 105–7
nonconsensual transplant surgery,
 71, 74
North American Free Trade
 Agreement (NAFTA), 41–44 passim
North Atlantic Treaty Organization
 (NATO). *See* NATO
Northrop Grumman, 155

Obama, Barack, 9, 183
O'Neill, Peter, 55
Operation Sophia (EU), 149–50
Operation Triton (Frontex), 30, 149,
 158
Operation Vaken (UK), 312
OPlatz movement (Berlin), 241, 249
organ trafficking. *See* transplant
 trafficking
ORS Service, 197
outsourcing of asylum housing. *See*
 privatization and outsourcing of
 asylum housing
Overseas Development Institute, 150

Pakistan, 313, 319, 324

Paladin Group (security company), 107, 108
Palestinian refugees, 72
Papua New Guinea (PNG), 47–65 passim, 101–11, 168, 325
Parenti, Christian, 282
parole, 184, 186, 205
performance of expertise, 203–15 passim
performance of victimhood, 268–70 passim
Petersen, Gregers, 245
Poland, 155
Portugal, 158
Pride Enterprises, 209
prison labor. See detention center inmates' labor
prisons, migrant. See detention centers
private prison corporations: 283; Australia and Papua New Guinea, 49–59 passim, 103, 107, 108, 127–45 passim; EU, 79–93; UK, 80
privatization and outsourcing of asylum housing, 193–201 passim
privatization and outsourcing of food services. See food services and catering, privatized
pro bono representation, 3, 25, 204–13 passim, 236
pro se representation, 3, 25–26, 204, 205, 213

Qatar, 71
Queer Detainee Empowerment Project (QDEP), 182, 187
Quick, Elan, 74
quotas, deportation. See deportation: quotas

RAF Brize Norton, 314
Rahim, Musa, 301
rape, 37, 80, 114–22 passim, 207
Red Cross, 246; Denmark, 219–29

refugee camps, 113; Calais, 256–58 passim; Cameroon, 117; Nigeria, 117–19 passim
refugee children: Europe, 257, 258, 260–61
Refugee Legal Centre (RLC) (UK), 232–33, 235–36
Refugee Relief Act of 1953 (United States), 6
refugees, climate. See climate refugees
refugees, internal. See internally displaced people (IDPs)
Refugees Emancipation (RE), 248
refugee shelters: Germany, 241, 330
refugee statistics, 13n3
refugee women workers, 301–2
Reid, John, 197
Reliance, 195
Republic of Nauru. See Nauru
Riles, Annelise, 175
Romania, 154, 158
Rosenbaum, Levy Izhak, 69, 73–74
Rudd, Kevin, 50, 61n18m, 168

Sahel Regional Action Plan, 151
Salvation Army, 48, 51
Sangaré, Mohammed, 303, 304
Save the Children Australia, 48, 51, 53
Schengen Facility, 150
Sea-Watch, 31
Selex, 155
"selfie Samaritans," 224
Senegalese refugees, 301
Serbia, 319, 327
Serco, 127–45, 195, 196, 197, 309
sexual abuse. See rape
Shapira, Zaki, 68, 69, 71
shelters, immigrant youth. See immigrant youth shelters
shelters, refugee. See refugee shelters
Shire, Warsan, 257
Sicily, 38, 155
Sierra Leone, 309
SIM cards, 246
Slovenia, 154

Soames, Rupert, 197
social workers: jargon, 258; UK, 253–65 passim
Social Workers Without Borders (SWWB), 253, 256–63
solitary confinement, 24, 25
SOS Méditerranée, 37
Soumah, Aboubacar, 181
South Africa: transplant trafficking, 70, 73
Southeast Asia, 49, 75n1. *See also* Indonesia
Southwest Key, 185–86
Soviet Union, 5
Spain, 26–27, 149, 152, 154, 156, 158
Sri Lanka, 168
Stierl, Maurice, 59
"suffering narratives," 7–8
surgical transplantation of organs, trafficking of. *See* transplant trafficking
surveillance technology, 79, 155, 156, 283. *See also* electronic monitoring
sweatshop labor, 44
Switzerland, 197
Syppli-Kohl, Katrine, 222, 226
Syrian refugees, 70–72, 319, 333n1

Tascor, 262, 311
Tati, Moshe, 67–69
Tator, Carol, 293
Telekom Germany. *See* Deutsch Telekom
Thales, 151, 152, 153, 156
Ticktin, Miriam, 222
Tofighian, Omid, 101–11 passim
Toll Group, 57
trafficking of humans. *See* human trafficking
Transfield/Broadspectrum, 48, 52, 54, 55, 57, 62n23, 62–63n29, 173
transgender asylum seekers. *See* LGBT asylum seekers
trans-Mediterranean refugees. *See* Mediterranean refugees
transplant trafficking, 67–76

trauma, 210–13
Trump, Donald, 41, 44, 45, 183, 209
Tsianos, Vassilis, 245
Tunisia, 154
Turkey, 72, 150, 156; Afghans, 319, 326, 328; transplant tourism, 68–69, 70

UK Immigration Advisory Service (UKIAS), 232
Ukraine, 154
unaccompanied asylum-seeking children (UASC), 253, 256, 258, 264n17
UNICEF Australia, 53
United Kingdom. *See* Great Britain
United Nations, 4, 6, 9, 198; Convention on the Rights of the Child, 257; Human Rights Committee, 49; 1951 refugee convention, 4, 6, 232; UNICEF, 53
United Nations High Commissioner for Refugees (UNHCR), 3, 5, 11, 38, 57, 122, 169, 174; ATD promotion, 185; Canada and, 295n3
United Nations Relief and Works Agency for Palestine Refugees in the Near East (UNRWA), 15n19
United States, 181–91, 203–15, 281–85 passim; Aramark, 195; DHS, 184, 186; ICE, 181–86 passim, 210, 274, 285; kidney trafficking and transplant tourism, 70, 71; KKR & Co., 154; Syrian refugees, 71
United States–Mexico border, 41–46, 74–75, 186
United States-Mexico-Canada Agreement (USMCA), 41–42, 45
Universal Declaration of Human Rights, 4
US Department of Homeland Security (DHS), 184, 186. *See also* US Immigration and Customs Enforcement (ICE)
US Immigration and Customs Enforcement (ICE), 181–86 passim, 210, 285; "infiltration" by, 274

USMCA. *See* United States-Mexico-
   Canada Agreement (USMCA)
USSR. *See* Soviet Union
Uzbekistan, 157

Venezuela, 44–45
Venligboerne (Friendly Neighbors),
   223–24
Vietnamese people, trafficked, 73
Vincennes detention center, Paris,
   81–86

Wackenhut Corrections Services
   (WCC), 60n7
walls and fences. *See* border walls
   and fences
Walmart, 210
Waqa, Baron, 166–67
Wilson Security, 48, 57
Windrush scandal (UK), 313, 316n13
wireless internet access: Germany,
   241–52
women, abduction of. *See* abduction
   of women and children
women IDPs: Nigeria, 113–25 passim
women workers. *See* refugee women
   workers
work permits: Malta, 297–308

Younge, Gary, 312
youth shelters. *See* immigrant youth
   shelters

Zambrano, Sandra, 204
Zammit, Alice, 303
Zelaya, Manuel, 209
Zimbabwean refugees and asylum
   seekers, 195

ABOUT PM PRESS

PM Press is an independent, radical publisher of books and media to educate, entertain, and inspire. Founded in 2007 by a small group of people with decades of publishing, media, and organizing experience, PM Press amplifies the voices of radical authors, artists, and activists. Our aim is to deliver bold political ideas and vital stories to all walks of life and arm the dreamers to demand the impossible. We have sold millions of copies of our books, most often one at a time, face to face. We're old enough to know what we're doing and young enough to know what's at stake. Join us to create a better world.

PM Press
PO Box 23912
Oakland, CA 94623
www.pmpress.org

PM Press in Europe
europe@pmpress.org
www.pmpress.org.uk

FRIENDS OF PM PRESS

These are indisputably momentous times—the financial system is melting down globally and the Empire is stumbling. Now more than ever there is a vital need for radical ideas.

In the years since its founding—and on a mere shoestring—PM Press has risen to the formidable challenge of publishing and distributing knowledge and entertainment for the struggles ahead. With over 450 releases to date, we have published an impressive and stimulating array of literature, art, music, politics, and culture. Using every available medium, we've succeeded in connecting those hungry for ideas and information to those putting them into practice.

Friends of PM allows you to directly help impact, amplify, and revitalize the discourse and actions of radical writers, filmmakers, and artists. It provides us with a stable foundation from which we can build upon our early successes and provides a much-needed subsidy for the materials that can't necessarily pay their own way. You can help make that happen—and receive every new title automatically delivered to your door once a month—by joining as a Friend of PM Press. And, we'll throw in a free T-shirt when you sign up.

Here are your options:

- **$30 a month** Get all books and pamphlets plus 50% discount on all webstore purchases

- **$40 a month** Get all PM Press releases (including CDs and DVDs) plus 50% discount on all webstore purchases

- **$100 a month** Superstar—Everything plus PM merchandise, free downloads, and 50% discount on all webstore purchases

For those who can't afford $30 or more a month, we have **Sustainer Rates** at $15, $10, and $5. Sustainers get a free PM Press T-shirt and a 50% discount on all purchases from our website.

Your Visa or Mastercard will be billed once a month, until you tell us to stop. Or until our efforts succeed in bringing the revolution around. Or the financial meltdown of Capital makes plastic redundant. Whichever comes first.

DEPARTMENT OF ANTHROPOLOGY & SOCIAL CHANGE

Anthropology and Social Change, housed within
the California Institute of Integral Studies, is a small
innovative graduate department with a particular focus
on activist scholarship, militant research, and social change. We offer both masters
and doctoral degree programs.

Our unique approach to collaborative research methodology dissolves traditional
barriers between research and political activism, between insiders and outsiders,
and between researchers and protagonists. Activist research is a tool for "creating
the conditions we describe." We engage in the process of co-research to explore
existing alternatives and possibilities for social change.

Anthropology and Social Change
anth@ciis.edu
1453 Mission Street
94103
San Francisco, California
www.ciis.edu/academics/graduate-programs/anthropology-and-social-change

We Are the Crisis of Capital: A John Holloway Reader

John Holloway

ISBN: 978-1-62963-225-4
$22.95   320 pages

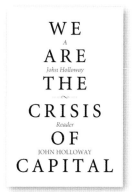

We Are the Crisis of Capital collects articles and excerpts written by radical academic, theorist, and activist John Holloway over a period of forty years.

Different times, different places, and the same anguish persists throughout our societies. This collection asks, "Is there a way out?" How do we break capital, a form of social organisation that dehumanises us and threatens to annihilate us completely? How do we create a world based on the mutual recognition of human dignity?

Holloway's work answers loudly, "By screaming NO!" By thinking from our own anger and from our own creativity. By trying to recover the "We" who are buried under the categories of capitalist thought. By opening the categories and discovering the antagonism they conceal, by discovering that behind the concepts of money, state, capital, crisis, and so on, there moves our resistance and rebellion.

An approach sometimes referred to as Open Marxism, it is an attempt to rethink Marxism as daily struggle. The articles move forward, influenced by the German state derivation debates of the seventies, by the CSE debates in Britain, and the group around the Edinburgh journal *Common Sense*, and then moving on to Mexico and the wonderful stimulus of the Zapatista uprising, and now the continuing whirl of discussion with colleagues and students in the Posgrado de Sociología of the Benemérita Universidad Autónoma de Puebla.

"Holloway's work is infectiously optimistic."
—Steven Poole, the *Guardian* (UK)

"Holloway's thesis is indeed important and worthy of notice."
—Richard J.F. Day, *Canadian Journal of Cultural Studies*

Building Free Life:
Dialogues with Öcalan

Edited by International Initiative

ISBN: 978-1-62963-704-4
$20.00   256 pages

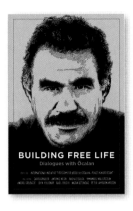

From Socrates to Antonio Gramsci, imprisoned philosophers have marked the history of thought and changed how we view power and politics. From his solitary jail cell, Abdullah Öcalan has penned daringly innovative works that give profuse evidence of his position as one of the most significant thinkers of our day. His prison writings have mobilized tens of thousands of people and inspired a revolution in the making in Rojava, northern Syria, while also penetrating the insular walls of academia and triggering debate and reflection among countless scholars.

So how do you engage in a meaningful dialogue with Abdullah Öcalan when he has been held in total isolation since April 2015? You compile a book of essays written by a globally diverse cast of the most imaginative luminaries of our time, send it to Öcalan's jailers, and hope that they deliver it to him.

Featured in this extraordinary volume are over a dozen writers, activists, dreamers, and scholars whose ideas have been investigated in Öcalan's own writings. Now these same people have the unique opportunity to enter into a dialogue with his ideas. *Building Free Life* is a rich and wholly original exploration of the most critical issues facing humanity today. In the broad sweep of this one-of-a-kind dialogue, the contributors explore topics ranging from democratic confederalism to women's revolution, from the philosophy of history to the crisis of the capitalist system, from religion to Marxism and anarchism, all in an effort to better understand the liberatory social forms that are boldly confronting capitalism and the state.

There can be no boundaries or restrictions for the development of thought. Thus, in the midst of different realities—from closed prisons to open-air prisons— the human mind will find a way to seek the truth. *Building Free Life* stands as a monument of radical thought, a testament of resilience, and a searchlight illuminating the impulse for freedom.

Contributors include: Shannon Brincat, Radha D'Souza, Mechthild Exo, Damian Gerber, Barry K. Gills, Muriel González Athenas, David Graeber, Andrej Grubačić, John Holloway, Patrick Huff, Donald H. Matthews, Thomas Jeffrey Miley, Antonio Negri, Norman Paech, Ekkehard Sauermann, Fabian Scheidler, Nazan Üstündağ, Immanuel Wallerstein, Peter Lamborn Wilson, and Raúl Zibechi.

"Öcalan's works make many intellectuals uncomfortable because they represent a form of thought that is not only inextricable from action, but also directly grapples with the knowledge that it is."
—David Graeber, author of *Debt: The First 5,000 Years*

Re-enchanting the World: Feminism and the Politics of the Commons

Silvia Federici
with a Foreword by Peter Linebaugh

ISBN: 978-1-62963-569-9
$19.95   240 pages

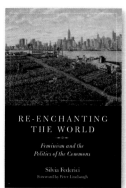

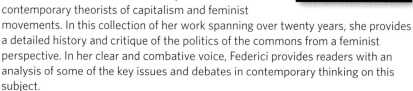

Silvia Federici is one of the most important contemporary theorists of capitalism and feminist movements. In this collection of her work spanning over twenty years, she provides a detailed history and critique of the politics of the commons from a feminist perspective. In her clear and combative voice, Federici provides readers with an analysis of some of the key issues and debates in contemporary thinking on this subject.

Drawing on rich historical research, she maps the connections between the previous forms of enclosure that occurred with the birth of capitalism and the destruction of the commons and the "new enclosures" at the heart of the present phase of global capitalist accumulation. Considering the commons from a feminist perspective, this collection centers on women and reproductive work as crucial to both our economic survival and the construction of a world free from the hierarchies and divisions capital has planted in the body of the world proletariat. Federici is clear that the commons should not be understood as happy islands in a sea of exploitative relations but rather autonomous spaces from which to challenge the existing capitalist organization of life and labor.

"Silvia Federici's theoretical capacity to articulate the plurality that fuels the contemporary movement of women in struggle provides a true toolbox for building bridges between different features and different people."
—Massimo De Angelis, professor of political economy, University of East London

"Silvia Federici's work embodies an energy that urges us to rejuvenate struggles against all types of exploitation and, precisely for that reason, her work produces a common: a common sense of the dissidence that creates a community in struggle."
—Maria Mies, coauthor of *Ecofeminism*

The Battle for the Mountain of the Kurds: Self-Determination and Ethnic Cleansing in the Afrin Region of Rojava

Author: Thomas Schmidinger with a Preface by Andrej Grubačić

ISBN: 978-1-62963-651-1

$19.95   192 pages

In early 2018, Turkey invaded the autonomous Kurdish region of Afrin in Syria and is currently threatening to ethnically cleanse the region. Between 2012 and 2018, the "Mountain of the Kurds" (Kurd Dagh) as the area has been called for centuries, had been one of the quietest regions in a country otherwise torn by civil war.

After the outbreak of the Syrian civil war in 2011, the Syrian army withdrew from the region in 2012, enabling the Party of Democratic Union (PYD), the Syrian sister party of Abdullah Öcalan's outlawed Turkish Kurdistan Workers' Party (PKK) to first introduce a Kurdish self-administration and then, in 2014, to establish the Canton Afrin as one of the three parts of the heavily Kurdish Democratic Federation of Northern Syria, which is better known under the name Rojava.

This self-administration—which had seen multiparty municipal and regionwide elections in the summer and autumn of 2017, which included a far-reaching autonomy for a number of ethnic and religious groups, and which had provided a safe haven for up to 300,000 refugees from other parts of Syria—is now at risk of being annihilated by the Turkish invasion and occupation.

Thomas Schmidinger is one of the very few Europeans to have visited the Canton of Afrin. In this book, he gives an account of the history and the present situation of the region. In a number of interviews, he also gives inhabitants of the region from a variety of ethnicities, religions, political orientations, and walks of life the opportunity to speak for themselves. As things stand now, the book might seem to be in danger of becoming an epitaph for the "Mountain of the Kurds," but as the author writes, "the battle for the Mountain of the Kurds is far from over yet."

"Preferable to most journalistic accounts that reduce the Rojava revolution to a single narrative. It will remain an informative resource even when the realities have further changed."
—Martin van Bruinessen, Kurdish Studies on *Rojava: Revolution, War and the Future of Syria's Kurds*